Diamond Classics II

ALSO BY MIKE SHANNON
AND FROM McFARLAND

*George Foster and the 1977 Reds: The Rise of a Slugger
and the End of an Era* (2019)

Hutch: Baseball's Fred Hutchinson and a Legacy of Courage
(written by Mike Shannon; illustrated by Scott Hannig, 2011)

Baseball Books: A Collector's Guide (2008)

*Coming Back to Baseball: The Cincinnati Astros
and the Joys of Over-30 Play* (2005)

*Diamond Classics: Essays on 100 of the Best Baseball
Books Ever Published* (1989; paperback 2004)

*Everything Happens in Chillicothe: A Summer in the Frontier League
with Max McLeary, the One-Eyed Umpire* (2004)

Diamond Classics II
The Best Baseball Books Since 1989

Mike Shannon

McFarland & Company, Inc., Publishers
Jefferson, North Carolina

ISBN (print) 978-1-4766-8463-5
ISBN (ebook) 978-1-4766-5816-2

Library of Congress cataloging data are available

Library of Congress Control Number 2026002577

© 2026 Mike Shannon. All rights reserved

No part of this book may be reproduced or transmitted in any form or by any means, electronic or mechanical, including photocopying or recording, or by any information storage and retrieval system, without permission in writing from the publisher.

Front cover image: by Tim Elliott (Shutterstock)

Printed in the United States of America

McFarland & Company, Inc., Publishers
Box 611, Jefferson, North Carolina 28640
www.mcfarlandpub.com

*For Robbie Franklin and Gary Mitchem:
publishing giants to whom baseball literature
aficionados owe a huge debt*

Acknowledgments

In terms of materially contributing to the writing of this book, there is one person above all others whom I must thank, and that is Mark Schraf, whose career in the chemistry department at West Virginia University is merely a front for his true vocation as a man of letters, with a specialty in baseball literature. There is no opinion about baseball books I value more than Mark's, and the list of candidates to be considered for inclusion in this sequel which he prepared was of considerable help. As the fiction editor of *Spitball: The Literary Baseball Magazine*, Mark has also been immensely helpful to me in running the CASEY Awards program which annually recognizes and honors the best baseball books of the year. If that were not enough, he has been my boon companion for decades on road trips to Cooperstown, New York, for Baseball Hall of Fame induction weekend, trips during which he has never tired of discussing baseball books and authors and all things related. To say that I am grateful for such friendship barely acknowledges the extent to which I am indebted to him.

I must thank Rich Puerzer, who also made a very thoughtful list of great baseball books to consider, and Ron Kaplan, another baseball bibliophile, whose opinion on baseball books I value. The man behind the best website dedicated to baseball books (*Ron Kaplan's Baseball Bookshelf*) and the author himself of several outstanding baseball books, Ron never fails to make intelligent nominations for the CASEY Awards. Al Turnbull, Bobby Plapinger, and Rob Langenderfer are cherished friends and baseball savants who also joined the conversation about books to be considered, and I thank them too.

My task was made a bit easier by several authors who spoke to me very candidly about the baseball books they have authored and even named their favorites. Book talk doesn't get more interesting than that, and so I gratefully acknowledge the help of Marty Appel, Herschel Cobb, Tim Peeler, Dennis Snelling, and Glenn Stout.

From a publishing standpoint, no one is more responsible for this book than Gary Mitchem. For a long time before I started working on this sequel, and absorbed as I have been in the annual reading and evaluating of thousands of newly published baseball books since 1989, I was nagged continually by the feeling that the book needed to be written. Knowing what needed to be done and actually doing it are two different things, and I freely admit that without Gary's support, I would never have had the fortitude to even begin the project. For Gary's support and patience, I am extremely grateful.

It may seem superfluous or even odd to say it, but I also thank the authors represented in this volume, for without their love of the game, admirable dedication, and wonderful writing talents, the books which I have enjoyed sharing my thoughts and opinions about with you would obviously not even exist.

Covers and dust jackets are very important components of the whole physical book experience, as identifiers and indicators of the contents, and so I must acknowledge the help of the following in gaining permission to reproduce the covers of some of the books I have written about here: Angela Tabor and Joe Rinaldi of St. Martin's Publishing Group; Emily Ferko of ECW Press; Leif Milliken and Rosemary Sekora of the University of Nebraska Press; David Allender of David R. Godine, Publisher; Gloria Castillo of the University of Texas Press; Marcy Hawley of Orange Fraser Press; Mary Dougherty and Scott E. Lodzieski of the University of Massachusetts Press; Brett Ortlen of Adventure Keen; Greg Rhodes of RoadWest Press; Tom Zappala; Jonathan Knight; DJ Stout; Tom Gilbert; Gary Cieradkowski; Henry W. "Hank" Thomas; Brett Friedlander; and David Pietrusza.

Finally, I must express my utmost gratitude to the following, just for always being there, in my corner: Donnie Pollard, without whose immensely important contributions *Spitball Magazine* would have ceased publishing years ago; my sisters Laura and Susie and my brothers Johnny and Tim; my wonderful adult children of whom I am so proud: Meg, Casey, Mick, Babe, and Nolan Ryan; and most of all, the beautiful Irish woman who has made my life, my wife, Kathleen Dermody Shannon. *Erin go bragh!*

Table of Contents

Acknowledgments	vii
Introduction	1
The Amazing Tale of Mr. Herbert and His Fabulous Alpine Cowboys Baseball Club: An Illustrated History of the Best Little Semipro Baseball Team in Texas	5
Ballpark: Baseball in the American City	9
Banzai Babe Ruth: Baseball, Espionage, & Assassination During the 1934 Tour of Japan	12
Baseball	17
Baseball & Bubble Gum: The 1952 Topps Collection	20
Baseball's Golden Age: The Photographs of Charles M. Conlon	24
Big Red Dynasty: How Bob Howsam & Sparky Anderson Built the Big Red Machine	28
Billy Martin: Baseball's Flawed Genius	33
Bleachers: A Summer in Wrigley Field	36
Bottom of the 33rd: Hope, Redemption, and Baseball's Longest Game	40
Bouton: The Life of a Baseball Original	44
The Bullpen Gospels: Major League Dreams of a Minor League Veteran	48
Cardboard Gods: An All-American Tale Through Baseball Cards	52
The Catcher Was a Spy: The Mysterious Life of Moe Berg	56
Center Field Grasses	60
The Chalmers Race: Ty Cobb, Napoleon Lajoie, and the Controversial 1910 Batting Title That Became a National Obsession	65
Chasing Moonlight: The True Story of Field of Dreams' Doc Graham	70

Table of Contents

The Church of Baseball: The Making of Bull Durham: *Home Runs, Bad Calls, Crazy Fights, Big Savings, and a Hit*	75
Cooperstown Verses: Poems About Each Hall of Famer	79
Crash: The Life and Times of Dick Allen	83
Cy Young: A Baseball Life	88
Dalko: The Untold Story of Baseball's Fastest Pitcher	92
Diz: The Story of Dizzy Dean and Baseball During the Great Depression	96
Dynastic, Bombastic, Fantastic: Reggie, Rollie, Catfish, and Charlie Finley's Swingin' A's	99
Fenway 1912: The Birth of a Ballpark, a Championship Season, and Fenway's Remarkable First Year	103
Fifty-Nine in '84: Old Hoss Radbourn, Barehanded Baseball, and the Greatest Season a Pitcher Ever Had	108
The Final Season: Fathers, Sons, and One Last Season in a Classic American Ballpark	112
The Further Adventures of Slugger McBatt: Baseball Stories by W.P. Kinsella	116
Gil Hodges: The Brooklyn Bums, the Miracle Mets, and the Extraordinary Life of a Baseball Legend	120
Gods of Wood and Stone	123
Heart of a Tiger: Growing Up with My Grandfather, Ty Cobb	127
How Baseball Happened: Outrageous Lies Exposed! The True Story Revealed	132
Jackie Robinson: A Biography	137
Joe DiMaggio: The Hero's Life	141
Johnny Evers: A Baseball Life	144
Judge and Jury: The Life and Times of Judge Kenesaw Mountain Landis	149
The Last Innocents: The Collision of the Turbulent Sixties and the Los Angeles Dodgers	153
The League of Outsider Baseball: An Illustrated History of Baseball's Forgotten Heroes	157
The Legendary Harry Caray: Baseball's Greatest Salesman	161
Let's Play Two: The Legend of Mr. Cub, the Life of Ernie Banks	165
Lords of the Realm: The Real History of Baseball	168
Luckiest Man: The Life and Death of Lou Gehrig	172
Mr. Wrigley's Ball Club: Chicago and the Cubs During the Jazz Age	176

Table of Contents

Moneyball: The Art of Winning an Unfair Game	181
Mover & Shaker: Walter O'Malley, the Dodgers, & Baseball's Westward Expansion	186
The Numbers Game: Baseball's Lifelong Fascination with Statistics	191
October 1964	196
Odd Man Out: A Year on the Mound with a Minor League Misfit	200
Oscar Charleston: The Life and Legend of Baseball's Greatest Forgotten Player	205
Pete Rose: An American Dilemma	210
Pie Traynor: A Baseball Biography	214
Pinstripe Empire: The New York Yankees from Babe Ruth to After the Boss	218
The Pitch That Killed: Carl Mays, Ray Chapman and the Pennant Race of 1920	222
Play for a Kingdom	227
The Pride of the Yankees: Lou Gehrig, Gary Cooper, and the Making of a Classic	231
Prophet of the Sandlots: Journeys with a Major League Scout	235
Sal Maglie: Baseball's Demon Barber	239
A Season in the Sun: The Rise of Mickey Mantle	243
Slouching Toward Fargo: A Two-Year Saga of Sinners and St. Paul Saints at the Bottom of the Bush Leagues with Bill Murray, Darryl Strawberry, Dakota Sadie and Me	246
The Soul of Baseball: A Road Trip Through Buck O'Neil's America	250
Spalding's World Tour: The Epic Adventure That Took Baseball Around the Globe—And Made It America's Game	253
Spitballing: The Baseball Days of Long Bob Ewing	257
Steinbrenner: The Last Lion of Baseball	262
Summer of Shadows: A Murder, a Pennant Race, and the Twilight of the Best Location in the Nation	266
21: The Story of Roberto Clemente (A Graphic Novel)	271
Walter Johnson: Baseball's Big Train	275
We Are the Ship: The Story of Negro League Baseball	280
The Wizard of Waxahachie: Paul Richards and the End of Baseball as We Knew It	283
Index	287

Introduction

This book is a sequel, if you will, of the first book I wrote, *Diamond Classics: Essays on 100 of the Best Baseball Books Ever Published*. McFarland published that book back in 1989, and for at least a decade I have been thinking about the need for a sequel because so many outstanding baseball books have continued to be released.

That abundance, of course, is what presented the greatest challenge, as both McFarland and I realized that it would be impossible to include all deserving books in a sequel. It is inevitable that deserving books get left out in any effort such as this, so an excellent place to look for more titles of baseball books worthy of your attention is the list of CASEY Award finalists, from 1983 to the present, which can be found on the website of *Spitball: The Literary Baseball Magazine* (*www.spitballmag.com*). In any event, it may interest you to learn exactly how I proceeded.

I started with lists, my own lists and those of my dear friend and colleague Mark Schraf, of "definites" and "maybes." But I knew full well that neither list would turn out to be cast in bronze, like the wording on a plaque in the Baseball Hall of Fame. It was inevitable that there would be crossings in both directions: some maybes becoming definites and some definites going the other way, which is to say that such titles have not been included in the book.

Lists are helpful but they can also be paralyzing, meaning that if I had waited until I was 100 percent certain of which books should be included, I might never have started the real work, which was the re-reading of the books and the writing of the essays. Once I decided that a beginning had to be made, I took a very simple and personal approach. I pulled down a book from one of the hundreds of shelves in my baseball library that I *wanted* to re-read. This was an exciting thing to do because I have found that book reading is similar to movie watching: because memory can often be unreliable and is certainly vulnerable to the effects of the passage of time, if you wait long enough, the re-reading (or re-watching) can seem almost as fresh and as enjoyable as the original experience.

This approach not only got me going but it also led to some surprising decisions. After re-reading some books that were on one of the lists, I was disappointed to discover that, for various reasons, they were just not as outstanding as I had remembered them being. I still considered them to be very good books—just not so outstanding as to deserve being named a "Diamond Classic," a very high standard indeed. And as I said, in other cases, some books turned out to be even better than I remembered. In fact, a couple of books included here were not on either of the original lists but called to me for some reason and then demonstrated, when given the chance, that they did belong. Yes, baseball books, like the players themselves, can be overlooked or underestimated, and we rightly take satisfaction in seeing them receive the recognition that is their due.

As the editor of *Spitball: The Literary Baseball Magazine*, I also must express a note of caution about which books are included or not included in this volume. As I write this, *Spitball* has presented the CASEY Award, the first, the oldest, and the most prestigious honor a baseball book can receive, to 42 books. Seventeen of those CASEY-winning books are included here, but no one should conclude that the absence of the other CASEY Award–winning books indicates in any way my regarding those books to be unworthy of inclusion in this or any similar work. There are several possible reasons any particular CASEY-winning book has not been included. For instance, in order to provide as much variety as possible, I tried to limit the number of books devoted to any one subject or topic. Once I had committed to including *Heart of a Tiger* by Herschel Cobb and *The Chalmers Race* by Rick Huhn, I regretfully felt compelled to omit not only Charles Leerhsen's fascinating and iconoclastic CASEY-winning *Ty Cobb: A Terrible Beauty* (Simon & Schuster, 2015) but also three other exceptional Cobb books, all of them in my opinion underappreciated: Richard Bak's illustrated biography *Ty Cobb: His Tumultuous Life and Times* (Taylor Publishing, 1994), *War on the Basepaths: The Definitive Biography of Ty Cobb* by Tim Hornbaker (Sports Publishing, 1995), and Steven Elliott Tripp's *Ty Cobb: Baseball and American Manhood* (Rowman & Littlefield, 1996). I imposed a similar limitation in regard to the subjects of the books included in the original *Diamond Classics*. For example, because Robert Creamer's *Stengel: His Life and Times* is included in the latter, I decided to pass over Marty Appel's CASEY-winning biography of the Professor, *Casey Stengel: Baseball's Greatest Character* (Doubleday, 2017), in favor of Marty's brilliant history of the New York Yankees, *Pinstripe Empire*, also a CASEY Award winner. For the record, five CASEY Award–winning books are included in the original *Diamond Classics* making for a total of 22 CASEY winners between the two books, and all but seven of the 68 books included here were at least nominated as finalists for the CASEY Award.

In addition, to exposing the reader to the work of as many outstanding authors as possible, I decided to include only one book by any particular author when, clearly, several authors represented in this volume deserved to have more than one book included, had time and page-count limitations not capped the number of titles feasibly to be included at 68. And, yes, I freely admit that there is more than one selection here that might be described as surprising or "unorthodox." After all, they haven't completely outlawed fun yet, have they?

Finally, I needed to feel I had something to say about each book that would pique the interest of the reader, that would explain why the book should be regarded as a classic, and that would cause the reader to want to read the book under discussion for himself. For that is the purpose of these essays: not only to recognize the stature of the books discussed but also to convince the reader that his baseball library is incomplete without these volumes on his shelves. There is also the fact that books are expensive. To go out and purchase every book included here would cost a pretty penny, I have no doubt. If nothing else, if such an expenditure would be a luxury, then this very affordable (by comparison) volume may serve as a "Reader's Digest" condensed substitute, as the essays provide, along with other components, the gist of each book included.

It is a fair question to ask of me or anyone else who presumes to write a book such as this: What makes me qualified to decide which books should be crowned "Diamond Classics"? The answer is nothing except a love of the game and a lifetime of experience. I have been carefully reading baseball books for more than 60 years and spending an obsessive amount of time and energy, as the editor of *Spitball Magazine*, evaluating them for more than 40 years. So while there is always a subjective element in the judging of literature, I hope that you will trust that I have done my homework and made myself through sheer hard work and persistence, if nothing else, a qualified guide capable of recognizing the very best that our many talented baseball authors have produced.

To paraphrase good old Harry, "Baseball lit fans … this book's for you!"

Ad Majorem Gloria Deum.

The Amazing Tale of Mr. Herbert and His Fabulous Alpine Cowboys Baseball Club: An Illustrated History of the Best Little Semipro Baseball Team in Texas

◆

DJ STOUT

◆

Austin: University of Texas Press. Cloth, 248 pages, ISBN: 978-0-292-72334-4. Foreword: My Father's Left Arm by DJ Stout, Introduction: The Cowboys of Summer by Nicholas Dawidoff. The Lineup (contributors).

Semipro baseball was once as ubiquitous in America as the obsolete service station attendants who used to pump our gas for us. Every small town had at least one such team; whose players, while not paid the salary of a professional, received compensation of some kinds not enjoyed by those who were strictly amateurs. The best book ever published about this hybrid version of the national pastime is an over-sized (12" × 10"), copiously-illustrated volume that more than lives up to its carnival barking title: *The Amazing Tale of Mr. Herbert and His Fabulous Alpine Cowboys: An Illustrated History of the Best Little Semipro Baseball Team in Texas*. Published by the University of Texas Press, the book chronicles in a season-by-season format the serendipitous combination of elements that produced an almost certainly unrepeatable baseball version of Camelot for those lucky enough to have experienced it.

The Mr. Herbert of the title is Herbert L. Kokernot, Jr., a multimillionaire cattle rancher, financier, and philanthropist whose empire (35,000 head of cattle on 400,000 acres at its peak) was headquartered near the tiny town (population 6,800) of Alpine, situated in the desolate Big Bend region of West Texas. A baseball fanatic and former semipro player himself who loved his home town of Alpine, Mr. Herbert, as he was affectionately called, bought the local semipro baseball team, the struggling Alpine Cats, in 1946 and re-named them the Cowboys. The Cats' rinky-dink wooden ballpark was part of the deal, but it was destined for the scrapyard as soon as Herbert Sr., visiting from his home in San Antonio, noticed the family's red and white "06" cattle brand painted on the fences. "Son, if you're going to put the 06 brand on something, do that thing right," he said to Herbert Jr.

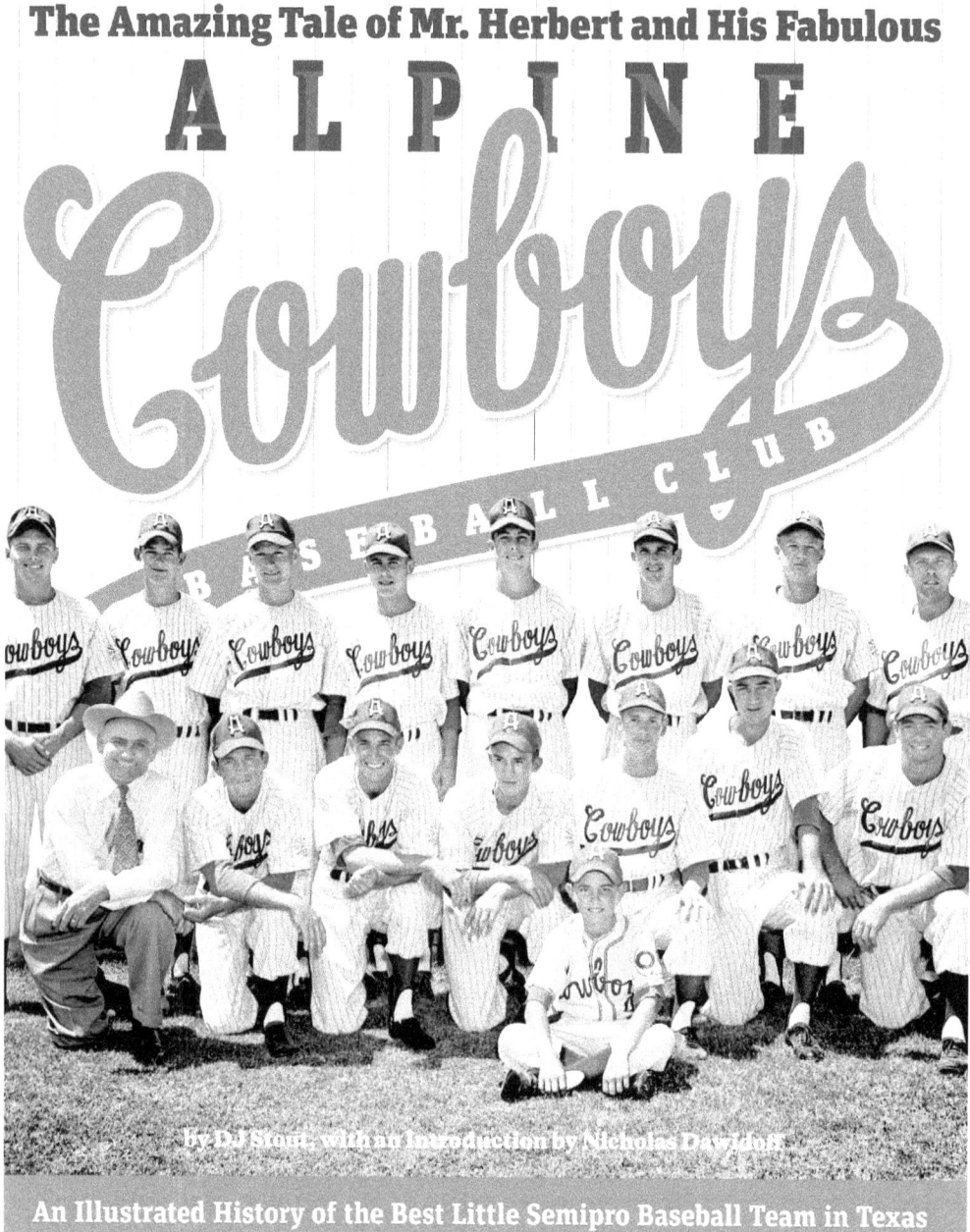

The Amazing Tale of Mr. Herbert and His Fabulous ALPINE Cowboys BASEBALL CLUB

By DJ Stout, with an Introduction by Nicholas Dawidoff

An Illustrated History of the Best Little Semipro Baseball Team in Texas

Buoyed by his father's blessing, Kokernot spared no expense in building a new 1,000-seat concrete and steel ballpark that was ready by May of the next spring. The $1.25 million tab was more than Wrigley Field had cost to build 33 years earlier. Truckloads of red stone blasted out of a quarry at the 06 ranch was used to construct the exterior walls of the roofed grandstands and gave the ballpark its distinctive face. The infield clay was imported from Georgia and hand pressed into a surface as smooth as a billiards table, and creek beds all over the region were searched for the heartiest grasses to become the field's turf. Kokernot Field was beautiful, the equal of the best minor league ballparks in the country, and visiting players and fans were stunned to find it in Alpine, in the middle of a desert. Kokernot Field itself was one of the reasons Mr. Herbert was able on several occasions to convince pairs of major league ballclubs to come to town for exhibition games

For 12 years (1947–58) the generous Kokernot spent his money as freely on his players as he did his ballpark. He employed the high school and college players who became baseball Cowboys on his ranch, provided scholarships for them to attend crosstown Sul Ross College, showered them with cash bonuses of $25–$100 for clutch performances, treated them to endless banquets and bar-b-ques and gifts (such as jackets and handmade cowboy boots) at the 06 ranch, and ran a first-class program for them in all respects; even flying them to distant tournaments and putting them up in fancy hotels. In short, he treated his players, including high schooler Gaylord Perry, who weren't even minor leaguers, as major leaguers … and as adopted sons. In return, the young men played their hearts out for Mr. Herbert and usually earned a trip to the prestigious National Semipro Baseball Tournament in Wichita, Kansas.

And then to complete the trio of elements which combined to create a near-Utopian baseball world, there were the knowledgeable and rabid fans; not just the citizens of Alpine but also those of neighboring small towns, such as Fort Stockton, Pecos, Fort Davis, Marathon, Sanderson, and Marfa. As a caption in the book explains: "The town supported the team because the team gave back to them. The game of baseball shares aspects with cowboy and ranching culture that resonated with West Texans in the '40s and '50s. They each have a strong work ethic and an innate quality of all-American wholesomeness. A bronze plaque that Mr. Herbert mounted on the wall at the entrance to the ballpark is inscribed with these words: 'Kokernot Field. Dedicated to the promotion of a clean and wholesome sport, our national game, baseball.'"

In addition to the pervasive and lengthy captions and the first-person remembrances called "Cowboy Tales," the text of the book consists of two highly informative essays. The first, called "My Father's Arm," is a loving family history and a tribute to former Cowboys pitcher Doyle Stout by son D.J. Stout, the author and gifted designer of the book, as well as the galvanizing force behind its publication. The second is a rich synopsis of the Cowboys' story, "The Cowboys of Summer," with an emphasis on the beneficent Mr. Herbert as a blessing to all those he encountered: an essay by Nicholas Dawidoff which first appeared in *Sports Illustrated* under a different title.

The writing in the book is indispensable in providing for the reader a full account of a complicated and heart-warming story, yet its more important function is to explain, elaborate on, and provide context for the black and white photos of "The Amazing Tale of Mr. Herbert," which are nothing less than spectacular. Included are photos of all types: posed individual shots of the players and other personages, group photos, team photos, action shots from games, aerial photos of Alpine and the nearby Davis Mountains, and, of course, ballpark photos galore. By virtue of its numerous appearances, as primary subject and as background, Kokernot Field rivals the various instances of humanity as the most important visual aspect of the book. Invariably, whatever the subject, the photos exhibit exquisite clarity, compositional brilliance, and an experienced eye for setting and timing: qualities that endow them with a sense of the artistic. Clearly cognizant of the exceptional nature of the photographs, the author and the Press employ numerous full-page and two-page spreads to enhance their beauty and their impact upon the reader.

As for the source of the photographs–there are no specific photo credits–only one photographer is mentioned in the book, Charles Hunter (1905-1963), the Cowboys official team photographer who ran a photography business for years on the bottom floor of Alpine's Holland Hotel. A photo of Mr. Hunter appears on the inside back dust jacket, along with the statement: "Many of his large-format images, housed at the Archives of the Big Bend at the Bryan Wildenthal Memorial Library at Sul Ross State University, appear in this book." It is a barely adequate recognition of the work that is the backbone of this Diamond Classic.

After the 1958 season, by which time major league-quality lights had been installed at Kokernot Field, Mr. Herbert reluctantly entered into an agreement to make the Cowboys a minor league affiliate of the Boston Red Sox. Mr. Herbert, who had never even tried to profit off his beloved Cowboys, did not make the change as a business decision but because semi-pro baseball had begun to die out and suitable competition on that level was no longer readily available. The professional Cowboys, including future major league star Norm Cash for one summer, played in the Class D Sophomore League for three seasons, before Mr. Herbert, dismayed at the methods and the different raison d'etre of the professionals, called it quits. The Sul Ross Lobos used Kokernot Field until the college disbanded its baseball program in 1968. Mr. Herbert then gave the ballpark to the local high school, and the place gradually fell into a state of disrepair. In 1983 Sul Ross re-instituted its baseball program and slowly returned Kokernot Field to its former glory. Then in 2009 professional baseball returned when the Big Bend Cowboys became founding members of the independent Continental Baseball League. Four years later, the Continental League morphed into the Pecos League, and the team, reclaiming its heritage as the Alpine Cowboys, continued their membership. Perennial contenders, the Cowboys won the Pecos League Championship in 2019, their second Pecos League title. Unfortunately, today's Alpine Cowboys do not have the privilege of meeting and playing for Mr. Herbert who died in 1987; however, they can certainly sense the spirit of this great baseball man whenever they look around themselves at Kokernot Field. Baseball bibliophiles can have a similar experience by immersing themselves in the words and images of the book which preserves his memory.

Ballpark:
Baseball in the American City

◆

Paul Goldberger

◆

New York: Alfred A. Knopf, 2019. Cloth, 364 pages, ISBN: 978-0-3077-0154-1. Prologue, A Word to the Reader. Acknowledgments, Notes, Bibliography, Index, 160 color and black & white photos scattered throughout the book.
   Comments: Goldberger was awarded the Pulitzer Prize for distinguished criticism of architecture while writing for *The New York Times*. At the time of *Ballpark*'s publication, he taught at the New School and lectured widely around the country on architecture, design, historic preservation, and cities.

   Baseball is the most photogenic of all team sports, and its aspect most made for the camera are the game's ballparks: the unique, inviting, often beautiful buildings dubbed "Green Cathedrals" by Philip J. Lowry. A number of alluring ballpark books have been published, and to the surprise of no one, photography has been the essence of most of them. The rich history involving the development of America's major league ballparks has been somewhat neglected and did not get its due, until the publication of *Ballpark* by Paul Goldberger: the first comprehensive, synthesizing, up-to-date examination of the subject by an acclaimed architectural critic, presented in graceful prose and supplemented by a slew of instructive illustrations and photographs.
   The main thesis of Goldberger's history is the concept of *rus in the urbe*, a Latin phrase coined by epigrammatist Martial, which translates to "country in the city." The idea being that the harried inhabitants of the dense urban environment, surrounded by man-made buildings and paved streets, yearn for and find relief in any rural oasis of natural beauty and simplicity, such as parks, cemeteries, and, of course, baseball grounds. "Baseball, parks, and cemeteries were all forms of psychic escape from the harshness of the city," says the author, "ways of establishing a connection to nature without physically leaving the city." When baseball's first ballpark, the enclosed Union Grounds of Brooklyn, was built in 1862 by entrepreneur William Cammeyer, the main interest of the fans, just as it is today, was in watching the competition while the ballpark's owner was motivated by the opportunity to make

money. Yet, even then, the author contends this deeper salutary benefit was in effect: "Union Grounds marked the beginning of the idea that baseball, the game of infinite space, should be played in an urban structure of very finite space, fitted and sometimes contorted into the urban grid. Union Grounds … was a green field of play, a thing apart from the city and at the same time intimately connected to it." The *rus in the urbe* concept is repeatedly referred to and emphasized, so that when indoor baseball stadiums with their lack of natural grass and their obliteration of views beyond the outfield (which negate the illusion that the dimensions of the fields run to infinity) are discussed, we grasp their inadequacy vis a vis the concept.

Other ideas influenced the development of ballparks, as well. In the second chapter entitled "Amusement Versus Virtue," Goldberger explains how the Jeffersonian vision of the nation as "agrarian and virtuous" competed with the Hamiltonian vision as "urban and transactional." These conflicting philosophies were represented during the last quarter of the nineteenth century by National League founder and owner of the Chicago White Stockings William Hulbert and his successor as owner of the White Stockings, Albert Spalding, on the one hand; and by St. Louis Browns owner Chris Von der Ahe, on the other. Determined to improve baseball's social standing, Spalding made the second version of Hulbert's Lakefront Park in Chicago in 1883 into "the first ballpark marketed as an attraction in its own right." He strictly segregated the lower classes from their betters and fashioned for the latter "private viewing boxes" that Goldberger calls the "precursor of the modern skybox." Von der Ahe conceived of baseball primarily as a way to sell more beer. He welcomed the lower-class ruffians and gamblers abhorred by Spalding and attempted to turn his ballyard (Sportsman's Park) into an amusement park offering more entertainment than merely baseball.

In addition to these foundational concepts, Goldberger discusses in turn other important factors that influenced the ways ballparks came into being. For instance, when ballparks were sited in developed neighborhoods, their shapes and sizes were often determined by the confines of surrounding streets and buildings that could not be sacrificed. For years ballparks were located strategically near street car lines; later on, proximity to railway lines became crucial (in fact, Goldberger points out that without railways, professional leagues would have been impossible). Formal ballpark architecture, we learn, was not something that suddenly appeared in full bloom but a process that developed over time. One of the first architects to build a ballpark was Jerome Deery of Philadelphia who constructed the second version of Boston's South End Grounds. The author credits Deery's ornate Grand Pavilion there as "the beginning of the ballpark as monumental Architecture." Other builders and architects are given their due in this history, as well, especially extremely important firms, such as the Osborn Engineering Company of Cleveland and Populous (formerly HOK Sport) of Kansas City. And early in the twentieth century the ubiquitous wooden ballparks, subject to destruction by fire, were replaced forever by those built of concrete, stone, and steel. Amazingly, this very first wave of improved building materials and techniques produced some of the most iconic ballparks ever built.

Perhaps the most useful contribution of *Ballparks* is its clearly-expressed demarcation of the history of the subject into four distinct periods. The first generation of ballparks were those which grew organically out of inner-city neighborhoods and were inextricably tied to them. Second generation ballparks fled the often-deteriorating inner city in favor of roomier urban sites with plenty of parking for the suddenly commonplace automobile. Unfortunately, these mostly doughnut-shaped monstrosities, built to serve pro football as well as baseball, were pretty much devoid of personality and any architectural flair. The construction of Camden Yards in Baltimore "brought baseball back to its downtown origins" and began a trend of viewing new ballpark construction as a key element of urban renewal. The implementation of classical design features throughout the facility ushered in what has become known as the "retro park" era. The fourth, and still emerging class of ballpark, represented by Atlanta's Sun Trust Park, is one which treats the ballpark, not as an integral part of an existing neighborhood, but as its own dominion, "the centerpiece of a developer-built theme park," replete with bars, restaurants, shops, apartments, and condos, all owned by the team itself. Goldberger considers this latest development inferior to the Camden Yards model but also acknowledges that its imitation by other teams, such as the St. Louis Cardinals, will probably continue for the foreseeable future. His appreciation for Camden Yards is so great that the chapter devoted to it serves as the spiritual heart of the book.

Ballpark is unquestionably the book for those who own no other books on the subject because Goldberger examines in some detail nearly every ballpark significant in major league history and because, while it is not a picture book per se, it offers a lot of wonderful images which are certainly sufficient to support the text. Especially useful too are the sections on the most recently built ballparks, such as San Francisco's Oracle Park, San Diego's Petco Park, New York's Citi Field, Minneapolis' Target Field, and Miami's Marlins Park.

The one aspect of the subject not addressed at any length in *Ballpark* is the costs of the new ballparks and the fundamental practical questions of whether these costs are justifiable and who should bear them: the taxpayers, the teams themselves, or some combination of the two. This omission though can be excused on the grounds that other books have already adequately dealt with the topic, books such as *Playing the Field: Why Sports Teams Move and Cities Fight to Keep Them* (The Johns Hopkins University Press) by Charles C. Euchner and *Field of Screams: How the Great Stadium Swindle Turns Public Money into Private Profit* (Common Courage Press) by Joanna Cagan and Neil deMause. More to the point, *Ballpark* can be fairly said to be occupied with more important matters. As long as baseball is played, ballparks will be a necessity. The right ballparks, properly sited and designed and built with an understanding of how the game's past can and should be reflected in the present, contribute mightily to the beauty and excitement of the competition that occurs within them. For the sake of the game, it is crucial to get it right when a new ballpark is built, just as Paul Goldberger got it right with this sparkling, definitive history.

Banzai Babe Ruth: Baseball, Espionage, & Assassination During the 1934 Tour of Japan

◆

Robert K. Fitts

◆

Lincoln: University of Nebraska Press, 2012. Cloth, 319 pages, ISBN: 978-0-8032-2984-6. List of illustrations, Recurring Japanese Characters, Prologue, Map of Japan with location and dates of the games. Appendix 1: The All American Touring Party, Appendix 2: Tour Batting and Pitching Statistics, Appendix 3: Tour Game Line Scores, Acknowledgments, Notes, Bibliography, Index, 35 black & white photos between pages 146–147. Other baseball books by the author: Remembering Japanese Baseball: An Oral History of the Game *(Southern Illinois University Press, 2005),* Wally Yonamine: The Man Who Changed Japanese Baseball *(University of Nebraska Press, 2008),* Mashi: The Unfulfilled Dreams of Masanori Murakami, the First Japanese Major Leaguer *(University of Nebraska Press, 2015), and* Issei Baseball: The Story of the First Japanese American Ballplayers *(University of Nebraska Press, 2020).*

Comments: *Banzai Babe Ruth* won the 2013 Seymour Medal awarded by the Society for American Baseball Research. It was a finalist for the 2012 CASEY Award.

Robert Whiting, author of *You Gotta Have Wa*: "An intelligent, well-crafted account of an important period in the history of U.S.-Japan relations. Painstakingly researched, rich in color and detail, it goes beyond baseball, illuminating the social, economic, and political life of a distant era, the impact of which can still be seen today."

Along with Robert Whiting, Robert K. Fitts reigns as our most knowledgeable and most trusted commentator on Japanese baseball, and the book which cemented his high place among authors of books worthy of being deemed Diamond Classics is *Banzai Babe Ruth: Baseball, Espionage, & Assassination during the 1934 Tour of Japan.* The book is fascinating in many respects and unique in that the main goal of the tour it recounts was different from similar American junkets previously undertaken. Because the Japanese had already enthusiastically adopted baseball (and adapted it to important elements of their culture), the tacit (if unofficial) mission of Ruth and company was to foster friendship and

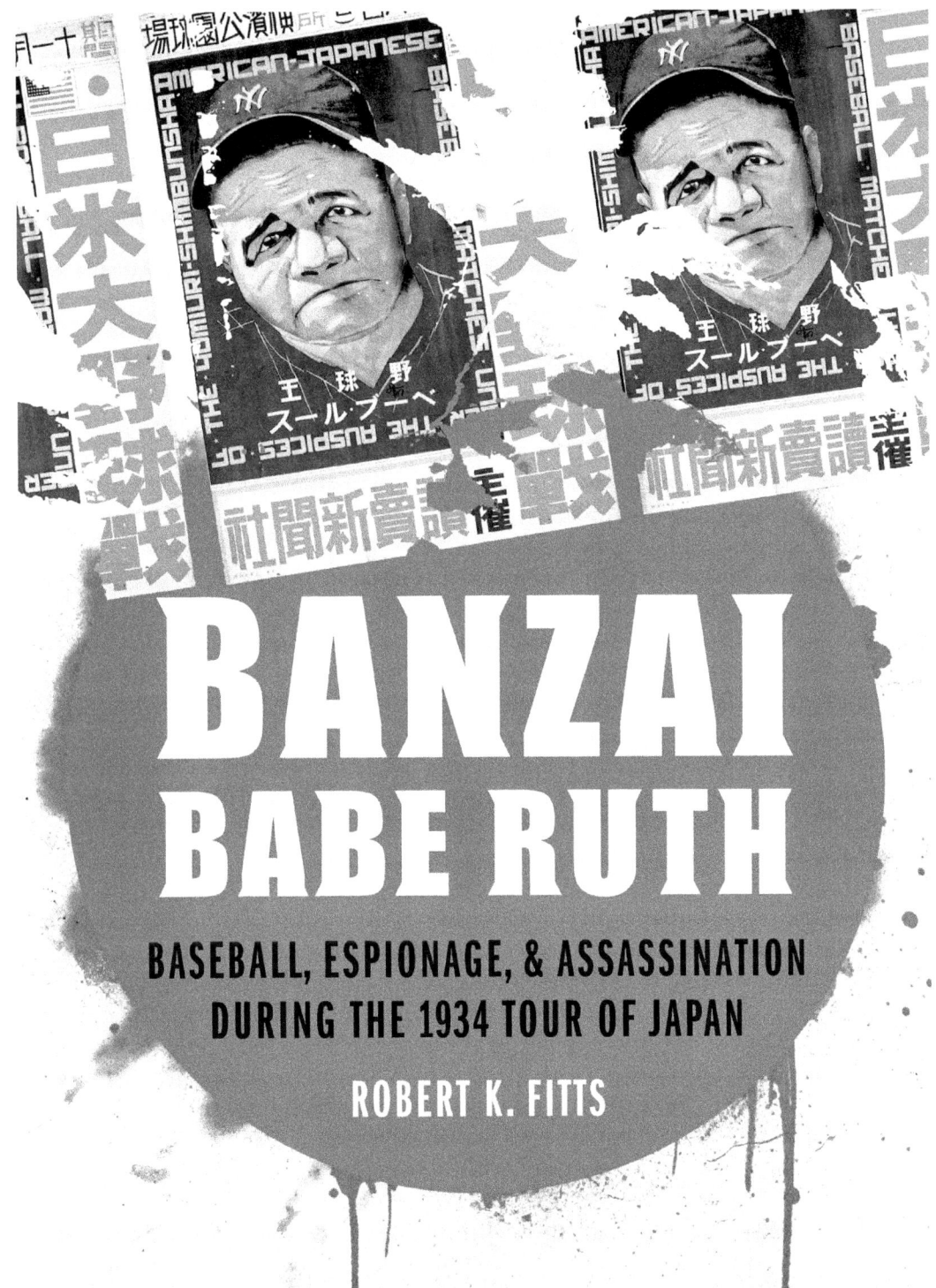

understanding between the United States and Japan and to defuse the tensions which were already drawing the two countries towards war. The catastrophe which became World War II simmers below the surface throughout Fitts' electric narrative (reading at times like a spy novel), and the book has become not only a lesson about the limits of baseball (or any sport for that matter) as a tool of cultural and political proselytizing, but also a cautionary tale for the perilous times in which we live.

Babe Ruth is featured in the book's title not only because it's such a catchy phrase, but also because Ruth was key to the entire adventure (*Banzai* translates to "May you live a thousand years"). The organizing force behind the tour was the owner of *Yomiuri Shimbun* newspaper, Matsutaro Shoriki, who was willing to underwrite it as a means of increasing his publication's readership. Shoriki came up with four non-negotiable conditions, the most important being that Ruth would be a member of the visiting major league all-star team, which came to be known as the All Americans. Even with the assistance of Lefty O'Doul, the legendary baseball ambassador to Japan, gaining approval for the tour, assembling a suitably star-studded team (another of Shoriki's conditions), and making all the necessary arrangements turned out to be a complicated and lengthy process full of fits and starts (all recounted in detail by the author). Encouraged by his wife and step daughter Julia who were keen to take the trip of a lifetime, Ruth at first agreed to join the tour, but, soured by his failure to secure the Yankees managerial job as his playing career wound down, he changed his mind. In the end it took a trip to New York by Sotaro Suzuki, a friend of O'Doul's and a sportswriter for *Yomiuri Shimbun*, to seal the deal. As a dejected Ruth climbed out of a barber's chair, Suzuki showed him one of the jackets with his image on it that *Yomiuri* newspaper hawkers planned to wear and a large poster with his mug on it bearing a caption that read "Baseball King Babe Ruth." This appeal to his vanity cheered the Big Bam no end and convinced him to grace the Japanese with his presence.

The 14-man major league all-star team that docked in Yokohama harbor on November 2, 1934, featured (in addition to Ruth) four future Hall of Famers (Lou Gehrig, Jimmie Foxx, Charlie Gehringer, and Lefty Gomez), but it was unquestionably Ruth who sent the Japanese into a frenzy. (In total the touring party consisted of 39 people and included wives, umpire John Quinn, sportswriter Stuart Bell, and assorted baseball dignitaries, such as Connie Mack and John "Bud" Hillerich.) When the motorcade transporting the tour members to their Tokyo hotel took a detour through the Ginza shopping district, the procession was brought to a crawl by a hundred thousand Japanese who flooded the wide streets and continuously roared, "Banzai! Banzai Babe Rusu!" while a beaming Ruth, standing in the rear of one of the limousines, waved Japanese and American flags which he'd grabbed from the crowd. This emotional outpouring of adulation, which was merely the beginning of an exhausting days-long reception, highlighted by banquets, speeches, and gift-giving, validated Shoriki's instincts and presaged the Babe's preeminent drawing-card status which never waned.

As expected, the All Americans dominated the All Nippon team (as the Japanese players were called), winning all 17 games; many of them by lopsided scores.

To allay the glaring mismatch of ability, several games were played with split squads (American and Japanese players on both teams), the All Americans on occasion tried to ease off the gas pedal, and Ruth further endeared himself to the fans by clowning. The fans' main interest lay in witnessing the power of the major leaguers, and they were content with a game if the All Americans clouted a few home runs. I.e., until Eiji Sawamura, the pitching star of the recently completed national high school championship in Koshien Stadium, held the All Americans at bay on November 20; losing 1–0 on a seventh-inning home run by Lou Gehrig. This performance gave the hosts hope, but Sawamura was battered in subsequent outings. Nevertheless, Connie Mack was so impressed he offered the youngster a contract to play for the Philadelphia A's, and Sawamura enjoyed national hero status for the rest of his life. After a slow start, Ruth lived up to the hype, leading all players with 13 homers and a .408 batting average. The disparity between American and Japanese baseball was most evident in the home run totals: 47 for the All Americans, three for All Nippon. Despite such results, the reader remains engrossed in the book's accounts of the contests; such is Fitts' most impressive narrative skills.

As alluded to earlier, unbeknownst to the All Americans, who were totally enthralled with the exoticness of Japanese culture and customs (though not so thrilled with the country's diet) as well as the natives' friendliness and hospitality, Japan was a deeply divided nation and a powder keg of competing philosophies and goals. Fitts intersperses with the baseball action incisive commentary on this complicated aspect of the Japanese zeitgeist that helps the reader understand the tenor of the times; particularly in Chapter 8 where he provides a dizzying review of numerous attempts in recent years to overthrow the government and restore total power to the Emperor and in Chapter 17 where he explains the government's leniency towards the violence carried out by the more than 150 ultranationalist groups, such as the War Gods Society, the Dark Ocean Society, and the Black Dragon Society, as long as the perpetrators claimed their actions stemmed from "love of country and emperor." Shoriki himself survived a brutal assassination attempt after the All Americans left the country for having "defiled the memory of the Emperor Meiji by allowing Babe Ruth and his team to play in the stadium named in the ruler's honor." The culmination of these dangerous revolutionary undercurrents occurred on the same day as Sawamura's great effort, when Japan's brutal secret police quietly but efficiently put down a military coup. "Only a handful of men knew that bloodshed, revolt, and maybe even civil war had nearly disrupted the All American baseball tour," writes Fitts.

Supplementing the two main thrusts of the narrative are a plenitude of gripping side stories: Jimmy Horio's unsuccessful efforts to become the first Japanese to play major league baseball; the visitors' voyage across the Pacific on the *Empress of Canada* and the salacious implications of Eleanor Gehrig's unaccompanied two-hour drinking session with Ruth in his cabin; the extensive sight-seeing done by the visitors, especially to Japan's most important shrines and temples; catcher Moe Berg's self-initiated espionage activities; the harrowing background of asylum-seeking Russian pitcher Victor Starfin; brief histories of baseball's introduction into Japan, China, and the Philippines; Japan's recent military conflicts and the brutality of its soldiers, especially during the Rape of Nanking; the efforts to use the 1934 tour as a springboard for the adoption of professional baseball in Japan; the four games the All Americans played in China and the Philippines on the way home; and Sawamura's total hatred of America once World War II got underway.

As Fitts explains, the tour was judged a complete success by every American participant. Many considered it to be a triumph of diplomacy, and Connie Mack predicted confidently that America and Japan would never go to war. Unfortunately, as everyone knows, it was all a mirage. The most poignant part of the book, which it was brilliant of the author to include, is Berg's short wave radio broadcast to the Japanese, expressing his disappointment at their betrayal of their American friends, his prediction that Japan would lose the war, and his naïve call for the Japanese people to rise up and demand an end to the hostilities. Equally unforgettable, though hardly poignant, is Babe Ruth's enraged reaction to Pearl Harbor: his throwing out the window of his high-rise New York apartment priceless souvenirs of the tour. The unsophisticated Ruth felt the betrayal as deeply as did the learned Berg, and true to form he tirelessly worked to raise money for the U.S. war effort. Nothing illustrates how completely the war changed things than Fitts' assessment that "the jovial, overweight, self-indulgent demigod of baseball, so welcome in 1934, had become a symbol of American decadence." Also true to form, when the Babe learned that Japanese soldiers were shouting "To hell with Babe Ruth" before suicidally charging American G.I. positions, he responded in kind, saying, "I hope every Jap that mentions my name gets shot—and to hell with all Japs anyway."

Later, right before his death in 1948, Ruth was able to articulate a more nuanced, less bitter view of the tragedy of World War II. For *The Babe Ruth Story*, he said to his as-told-to co-author Bob Considine, "No doubt there were plenty of stinkers among them; but looking back at the visit I feel it is another example of how a crackpot government can lead a friendly people to war." It is admittedly useless to say it, but if any sports book might benefit foreign policy makers in Washington, D.C., then surely that book would be *Banzai Babe Ruth*.

Baseball

◆

DAVID LEVINTHAL (*photographs*);
JONATHAN MAHLER (*text*)

◆

New York: Empire Editions, 2006. Cloth, 143 pages, ISBN: 0-9779008-00. Foreword. Player identification key to the photographs, Acknowledgments.

    Using a special Polaroid camera that produces huge 20" × 28" images, David Levinthal has built a brilliant career taking photos of children's toys and household objects to create startling and evocative versions of the adult world. Plastic army men and their weapons, cowboy and Indian figures, X-rated dolls and Barbies, and African American memorabilia have been the materials used by him to create series of arresting photographic scenes and images, such as *Hitler Moves East*, *Modern Romance*, *Wild West*, *Desire*, and the highly controversial *Blackface*. When Levinthal turned his attention to the national pastime, he found scores of plastic and ceramic statues and figurines brimming with hitherto unsuspected vitality and nostalgic value, and his masterfully executed color photos of these pieces resulted in *Baseball*, the most alluringly beautiful, exotic, and original book of consciously artful baseball photography ever published.

    Almost without exception, the photographs in *Baseball* are closeups of individual player figures, designed to accentuate telling details, but even when it broadens into a scene of more than one player, the field of our vision is comparatively restricted, a mere slice of the insinuated game in progress. The figurines are immersed in darkness, but darkness partially illuminated by background lighting of varying colors, and they stand in carefully constructed sets (all of them the work of Lori Jacobs of bloofoolz design). At ground level these sets, realistically reproducing clay granules, batters' boxes, baselines, and bases, are wonderfully life-like and easily apprehended, but at eye level the backgrounds are intentionally blurred so as to increase the focus on the figures. (Nevertheless, the detail discernable in the backgrounds varies, and in a scene depicting Joe DiMaggio completing his powerfully smooth, classic swing, we can make out behind him the blurry Yankee Stadium grandstands including a large swath of second-deck seating and an imposing, view-blocking support column.) Even parts of the player figurines are blurred, again to highlight certain aspects and to contribute to the illusions of motion, immediacy, and reality the artist seeks to create. The best example of this technique is found in the two-page photo of the figurine of Cincinnati Reds catcher Johnny Bench (from the waist up) looking upwards to track a Major League popup with his glove hand outstretched before him, while holding his mask in his right hand. Everything is slightly out of focus except for the part of the figure closest to us, Bench's catcher's mitt, so sharply captured that we can see the lacing in the mitt. On the other hand, sometimes an entire scene is blurred, as in the case of Jackie Robinson sliding into a base towards our viewpoint, with an infielder approaching the base from the right too late to make a difference. This is the artist's way of suggesting how quickly such a play ends: in a blur.

Levinthal used player figurines made by seven different companies: the Danbury Mint, Hartland plastics (& Hartland Collectibles), Gartlan U.S.A., Romito Enterprises, Salvino Sports Legends, Sports Impressions, and Upper Deck Historical Beginning. A total of 112 photos appear in the book, most of them utilizing Danbury Mint figurines, and for good reason: the superior attention to detail, the high quality of craftsmanship, and the exceeding verisimilitude exhibited by their products. Another reason Danbury Mint figurines were best suited for the artist's purposes is that they come separate from their wooden bases, a pin beneath each shoe of the player figurine fitting into a hole in its base. Because this feature enabled Levinthal to easily imbed the Danbury Mint figurines into the sets, he was always able to photograph these figures in their entirety when he desired to do so; something much harder (or even impossible) to do when the figurine comes securely attached to its base as is the case with most of the other manufacturers. For example, as the Bob Feller figurine (made by Romito and depicting the great Cleveland Indians right-hander rearing back, left foot pointing to the sky, prior to unleashing a blazing fastball) comes attached to a wooden base, Levinthal shot this figurine from the waist up, even though the drastic lean backwards of Feller's upper body in the full-page photo seems a bit disconcerting.

In the very best of these photos, the difference between art and life is very thin indeed, and the viewer is not only astounded by this slim discrepancy but happy to ignore it completely, if only momentarily. Included in this group of astonishingly realistic images are: Babe Ruth, Mark McGwire, Joe DiMaggio, Ichiro Suzuki, Derek Jeter, Willie McCovey, Don Mattingly, Hideki Matsui, Willie Stargell, Roger Maris, Bill Mazeroski, Kirk Gibson, Bobby Thomson, Willie Mays, Sammy Sosa, Carlton Fisk, Rod Carew, Al Kaline, and Barry Bonds ... all in one stage or another of the batting process; and Rollie Fingers, Tom Seaver, Roger Clemens, Pedro Martinez, Don Drysdale, Bob Gibson, Catfish Hunter, and Randy Johnson ... all in one stage or another of the pitching process (in a few cases Levinthal even gives us multiple shots of the same player batting or pitching from different angles). Other highly realistic images depict player figurines involved in other baseball actions, such as fielding (the Indians' Omar Vizquel and the NY Giants' Willie Mays), throwing (Roberto Clemente), chasing after a pop up (Tim McCarver), base running (Rickey Henderson), and blocking home plate (Thurman Munson). In most cases, the illusion created by these images is heightened by the fact that we easily recognize these famous players by the forms of their actions and movements, as well as by their uniforms, their jersey numbers, and the logos of the teams they represent. (A player identification key of small photos is included at the back of the book, but it is needed by knowledgeable fans in only a small number of instances.) In most of the above cases the player is depicted in typical form that might represent any moment of his career; at other times, specific, historic moments are referenced, such as Carlton Fisk waving his 1975 World Series home run fair, Bill Mazeroski stepping on home plate to complete his 1960 Series-winning home run, and Brooklyn's Jackie Robinson sliding in on an attempted steal of home as Yankees catcher Yogi Berra prepares to apply the tag in Game One of the 1955 World Series. Levinthal was so enthralled with this moment of baseball history, one during which Robinson was deemed safe on a highly controversial call, that he photographed it from four different angles, each providing a slightly different perspective.

With only an exception or two, the photos of the plastic statues made in the 1960s by the Hartland company are the least realistic of the bunch; yet they too are wonderful in their relative artificiality and serve as tributes to the figures as iconic toys which gave hours of enjoyment to us as children, and which we can now enjoy once again nostalgically through the artistry of Mr. Levinthal.

It may be a bit ironic to consider a work which contains no images of actual major league baseball players to be the greatest book of modern baseball photography ever produced. And one may legitimately ask what the purpose is of spending so much time, talent, expense, and effort on photographing ersatz representations of athletes who, in their actual persons, have been among the most frequently photographed people in the world. The answer to such a question is that in focusing our attention on these plastic and ceramic figurines and inviting us to really see what is before us, Mr. Levinthal offers us a greater appreciation for the cultural significance of these toy-like objects, for the stature of the baseball heroes we feel already well-acquainted with, and for the possibilities of the art of photography in the hands of practitioners willing to step outside the bounds of conventionality. If nothing else, after spending time being thoroughly mesmerized by his stunningly original and unique photos, most fans will find themselves unable to disagree with the belief expressed by Mr. Levinthal in saluting the book's designer that *Baseball* is a "remarkably beautiful book that will doubtless stand the test of time and serve as a testament to illustrated books and to the sport of baseball itself."

Baseball & Bubble Gum: The 1952 Topps Collection

◆

Tom Zappala *and* Ellen Zappala, with John Molori

◆

Portsmouth, NH: Peter E. Randall Publisher, 2020. Cloth, 235 pages, ISBN: 978-1-942155-31-7. Acknowledgments, Foreword by Joe Orlando, A Tribute to Sy Berger by Glenn Berger, Introduction. Player Index, About the Authors and Contributors. Other baseball books by the authors: The T206 Collection: The Players & Their Stories *(2010),* The Cracker Jack Collection: Baseball's Prized Players *(2013),* The 100 Greatest Baseball Autographs *(2016),* Legendary Lumber: The Top 100 Player Bats in Baseball History *(2017),* An All-Star's Cardboard Memories *(2018), and* The Diamondbacks Collection: 50 of the Greatest Cards in Sports Collecting History *(2022), all published by Peter E. Randall.*

Comments: *Baseball and Bubble Gum* won the 2021 Ben Franklin Award Silver Medal.

With former Red Sox third baseman Rico Petrocelli, Tom Zappala co-hosts *The Great American Collectibles Show*, aired nationally every week.

When baseball cards were given away free with the purchase of tobacco or snack products or sold for a penny a piece as an incentive to buy a stick of gum, no one could have foreseen the day that the cardboard photos of mere ballplayers would be regarded as so valuable and precious that photos of *them* would be gathered into sumptuous books treating them as iconic treasures of American popular culture. But that is exactly what has happened, and there is no finer example of a beautiful book of photography devoted to American baseball cards than *Baseball & Bubble Gum: The 1952 Topps Collection* by Tom & Ellen Zappala with John Molori.

When *Baseball & Bubble Gum* was published, the Zappalas were no rookies at treating significant baseball cards with due reverence, having earlier released similar books on two older sets of cards: *The T206 Collection: The Players & Their Stories*, in 2010, and *The Cracker Jack Collection: Baseball's Prized Players* in 2013. Yet the authors truly barreled up the ball with their third swing, as the 1952 Topps set has arguably become the most sensational and desirable set of baseball cards ever produced and certainly of the post-war period.

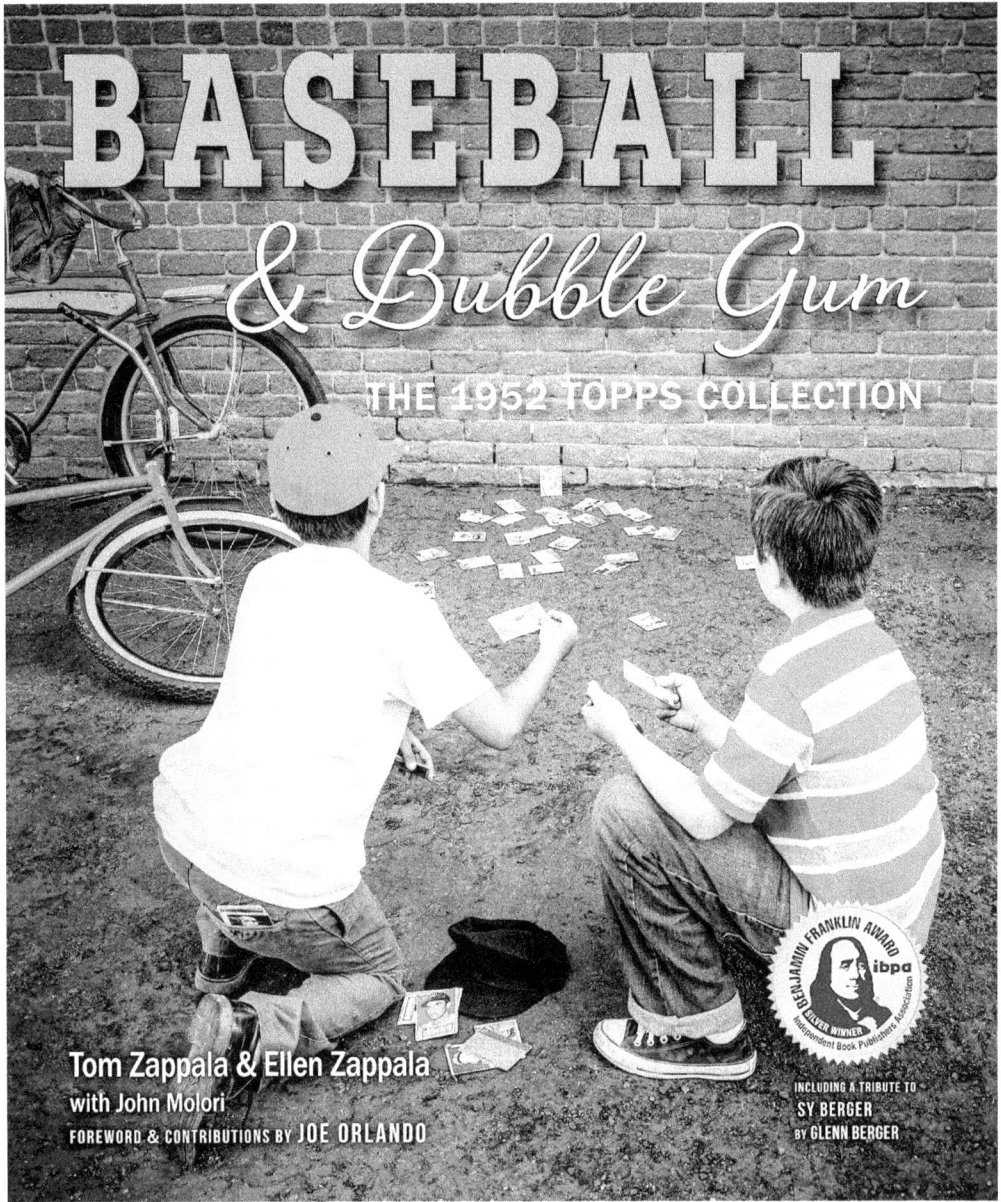

While the '52 Topps set has many virtues, one card in the set is most responsible for the veneration in which it is held: card # 311 of a very young New York Yankees superstar Mickey Mantle, glancing to his right while both hands grip a bat laying across his right shoulder. The Yankees dominated baseball in the 1950s, and Mantle was the team's cynosure, the fair-haired, broad-shouldered idol of boys across the country who recognized in Mantle's Olympic sprinter-speed and Herculean power hitting a combination of talents rarely seen in one mortal. Mantle actually made his baseball card debut the previous year on a card put out by the Bowman company, but his '52 Topps card, his Topps "rookie card," completely overshadows it. In fact, the '52 Mantle has become, along with the Honus Wagner tobacco card from the T206 set, the so-called Holy Grail of baseball cards. The Mantle card is so expensive that it is beyond the purchasing capability of all but the most deep-pocketed collectors, even in the lowest grades.

However, for the authors, *Baseball & Bubble Gum* is a book about appreciation, not values. Thus, every card in the 407-card set is depicted and treated with respect. The cards are grouped into three chapters: Chapter One displaying cards of 26 Hall of Famers; Chapter Two, cards of 142 "Uncommons"; and Chapter Three, 239 "Commons." A brief biography, "Career Stats," and the teams (and years) for which the player labored are included with the photo of each card.

Yet, there is no denying the ultra-lofty status of the Mantle card, and that is why it receives extra attention in the fourth and final chapter about the history and various other aspects of the set. In describing the allure of the Mantle card the authors write:

> The player and the card are almost too good to be true. The unforgettable pose, the beautiful blue and yellow colors, and even the name "Mickey Mantle" combine to create a card that only a Hollywood casting executive could dream up. The image has become more akin to pop culture art than a mere baseball card, which is why it has such powerful symbolic value alone.

The authors clearly wanted to keep the focus on the beauty and cultural importance of the cards rather than their values; plus, they realized all too well the futility of stating values that would be outdated as soon as the book was published. Nevertheless, price does come up once and in regard to the Mantle card. In a story about "finds" of 1952 cards, we are told that a New Jersey man was inspired by the 2018 sale of an almost perfect condition (MT 9) '52 Mantle for nearly $3 million to look though his stash of old cards which had lain undisturbed in an attic for seven decades. Among the man's cards were five 1952 Mantles which received grades from PSA (Professional Sports Authenticator), the leading card-grading service, of EX 5, EX 5, NM (Near Mint) 7, NM+ 7.5, and NM-MT+ 8. The five cards sold at auction for a combined $1,273,200. Such prices may not be the point of the book, but they do justify its publication as a wonder of the art of bookmaking and serve as a comforting consolation for collectors for whom putting together the set is prohibitively expensive.

Aside from the eminence of the Mantle card, as the authors explain, the 1952 Topps set is special also because it was Topps' first major release in their duel-to-the-death competition with Bowman, an established baseball card producer that Topps bought a few years later. Topps came out fighting by making bigger cards and a bigger set. At 2⅝" × 3¾"," the Topps card was considerably larger than the 1952 Bowman card which measured 2¹⁄₁₆" × 3⅛" as was the Topps set at 407 cards compared to the 252 cards which comprised the Bowman set. And Topps wasn't shy about publicizing the differences either; bragging about their new "GIANT-SIZE BASEBALL CARDS," "New Big Size," and "Giant Baseball Picture Cards" on wrappers and boxes.

Of more importance today is the beauty of the cards themselves. In its design the 1952 card is unsurpassable. Other than the white border around the edge of each card, only two elements prevent the '52 Topps card from being a "pure" card: a rectangular, yellow stars-on-black bordered box at the bottom of each card with the player's name and his facsimile autograph inside of it and a team logo perched on the upper left-hand corner of the box (another and most welcome Topps innovation). The absence of team names and player positions, wording that is a staple of modern card design, leaves the focus on the player photos. And here too, in its photography, the cards are exemplary. Closeups that familiarize the collector with the faces of the players predominate, and among these cards there is a judicious mixture of real world (ballpark) backgrounds and solid color-tinted ones, some of them enhanced by white auras around the head. There are enough action or posed-action photos to keep things interesting and, happily, no air-brushed caps or jerseys of traded players, a bane of later Topps offerings. In short, the cards seem like miniature works of art, and there are any number of cards that rival the Mantle card in attractiveness; such as the card of Cardinals outfielder Enos Slaughter (himself a Hall of Famer) depicted in a bat-over-the shoulder pose very similar to that of the Mantle card.

Given the age of '52 Topps cards, condition is always a major concern, and in order to present the set in the best possible light, the authors arranged to have photographed for the book only cards graded by PSA, with 8 NM-MT being the lowest grade included. That alone makes the book the best opportunity anyone will ever have to view the entire set in such outstanding condition.

Finally, in that fourth and concluding chapter, the authors discuss several other pertinent and intriguing matters, such as the "Bookends" (the first and last cards in the set which have usually been subject to additional abuse); the decision of Topps president Sy Berger to dump cases of unsold high-number (thus, more scarce) 1952 cards into the ocean in 1960; variations and errors in the set; and the reason Hall of Famers Whitey Ford, Stan Musial, and Ted Williams are absent from the set. A note about the photo on the cover is also in order. Yes, it shows two youngsters flipping 1952 cards (reprints, surely) against a brick wall, a common enough occurrence back when the cards were originally sold. Such an activity seems like nihilistic vandalism today, but the authors are making an ironic comment upon which they later enlarge after recounting the cringe-worthy deed of Mr. Berger.

After you are finished drying the tears from your eyes, keep in mind that part of the reason high-grade vintage cards are worth so much today is because of stories like this. If moms kept all their children's cards, kids never put them in bicycle spokes and Topps archived everything that didn't sell, then scarcity would play a much more limited role. Like the sport of baseball itself, part of the appeal is that it's not easy. It's hard to hit a Major League breaking ball and it's hard to find top-quality collectibles. The truth is that no one knows how the preservation of all those cards would have impacted the market today. What we do know is that collectors may decide to cut moms across the country a little more slack for cleaning out their rooms and taking out the trash. Remember, it wouldn't be considered treasure today if it was common.

This is a thoughtful, sensible assessment of the situation but one that may not comfort all that much the average collector who no longer owns the baseball cards of his youth. At least, in regard to Topps' greatest achievement, and thanks to Tom and Ellen Zappala and their team, he has *Baseball & Bubble Gum* to ease his pain.

Baseball's Golden Age: The Photographs of Charles M. Conlon

◆

NEAL McCABE *and* CONSTANCE McCABE

◆

New York: Harry N. Abrams, 1993. Cloth, 198 pages, ISBN: 0-8109-3130-3. Preface, Acknowledgments, "The Base Ball Photographer." Index to the plates. Other baseball books by the authors: The Big Show: Charles M. Conlon's Golden Age Baseball Photographs *(Abrams, 2011).*

For true bibliophiles, every book is something of a miracle. On rare occasions, everything about a particular book is miraculous, and such is the case with *Baseball's Golden Age: The Photographs of Charles M. Conlon* by Neal and Constance McCabe.

Consider the elements involved in the creation of the book. We begin with Conlon himself, a self-effacing newspaper proofreader and self-taught *amateur* photographer who, using an unwieldy box-like Graflex camera, took more photos of dead-ball era players than anybody else. Next, many of the heavy but delicate glass plate negatives from which Conlon's photos were printed did not survive (Conlon himself threw away thousands of them), but more than 8,000 of them did. Then, intelligent archivists/conservators such as Steve Gietschier of *The Sporting News* and Constance McCabe of the National Gallery of Art needed to recognize the importance of and properly care for the surviving negatives. It was necessary for a talented writer like Neal McCabe to see not just the potential for such a book but the *necessity* of producing it, in order to share Conlon's artistry with the public and to facilitate, at last, the wide-spread acclaim he so richly deserves. And finally, there had to be a classy publisher like Abrams in business for the express purpose of publishing handsome books on the finer things in life, such as great art, architecture, photography, and other cultural treasures. Thus, this greatest of all baseball photography books came about through the confluence of a number of unlikely factors and was a long time in coming, but then again, such miracles don't happen every day.

In a short Preface and a biographical essay of approximately 4,600 words, McCabe tells us how in the beginning (1904) Conlon's photos appeared in newspapers and magazines "haphazardly and anonymously." By 1909 his photographs filled the pages of the two prominent baseball Guides of the day, and by 1920 when his work was appearing regularly, and attributed to him, in the *New York Telegram* and *The Sporting News* he "had become, de facto, the official photographer of baseball." During his time and in his milieu, Conlon was well known and well liked–John McGraw even had one of his players attempt an ill-advised steal of third one day, just to make sure Conlon got at least one photo in the game he could use—yet he remained so completely anonymous to the public at large until the publication of this book that his name "has never appeared in any history of American photography." Given the paucity of information published about Conlon before the McCabes began work on the book, Neal's essay is extremely important, as it fleshes out Conlon's career, describing how he worked and detailing the difficulties and dangers he faced while engaged in his art.

Equally challenging for McCabe was the composition of the captions for the more than 200 photos in the book. There is an art to writing captions, and it is one mastered by Mr. McCabe. The trick for the most part is saying a lot in a few words and saying something interesting as well; not an easy thing to do when, in the case of photographs like these, the subject must be identified and the significance of each photo explained. Early in the book (page 26) we get a prime example of McCabe's skill through his caption for a photo of Ty Cobb stealing third base in a 1909 game against the New York Highlanders (a name later changed to Yankees). As he often does, McCabe begins with a confident declaration, demonstrating that he'd done his homework. Next, he explains the history and status of the original photo and then lets Conlon (based on a couple of magazine articles, the only writing ever produced by the photographer) himself explain how the great photo came to be:

> This, Conlon's most famous image, is the greatest baseball action picture ever taken. Miraculously, the priceless glass negative still exists, having somehow survived the careless treatment the photographer gave it. Curious visitors were asked: "Would you like to see the original glass plate of that picture?" And the fragile negative would be passed from hand to hand.
>
> Charles M. Conlon: "The strange thing about that picture was that I did not know I had snapped it. I was off third, chatting with Jimmy Austin, third baseman for the New York club. Cobb was on second, with one out, and the hitter was trying to bunt him to third. Austin moved in for the sacrifice. As Jimmy stood there, Cobb started. The fans shouted. Jimmy turned, backed into the base, and was greeted by a storm of dirt, spikes, shoes, uniforms— and Ty Cobb. My first thought was that my friend, Austin, had been hurt....
>
> But in a moment I realized he wasn't hurt, and I was relieved.... Then I began to wonder if by any chance I had snapped the play. I couldn't remember that I had, but I decided to play [it] safe and change plates anyway. I went home kicking myself. I said, 'Now there was a great picture and you missed it.' I took out my plates and developed them. There was Cobb stealing third. In my excitement, I had snapped it, by instinct."

Conciseness being so important, McCabe also sometimes sums things up in one opening sentence. The caption for a photo of Fred Merkle begins: "On September 28, 1908, this man's life was ruined." What follows is the best possible two-sentence summary of the boner which ultimately cost Merkle's New York Giants the 1908 National League pennant. Similarly, the caption for Boston catcher Bill Bergen begins: "This man is, without question, the worst hitter in the history of baseball"; while that for

Jack Dunn, a utility infielder posing in his 1904 Giants uniform starts: "This man discovered George Herman Ruth and signed him to his first professional contract on Valentine's Day, 1914." Dunn is famous for doing just that, but even knowledgeable fans may be surprised to see that he was a major leaguer and an old Orioles teammate of John McGraw before he became a minor league team owner. There is even more to the story which McCabe gives us, the fact that McGraw never forgave Dunn for later selling Ruth to the Red Sox without offering him to the Giants.

McCabe points out subtle things we might miss (like Ruth parking his ABC wad of chewing gum on the top of his hat for a Conlon closeup) and a bent-over Giant sitting in the dugout background being caught in the first photo of a player spitting. And time and time again, he smartly interprets the expressions on the faces of Conlon's subjects: describing, for example, Wee Willie Keeler's "sad eyes gazing skyward with a look of foreboding and resignation" and Yankees manager Miller Huggins's face showing "the strain of trying—and failing—to tame Babe Ruth and the other members of Murderer's Row."

As skillful and informed as McCabe's captions are, it is Conlon's pictures of course which steal the show. These are all black and white, a matter of necessity which became a virtue in the hands of a master like Conlon. Somehow, Conlon always found the perfect lighting so that the faces of his subjects are never obscured by shadow. His subjects are invariably perfectly framed, and the crispness of his pictures is unimprovable, making debatable McCabe's puzzling statement that Conlon "never fully mastered the mysteries of focus." Conlon took every conceivable type of photo and all are present in the book. While closeups were not his favorite type of picture, the book contains more than a few: for example, of Honus Wagner's batting grip, Eddie Cicotte's knuckleball grip, catcher Jimmy Archer's oft-broken fingers, and, most intimate of all, the sober faces of the players who composed the '27 Yankees Murderers' Row. Although Conlon took hundreds of action photos from actual games, only a handful of the negatives survived, and the Cobb sliding photo along with an amazing shot of Hack Wilson throwing himself backwards to avoid a brushback are the only such pictures in the book. Conlon took the vast majority of his photos before the games, and so the bulk of the photos in the book are still portraits and photos of players posed to simulate their batting, pitching, and fielding motions. They are exquisite images nevertheless that show us much about the players depicted and which preserve an era of the game which is indeed appropriately dubbed "golden."

As he did with the Cobb sliding photo, McCabe singles out other photos for special recognition, calling one of the Brooklyn Superbas' Tim "Big City" Jordan at the end of his swing "one of the most graceful batting photographs ever taken" and another of a young Mel Ott twisted in a batting practice follow-through "one of his [Conlon's] most beautiful photographs." Readers will have no difficulty selecting their own favorites; some of which are certain to be those which have attained iconic status: a photo of a broadly smiling rookie named Lou Gehrig (happy, we are told, because Yankees first baseman Wally Pipp is being benched); a portrait of the Cubs' Johnny Evers, his off-the-charts baseball IQ evident in his face and the way he is choking up on the bat laid across his left shoulder; another showing us the dreamy look on the face of every batter's worst nightmare, the Giants' screw-balling Carl

Hubbell; and the absolutely arresting image of a "pitcher's-eye view of one the most fearsome batters ever to step up to the plate, the man who inspired Babe Ruth's batting style," Shoeless Joe Jackson of the 1913 Cleveland Naps.

Throughout this book, McCabe sings Conlon's praises, concluding that Conlon "deserves to be ranked with the acknowledged masters of twentieth-century documentary photography." He will get no argument here, nor I suspect from anybody else who immerses himself in the extraordinary visual pleasures provided by this book.

Big Red Dynasty:
How Bob Howsam & Sparky Anderson
Built the Big Red Machine

◆

GREG RHODES *and* JOHN ERARDI

◆

Cincinnati: Road West, 1997. Cloth, 298 pages, ISBN: 0-9641402-2-5. Forewords by Bob Howsam and Sparky Anderson, Introduction by Marty Brennaman. Appendix: Big Red Machine Scrapbook, 1970–1978, References, Subject Index, About the Authors, 158 black & white and color photos throughout. Other baseball books by the authors: The First Boys of Summer: The 1869–1870 Cincinnati Red Stockings, Baseball's First Professional Team *(Road West, 1994),* Cincinnati's Crosley Field: The Illustrated History of a Classic Ballpark *(Road West, 1995), and* Opening Day: Celebrating Cincinnati's Baseball Holiday *(Road West, 2004).* Baseball Revolutionaries: How the 1869 Cincinnati Red Stockings Rocked the Country and Made Baseball Famous *(Baseball Revolutionaries Press, 2019) by Greg Rhodes, John Erardi, and Greg Gajus.* Reds in Black and White *(Road West, 1999) by Greg Rhodes and Mark Stang.* Redleg Journal: Year by Year and Day by Day with the Cincinnati Reds Since 1866 *(Road West, 2000) by Greg Rhodes and John Snyder.* Cincinnati Reds Hall of Fame Highlights *(Road West, 2007) by Greg Rhodes.* Redleg Memories: The Reds of the Fifties and Sixties *(Road West, 2021) by Greg Rhodes.* Pete Rose 4,192 *by John Erardi (The Cincinnati Enquirer, 1985).*

Comments: The 8 ¾" × 10 ¼" size of the book is conducive to the many charts, lists, sidebars, and photos included. The cover features a photo of an autographed Reds team baseball, the red stitches of which are raised and can be felt by the reader's fingers.

Numerous teams throughout the long history of major league baseball have dominated the game for a sufficient period of time to deserve the title "dynasty." A handful of such teams vie for the honor of being recognized as the game's greatest team: the '27 Yankees, Mr. Mack's '29–31 A's, the Brooklyn Dodgers of the 1950s, etc. While the debate may never be settled to everyone's satisfaction, one thing is certain: no contender has been chronicled and dissected as brilliantly as the 1970s' Cincinnati Reds in *Big Red Dynasty: How Bob Howsam and Sparky Anderson Built the Big Red Machine* by Greg Rhodes and John Erardi. Chief among the authors' numerous revelations and insights, gleaned from extensive interviews with the principals,

is the fact that Cincinnati's powerhouse ballclub was envisioned and constructed as carefully as a skyscraper; and their detailed, behind-the-scenes account of how it all happened, including the dynasty's demise, not only makes for enthralling reading but also delineates the defining characteristics of one of baseball's most important, transitioning eras.

The heroes of *Big Red Dynasty*, as the book's subtitle indicates, are Reds GM Bob Howsam and field manager Sparky Anderson; and particularly, Howsam, as it was he who stuck out his neck to give Anderson his first managing job in the big leagues. Given Howsam's accomplishments and his importance to the emergence of the Reds' dynasty, it is amazing that so little about him had been previously published (Myron J. Smith, Jr.'s *Baseball: A Comprehensive Bibliography* contains exactly one entry on him). And there was a lot to know about Bob Howsam. A native Coloradan, Howsam grew up working in the family's honey bee business in La Jara. He found his entrée into professional sports through marriage, when his father-in-law, Colorado Senator and titular head of the struggling Western League, Ed Johnson, appointed him the League's actual working president. Howman turned the League around and then, with his father and brother, formed Rocky Mountain Empire Sports and bought the Denver Bears. The Bears set attendance records, which enabled the Howsams to build Bears Stadium, "the first modern ballpark in the history of Denver." Through the Bears' affiliations, first with the Pirates and later with the Yankees, Howsam learned the ins and outs of baseball front office management from two masters, Branch Rickey and George Weiss; and he was twice named Minor League Executive of the Year by *The Sporting News*. (Meeting Weiss instilled in Howsam a desire to earn a World Series ring. He figured Weiss had about ten such rings and was surprised to learn the number was nineteen.) Howsam later worked with Rickey on the proposed third baseball major league, the Continental League. While the league never got off the ground, it did lead to expansion, just not in Denver. Howsam landed on his feet when he was offered a franchise in another upstart sports league that did succeed, the American Football League. Enlarging Bears Stadium for pro football and funding the Broncos from the ground up proved to be more costly than the Howsams could afford so the family sold out, and Bob started an investment firm. Fortunately for the Cincinnati Reds, Howsam longed to return to baseball; and it happened when Rickey, a special consultant to August Busch, Jr., convinced the owner to hire Howsam as a replacement for Cardinals GM Bing Devine. Howsam was in St. Louis less than three years before the Reds, under new ownership, came calling in 1967; seeking someone "with major league experience, who was promotions-minded and committed to a vigorous farm system."

Howsam brought trusted lieutenants with him (hatchet-man and personal assistant Dick Wagner and farm director Chief Bender) and immediately began to put his stamp on the entire Reds organization. Rolling out a philosophy that "you have to spend money to make money," he strove to turn the Reds into a first-class operation and to create a family atmosphere in the front office as well as at the ballpark (he fixed up old Crosley Field even as plans to build its replacement, Riverfront Stadium, were well underway). He expected employees to work long hours and to show loyalty to him and total dedication to the Reds and the game of baseball. Most important of all, he went about assembling perhaps the best scouting department in the game. Years earlier he had learned that "nothing is more important or satisfying than scouting, developing and evaluating players, and forming a network of skilled baseball men whose decisions he could trust."

Howsam's emphasis on "thorough research and preparation" manifested itself dramatically prior to his first June draft with the Reds in 1967. With the Reds supposedly set to make pitcher Wayne Simpson their first pick, holdover scouting director Jim McLaughlin threw into the mix a player "he had seen only in a couple of games at a tournament." The "haphazard recommendation" shocked Howsam and convinced him to replace McLaughlin. Other key elements of Howsam's scouting and player evaluation philosophy were the idea of obtaining "quality through quantity"; an emphasis on speed; honesty and openness in discussions of players but unity once a final decision had been made; and patience with young players (if even one man in Howsam's inner circle stood up for a player, the Reds would give that player more time to develop). In short, Howsam loved his scouts and understood their importance in contrast to future Reds owner Marge Schott, who dissed them by the comment that all they did was sit around and watch baseball games. When other cost-conscious teams put their scouts in compact cars, Howsam went with gas-guzzlers to afford better protection for his scouts. Howsam particularly relied on the judgments of super-scout Ray Shore, the previously unsung hero of the Big Red Machine's success, who finally gets his due in the book. It was Shore who helped bring about the most important trade in team history, the one which brought Houston Astros second baseman Joe Morgan to Cincinnati, giving the team a Hall of Fame-quality Big Four unit of Pete Rose, Johnny Bench, Tony Perez, and Morgan which no other team could match. The Reds scouting crew did such productive work that Howsam realized he usually knew more about the ballclubs he was trying to trade with than the people running those teams.

As for Anderson, who elicited newspaper headlines of "Sparky Who?" upon his hiring, he proved himself to be the perfect complement to Howsam. Like Howsam, Anderson understood that the game was changing, and he was completely on board with the plan to tailor the roster to take advantage of Riverfront Stadium's faster Astro-turf surface. The Reds were at the forefront of two monumental shifts in the game. In 1976, for the first time since 1927, there were more stolen bases in the National League than home runs. And as "Captain Hook," who went to his bullpen quickly and often, Anderson was way ahead of his time. "By 1977," say the authors, "saves had surpassed complete games in the National League. But Anderson and the Reds had made the transition seven years earlier." Anderson had great talent to work with, yes, but he also knew how to get the most out of it; the best example of his ingenuity and flexibility being the move of Pete Rose to third base in order to get the big bat of George Foster into the lineup on a daily basis.

The authors review the decade of the 1970s year by year, covering the key moments on the field and the heroics of individual players, while paying close attention to the player comings and goings that show how the organization slowly built the powerhouse that finally proved its greatness by winning consecutive World Series. The confidence felt by everyone involved as the climax approached, the '76 World Series against the Yankees, was best exemplified by Anderson, who said he thought the Reds would win in seven games; meaning not a seven-game World Series but a four-game sweep of the Yankees to go along with the three-game sweep of the Phillies in the NLCS. Along the way, the authors also perform analyses that result in information of revelatory quality. In discussing the disastrous trade of Tony Perez after the 1976 season, for example, they explain that it was the loss of Perez's calming influence in the clubhouse that hurt the team; not the play of his replacement, Dan Driessen, who turned in a 1977 season comparable to what Perez did with the Montreal Expos. We also learn, incredibly, that the Reds considered trading Perez earlier, right after the 1974 season. Even more startling: the revelation that the so-called Great Eight (Rose, Griffey, Morgan, Perez, Bench, Foster, Concepcion, and Geronimo) started only 87 games in the 1975 and '76 seasons combined, including the post-season; as most fans remember the group always taking the field together. Not so startling, the winning percentage of that lineup in those 87 games: .793 (69–18)!

From 1970 through 1976, the Howsam/Anderson-led Reds won five Division titles, four NL pennants, and two World Series. It was an achievement to be immensely proud of, but it all fell part as suddenly as free agency changed the rules governing the retention of players and the dynamics governing the power struggle between ownership/management and the players. Howsam despised the new order, and whether or not his refusal to allow the Reds to join in on the bidding for free agents cost the team further championships is a legitimate question to ask. Other routine problems, "potholes" the authors call them ... injuries, bad trades, the aging of veterans, the failure of prospects ... appeared in the road; and while Howsam and Anderson had steered the Big Red Machine around most of them for seven seasons, in 1977 and 1978 "the Reds hit every one." At the end of the book, a reminiscing Howsam gets the last word about the legacy of the Reds dynasty: "You couldn't replace them (the talented players). Just be happy you had the ballclub like the Big Red Machine." Howsam spoke as if he were addressing Reds fans; who should also be happy, we venture to add, to have a tribute to those teams as superb as *Big Red Dynasty*.

Billy Martin: Baseball's Flawed Genius

◆

Bill Pennington

◆

Boston: Houghton Mifflin Harcourt, 2015. Cloth, 530 pages, ISBN: 978-0-544-02209-6. Introduction. Epilogue, Acknowledgments, Notes on Research and Sources, Bibliography, Index, 43 black & white photos between pages 242 and 243.

    Comments: *Billy Martin* won the 2016 Seymour Medal and was a finalist for the 2015 CASEY Award.

    Publishers can get carried away using lengthy subtitles as explanatory, promotional teasers, but if ever the subtitle of a baseball book bears paying attention to, surely it is the succinct one selected by Houghton Mifflin for *Billy Martin: Baseball's Flawed Genius*; Bill Pennington's biography of the New York Yankees' most controversial manager. Seldom have three words captured so poignantly its subject as the subtitle of *Billy Martin* or indicated so accurately the tenor of such a complex and multi-dimensional biography. Such a subtitle promises much in the way of fascinating reading, and the book delivers in a big way from its first to final pages; making *Billy Martin* an unforgettable account of a frenetic life lived like an endless roller coaster ride.

    For Alfred Manuel "Billy" Martin, Jr., the genius half of the equation was the easy part. Almost as soon as Martin could pick up a baseball, his goal in life was to play for the New York Yankees. Despite a scrawny frame, he made that extremely unlikely dream come true by totally dedicating himself to the game. Having been mentored while growing up by a series of wintering major league players at the park near his modest home in West Berkeley, California, the precocious 19-year-old Martin was named MVP of a tough minor league circuit in only his second year as a pro. The next year he helped the Triple A Oakland Oaks win the PCL championship and, more importantly, received graduate school baseball training at the side of Casey Stengel. He became known as "Casey's boy," and a year after Stengel was named manager of the Yankees, "The Professor" brought his protégé to New York to play second base. Martin made the most of it, becoming the team's infield sparkplug and playing a crucial role in the Yankees' World Series championships of 1952 and '53 (in the latter Fall Classic, Billy hit .500

and set a record for hits in a six-game Series with 12). His trade to Kansas City in 1957, supposedly because he was a bad influence on Mickey Mantle and Whitey Ford, emotionally devastated him, ruined his relationship with Stengel for years, and turned him into a journeyman who labored briefly for five more teams before he retired.

It was all merely an apprenticeship for the job he was born to do, being the manager of a major league baseball team. In 1969 Martin won an unexpected divisional title with the Minnesota Twins in his first shot and another, even more unexpected one, in 1972 with the Detroit Tigers. He was finally called home by Yankees owner George Steinbrenner two thirds of the way through the 1975 season. The very next year under Martin's tutelage, the Yankees won their first American League pennant in eleven years. They lost the World Series to the Cincinnati Reds but came back even stronger in 1977 to win 100 games and beat the L.A. Dodgers in the World Series. With that championship, his status as an all-time Yankees great was assured.

No one has chronicled these glories and the following years of Martin's baseball career better than Pennington; who, for instance, deftly identifies and gives numerous examples of the sources of Martin's success: his superb player evaluations; his constant teaching of fundamentals, especially in spring training; his setting high goals for his players and convincing them they were able to achieve them; his hyper awareness of everything happening on the field; his philosophy of putting constant pressure on the opposition (the basis of what came to be known as "Billy Ball" when he later managed the Oakland A's); his fondness for the hidden-ball trick, the squeeze play, and the double and even triple steal plays (especially those involving steals of home); his uncanny ability to steal the opponents' signs; and his unmatched knowledge of the rule book and his ability to use it for his team's advantage (e.g., the infamous Pine Tar Game during which he had a George Brett home run nullified).

But what really sets the author's narrative apart from all other Martin biographies is his handling of the other side of the story: Martin's drinking and his inability to stay out of trouble, especially away from the ballpark. Martin's self-destructive tendencies were apparent from the beginning, and Pennington's thorough examination of Martin's early life enables the reader to perceive that to Martin they were merely examples of his determination to survive. Martin was raised by a foul-mouthed mother who, abandoned by her first two husbands, was a tough survivor herself. "Don't take shit from anybody!" she drummed into him. And according to several of the close friends and relatives whom Pennington interviewed, fist fights were almost a daily occurrence for everybody in the Martin adolescence milieu. Although Pennington does not say so, the fighting as a matter of pride and self-preservation became an ingrained part of Martin's psyche and identity. For example, Martin was kicked off his high school baseball team his senior year after he TKO-ed a rival who attacked him in a post-game fight. When the principal said he should learn to turn the other check, Martin told him "…in my neighborhood I wouldn't be alive if I turned the other cheek." Whereas most males leave them behind with adolescence, fist fights became for Martin an unbelievably regular part of his adult life. Amazingly, Billy's pugilistic scorecard was seldom blotted with a defeat. Bar flys who imagined themselves tough guys looked at the slim Martin, especially during his stints as Yankees manager, and thought they saw a pushover; but what they failed to consider was the training Martin had received as a kid from former professional prizefighter Dick Foster. Martin knew how to throw devastating punches, and in his defense he often acknowledged that while he never started a fight, he ended many.

While the endless fights and drunken episodes marred both his playing and managerial careers, Martin was a highly likable person. He was extremely generous and sincere about his Catholic faith, despite his numerous sins of the flesh. Women also found him charming and irresistible. Martin's first marriage was a youthful indiscretion, but in the case of his subsequent three marriages, the women all loved him deeply, and their love was reciprocated. Pennington's triumphant interviews with these women provide great insight into the subject as a person and lend heft to the narrative not found in previous Martin biographies. Above all, Martin was adored by Yankees fans who showered him on numerous occasions with adulation usually reserved for superstars the caliber of DiMaggio and Mantle.

There is a sadness to this biography in the sense the reader gets that while Martin achieved much, his was an unfulfilled life. Billy lived not just for baseball, but baseball as a New York Yankee. Pennington is quite correct when he says that the most meaningful statement the subject ever uttered was what Martin said at the ceremony unveiling his plaque in Yankee Stadium's Monument Park: "I may not have been the greatest Yankee to put on a uniform but I was the proudest." Martin was happiest when he was manager of the Yankees, but the job also stressed him out, drained him, and left him vulnerable to challenges he was unable to meet without damaging his health, his job security, and his reputation. Nothing better exemplifies Martin's "flawed" nature than the fact that, hired and fired five times, he was unable to keep his dream job. On top of this, although many of Martin's numerous close friends did not like his fourth wife whom they regarded as "controlling," there's no doubt that she provided some much-needed stability in his life and brought his finances under control. The fact that the 61-year-old Martin died in a car wreck near his Binghamton, New York, farm on Christmas Day 1989 after a night of drinking with an old friend reeks with irony, as he and Steinbrenner had agreed upon yet another comeback at some point in the 1990 season. There was controversy about whether Martin was driving at the time the car slid off the road and into a ditch; but Pennington, who handles the whole incident dispassionately, says the evidence clearly exonerates him. And the main reason Martin died of a broken neck is that he wasn't wearing a seat belt.

After detailing the effect of Martin's death on various people and describing his funeral which drew crowds comparable to the ticker tape parade that celebrated the Yankees 1977 World Championship, Pennington considers the Hall of Fame question and suggests that it is Martin's reputation as a drunken brawler which has kept the doors closed. This leads to the more relevant point that in a way Billy Martin was let down by society which at the time did not recognize alcoholism as a disease. Martin got no help whatsoever with his drinking problem, and there is no guarantee that it would have made much difference if he had. On the other hand, it seems unfair to hold against him what Martin was physically and perhaps psychologically unable to control. For on balance, as this penetrating biography demonstrates, Billy Martin gave much more to baseball and to life than he took from them.

Bleachers:
A Summer in Wrigley Field

◆

LONNIE WHEELER

◆

Chicago: Contemporary Books, 1988. Cloth, 238 Pages, ISBN: 0-8092-4641-4. Acknowledgments, Introduction. Postlude. Other baseball books by the author: The Cincinnati Game *(Orange Fraser Press, 1988),* I Had a Hammer: The Hank Aaron Story *(Harper Collins, 1991),* Stranger to the Game: The Autobiography of Bob Gibson *(Viking Penguin, 1994),* Sixty Feet, Six Inches: A Hall of Fame Pitcher & A Hall of Fame Hitter Talk About How the Game Is Played *(Knopf Doubleday, 2011),* Long Shot *(Simon & Schuster, 2014),* Intangiball: The Subtle Things That Win Baseball Games *(Simon & Schuster, 2015),* Pitch by Pitch: My View of One Unforgettable Game *(Flatiron Books, 2015), and* The Bona Fide Legend of Cool Papa Bell: Speed, Grace, and the Negro Leagues *(Harry N. Abrams, 2022).*

Comments: *Bleachers* was nominated as a finalist for the 1988 CASEY Award for Best Baseball Book of the Year, along with *The Cincinnati Game*, the first and only time that the same author has had two CASEY Award finalists in the same year.

With the enveloping sense of place that almost every one of them offers, its ballparks give baseball a huge emotional and aesthetic advantage over other sports and the often soul-less venues in which their contests unfold. The crown jewel of major league ballparks is Wrigley Field, home of the Chicago Cubs, and the most special space in this most special of baseball places is the bleachers, the rows of hard, green, backless benches that run in rows behind the outfield walls from left to right fields; the bleachers, where one finds the most passionate, the most knowledgeable, the quintessential fans. Lonnie Wheeler, a native of St. Louis who spent most of his adult life in Cincinnati, instinctively knew these things and set out to illustrate them by spending a season in the Wrigley Field bleachers, as a fan, an observer, and a reporter. Wheeler's vivid, six-month guided tour of the ordinary 1987 Cubs season among the heralded "Bleacher Bums" vicariously provides an extraordinary experience for the reader and validates his beliefs that "the bleachers at Wrigley Field were what baseball was all about, and that if a book could capture the bleachers, it could capture baseball."

Naturally, a writer as curious and perspicacious as Wheeler could not spend half a baseball season in the Wrigley Field bleachers without delving into the various aspects that combine to make them such a distinctive place to be and the Cubs such an irresistible team to follow. There was a lot to cover, and the author judiciously doles out scoops of information and history about these aspects in well-spaced intervals (often segueing into them via something that happened or was said during a ballgame). For instance, he begins the chapter devoted to the month of May with a look at the history of the ballpark's most famous physical feature ("The ivy turns in May," he begins), and he goes on to provide succinct and fascinating ruminations on the scoreboard and the park's semaphoric baseball flags. Happily, with Wheeler, we get the facts along with their significance. After pointing out the simplicity of Wrigley's massive center field scoreboard (which he notes had never been reached by a home run), he writes: "Wrigley's scoreboard is what it purports to be—a board for scores." As for the won-loss flags that fly after each game, they are "more indulgent than informative, because any Cub fan worth Rich Nye's resin bag knows what the boys have done before he starts home."

Other topics which serve as welcome digressions include the origins of the name and concept of the Bleacher Bums (founder Mike Murphy says that they were a media creation, born during the excitement of the 1969 doomed pennant run); television's impact on the popularity of the Cubs in general and the bleachers in particular; the Cubs' questionable preference for plodding power-laden ballclubs that could take advantage of Chicago's frequently windy conditions; the extreme density and diversity of Wrigley's Lake View neighborhood (Wheeler calls the area "Chicago's Ellis Island"); the lingering hangover from the team's long stretch of mediocrity (upon the book's publication in 1988 the Cubs had still not been back to the World Series since 1945); the Cubs-White Sox competition for supremacy in Chicago; whether Andre Dawson's great season qualified him for the MVP Award he did win; and the controversy over the team's desire to install lights at Wrigley which simmered all season long and drew close to a resolution in favor of lights, only to have those pro-lights hopes dashed upon the death of Mayor Harold Washington the day before Thanksgiving.

As intriguing as these mini-essays are, the book revolves around the games being played and the fans there, in the bleachers, to watch them. Wheeler keeps play-by-play to a minimum; sometimes summing up the action in one sentence: "Trout pitched his second straight shutout, the Cubs won 7–0, and things didn't look so bad." He focuses instead on key moments and the ends of ballgames, the last couple of innings when, time after time, things were decided. Often the drama centered on the Cubs closer, Lee Smith, with whom the fans in the bleachers had a love-hate relationship. When Smith was called on in the bottom of the ninth of an August game against the Mets, Wheeler writes, "Then with two outs and no runners, it became a Smithian game." Smith gets the last out, whiffing Dave Magadan for his 29th save, but not before loading the bases and driving the entire crowd to distraction.

Although the Cubs stood atop the NL East Division standings in May, they slowly lost ground until they finished dead last. It is a tribute to Wheeler's abilities that we never lose interest in the Cubs' season. And a lot of interesting things did happen at Wrigley Field in 1987. In April catcher Jody Davis hit the Cubs' 4,000th

Wrigley Field home run, and in August Houston's Bill Doran hit Wrigley Field's 8,000th. Right fielder Andre Dawson hit for the cycle in one game and in another threw out a batter at first who had (for a moment) singled. The Cubs hit six homers in a 22–7 win against the Astros on June 3, and seven Cubs were ejected from a game in July as a result of a bean ball battle with the Padres. Rookie Greg Maddux, starting his Hall of Fame career as the youngest player in the National League, was demoted mid-season to the minor leagues, and veteran first baseman Leon Durham was credited with nine unassisted putouts in a single September contest. While any fan might have noted these events, Wheeler astutely calls our attention to more subtle occurrences. For instance, he points out that the first and last pitches of a Cubs win against the Reds in May resulted in home runs. Musing on Wrigley's track record as a Zephyrus-abetted launching pad, he reminds us that while the ballpark was the site of the highest-scoring game in history (26–23, in 1922), it also hosted the only double no-hit game ever pitched (by Fred Toney and Hippo Vaughn). Most strangely of all, when the Cubs complete a suspended game against the Dodgers from the day before and then have the scheduled game suspended too, he recognizes the oddity by writing, "Thirty-six thousand people had seen portions of two games and all of none."

Ultimately, Wheeler finds the essence of the bleachers experience in the fans with whom he shared the summer, and a motley crew they were: ballhawks, gamblers, sun bathers, body builders, drunks, hooky-playing businessmen and women, characters like the screaming Ronnie "Woo Woo" Wilkers, scorecard keepers (many as diligent as scholars), blind guys with super-charged powers of recall, fans of both sexes on the make, frisbee tossers, chanters ("Right field sucks!"), and beer drinkers, beer sprayers, and beer dousers. Many of these bleacherites were also at one time or another vociferous bench jockeys and unabashed critics. Wheeler records much ragging on the opposition, some of it crude, much of it humorous. He also overheard and preserves a great deal of criticism of GM Dallas Green's leadership and manager Gene Michael's in-game strategy; both of which demonstrate real knowledge of the game. What characterizes the fans in the bleachers best though is their devotion to the Cubs and their eternal, indefatigable optimism.

Scoreboard operator Art Sagel was born four blocks from the ballpark. Terry Hemstreet tells Wheeler about his dad who kept hoping for a Cubs pennant to his dying day ("At the end, I'd tell him the Cubs were winning, and that would perk him up.") Leonard Becker, a 50-year denizen of the bleachers, tells the author and other doubters the Cubs will finish a June game despite a downpour that lasts almost three hours … and they do. And Jerry Pritikin, the self-promoting "Bleacher Preacher" always looking for ways to monetize his fan-ship, has been stuck on the Cubs since 1945 when his father said he was too young to go to the 1945 World Series. "I'll take you the next time the Cubs are in it," Henry Pritikin told his son. This legacy of loyalty is what Wheeler means when he writes that Wrigley Field is a "hand-me-down ballpark." Undying hope is part of the deal too. At the end of June Steve Schanker admits he was about to give up on the season; "Then they won a couple of games and sucked me in again," he says. And in August when Wheeler overhears one fan tell another that the fading Cubs are "making their move," he remembers the earlier words of Gary Grosskaus: "Being a Cubs fan is like getting married for the second time–hope wins out over experience."

At one point in mid-August when a sparse crowd allows Wheeler to relax and enjoy an inconsequential game without the usual crazy atmosphere, he opines that the bleachers had become perhaps too popular, a "caricature of themselves." He springs from this idea into a consideration of baseball's special allure, referring to:

> "…the way it plays itself out over a season, unfolding with patient, playful deliberation, nothing meaning everything and everything meaning something. For every game to be a circus is to have baseball's rambling rhapsody drowned out by drums and cymbals. Game by game, it doesn't compare with football, and yet the sum total of a football season is but a box of chocolates next to baseball's pig on the spit."

This is vintage Wheeler, and while he enjoyed a bit of peace and quiet, the thoughtful, poetic riff serves as a mere interlude for the reader, whom he has completely sold on the indispensability of the Wrigley Field bleachers. In the Postlude, the author disagrees with people who thought it a shame he picked such a lousy season to cover. "I thought it was a quintessential Cub summer—and, in that sense, a quintessential baseball summer," he writes. Readers, sorry to run out of ballgames to share with the author, will surely agree.

Bottom of the 33rd: Hope, Redemption, and Baseball's Longest Game

Dan Barry

New York: Harper, 2011. Cloth, 255 pages, ISBN: 978-0-06-201448-1. Prologue. Sources, Thank-Yous, and Cracker Jack; Official Box Score, About the Author, 12 black & white photos throughout.

    Comments: End papers are a photo of Pawtucket's McCoy Stadium in winter. New owners of the Pawtucket Red Sox franchise moved it to Worcester, Massachusetts, for the 2021 season, spelling the end for the ballpark which had opened in 1942. Demolition of McCoy Stadium began in March 2025 and was scheduled to be completed in July.

    Bottom of the 33rd by Dan Barry is the best book ever written about a single game of professional baseball. Unsurpassed in its keen understanding of the ways a minor league team can insinuate itself into the fabric of its host city, the book drapes a heroic mantle over the ambitions, achievements, and disappointments of its subjects; the numerous people who played, umpired, watched, and supported behind the scenes the longest game of professional baseball ever played. And in dissecting so brilliantly the surreal 33-inning 1981 contest between the Rochester Red Wings and the Pawtucket Red Sox in literate, at times lyrical prose that never flags for even a paragraph, it represents the single book best suited to make converts out of non-fans, those readers who come to it not already enthralled by the fascinating human and historic elements always at play in even the most ordinary of baseball games.

    And the International League game begun on the cold and windy Easter Saturday night of April 18, 1981, finally suspended after 32 innings at four o'clock in the morning, and concluded on June 23, 1981, at Pawtucket's McCoy Stadium was, after all, just another early-season Triple A matchup; despite its featuring in the two teams' starting lineups a number of past and future major leaguers, including the now famous pair of third basemen, anointed with super-hero drive and ability, who would eventually ascend to Hall of Fame heights: Cal Ripken, Jr., and Wade Boggs. It was just one more bush league scrimmage, that is, until it wouldn't end … until it seemed to acquire a life of its own that the players were powerless to extinguish.

Besides the length of the game, records were set, to be sure: time of game was 8:25; there were 219 at bats and 60 strikeouts; Rochester center fielder Dallas Williams went 0–13 and Pawtucket's DH Russ Laribee whiffed seven times ... seven times! ... (while going 0–11); and Scott Luebber and Jim Umbarger, both of Rochester, pitched eight and ten innings of *extra-innings* relief. As noteworthy as all these additions to the record book were, however, Barry realized that his story did not reside in these statistical oddities, nor was a detailed account of the play-by-play in order. In a 33-inning game that finally ended with a score of 3–2, such a recitation would have been stultifyingly boring. And that's why Barry used a sort of shorthand summary more than once to convey the repetitive, unexciting action that took over the contest, as he did for the 30th inning:

> ROCHESTER: groundout; strikeout; strikeout.
> PAWTUCKET: groundout; groundout; single; fly out.

No, Barry was not interested in translating into prose the epically over-documented scorecard of official scorer Bill George, who used four different colors of ink in an attempt to keep straight his record of the marathon action. What interested Barry was the human factor, and it is his weaving together the many divergent strands of personal, political, civic, and baseball history which impacted the game into one beautiful tapestry that creates the masterpiece that is *Bottom of the 33rd*.

While narrating the ebb and flow of the game in the present tense, Barry expertly uses both the past and the future to provide background and context to the events unfolding before the readers' eyes. For instance, after Rochester takes a 1–0 lead in the seventh inning, he utilizes the pause in the action of the seventh inning stretch to present the bizarre history of well-worn McCoy Stadium having been built on a most unsuitable site: Pawtucket's Hammond Pond which had to be drained and repeatedly filled in and bolstered with hundreds of wooden and concrete pilings. As introduction to this history, the author provides a most irresistible lead-in, imagining the laborers who built the ballpark, the first minor leaguers to call the place home (they were named after the king of the city's one-time important textile industry), and the mayor whose determined vision forced the stadium into being to be ghosts, haunting McCoy and joining the actual fans in the common leg-stretching ritual:

> Standing at the very back of section 1, on the first-base side, watching from the concourse, Depression-hardened men in battered cloth caps and mud-flecked overalls shaking their heads in disbelief that the thing ever got built. Standing in the blue general-admission seats, in section 12 along the third-base side, ballplayers in woolen uniforms with red-and-navy piping and the word "Slaters" scripted across the chests, itching to snag the next foul ball to show they still have what it takes. And standing before the best box seat in the house, white hair crisply parted and bristle-short on the sides, wearing a dark suit offset by a shamrock-patterned tie and a red rose in his left lapel: Himself, The Prince of Pawtucket, Mayor Thomas P. McCoy, Dead since 1945, but looking out upon his handiwork, all aglow, and sniffing:
> "McCoy's Folly, indeed."

In a similar way, Barry not only brings the reader up to date on the past of each person integral to the story, but he also discloses what the future holds for him;

knowledge which adds understanding and often much pathos to our perceptions of the participants. For instance, as the game appears to reach its conclusion with Rochester still ahead 1–0 in the bottom of the ninth, the Pawtucket clubhouse "boy" nicknamed "Hood" finishes preparing a special post-game meal for the Rochester players that will go cold and unappreciated when Pawtucket ties the game with two outs to send it into extra innings. Barry tells us that this totally dedicated young man will one day become Deputy Police Chief Michael Kinch and, we learn towards the end of the book, a pall bearer at the funeral of the beloved team owner who hired him, Ben Mondor. Pawtucket's right fielder Sam Bowen, with nothing left to prove at the Triple A level, comes to bat in the bottom of the 26th inning with the game tied 2–2. We learn that a couple of years before this game, Bowen had been on his way to the big leagues via a trade to the Tigers, until he inadvertently sabotaged his promotion (and the trade) by being honest with Detroit GM Jim Campbell about a minor injury from which he was recovering. Bowen crushes a pitch for a game-ending home run, until a gale force wind knocks it down, turning it into a harmless fly ball: a piece of bad luck symbolic of the trajectory of his career. And on the day of the suspended game's resumption gung-ho former unpaid intern Lou Schwechheimer, now working as only the team's third full-time employee, hustles to meet the needs of the 140 media members who show up for the resumption of the game on June 23. He later rises, we are told, to the position of senior vice president and serves with Mondor and GM Mike Tamburro as the PawSox's brain trust for three decades. Barry finds just the right spot to flesh out the personal stories of these three participants and those of many many more to invest the drama with the utmost human interest appeal.

When the narration reaches the point of the game's suspension after 32 innings, Barry refers to the game, which has settled nothing, as "this protracted demonstration of endurance, commitment, and that great engine of human existence, ambition." The player Barry chooses as the standard bearer of this collection of virtues is Pawtucket first baseman Dave Koza, who functions as the book's protagonist. Koza is an excellent fielder and power hitter who nevertheless languishes year after year in Pawtucket as teammates get late-season call-ups to Boston. Barry devotes more space to him than any other player in the book, and we learn much about his home town of Torrington, Wyoming (where he is regarded as a hero despite his failure to complete the final leg of his journey) and his supportive wife Ann, who is one of the fewer than 20 exhausted fans who stick out the first 32 innings to the bone-chilling end. When Koza finally works up the courage to ask Pawtucket manager Joe Morgan why he is never the guy who gets promoted, Morgan tells him that he is just not consistent enough. It's highly satisfying poetic justice then when Koza is the player who gets the hit to end the famous game: not one of his towering home runs hit off a fastball but a little dinker over the third baseman's head hit off a curveball, low and away. And it's Koza and his post-career struggles whom Barry focuses on in the Epilogue that checks in on some of the game's mainstays 30 years later.

There remains the question of how the game happened in the first place. It was certainly an aberration of the first order. The mother of Pawtucket's AWOL bat boys becomes worried sick and treks to McCoy to demand their return. Hours after hurling his four innings of relief, Pawtucket's Luis Aponte trudges home at three in the morning, only to be denied entrance by his wife who is convinced he's been out drinking. And Rochester's play-by-play radio broadcaster Bob Drew, who called every pitch from McCoy's unheated press box, is completely cognizant of the irony of his efforts, when he tells his listeners back in New York that it's "Inning number thirty-two. It's been tied since the twenty-first, for ten innings. My goodness. What a beautiful morning for baseball here in Pawtucket. We'll hear birds chirping anytime now."

It happened this way. A page got left out of the 1981 International League rule book: the page about a curfew, about no inning starting after midnight, and so the umpires believed the show had to go on. IL President Harold Cooper at first ignored Pawtucket's desperate phone calls, believing they were prank or nuisance calls (when Cooper finally returned the calls, he ordered the game, if still tied, suspended at the bottom of the inning, the 32nd). Pitchers on both teams pitched well, and the cold weather and high winds further conspired against effective hitting. Thus, this miraculous event, witnessed by so few people, came about through the confluence of mistakes and fateful factors, and it happened on the holiest evening of the year; the symbolic significance of which was not lost on the author who makes numerous knowing and respectful references to Christ and to His triumph. A triumph, the celebration of which was being joyously, if unconsciously, awaited by hundreds of millions outside the walls of McCoy Stadium. Readers can rejoice that Dan Barry achieved his own triumph in telling so well the story of all the people who participated in and endured the longest game in professional baseball history.

Bouton: The Life of a Baseball Original

Mitchell Nathanson

Lincoln: University of Nebraska Press, 2020. Cloth, 407 pages, ISBN: 9781496217707. Acknowledgments, Prologue: Publication Day. Epilogue: The Cool of the Evening, Notes, Bibliography, Index, 32 black & white photos between pages 200 and 201. Other baseball books by the author: The Fall of the 1977 Phillies: How a Baseball Team's Collapse Sank a City's Spirit *(McFarland, 2007),* A People's History of Baseball *(University of Illinois Press, 2012),* God Almighty Hisself: The Life and Legend of Dick Allen *(University of Pennsylvania Press, 2019), and* Under Jackie's Shadow: Voices of Black Minor Leaguers Left Behind *(University of Nebraska Press, 2024).*

According to Mitchell Nathanson, and it is difficult to argue with his premise, the three most influential baseball players of the 1960s were Dick Allen, Jim Bouton, and Curt Flood. As the basis of such an opinion, Nathanson is alluding not to the players' on-field performances and accomplishments, as significant as they were, but to the impact each had on the game as a profession, a business, and an American cultural institution. Bouton is most famous as the author of *Ball Four*, a highly controversial book at the time of its publication which has not only stood the test of time but remains perhaps the most popular baseball book ever published. Yet, as ground-breaking and impactful as the book was, it did not come close to defining Bouton. Few players have led as rich, as interesting, and as accomplished a life after baseball as Bouton, and Nathanson having captured it all so perfectly in *Bouton: The Life of a Baseball Original* makes the book one of the undisputed masterpieces of baseball biography.

Putting on the cover a photo of Jim Bouton, slouching bare-footed on a beach, hands jammed into the pockets of tight white jeans, was a stroke of genius, as it announces right off the bat that the book is not going to be the typical baseball biography based primarily on events that transpired between the white lines. Nicknamed "Bulldog," Bouton *was* a terrific starting pitcher with the New York Yankees but for a very short period of time. He threw hard, the effort expended often jarring the cap off his head, and his moniker paid tribute to his ultra competitiveness. And pitching was in his blood. Like the "Spaceman" Bill Lee, Bouton continued to play amateur baseball long after he hurt his arm and his career fizzled out, first with the

one-year Seattle Pilots and then with the Houston Astros. And despite success off the diamond, Bouton was unable to accept his retirement until after he had accomplished his most unlikely come back to the major leagues as a knuckleball-throwing relief pitcher with Ted Turner's hapless Atlanta Braves; a quixotic odyssey which drained his bank account and caused his first wife (Bobbie) and young family to move around like vagabonds.

Bouton's playing career then, it could be argued, was important not so much for helping the fading Yankees dynasty extend its run of domination for another couple of years but for giving him the material and platform to produce *Ball Four*; and Nathanson skillfully keeps this dynamic before the reader's eyes as he documents the particulars of Bouton's pitching career on all levels, including his compatible stints with the independent and perfectly named Portland Mavericks (known as the "Bastards of Baseball") and the Durango Alacranes of the Mexican League.

Just as importantly, the author explains how the new breed of younger, less starry-eyed sportswriters known as "Chipmunks" were drawn to Bouton and his counter cultural views and attitudes; clarifies the role of sportswriter Leonard Schecter as an editor, not the primary author, of *Ball Four*; and reviews the "tell-some" predecessors to Bouton's inaugural sports "tell-all." Most deliciously, he recounts the highly polarized reaction to the book, especially Commissioner Bowie Kuhn's officious and outraged condemnation which ironically served to boost interest in and sales of the book.

As Nathanson demonstrates, the mindset that produced *Ball Four* did not suddenly break forth like a torrential thunderstorm on a sunny day but had been formed during a youth and adolescence marked by the habit of charging to the beat of a different drummer. From an early age, Bouton stood out among his peers. With a family history of like-minded souls, Bouton was a born hustler, innovator, entrepreneur, and leader … one who questioned everything, challenged the status quo, and insisted on doing things his own way. For example, while the typical kid earned money delivering newspapers or mowing lawns, Bouton made and sold jewelry and water color paintings. And he never led the post-career life of most ballplayers. He went into television sports broadcasting at a time when ex-jocks were still a novelty in the field; and, breaking all the rules and tormenting his bosses, quickly became the most popular sports news broadcaster in the New York City area. He later toyed with the idea of running for public office, acted reasonably well as the villain in the Hollywood movie *The Long Goodbye* (starring Elliot Gould), became a motivational speaker, and made a small fortune off "Big League Chew," the shredded bubble-gum in a pouch product that he went into business producing and marketing with minor league teammate Rob Nelson who originally came up the idea (actually, Nelson mentioned the idea in passing). And then there was what turned out to be a real career as an author: Bouton churning out a succession of other noteworthy if not particularly lucrative baseball books, in addition to updates of *Ball Four*, that proved his prowess as a writer. Not everything Bouton touched turned to gold, of course. Failures include a proposed TV adaptation of *Ball Four* and his disastrous involvement in a scheme to organize, regulate, and market on a national basis the playing of vintage "base ball." Yet, until dementia put a stop to it, it was his ceaseless searching for the next big idea which made him so different from his colleagues and so attractive as a subject of biography.

Bouton's fame rests on his authorship of *Ball Four*, but as Nathanson shows, he paid a heavy price for daring to break one of professional baseball's most sacred taboos: transgressing the privacy of the clubhouse and revealing the peccadillos of his teammates, especially sexual ones. He was denounced by many of his former teammates who became important figures in the book, most of whom had always considered him to be an odd bird, and he essentially became a persona non grata in baseball circles. Although he was never officially banned from Old-Timers Day celebrations at Yankee Stadium, he never appeared at one until 1998 when his son Michael appealed to the team to invite him as a means of helping him cope with the tragic accidental death of his sister and Jim's daughter Laurie. The chapter devoted to these two related circumstances is typical of the entire book in its being extremely insightful and empathetic, rich in painstakingly unearthed detail, and characterized by singing, perfectly-pitched prose. About the effect of Laurie's demise on Bouton, for instance, Nathanson writes: "Her death left him in a fog he had trouble emerging from."

Today, there is little in *Ball Four* that would shock the average reader. Yet it is still an exceptionally funny and entertaining book to read. Its power resides in its humanizing ballplayers who were once put on pedestals, portrayed as demi gods. Bouton changed that perception with one fell stroke, showing the world that apart from their rare physical abilities, ballplayers are just like the rest of us, flawed in various ways. It was a service for which Bouton still receives much credit.

In a similar fashion, Mitchell Nathanson (who received the full cooperation of Bouton and his second wife and caretaker Paula Kurman) has done the world a great service in composing not just one more baseball biography but baseball's first literary biography, the life story of an author who just happened to also be a ball player. While easily ploughing through this wonderous tale, many readers will not even realize how much they are absorbing about the art of writing, its challenges, its methods, its pitfalls, and its joys. But if they reflect on the experience, they may come to the conclusion that *Bouton* is such a great book because it was written by an author who is a kindred spirit with his subject. Finally, if *Bouton* does nothing else, it will (as the book in your hands attempts to do for the works it examines) make you determined to read (or re-read) for yourself the classic baseball book that inspired it.

The Bullpen Gospels: Major League Dreams of a Minor League Veteran

◆

Dirk Hayhurst

◆

New York: Citadel Press, 2010. Paper, 340 pages, ISBN: 978-0-8065-3143-4. A Note from the Author, Prologue. Other baseball books by the author: Out of My League: A Rookie's Survival in the Bigs *(Citadel Press, 2012),* Wild Pitches: Extra Innings from Out of My League *(Citadel Press, 2013), and* Bigger Than the Game: Restitching a Major League Life *(Citadel Press, 2014).*

Comments: In the *New York Times Book Review* Jonathan Eig called the book "an American classic." The book, he continued, "may be the funniest baseball memoir since Jim Bouton's *Ball Four.*"

"This is the long-awaited, much-needed minor-league equivalent of *Ball Four*. It's eloquent. It's insightful. It's poignant. It's hilarious. Sometimes all in the same paragraph. I love it. All of it."—Jayson Stark, ESPN.com

Few baseball literary debuts have been as spectacular as the one Dirk Hayhurst made in 2010 with the publication of *The Bullpen Gospels: Major League Dreams of a Minor League Veteran*: his beautifully-written, highly introspective, and hilarious account of his 2007 season laboring in the farm system of the San Diego Padres. With a bus load of original expressions, a remarkable facility with language, and an uncanny ability to re-create lively conversations and unforgettable scenes, Hayhurst demonstrates on every page that he is a real writer; a fact supported by his subsequent publication of three equally engaging sequels. In its depiction of the minors as a combination weeding-out process and halfway house for talented but immature athletes obsessed with scatological humor, the book is like other minor league memoirs; it is unique in its moving account of the author's struggle, not only to succeed as a pitcher, but to understand and live up to the true meaning of the role of a professional baseball player; an effort rarely undertaken in the literature.

In the early chapters of the book, Hayhurst gives us a good look at the circumstances of his life in his hometown of Canton, Ohio, and they aren't pretty. He lives with his grouchy, misanthropic grandmother, and his bedroom consists of an air mattress on the floor of her laundry room. He puts up with this arrangement because, as a four-year veteran minor leaguer, he's basically broke and, more importantly, because he is a member of a totally dysfunctional family: one consisting of a withdrawn father, perpetually angry over an accident that has left him disabled, unable to work, and barely capable of tying his own shoes; a violent and abusive older brother who has become a mean alcoholic due to his ADD, cleft pallet, poor self-image, and jealousy over his younger brother's prowess as an athlete; and a victimized mother so stressed out by being caught between two such unhappy people and by having to shoulder the family's financial burden that she can offer Dirk only the meagerest of emotional support. At this point in his career, Hayhurst finds himself at a crossroads, wondering if he should continue to chase the dream of making it to the big leagues and feeling as if he really doesn't want to continue. "I know folks would say that walking away from such a great opportunity would be a mistake," he says. "But what if giving up some of the best years of your life for something that may never happen is the mistake? There comes a moment in life, no matter what your line of work is, when you have to step back and wonder if you're heading in the right direction." It is clear that nobody in his family is capable of helping him deal with this existential question; and so, as much to escape familial chaos as to take his destiny by the horns, he heads off to one more spring training.

Before he leaves, Hayhurst spends a couple of hours at the local homeless shelter, working the door and handing out lunch tickets. Hayhurst regards the volunteering as a harmless image-boosting activity, but on this day it turns into something much more. When an old man wearing filthy clothes and worn-out, rain-soaked boots shows up, Dirk assumes the man will be suitably impressed to meet a professional baseball player and even offers him a signed Dirk Hayhurst baseball card. When the old man throws Hayhurst's arrogance back into his face, Dirk drops a handful of cards and meal tickets on the floor. Bending over to pick them up, he finally notices the old man's footwear. Chastened and suddenly desiring to actually help his fellow man, Hayhurst offers his "fancy leather workman's boots" in exchange for the old man's ratty boots; an offer the old man gratefully accepts. It's an important scene, a moment of foreshadowing epiphany for the rest of the book:

> I didn't know that man in rags, and he didn't know me, but we knew how to treat each other because of the clothes we wore. Yet, something deeper than stained rags, dirty hands, glossy pictures, and clean uniforms took place between us. In that moment, both awkward and perfect, something happened I didn't quite understand. For a moment the burden of baseball left my shoulders, and I wasn't a player to be labeled. Though I didn't understand it all right there, I knew my life in the game was going to change.

What happened, of course, was that Hayhurst observed the second commandment, which is to Love Thy Neighbor as Thy Self. He began, in other words, to live out the Biblical Gospel. That word, "Gospel," is not in the book's title by accident, but Hayhurst hardly wears his beliefs on his sleeve. In fact, he fits in so well with his teammates that they are shocked to learn he is a teetotaler and a virgin, saving himself for marriage. Nevertheless, while Hayhurst never references it, the Christian faith and its beliefs are what underpin the transformation he undergoes throughout the time period covered by the book.

Hayhurst, who previously got as high as Triple A for a brief unimpressive stint, pitches well in the spring but becomes a victim of the numbers game. Hoping to be assigned to the Padres Double A team in San Antonio, he is offered instead a take-it-or-leave-it spot in the bullpen of the Lake Elsinore Pirates team of the High Single A California League, which he grudgingly accepts, for his fourth round with the team. Sucking it up, he pitches well, and quickly earns a promotion to San Antonio, where he continues to pitch better than ever. His once unpromising season is crowned when the Missions rally to win the Texas League championship. This triumph and Dirk's improvement on the mound though pales in comparison to the series of events that bring about his growth as a person.

Speaking at a Lake Elsinore meet-the-team party, a vision he has of himself pitching against the "Baseball Reaper" makes him realize that he has been his own worst enemy. Later, as a Missions player, he rues his inability to provide any joy via the gift of a baseball to a totally disabled boy in a wheelchair. And then when asked why he is pitching so much better than the year before he tries to explain that he no longer pins his entire self-image on his being a baseball player. The Missions pitching coach doesn't quite understand this answer, but the reader does.

The book reaches its thematic climax in its most powerful scene, when Hayhurst's brother, trying desperately to recover from his alcoholism, apologizes and begs Dirk's forgiveness over the phone. Upset by the poor performance he has just turned in before the Padres major league brass, Hayhurst initially lets his anger get the best of him and refuses to forgive his brother; but he is already a new man and ultimately follows the command of Jesus who, when asked if one should forgive his brother seven times, says, "I do not say to thee seven times, but seventy times seven (Matt. 18:22)." Near the end of the season, Hayhurst's probings into the philosophical dimensions of his profession come to a head during a second life-changing encounter with a fan. A heart-broken mother of a 3-year-old boy dying of liver cancer asks not for a free baseball, like so many other annoying, entitled fans, but only that Dirk "be a real person to him." When Hayhurst realizes the situation, he and his teammates adopt the kid and for a couple of innings turn him into the happiest person in the ballpark by treating him like a real member of the San Antonio bullpen. "I'd wondered all year how the power of baseball should be wielded," he says. "And now I knew.… The burden of the player isn't to achieve greatness, but to give the feeling of it to everyone he encounters."

The scene of the book's final chapter is Hayhurst's wedding day, a year later, after he'd begun the 2008 season in Triple A and finally made it to the major leagues. He recounts how during the reception he spoke about all that he had learned during his journey to the big leagues and to this special day with his new bride Bonnie. Especially important to him was his relationship with Trevor Hoffman, the Padres Hall of Fame closer. Hoffman told Dirk that their conversations had made him think about baseball in ways he never had before, and Hoffman's greatest insight was very much like Hayhurst's: that there is "more to a person than just what they do, and that only a real person, not an icon or an image or a jersey, can take a job that puts a man on a pedestal and use it for something selfless." It's not much of a stretch to see in this idea an echo of one of the most well-known paradoxes of the Biblical Gospel, our Lord's saying "For he who would save his life will lose it, but he who loses his life for my sake will find it. (Matt. 16:25)"

It takes a close reading of the book to discern its seriousness, belied as it is by the author's self-deprecation and old-pro jadedness. Even more distracting is the ever present humor, and juvenile as much of it is … the insults, the pranks, the obsession with body parts and smells, and the stupid discussions (such as whether guys or girls are bigger sluts) are truly laugh-out-loud funny; at least to male readers whose standards of decorum are admittedly lower than those of their female counterparts, excepting perhaps Chaucer's Wife of Bath. But this is as it should be, for Hayhurst was not an evangelist, nor did he have any desire to become one. No, he was just a disciple trying to discover his true self and his life's purpose. He clearly succeeded in that mission, and *The Bullpen Gospels* is his inspiring written testimony.

Cardboard Gods: An All-American Tale Through Baseball Cards

Josh Wilker

New York: Seven Footer Press, 2010. Cloth, 243 pages, ISBN: 978-1-934734-16-2. Color photos of 60 Topps baseball cards from the 1970s, plus one color photo of a Topps basketball card and nine color photos of the author and members of his family. Front end papers are a collage of the fronts of Topps baseball cards; the rear end papers, a collage of the backs of Topps baseball cards.

Comments: As tributes to the baseball cards Wilker writes about, the publisher covered the book in a wax paper DJ that resembles a baseball card wrapper from the 1970s and inserted a photo of an old baseball card slab of gum on the page opposite of the copyright page, to fulfill the promise "With 1 Stick of BUBBBLE GUM" that appears beneath the title of the book on the DJ.

The Chicago Tribune called the book "clever, witty, self-effacing, fun and poignant" and said that it is "too good to be classified as mere blog-to-memoir," a reference to the fact that Wilker first wrote about his childhood and baseball cards in a blog: most recently to be found at cardboardgods.net.

Wilker is a winner of the Howard Frank Mosher Prize for Short Fiction.

Anyone who thinks that baseball cards are nothing more than a type of children's amusement that inexplicably morphed into a class of investments should read *Cardboard Gods: An All-American Tale Through Baseball Cards* by Josh Wilker. The autobiography of a sensitive, thoughtful boy, hampered by a challenging family situation and terrified by life's uncertainties, the book does not say one word about the monetary value of cards, but it demonstrates as no other sustained piece of writing ever has the other kinds of benefits, especially emotional assuagement, often derived from baseball cards by devoted collectors. No one who reads this moving, often hilarious account will ever doubt again the important connections that can be made between young collectors and the talismans of hero worship we conveniently refer to as baseball cards.

While Josh Wilker may have been a bit naturally neurotic, life certainly gave him from an early age plenty to be anxious about. He and his older brother Ian became part of a three-parent experiment when their father Louis Wilker moved into the spare bedroom while a younger man, Tom Byrne, became mom Jenny Wilker's paramour. This arrangement was amazingly rancor free–Josh's parents never did divorce, even after Louis moved out to live by himself–and Tom functioned about as well as a surrogate parent can; yet the situation caused considerable pain nevertheless, pain that was borne stoically by Josh's father, resentfully by Ian, and subconsciously by Josh. The difficulties of dealing with this less-than-ideal family structure were compounded by the quixotic decision of the new couple to engage in another doomed experiment, an attempt to "live-off-the-land," which caused them to shun boring but reliable employment and move from New Jersey to rural Vermont where they bought a rundown farm house foreclosure.

Shy, tormented by older local kids who considered him and the rest of his family to be hippie weirdos, and desperate for attention and understanding, Wilker struggled mightily to adjust to his circumstances. He continually leaned heavily on his beloved brother for guidance and reassurance and suffered from "night terrors," fits of undefined fear that caused him to awake and run screaming through the house. Fortunately, Josh and Ian both loved something which bonded them tightly forever: baseball and baseball cards. Buying and opening packs of cards became a ritual and a refuge which Wilker longed for. He found solace in the cards–he says he *needed* the cardboard gods–and it would not be an exaggeration to say that baseball cards saved his life, psychically speaking.

Fifty-nine of Wilker's childhood Topps card, from the years 1975–1981, are reproduced in the book, and an essay accompanying each card tells a little piece of the story. For instance, after we have gotten the basic idea of the challenges faced by young Josh Wilker, the author uses the 1978 Wilbur Wood card to provide an important insight into the appeal that baseball cards had for him: "Even during my earliest years of consciousness, when I generally understood the experimentation of the adults in my family as simply the way life was, I instinctively began to reach for things that had clear rules and distinct lines between what was good and what was bad." Wilker says that the "clean, well-defined system of statistical landmarks" found on the backs of cards was one of the things that would "draw me into the world of the cardboard gods as much as anything else.… You knew where you stood with the numbers on the back of a baseball player's card.… It was as simple as that, no gray areas, no confusion."

Cards of both All-Star players and bench warmers would have illustrated the author's point, but Wilbur Wood was a better choice; precisely because the White Sox pitcher's mediocre won-loss records perplexed Wilker and, more importantly, because it reflected the tenor of Josh's personal life. In reviewing Wood's record, Wilker says, "The most confusing year of all was one of the years when all three of my parents lived in the same house, 1973, when Wilbur Wood won 24 games and lost 20.

I never could figure out if Wilbur Wood was bad or good.…"

While making connections between the characteristics of the cardboard gods and his own evolving life is a technique Wilker employs throughout the book, he also often goes on riffs that simply pay tribute to the players. The conclusion of the Wood rumination is a good example of this, as well as his ability to paint insightful, beautiful word pictures:

…eventually I came to see him as being, in both name and deed, some kind of throwback to the rugged, spike-gashing dawn of major league baseball, when hurlers started both ends of a doubleheader and then came on in relief the next day at dusk despite massive corn liquor hangovers to strand the go-ahead and winning runs in scoring position. Wilbur Wood was beyond Old School. He was Old Testament. He was the last vestige of a time when men named Mordecai and Smokey Joe and Grover strode as giants upon the land, their won-lost records both gleaming and gory, good and bad entangled.

When Wilbur Wood hung it up, it left no one to stop the meek five-inning starters and one-out lefty bullpen specialists from inheriting the earth.

Other memorable examples of Wilker making connections between cardboard gods and his own life include his rumination about the 1975 card of shortstop Eddie Leon; a major league nobody, whom Wilker says he needs nonetheless. Leon's card associates him with three different teams. He is posed in a Chicago White Sox uniform, but via a mis-cutting he is identified erroneously as a St. Louis Cardinal, while the back of the card declares that he is neither a White Sox nor a Cardinal but a New York Yankee. This confusing sloppiness is a perfect spring board for Wilker's description of the shock and disgust felt by all, especially the author, when they first explored the dilapidated, vandalized, obscenity-marred Vermont property Jenny and Tom won at auction. After noting that the highest praise the Topps biographers could give Leon was the fact that he was among the Sox leaders in sacrifice bunts in '73 and '74, Wilker concludes on a note of optimism: "…if a fallible, forgettable guy like Eddie Leon in the wrong uniform on a defective card is capable of not only be*ing* sacred but *making* sacred, then who in our own damaged world is beyond the reach of hope?"

In a similar vein Wilker sees Johnny Bench (1976 card) as the embodiment of a dying breed, the tough male (which neither Josh nor his dad were); the 1975 card of Tigers outfielder Dick Sharon leads to introspection about his Jewish heritage; the 1978 card of Lyman Bostock, murdered in the prime of life, helps him confront his own mortality; and the 1978 card of Ivan DeJesus, posed in a bunting stance, offers a life lesson especially important for someone like Josh. "I learned from my cards that some people are special. Some people aren't," the DeJesus essay begins. Wilker goes on to describe the last game of baseball he ever played, when he ignored his Babe Ruth League coach's signal to bunt in a meaningless situation. The ringing double that he hits is symbolic of his first halting steps into adulthood.

Even after Wilker left childhood behind and stopped actively collecting new cards, he continued to see his old cards as a lens through which his own struggles could be brought into perspective. His amusing ignorance of sexual matters, his difficulties fitting into the narrow public and boarding school parameters, his aimless shifting in New York City from one dead-end job to another and from one temporary lodging (almost always with a family member) to another, his need to become emotionally independent of Ian, and his frustrating attempts to prove his worth by becoming a successful writer … all these wrenching experiences too are chronicled with humor, self-deprecation, literary panache, and reference to the cards of specific cardboard gods.

When Wilker's melded family moved to Vermont, Josh and Ian became Red Sox fans. Carl Yastrzemski became their idol, they suffered over Boston's repeated failures to end their championship drought, and their hopeful refrain "Come on, Yaz" uttered at numerous critical junctures they were witness to became a mantra for their lives together as baseball and baseball card-loving brothers. It is fitting that a 1980 card of Yastrzemski accompanies the final essay in the book, which recounts an awkward family therapy session and a diminished closeness between Josh and his brother. Their relationship is repaired and made stronger than ever when they meet in Boston in the fall of 2004 and celebrate the World Championship for which Red Sox fans had waited so long. The last sentence in the book begins "Winter was on its way, but for the first time in our lives my brother and I were going into it side by side as champions...." Readers who have made the journey with Wilker realize that the Red Sox victory was a validation of so much more than Boston fielding the best baseball team for one passing season. Just as they realize that *Cardboard Gods*, with all its talk about fear, frustration, and failure, is the brilliant, grand fulfillment of one humble man's literary destiny.

The Catcher Was a Spy:
The Mysterious Life of Moe Berg

◆

NICHOLAS DAWIDOFF

◆

New York: Pantheon Books, 1994. Cloth, 453 pages, ISBN: 0-679-41566-1. Prologue: Who Was Moe Berg? A Note on the Sources, Notes, Selected Bibliography, Index, 30 black & white photos between pages 150 and 151. Other baseball books by the author: editor, Baseball: A Literary Anthology *(Library of America, 2002) and* The Crowd Sounds Happy: A Story of Love, Madness, and Baseball *(Pantheon, 2008).*

The Catcher Was a Spy by Nicholas Dawidoff is one of the greatest achievements in baseball biography because it deals so brilliantly with the most accomplished, complex, and secretive individual to ever play major league baseball: Morris "Moe" Berg. One of the many ironies of Moe Berg's multi-faceted life is that he craved secrecy and obsessively guarded the details of his personal and professional life, even before he became a spy for the U.S. government, while at the same time he enjoyed and exploited the fame that made him instantly recognizable not only to hundreds of friends and colleagues but to many in the general population as well. Dawidoff's ability to uncover and chronicle the numerous shrouded paths down which Berg trod and to plumb the depths of the man's complicated personality results in a story that is a triumph of research, narration, and understanding.

What makes Berg such a fascinating figure is the fact that his 15-year major league career was hardly the pinnacle of his success, not for a man of his talents and accomplishments in other fields. Berg was educated at Princeton, the Sorbonne, and Columbia and passed the New York bar exam, although he practiced law only briefly. He was much more passionate about language. He studied numerous languages, could have had a university career teaching linguistics, and inspired an oft-quoted quip by a Washington Senators teammate. Told that Berg could speak seven languages, the teammate said, "Yeah, I know, and he can't hit in any of them." Dawidoff deftly sums up Berg as a major league player by saying: "He was many things ballplayers are not supposed to be: educated, intelligent, cosmopolitan, well-spoken, Jewish, and slow-footed."

Berg was curious about everything and he never stopped learning, never quit educating himself. He read as many newspapers as he could get his hands on virtually every day of his life, and his insistence that a newspaper was "alive" and not to be touched by others until he had read it front to back was merely one of his many quirks. While his major league teammates went out drinking or slept in after a night out carousing, Berg visited museums, attended academic lectures, and haunted libraries and book shops. He was a loner, and while he genuinely loved baseball, he enjoyed the lifestyle and freedom afforded him by the game even more. Berg was not without baseball ability–he had a great arm–but he had a major deficiency, encapsulated by Mike Gonzalez's famous scouting report of him as a minor league shortstop: "Good field, no hit." Dawidoff does Gonzalez one better, saying that, after a knee injury limited Berg to 20 games, 61 at bats, and a .115 batting average for the Chicago White Sox in 1930, he didn't become a full-time lawyer but "made a life for himself as that consummate baseball mediocrity, the third-string catcher." Berg's love for the game never left him; his dying words were a question: "How'd the Mets do today?"

It takes Dawidoff only a third of the book to cover Berg's baseball career; nevertheless, by the end of that stage of the life we have become familiar with many of the habits, propensities, and interests that made Berg such an unusual person. Berg, we learn, never owned a house or a car and was an indefatigable walker. He frequented cafes where he devoured his newspapers and downed gallons of coffee (but never alcohol). He never had much money but always until the end of his life dressed formally and seemed to be able to stay and eat in the best hotels. He was a raconteur of the first order who held listeners spellbound; the subject of his stories always his own numerous world travels and adventures. He liked to amuse himself and amaze others by telling strangers what country (and often what part of a country) the stranger hailed from, based on the person's last name. He astonished friends by flawlessly translating aloud Latin inscriptions come upon and, after reading them, repeating word-for-word entire pages of books. Most indicatively of all, he seldom revealed anything about himself, kept his movements and locations to himself, and routinely vanished like a ghost without even saying goodbye.

Berg, who came to love Japanese culture, made two trips to Japan, one in 1932 to teach baseball, and the second in 1934 as part of an American All-Star team. It was during the second junket that he gained admittance to St. Luke's Hospital dressed in a kimono, sneaked atop the building, and filmed panoramic views of Tokyo. Previous writers have claimed that these films were used to plan Doolittle's World War II bombing raids of the Japanese capitol, but Dawidoff debunks that notion; explaining further that Berg acted on his own volition and not at the behest of the U.S. government. Nevertheless, Berg's foresight and the real risks he took to pull off the caper were an early indication of his aptitude for espionage work.

Throughout Berg's baseball career, sportswriters, such as John Kieran and Shirley Povich, delighted in boosting the bench-warming catcher as a savant in knickers and referring to him as "Professor Berg." Berg contributed to this persona by doing things like authoring a perceptive article on pitching and catching for the *Atlantic Monthly* and showing off his erudition on the popular quiz show of the day,

Information, Please! There was certainly some truth in Judge Landis' admission after Berg's appearance on the radio program that he'd done more to elevate the baseball profession in the minds of the public than the Commissioner had done in his entire tenure as the game's grand pooh-bah. Thus, Berg's reputation as a gifted person greased his way into the profession which most interested him: spying.

Berg first joined the war effort in January 1942 as a "special consultant" for the Nelson A. Rockefeller-led Office of Inter-American Affairs (OIAA), an organization begun to help keep Central and South American countries in the allies' camp. In this position Berg immediately established the M.O. that would characterize all his undercover work: he employed great initiative in determining his assignments and great latitude in carrying them out. Much to the consternation of his handlers, they often had no idea where he was, and he spent whatever sums of money he deemed necessary, often keeping little track of his expenditures. (After the war officious bureaucrats sent him a large bill, but wiser heads took care of it.)

When everyone realized that south of the border was a "back eddy," Berg yearned to get involved in the real theatre of action, and he was eventually hired by the Office of Strategic Services (OSS), the first U.S. intelligence agency and a forerunner of the CIA. Berg did a number of things, but most of his work involved two missions connected to the atomic bomb (Dawidoff's detailed accounts of which take up large portions of the book). First, he traversed Europe tracking down the world's leading nuclear physicists to determine their allegiance and to find out what they knew (if anything) about Germany's progress towards developing the bomb. And, second, he attended a lecture in Zurich, Switzerland, delivered in German (of course) by Germany's leading physicist Werner Heisenberg in order to assess Germany's progress. Berg, who according to the author posed as either "a Swiss physics student, an Arab Businessman, or a French merchant from Dijon," went equipped with a cyanide capsule (to be used on himself in the event of capture) and a pistol to be used to assassinate Heisenberg, if necessary. Neither drastic step *was* necessary, as Berg realized that English intelligence had been correct all along: Germany was not close at all to developing a nuclear weapon. Still, the allies had to be certain, and Berg's brave mission, undertaken at considerable personal risk, was an important contribution to the war effort. In carrying out these missions Berg had to educate himself in physics, and he became so conversant in the subject that he later astonished professionals in the field, especially when they realized he had once been a major league baseball player.

Dangerous though it often was, espionage suited Berg like one of the nylon dress shirts he nightly washed in the bathroom sinks of the places where he laid his head, and Dawifoff says that he was actually disappointed to see the war come to an end. Berg desperately wanted to continue his real vocation by working for the newly-formed CIA in the cold war struggle against communism, but he ultimately was found lacking. He was considered to be too much of a maverick, a good amateur but not capable of operating as a professional spy. The final third of the book chronicles the remaining twenty-five years of his life; a period during which he held no job but gave everyone the idea that he was still engaged in important espionage work. He became a bigger vagabond that ever, lived off the free dinners and short-term lodging of friends (always in his mind in exchange for his company and conversation), traveled around the country by rail as the guest of porters with whom he'd become pals, and spent his time beholden to no one and doing exactly what he wished to do. While admirable in many ways, this existence naturally led to a decline in his health, wealth (such as it was), and general well-being (he walked around with an enormous umbilical hernia for years before getting it removed, for free, by a befriended doctor); and this decline lends a melancholy to his story.

Berg had one true love in his life (Estella Huni) but allowed her to get away, and Dawidoff reveals several strange incidents and episodes with the opposite sex which indicate if nothing else the understandable loneliness the man endured. That loneliness was compounded by the mysterious life-long estrangement he experienced with his brother Sam, an accomplished doctor, and his sister Ethel; both of whom, in turn, took him into their Newark, New Jersey, homes for long periods in the last stages of his life.

Dawidoff not only recognizes Berg's lonesomeness but also his surprising lack of self-esteem. Berg was put up for the Medal of Freedom but declined it; believing, once the atomic bomb had become common knowledge, that nobody would really understand what he'd done to deserve the award. He met and enthralled hundreds of people, many of them important in their own right, but had trouble maintaining any lasting friendships. And, despite secrecy being the governing principle of his existence, after the war he exaggerated and embellished more than ever his tales of adventure and derring-do; not something done by people confident of their place in the world and history. While few of us who lead conventional lives would willingly give up our comforts and security in exchange for the freedoms Berg enjoyed, any reader can admire what Berg accomplished. Dawidoff concludes this great biography by pointing out: "In the end, there are few men who find ways to live original lives. Moe Berg did that."

Center Field Grasses

Gene Fehler

Jefferson, NC: McFarland, 2012. Paper, 192 pages, ISBN: 978-0-7864-6705-1. (Cloth edition published in 1991.) Acknowledgments, Preface. Other baseball books by the author: I Hit the Ball: Baseball Poems for the Young *(McFarland, 1996),* Tales from Baseball's Golden Age *(Sports Publishing, 2000),* Dancing on the Basepaths: Baseball Poetry and Verse *(McFarland, 2001),* More Tales from Baseball's Golden Age *(Sports Publishing, 2002),* Change-Up: Baseball Poems *(Clarion, 2009),* Never Blame the Umpire *(Zonderkidz, 2010),* Forced Out: Travel Team Series *(Darby Creek, 2012), and* When Baseball Was Still King: Major League Players Remember the 1950s *(McFarland, 2012).*

Comments: Beanball *was named 2008 Best Book by the Society of School Librarians International, and* Change-Up *was the co-winner of the Paterson Prize for Books for Young People in Grades 4–6.*

Fehler was interviewed by Spitball: The Literary Baseball Magazine *(#5) in 1983, with Gene's baseball poetry being the focus of the discussion.*

During the great revival of the 1980s and '90s when baseball poetry began to flourish again, as it had once flourished as a common part of newspaper baseball reporting, one of the most important and prolific practitioners of the art was Gene Fehler, a college professor of literature who in retirement traveled about teaching poetry writing to grade schoolers. As with Paul Weinman and Tim Peeler, baseball poetry for Fehler was experiential, a great many of the more than 800 ball poems he published being descriptions of or reflections on the playing of the game, whether actual or imagined. Regardless of the calendar, it was always baseball season for Gene, as it is for all those who happily never outgrow their childhood/adolescent obsession with the game.

Fehler's first collection of baseball poetry was his best, and *Center Field Grasses* remains one of the most significant volumes of baseball poetry by a single author. Part Three: The Players consists of 87 alphabetically-arranged poems about specific major league players, and the poems here are attempts to memorialize each of them by highlighting some characteristic or defining moment. Examples of arresting metaphors used by Fehler to begin some of these poems are his calling Denny McLain "A modern Tantalus" (referring to McLain's tantalizing inability to sustain greatness) and

Center Field Grasses

Poems from Baseball

Gene Fehler

Mickey Mantle "A mummy in pinstripes" (a reference to the extensive taping Mantle's numerous injuries required). While most of these poems celebrate greatness and high achievement, the positive is often balanced with the other side of the coin, as in the poem about Mel Stottlemyre, who is remembered for being the best pitcher on a string of bad Yankees teams (1965–74). The poem's opening lines remind us, as it purports to repeat a question asked of all players (not just Stottlemyre), that major league baseball is first and foremost a serious business: "but what have you/done for us lately?" This and the following images ("they asked him, the knife/ hidden in one hand,/ the release clear as a bell/ … in the other") set up the poem's startling conclusion, which conveys just how difficult if not cruel the final separation can be for a player:

> Like a mistress
> they don't want
> you for your mind—
>
> at the end they
> send you out with
> the garbage
> only
> to tell you,
> too late,
> that you
> ARE
> the garbage.

There is also much concrete poetry in this section, Fehler's use of unorthodox spacing and manipulated letter and word arrangement to accentuate meaning. Consider "Satchel Paige," for example :

> He might have pitched
>
> forever
>
> If Boston hadn't bunted.
> Brought to Cleveland to get
> his pension,
> he surprised skeptics who
> didn't believe in
>
>   *
>   a * i
>   t * n
>   n * o
>   u * f
>   o * y
>   f * o
>   the uth
>
> When we wanted to think of
> "what might have been"
> he called out from his
>
>   rockingchair
>
> and told us
> not to.

The book's most original section, oxymoronically speaking, is Part Two: Baseball Parodies—Poems from the Classics. While by definition a parody is an imitation of a prior work, I say "original" out of astonishment at the number of poems included. To write one or two superb parodies on a subject is something; to compose 59 of them is something else indeed! From William Wordsworth, Alfred Lord Tennyson, and Robert Browning to Walt Whitman, Emily Dickinson, and Edwin Arlington Robinson, the most famous British and American poets are represented; and no matter the poem chosen, Fehler somehow brilliantly adapts its rhythm, rhyme, and tone to baseball. Frost's "Stopping by Woods on a Snowy Evening," for example, is one of America's most well-known and loved poems, and surely almost every high school graduate can recognize Fehler's tribute to it in a poem satirizing the infamous George Brett Pine-Tar Bat fiasco. Entitled "Grabbing an Illegal Bat at Yankee Stadium," the poem, spoken presumably by Yankees manager Billy Martin, concludes:

> The pine tar's lovely, dark and deep
> Enough to make the Royals weep.
> This victory is ours to keep,
> This victory is ours to keep.

Fehler's parody of lesser known poems such as Richard Lovelace's "To Lucasta, Going to the Wars" will strike a chord even if one has never heard of the author of the original poem; familiarity with the original simply multiplies the satisfaction.

> **To My Fans, on Becoming a Free Agent**
>
> Tell me not, fans, I am unkind
> For saying my good-bye
> And leaving your kind cheers behind
> While I to new fans fly.
>
> True, I have lost your sweet embrace
> While on your rival's field;
> But I have viewed the market place
> And seen what it can yield.
>
> Though my disloyalty is such
> That all you fans abhor,
> It's not that I don't love you much:
> I just love money more.

Finally, the 58 poems in Part One: Up Close and Personal are those which touch most directly on Fehler's own experiences wielding bat, ball, and glove. Thematically, they tend to fall into four categories: those about father-son relationships, the ones about dealing with the absence of baseball during the winter, the poems about playing ball while aging, and those about the similarities between playing baseball and writing poetry. As with the parodies, the pleasures they offer abound to such an extent that one example, the title poem, will have to suffice. "Center Field Grasses" is not a sentimental expression of disappointment that the baseball diamond on which the speaker once performed heroic deeds has transformed into the prosaic cow pasture at which he has stopped the family automobile but a melancholic rumination on the speaker's vanished youth. The moment so meaningful to the speaker is lost on his impatient sons who "…will not believe that I wanted/ more than what I have. They do not know/ that compromises must be made." The speaker's sadness is deepened because he can foresee that his sons' future will mirror his own:

> They do not think that twenty-five years
> from now THEY will reminisce
> at a long deserted bandstand
> while my grandchildren sit amused
> unwilling to believe that THEIR FATHER
> once played a guitar before ten thousand
> pot-smoking, half-dressed, long-haired…

Keenly aware that nothing he can say will reverse the effects of time nor convey to his sons his knowledge that such effects should serve as a bond between them, the speaker keeps his thoughts and feelings to himself:

> I let them honk.
> I turn my back to them,
> fighting tears,
> cursing silently, wishing I could go back
> to voices from long ago,
> because my sons are in a hurry:
> they don't know who I am.

In the Preface, Fehler cites as the motto for his own work what Dylan Thomas said of poetry, that "All that matters is the enjoyment of it." In each and every one of its poems, *Center Field Grasses* offers the reader the chance to see its author fulfilling the promise of that motto.

The Chalmers Race: Ty Cobb, Napoleon Lajoie, and the Controversial 1910 Batting Title That Became a National Obsession

◆

RICK HUHN

◆

Lincoln: University of Nebraska Press, 2014. Cloth, 283 pages, ISBN: 978-0-8032-7182-1. Foreword by Charles Alexander, Preface, Prologue. Acknowledgments, Notes, Bibliography, Index, 25 black & white photos between pages 134 and 135. Other baseball books by the author: The Sisler: George Sisler, Baseball's Forgotten Great *(University of Missouri Press, 2004) and* Eddie Collins: A Baseball Biography *(McFarland, 2008).*

Comments: Reed Browning, author of *Cy Young: A Baseball Life*: "This is the kind of baseball history we need more of–a book grounded in a great story, shaped by intelligent assessments of the evidence, committed to accuracy and truth-telling, and presented in vigorous prose."

Baseball takes its statistics and records seriously. Very seriously, and there is no greater proof of this than the competition for the highest batting average in the 1910 major league season, which boiled down to a spirited and ultimately disputed contest between two American Leaguers, Ty Cobb of the Detroit Tigers and Napoleon Lajoie of the Cleveland Naps, both of whom already had three batting titles to their credit. The battle for the batting crown was greatly invigorated by Detroit carmaker Hugh Chalmers who, with the baseball establishment's uneasy blessing, had put up one of his brand-new touring automobiles as the prize to be awarded the winner. The race went down to the final days of the season, with Cobb being declared the winner, but not before suspicious play and accusations of dishonesty, favoritism, and a coverup became a raging controversy that has not been resolved to this day to everyone's satisfaction. While a cloud of ambiguity remains over the 1910 AL batting title, we at least now know the complete multi-faceted story behind it, thanks to the publication of Rick Huhn's marvelous history, *The Chalmers Race: Ty Cobb, Napoleon Lajoie, and the Controversial 1910 Batting Title that Became a National Obsession*.

The basic facts of this unseemly diamond melodrama were well-known right from the beginning; however, they were also anything but simple or incontrovertible. Assuming that he enjoyed a lead too big for his rival to overcome and with Detroit

THE CHALMERS RACE

TY COBB, NAPOLEON LAJOIE,

and the Controversial 1910 Batting Title

That Became a National Obsession

RICK HUHN

Foreword by CHARLES C. ALEXANDER

clearly out of the pennant race, Cobb (with his team's permission) declined to play the final two games on the Tigers' schedule in Chicago. He instead joined a group of all-stars who came together in Philadelphia to help the pennant-winning A's prepare for the upcoming World Series against the Chicago Cubs. As Huhn carefully explains, Cobb's assumption was flawed because of the state of scoring and record keeping at that time. Scorers (usually reporters covering the home team) were neither well-trained nor independent; and "official" statistics, particularly batting averages, were compiled haphazardly and slowly by the league, infrequently reported, and sometimes not audited. Cobb had a lead but no one really knew how big it was, as different newspapers reported different averages for him and his rival. Huhn says that by sitting out his final two games essentially all Cobb did was "lock-in" his final average, whatever it was.

For his part, Lajoie, who wanted the Chalmers automobile as much as if not more than Cobb who already owned several vehicles, was not ready to throw in the towel. He had one last chance to catch and overtake Cobb, as Cleveland was scheduled to play a doubleheader in St. Louis on the last day of the season against the cellar-dwelling Browns. Despite all the uncertainty, the St. Louis newspapers thought they had a pretty good idea of how many hits the "Big Frenchman" needed. Huhn writes: "One in particular, the *Post-Dispatch*, told readers seven hits in eight tries would do the trick, but no less."

Apparently, Browns manager "Rowdy Jack" O'Connor and some of his players believed the *Post-Dispatch's* estimate and set out to help Lajoie rack up the safeties he reportedly needed. Their motivation, as explained by Huhn, was not a hatred of the fierce Cobb (although there was some bad blood between O'Connor and Cobb), but a desire to aid the universally popular Lajoie. Supposedly, the team felt bad about having ended Cleveland's pennant chances two years earlier and denying Lajoie the best chance he ever had at playing on a pennant winner. As Lajoie's career was winding down, they also realized that 1910 would probably be the great second baseman's last chance to win another batting title. Lajoie went eight for eight in the doubleheader and left the diamond hoping that he had done enough to overtake Cobb, but what actually happened was subject to dispute and immediately enflamed a blazing controversy, as every one of those eight hits was tainted by the play of the Browns. In the first game, Lajoie went 4–4 on, in succession, misplays on a fly to left and a grounder to short and two bunts down the third base line with Browns third baseman, rookie Red Corriden, playing on the outfield grass; and then Lajoie picked up four more bunt hits to third in the second game.

By carefully citing published accounts of reputable eyewitnesses, Huhn makes it clear that both of Lajoie's first two hits were intentional misplays on routine chances. However, at this distance, some things about the game are impossible to know with certainty; such as exactly when Corriden moved so far back as to extend Lajoie an engraved invitation to lay down bunts. Was Red out of position from the start of Game One and did Lajoie only notice this when he came to bat for the third time, or did Corriden move back only after it appeared that Lajoie was not hitting the ball as authoritatively as usual? No one knows for sure. In any case, the idea that any major league player could legitimately beat out six consecutive bunt hits is preposterous.

Browns fans in attendance knew this, as Huhn tells us that after Lajoie's first bunt hit in the second game of the doubleheader "There was the usual chorus of cheers, but now there was a smattering of hisses as well. It seems some in the crowd, including Lajoie rooters, only wanted to see the venerable Naps' star win his Chalmers legitimately."

To complicate matters, the Browns used a replacement scorer that day, Victor Parrish, who found himself in the thick of the controversy. When Lajoie came to bat for the second time in the second game, there was a runner on first with no outs. He once again bunted down third. Corriden "briefly fumbled the ball" before throwing to first, too late to retire Lajoie. Parrish gave Corriden an error but also credited Lajoie with a sacrifice, as the runner advanced safely to second, which meant that Lajoie's perfect day at the plate continued. The ruling became more unsavory grist for the farce unfolding before the Browns fans when Parrish was pressured to change the sacrifice to a hit, first by a Browns former pitcher-turned-scout and later via the Browns batboy who delivered a bribe from an anonymous source. Even more galling, hours after the game Lajoie himself phoned Parrish to ask if the sacrifice could not be changed to a hit in order to give him a 9-for-9 day instead of the 8-for-8 he received. Throughout the aftermath Cobb took the high road, and his public statements and attitude reflected more honorably on him than Lajoie's did on himself.

After the three-man National Commission declined to get involved, AL President Ban Johnson investigated the matter, interviewing many of the doubleheader's participants. Worried about charges of dishonest play (known back then as "hippodroming") rampant in the press and determined that a scandal not upstage the approaching World Series, Johnson issued a white-washed report that was a foregone conclusion. He supposedly accepted Corriden's defense that his ridiculous positioning was due to how hard Lajoie hit the ball, as well as O'Connor's laughable explanation that "Lajoie outguessed us. We figured he did not have the nerve to bunt every time. He beat us at our own game." Not as easy to paper over were the comments of umpire Billy Evans, an arbiter of unquestioned probity who initially opined that many of Lajoie's hits in the doubleheader were questionable, yet Huhn concludes that Johnson was able to pressure him to change his view. The key finding of the report: Cobb was the champ, edging Lajoie by percentage points .384944 to .384084. These figures were not accurate as a later audit revealed, but the corrected figures still gave Cobb the edge. In a further attempt to put the whole mess to bed and smooth the feathers of the disappointed Lajoie, Johnson got Chalmers to give both players a new car, claiming that he had first offered to buy a car for the runner-up. Certainly, Chalmers needed little arm-twisting, as he could not have afforded to buy all the publicity the controversy generated for his product. And although Johnson did not publicly accuse anybody of wrongdoing, he saw to it that Browns owner Robert Hedges discharged Jack O'Connor as the team's manager.

Much important and engrossing detail has inevitably been left out of this summary of the events of 1910 (including Huhn's surmise that it was members of the Cleveland team who suggested that the Browns help Lajoie), and it is this mass of relevant facts unearthed by the author which makes the book such a pleasure to read. Yet Huhn's greatest contribution is his giving us, a la Paul Harvey, "the rest of the story." As he writes at the end of Chapter Nine: "It now appeared that the last dangling shoelace [O'Connor's dismissal] would be tied in what had started out as a rather simple affair designed to reward baseball's best batsman. For all intents and purposes, the Cobb-Lajoie affair was all set to become just another footnote in baseball history. But it was not over, not by a long shot."

While including accounts of many related matters, such as how baseball attempted to avoid another such snafu, what happened to the key figures after 1910, and instances of similar shenanigans in succeeding years, the rest of the story involved most importantly two developments: the lengthy, revelatory law suit brought by O'Connor against the Browns which brought the whole matter back before the public (and fairly demonstrated the culpability of Corriden, Browns pitchers, and O'Connor himself) and the discovery decades later by diligent researchers that Cobb's stats for 1910 were still incorrect; one of his base hits having been unintentionally counted twice. Rightly or wrongly, Commissioner Bowie Kuhn decided not to disturb Ban Johnson's ruling, yet today the record books acknowledge the mistake, listing Cobb as the batting champion and Lajoie as having a higher batting average. It is an amazing, probably unparalleled phenomenon that can be truly understood only be reading and savoring every word of this delicious history.

Chasing Moonlight: The True Story of Field of Dreams' Doc Graham

◆

Brett Friedlander *and* Robert Reising

◆

Winston-Salem, NC: John F. Blair, Publisher, 2009. Cloth, 220 pages, ISBN: 978-0-89587-369-9. Foreword by Bobby Brown, Introduction. Appendix 1: Career Statistics of Archibald Wright "Moonlight" Graham, Appendix 2: 1905 New York Giants Statistic, Appendix 3: Standings and League Leaders from Graham's Minor League Seasons, Appendix 4: Field of Dreams: Film vs. Fact, Acknowledgments, Index, 27 black & white photos scattered throughout the book.

    Comments: The cover photo is the only known full-figured photo of Moonlight Graham practicing in a New York Giants uniform. In its Summer 1987 issue (#22), *Spitball: The Literary Baseball Magazine* became the first to publish a portrait photo of Graham in his Giants uniform which had hung for decades in the offices of Veda Ponikvar, the editor of the newspaper in Chisholm, Minnesota.

    Other than midget Eddie Gaedel, the most famous man to make a single appearance in a major league baseball game is Archibald "Moonlight" Graham. W.P. Kinsella, the author of the novel *Shoeless Joe*, stumbled across Graham's entry in the *Baseball Encyclopedia* and was immediately intrigued by Graham's nickname and the fact that the former New York Giant did not bat in the one major league game he played. Then, when the time came, Kinsella gave a fictionalized Graham a starring role in his novel. Kinsella's genius was his curiosity, the nagging suspicion that a story of wonderous import hid behind that mysterious moniker. Kinsella's work ethic resulted in his making a research trip to Chisholm, Minnesota, the small mining town where Graham lived most of his life to find out more about the ex-ballplayer. And Kinsella's artistry lay in his filling in the details so brilliantly, in molding a fictional Graham to fit the needs of his plot and in so doing creating a character so beloved and so seemingly real that he rivals the historical Joe Jackson who is the focal point and driving force of the narrative. The genius of Brett Friedlander and Robert Reising, the authors of *Chasing Moonlight*, is their recognition that there were crucial differences between the fictional and actual Graham, as well as a need for a sympathetic biography of the latter which would not diminish the

achievement of Kinsella in the slightest but would inform and elevate the historical Graham; who, it turns out, is even more interesting than his fictional counterpart.

Kinsella's portrayal of Moonlight Graham is fairly accurate though not completely. In *Shoeless Joe*, Graham plays one inning in the last game of the 1922 season, when in fact he played two innings (and was on deck when the game ended) in a game on June 29, 1905. Graham tells the protagonist of the novel, a novice farmer named Ray Kinsella, that he retired after his one major league appearance rather than return to the minor leagues; actually, Graham reported to Scranton, Pennsylvania, where he finished out the year and then played three more seasons for the hometown Miners before leaving professional baseball for good to devote himself fulltime to medicine. There are a few other discrepancies too, such as the fact that Graham was born in Fayetteville, North Carolina, not Chisholm, and that his father was not a doctor, like Graham, but a distinguished educator who'd obtained a law degree from Columbia University.

Of course, as a novelist, Kinsella was entitled to the plot-simplifying fabrications, especially since they did not obscure the truth of the man, which was the high moral character of Dr. Archibald Wright Graham. This essence is captured poignantly in the novel when Doc Graham saves the life of Ray Kinsella's young daughter who takes a nasty fall from the bleachers and most succinctly in the movie *Field of Dreams* when screenwriter Phil Alden Robinson has Graham respond to the suggestion that his curtailed career as a big leaguer might be considered a tragedy. "Son," the silver-screen Graham (played by Burt Lancaster) replies contentedly, "if I'd only gotten to be doctor for five minutes, now that would have been a tragedy."

The significance of these noted differences and a few others between the fictional and actual Graham pale in comparison to the importance of the rest of the story, which is supplied by *Chasing Moonlight* while being only hinted at by the novel and movie. As noted above, Graham was a Southerner, born into a large genteel family of accomplished persons (his younger brother Frank, for example, became president of the University of North Carolina and an ambassador to the United Nations). He played college baseball and football and made a name for himself as a very speedy fly chaser during his seven-year minor league career; playing on a Charlotte Hornets Carolina League team that won 25 games in a row and winning the 1906 New York State League batting title (.335) as a Scranton Miner. He loved Scranton, was the most popular baseball player in the area, and probably would have settled there if not for the industrial air pollution which had begun to cause him respiratory problems. It was the pure air and water of the famed Iron Range area in Northern Minnesota which led Graham to visit Chisholm in the first place. While Graham could have started a lucrative and comfortable practice in any large city back east, he chose to put down roots in Chisholm, a small town of poor immigrant farmers, miners, and loggers, which had just been devastated by a fire, because he knew that the area needed him.

The young Graham struck up a close friendship with the superintendent of schools and became the official physician of the school system. He became a huge booster of the sports teams at Chisholm High School and served as the first de facto practitioner of sports medicine. He conducted a massive years-in-the-making study of children's blood pressure, which not only made a name for him but also a very important contribution to the profession's understanding of the issue. His expertise and preparedness helped the entire area survive a succession of epidemics with minimal loss of life, and when he retired from medicine he won election to the local school board.

The authors cover all these aspects of Graham's life in satisfying detail and bolster the historical record with winsome anecdotal information about the good doctor's personality and habits. Doc Graham, as everyone in Chisholm called him, walked to work each day and stopped every morning at the same shop for coffee and a doughnut. A friend to all, he loved the area's children especially, and he always kept candy and change in his coat pockets to freely distribute to them. He accepted all comers as patients and never asked for monetary payment. His generosity extended to his tenants, whose rent checks often went uncashed. His idiosyncrasies included chewing paper and dreaming of inventing a perpetual motion machine. In Chisholm Doc Graham met, married, and stayed true to the love of his life, a pretty young school teacher named Alecia Vicentia Madden. Unable to have children of their own, the couple adopted (in spirit) the youngsters of the entire town; and whenever any of these natives became successful as adults, Graham beamed as proudly as if they were his own flesh and blood. It's little wonder that the man was loved by all.

And what of the exotic nickname that, years after Graham's death, led to his discovery? In *Shoeless Joe*, the name is hung on him by a teammate who awakens to find an insomniac Graham taking a walk, dressed in the first clothes he pulled out of the closet. "Graham," the roommate hollers, "what the heck are you doing standing out there in the moonlight?... And you got your uniform on. What are you doing, playing ball out there in the moonlight?" The authors explain that the name almost certainly was derived from Graham's moonlighting as a medical student while he pursued a career in professional baseball. This dual focus, in fact, was greatly responsible for the brevity of Graham's career with the Giants. John McGraw, the Giants' Napoleonic manager, simply didn't like Graham, the son of a Confederate soldier and a college boy. Worse, in McGraw's eyes, Graham, who missed the first two months of the 1905 season attending to his medical school studies, just wasn't as dedicated to baseball as McGraw demanded all his players to be. (Graham, who sat on the Giants' bench for a month before his big moment in the sun, was also still hampered by a leg injury he'd suffered the previous fall playing football at the University of Maryland.) It also didn't help Graham's chances that the Giants in 1905 were loaded; defending National League champs, they went on to another pennant and a victory in the World Series over the Philadelphia Athletics.

In the book's final pages the authors provide a thorough account of the influence that Graham had on others–the high school yearbook was dedicated to him on two different occasions–and the belated efforts Chisholm has undertaken to honor his memory in suitable ways. It is a bit ironic that the fame Graham dreamed of achieving through his efforts as an inventor has come to him posthumously, because of a movie and the fantasy novel on which it was based. And, amazingly, it all happened because of a nickname. Just as W.P. Kinsella used an obscure minor leaguer to enrich his fiction and create one of the most captivating characters in baseball literature, Brett Friedlander and Robert Reising took a minor character in a novel and through diligent research and empathy created a fully fleshed-out portrait of a real man whose actual life of sacrifice and service to others made him one the most beloved persons to ever personify the goodness of small-town America.

The Church of Baseball: The Making of Bull Durham: *Home Runs, Bad Calls, Crazy Fights, Big Savings, and a Hit*

◆

RON SHELTON

◆

New York: Alfred A. Knopf, 2022. Cloth, 241 pages, ISBN: 9780593319772. Introduction. Afterword, A Note about the Author.

Comments: For the *Bull Durham* script Shelton received an Academy Award nomination for Best Original Screenplay, and the success of the movie launched his career as an important screenwriter and director. He has directed several other sports films, including the classics *White Men Can't Jump* and *Tin Cup*. In 2017 he was inducted into the Rochester Red Wings Hall of Fame, and he was included in Little Sun's 1990 baseball card set of Major League Writers, along with fellow literary baseball stars such as Grantland Rice, Lee Allen, Red Smith, Jim Brosnan, Roger Kahn, W.P. Kinsella, John Holway, and John Thorn.

"The Church of Baseball may present itself as solely for a small intersection of readers: Bull Durham fans, sports fans, writers, and film nerds. In reality, the book is so multifaceted that it appeals to non-overlapping sections of the Venn Diagram. Shelton's writing voice is clear and good-humored, and while nothing groundbreaking, the book embodies the vintage wistfulness and romance that the movie continues to represent"— Malavika Praseed, *Chicago Review of Books*

Bull Durham, written and directed by former minor league baseball player Ron Shelton, won a host of major film awards, jump-started the directing career of the struggling Shelton, and inspired *Sports Illustrated* to call it the best sports movie of all time. Remarkably, *The Church of Baseball*, Shelton's sage and entertaining account of the making of *Bull Durham*, perfectly illustrates a most amazing phenomenon: the fact that sometimes such a book is even better than the terrific film it seeks to illuminate. If devotees of the 1988 movie find such a claim to be a bridge too far, there can be no denying the great extent to which the book enhances one's appreciation for the film, as well as for the multitudinous talents of Mr. Shelton.

Although *Bull Durham* is not a primer on the art of movie making … it is far too well-written for that.... Shelton's mind is too disciplined for him not to have imposed an order on his narrative that replicates that of the movie-making process. Thus, he divides the story into four major parts: Development (conceiving of the story and theme, writing the script, selling the script to a studio), Preproduction (hiring producers, editors, camera crew, etc.; conducting auditions; holding rehearsals), Production (filming), and Postproduction (editing the film, setting it to music, screenings); a tactic which educates the reader by osmosis.

Shelton begins by outlining his background and explaining how he was deeply influenced by a conservative Baptist upbringing and its frowning upon "forbidden fruit"; i.e., life's trivial pursuits, such as the watching of movies and television, a disdain which only heightened his fascination with them. (He even remembers the first three films he ever watched: *Winchester '73*, *Here Comes the Nelsons*, and *A Man Called Peter*.) He also contracted a bad case of baseball fever, and in college had his eyes opened to the glorious world of literature. Life, it seems, could not have prepared him any better for his career as a film director.

The author never played major league baseball, but he was good enough to reach Triple A in the Baltimore Orioles organization; and, again, his experiences as a minor leaguer made it almost a certainty that he would turn to baseball as a subject for a feature film. The most important of those experiences was Shelton having played with the legendary Steve Dalkowski, the reputed fastest pitcher of all time whose downfall was his inability to throw strikes. It was Dalkowski who became the model for one of *Bull Durham's* trio of main characters: Ebby Calvin "Nuke" LaLoosh (played by Tim Robbins), the rube of a pitcher with a million dollar arm and ten cent brain.

As Shelton explains repeatedly, the story of the movie is a simple one: the heroine and narrator, Annie Savoy, is sleeping with the wrong guy. Annie, played by the gorgeous Susan Sarandon, is a free spirit and pseudo-intellectual who carries her love of baseball into the bedroom. Each year she selects a promising young Bull to mentor in the ways of life and love, as a way of maturing the young man and speeding his progress up the professional baseball ladder. Super pitching prospect Nuke LaLoosh appears to be her obvious choice for the new season until veteran catcher Crash Davis (played by Kevin Costner) arrives shortly after the start of the season to educate Nuke in the ways of pro baseball. That's when things get complicated. The proud Crash, who once spent 21 days in the bigs, bows out of the competition, leaving the field to Nuke, who winds up being tutored by *two* older pros who were made for each other. Crash and Annie soon realize that they long for each other, but they find it difficult to admit their feelings to themselves and each other.

One of Shelton's favorite scenes in the movie is the "meeting at the mound" scene, whereby several players interrupt the game to discuss things worrying them. The Bulls manager sends Larry, the pitching coach, out to speed things up. When Larry asks what the holdup is, Crash gives him a summary.

> **CRASH:** Nuke's scared 'cause his eyelids are jammed and his old man's here.... We need a live rooster to take the curse off Jose's glove, and nobody seems to know what to get Millie or Jimmy for their wedding present.... We're dealing with a lotta shit.
> **LARRY:** Candlesticks always make a nice gift or you can find out where she's registered and perhaps a place setting or a silverware pattern might be nice.

(beat)
Okay. Let's get two.

It's a funny scene, providing a spoof on what fans assume are serious strategy sessions; however, after filming had been completed, an "Unnamed Executive," who gave Shelton trouble from the very beginning, wanted the scene deleted. (The same Unnamed Exec. insisted that Anthony Michael Hall, who blew two aborted auditions because it was too much trouble for him to have read the script, would be a better Nuke than Tim Robbins.) When the U.E. complained that the scene didn't advance the plot, Shelton said, "There is no plot!" Perhaps; but there is, as Shelton emphasizes, a series of complications of the main story, which are necessary to keep things moving. And the most important of these complications is Annie's convincing Nuke to forego an afternoon roll in the hay one day in order to channel his energy into that night's ballgame. Her suggestion works better than she bargained for. Nuke starts pitching better, the heretofore impotent Bulls go on a roll, and Nuke vows to stay the course until the team loses. When he begins to weaken because Annie gets horny, Crash delivers another bit of hard-earned advice. "Never fuck with a winning streak," he tells Nuke. Never mind that the advice keeps Nuke out of Annie's bed, a consequence Annie actually accuses Crash of intending when she angrily storms into his apartment, sexually frustrated. When Crash tells her it's her own fault and declines her tacit advances, she delivers one of the greatest lines of a script full of great lines. "This is the damnedest season I've ever seen-I mean, the Durham Bulls can't lose and I can't get laid!" It is the script above all other virtues that makes *Bull Durham* such an engaging film.

Of course, Crash and Annie eventually fall into each other's arms; Nuke gets called up to the major leagues and finally appreciates everything Crash has tried to teach him; after getting released by the Bulls, Crash catches on with the Asheville Tourists just long enough to hit the long ball that makes him the career minor league leader in home runs; and he returns to Durham, tired but ready to try his hand at managing the Visalia ballclub the next spring in an attempt to earn his way back to the majors … as long as Annie will be at his side. In other words, *Bull Durham* has a very happy ending, one which none but the grumpiest of movie-goers would object to. As Annie and Crash sit on the porch swing of her house during a downpour, we hear Annie's voiceover proclaim:

> **WALT WHITMAN ONCE SAID,** "I see great things in baseball. It's our game—the American game."
> (beat)
> **HE SAID,** "It will repair our losses and be a blessing to us."
> (beat)
> You could look it up.

The lines are a perfect conclusion to a movie that is romantic, funny, and, as Shelton insists, also about baseball.

While it's beyond the scope of this essay to enumerate all the delights the book offers, we must point out a few, such as: Shelton's pithy sayings (e.g., "There are few things less sexy than shooting a sexy lovemaking scene."); his use and explanation of numerous film industry terms (e.g., "making the day" which means actually filming all the scenes that are scheduled to be filmed on any particular day); his subtle sense of humor (e.g., his characterizing several lies, his own and those of others, as "within industry standards"); his numerous literary and film references which are related to the topic under discussion; the fascinating insights we get into how the names of the three main characters came about (e.g., Shelton was served by a vivacious young waiter who introduced himself by saying, "My name's Ebby Calvin LaRoosh, but you can call me 'Nuke.'"); and the kindness and cooperativeness of Sarandon and Costner, both of whose careers were greatly enhanced by their performances in the movie.

Also fascinating are the many things that Shelton himself learned: that actors who claim to also be athletes cannot be taken at their word; that a baseball movie can succeed without the "big game" scene; that a good director often has to "kill his darlings" (meaning that sometimes a beloved scene *does* need to be cut, in this case, a scene during which Annie delivers a long soliloquy about the details of her past; it turned out that audiences didn't care about her past); and that sometimes "the numbers *do* lie" (meaning that the low scores the movie received from viewers in numerous screenings were clearly an aberration and, furthermore, that the ultimate grand success of the movie was not due, as a "Test Screening Expert" insisted, to "great marketing" and "great word of mouth.")

The Church of Baseball: The Making of Bull Durham: Home Runs, Bad Calls, Crazy Fights, and a Hit, it turns out, is such an edifying work that perhaps it should be used as a textbook in college film and drama classes. The guess here is that it would be the one book the students would hang onto for life and not sell back to the college bookstore.

Cooperstown Verses: Poems About Each Hall of Famer

Mark Schraf

Jefferson, NC: McFarland, 2001. Paper, 150 pages, ISBN: 0-7864-1148-1. Acknowledgments, Foreword by Mike Shannon, Preface. Index of Titles and First Lines.

Cooperstown Verses by Mark W. Schraf is one of baseball literature's most unique and accomplished volumes as it includes a well-wrought poem about every member of the National Baseball Hall of Fame (in alphabetical order) up to the date of the book's publication: 253 entities altogether. In undertaking what was as ambitious a task as any baseball poet has set for himself, Schraf faced a considerable, double-sided problem. On the one hand, he faced the challenge of avoiding cliché while writing about the greatest and most familiar of baseball greats; while on the other hand, he was required to find something worth saying about the lesser-known immortals, those we might paradoxically refer to as "obscure" Hall of Famers, about whom it can be difficult to say much at all that is interesting, much less poetic.

After only a few pages, the reader is struck by the variety of forms, techniques, and voices employed by the author, as well as by the considerable wit, intelligence, humor, baseball knowledge, and verbal ingenuity displayed. In *Cooperstown Verses* one finds a dizzying assortment of haiku, limericks, ballads, parodies, monologues, all manner of free verse, shape poems, and traditional rhymed poems. It is clear very early on that Mr. Schraf has an almost endless number of tricks up his sleeve, and it is this continual attempt to keep his approach fresh, unrepetitive, and even surprising that motivates the reader to keep turning the pages with delighted anticipation.

Saddled as he was with the impossibility of saying everything about his subjects, Schraf had to choose one thing or idea to represent his subject, his career, personality, character, or legacy. On occasion, such as the poem about reliever Rollie Fingers called "Save," he focuses on the skill for which the player is famous:

> you came in when
> a save was a save
> and killed instead

you twirled your Dick
Dastardly curls
tied the rally
to the tracks
and let the A-train
run her over

As the title indicates, Fingers is known for the saves he racked up, yet the poem suggests that there was more to it than that; the first two lines conveying the fact that Fingers often pitched two and sometimes three innings, working much harder for his saves than the closers of today who prefer to delay their appearance until the start of the ninth inning and sometimes are even called upon to retire one batter! Thus, Fingers didn't merely save games, he "killed" rallies. After subtly making this important point, the poet shifts into fun mode, comparing Fingers to the Hanna-Barbera cartoon character Dick Dastardly who sported a thin curling moustache similar to Fingers'. The final jest about the A-train refers to the team Fingers helped make famous, the rowdy three-time World Champion Oakland A's, and ties a neat bow on the poem, alluding as it does to Fingers' key contributions to the team's success.

A good contrast to the Fingers poem is the one about New York Yankees catcher Bill Dickey, which doesn't even mention any of the baseball skills and achievements which got Dickey enshrined in Cooperstown:

Was It Rougher
watching him
on the set
repeat his
grandma throws
molasses
swings
or remembering
near the end
when the
real
man
wasn't
much
better

This entire spare poem is one question, hypothetically addressed to the ostensible subject of the poem who is not even mentioned in it. Bill Dickey's best friend, "the real man" of the poem, was Lou Gehrig, who died in the prime of life from ALS. The actor who played Gehrig in the movie "The Pride of the Yankees," Gary Cooper, was not a natural athlete, and it took extensive coaching for him to perform in a barely acceptable way the baseball actions required by the film: hence, the "grandma throws" and "molasses swings." While Dickey is barely present, a great deal is said about him nevertheless in the poem ... and about friendship, honor, and how the company a man keeps is a reflection of his own character, as well. Such is the skill of the poet.

Mr. Schraf's use of the title as the first line of a poem (as in the Bill Dickey poem), a literary device which we might call a "titular line," is one of the most common devices used throughout *Cooperstown Verses*; along with rhyme, apostrophe, irony, and ellipsis. The latter in particular characterizes the poet's style, as he likes to require the reader to supply omitted words as a means of involving him more intimately in the meaning of the poem. The poem about Robin Roberts, for example, is about the pitcher's overcoming his penchant for allowing home runs, and it begins and ends with ellipsis:

Gopher
505 times
once a game
you watched as
they sauntered the
bases knowing they'd
won the battle yet
confident that you'd

As the poems unfolds and the reader realizes what "sauntered the/ bases" refers to, he is then able to add for himself the implied concluding line, "win the game" (or "win the battle") and to complete the title: "Gopher Ball," a synonym for home run.

Three motifs run throughout the book. Poems about Joe Tinker and Enos Slaughter are only two of several which question the subject's worthiness for the high honor represented by election to the Hall of Fame. (In a variation of the theme, the Billy Herman poem questions why Buddy Myer, whose statistics mirror those of Herman, is not in the Hall of Fame.) Numerous poems have fun with the subjects' names and nicknames, and even more poems discuss in one way or another the injustice of the color line; perhaps an inevitability given the concerted efforts the Hall of Fame has made to make amends, as far as possible.

The most common denominator of all is humor which enlivens so many of the poems. And here too, Mr. Schraf displays uncommon versatility, inducing degrees of mirth ranging from: the smile-inducing concluding tribute to Juan Marichal ("could also be dangerous/ on occasion with/ the bat") to the chuckle elicited by his reference to Gaylord Perry's signature pitch ("The reason why he holds a Cy Young/ trophy in both hands/ is Gaylord Perry's Hall of Famer/ salivary glands") to the horse-laughter prompted by the poem about Will Harridge, president of the American League when maverick Bill Veeck sent four-foot tall Eddie Gaedel to bat for the St. Louis Browns. The romp in couplets, entitled "***An Ode to Will Harridge*** by Eddie Gaedel as related by the author," concludes;

> But how could you remove my single stat,
> you jealous, pompous, midget-hating rat!
> You always were a frumpy gloom and doomer.
> It's clear you never had a sense of humor.
> You'll see: there'll be a special place in hell
> for wiping out the walk of Ed Gaedel!

Every poem in this book is not a home run, but Mr. Schraf complies a very high batting average indeed. And when the Baseball Poets Hall of Fame is finally established, he will undoubtedly by virtue of the book earn distinction as a first-ballot inductee.

Crash: The Life and Times of Dick Allen

◆

Dick Allen *and* Tim Whitaker

◆

New York: Ticknor & Fields, 1989. Cloth, 189 pages, ISBN: 0-89919-657-8. Acknowledgments, Preface. Epilogue, Dick Allen's Major League Playing Record, 13 black & white photos between pages 90 and 91.

If any "As Told To" collaboration between a player and an author rises above the expected parameters to expand our understanding of what a baseball autobiography can be, surely it is *Crash: The Life and Times of Dick Allen* by Dick Allen and Tim Whitaker. Reading at various times like an essay, an interview, investigative journalism, a travelogue, Boswellian reporting, and an apologia, the book defies definition; yet it succeeds brilliantly in the main purpose of all biography: the establishment of exactly who the subject was (or is) to the best of another human being's ability to determine such elusive knowledge.

By the time Whitaker began work on the book about a decade after the subject's retirement from the game, much about Allen had become cemented in the public's perception of him. Simply put, Dick Allen was widely regarded as one of the most fascinating and troublesome ballplayers of his era, a unique character who seemed to be a mass (or "mess" according to his sportswriting critics) of peculiarities and defects. He was raised not in a big city ghetto but in the small Western Pennsylvanian country town of Wampum, located about a half hour northwest of Pittsburgh. One of five brothers, all of whom became all-state basketball players in high school, Allen was so gifted at roundball that he could have played in the NBA (he did, we learn in the book, sometimes practice with the Philadelphia 76ers when he was a Phillie). One of the most impressive physical specimens to ever play major league baseball, Allen was a born slugger who launched long distance home runs wielding a 42-ounce pole of a bat and also often hit for high average, all the while wearing glasses. He loved horses, fantasized about becoming a jockey (he actually raced on his horse around a Philadelphia city park), and loved to wear cowboy hats and lizard-skinned boots. He was never called by the name he detested, "Richie," a day in his life until he got to Philadelphia; picked up the nickname which entitles the book after teammates said the batting helmet he began wearing in the field to protect himself from things thrown out of the stands looked like a crash helmet; smoked cigarettes in the dugout while in uniform; wore a golf glove at bat; loved to sing do-wop songs in harmony with members of the Phillies grounds crew; and generally dressed and behaved to the beat of his own bongo drums.

He was also labeled and widely regarded as a malcontent, an albatross hung around his neck partly due to his insistence on indulging his individuality and penchant for flouting rules but due more to racism, which he undoubtedly faced. The latter, in fact, is the overriding issue addressed in the book. In the Preface Whitaker admits that he came to the project from a position of prejudice ... in favor of the subject. He had grown up a Phillies fan and been awed as he'd watched the ebony third baseman play many games at Philadelphia's old Connie Mack Stadium; which like virtually every other major league ballpark could not hold the slugger's parabolic blasts. Whitaker personally witnessed the palpable current of unrealistic expectations, the racist name-calling, and the booing which was directed at Allen by Philadelphia's notoriously vicious fans, and his desire to write the book was motivated mainly by his desire to give Allen a forum to tell his side of the story; something which, ironically, the intelligent, well-spoken Allen had never been able to accomplish to any substantial degree on his own. The danger in all such approaches, of course, is a lack of objectivity. Whitaker was aware of this trap, and one of the devices he employs to counteract it is that, at various times, he puts psychological and nominal distance between himself and the subject by referring to Allen as "The Ballplayer" and to himself as "The Writer." Allen too was aware of this dilemma, and after numerous rebuffs of Whitaker's overtures, when he finally agrees to cooperate on the book, he insists that Whitaker not just take his word for what happened during his career. "I don't want to just tell my story," Allen says. "I want you to live it. I want you to walk in my shoes." This condition is what puts the pair of them on the road, visiting the actual places where Allen's life and career unfolded and Whitaker on the trail of interviewees, such as family friend Chuck Tanner who managed Allen in Chicago, who are able to speak authoritatively about the key moments and events of that life and career. Indicatively, they travel in "Big Blue," Allen's meticulously-cared for baby-blue 1974 Lincoln Continental; an automobile, Whitaker realizes, that has served for years as Allen's road-trip equilibrium-restoring escape vehicle.

The book opens with an account of the incident which more than any other branded Allen as a troublemaker: the fight with the white Frank Thomas on July 3, 1965; half a year after Allen had won the National League Rookie of the Year Award for batting .318 with 29 home runs and 91 runs batted in. On the downside of his career, Thomas could still supply much-needed power off the bench. Popular with the fans, Thomas had an annoying habit of constantly "agitating" other players, which made him a thorn in the side of Phillies manager Gene Mauch. Thomas especially liked to harass young black players, but Allen tried to make it clear he was not one to be trifled with. As Thomas took batting practice on that fateful afternoon, outfielder Johnny Callison got under Thomas' skin, and Thomas responded by calling out Allen, who'd been taking grounders next to Callison down at third base. When Allen went in to hit with the regulars, Thomas lingered around the cage; and Allen, who claims that Thomas knew what was coming, admits he punched Thomas in the jaw. Thomas then swung the bat he was holding at Allen and delivered a blow to Allen's shoulder which caused it to swell like a balloon. As Callison later said, "In baseball, you don't swing a bat at another player—ever." The Phillies, still reeling from their infamous collapse in the pennant race the year before and intent on evincing decisiveness as well as immediately snuffing out any residual inter-club effects of the incident, released Thomas the next day and issued a gag order among the players. Thomas was able to tell his side of the story to a sympathetic media while Allen was not, and so all the blame landed on Allen. According to Callison, "Thomas rubbed a *lot* of people the wrong way. Mauch wanted him gone—and here was his excuse. People just assumed that Allen was the guy who got Thomas fired. But Thomas got himself fired when he swung the bat at Richie." Whitaker gives the last word to Bill White, Allen's teammate and roommate, who explains that the result of the fight and the Phillies' handling of the incident was that it robbed Allen of the joy of playing the game.

Not surprisingly, the racism Allen faced didn't begin in Philadelphia but in Little Rock, Arkansas, where Allen, playing for the Triple A Travelers, served as an unwilling pioneer, integrating professional baseball in the state the year before his promotion to the big leagues. Arkansas was well known as the Southern state which most vehemently opposed integration. It had gained national infamy with its campaign, led by Governor Orval Faubus, to prevent the admission of black students to Little Rock's Central High School in 1957. While public education was integrated in the city, racism against blacks did not suddenly vanish. When he got off the airplane at the airport and when he arrived for his first game at Ray Winder Stadium, Allen saw evidence of this: marchers carrying signs that said, "DON'T NEGRO-IZE BASEBALL" and "NIGGER GO HOME." In a remarkably restrained display of wit, Allen explains to Whitaker what his reaction to such a reception was by saying, "Here, in my mind, I thought Jackie Robinson had Negro-ized baseball sixteen years earlier." Playing left field on Opening Night, the nervous Allen badly misjudged the first fly ball hit to him, drawing the disgust and mockery of many in the crowd. He redeemed himself later in the game by hitting a pair of doubles. He began to relax and think things might work out. Then, after the game after everyone else had departed, he walked into the dark parking lot and found a note taped to the windshield of his car: "Nigger, don't come back." That set the tone for his time in the city. He would be cheered when he succeeded but never really accepted by many. Allen gives examples of the prejudice he faced, including harassment by local police, while laying a good part of the blame for his difficulties that season on the Phillies. He opines that the Phillies, well aware of what he was facing, were willing to let him face this trial by fire because they were intent on integrating their farm team in Little Rock. That was okay with Allen, but he says they should have prepared him better for the trial, just as Branch Rickey prepared Jackie Robinson. Things got so bad that at one point Allen was ready to give up and return home, and it took intervention by his family, a close family friend, and Phillies executives to convince him to stick it out. Near the end of the season, he was voted the team's Most Popular Player. Whitaker recounts the trip he made to Little Rock in performing due diligence to determine for himself the accuracy of Allen's portrayal of the time he spent as a Traveler. He confers with a sportswriter, Orville Henry, who not only covered Allen in those days but also composed an in-depth personality profile of Allen for the files of *Sports Illustrated*. Henry sums up Allen by telling Whitaker that he was "A frightened kid, and unduly so." As Henry's downplayed characterization of the difficulties Allen confronted conflicts with Allen's version of the same, Whitaker finds another sportswriter with the *Arkansas Gazette*, a young black man and native of Little Rock named Wadie Moore, Jr., who provides a perspective that validates Allen. "Understand, I'm not saying there aren't good people in Little Rock, then or now," he says. "But this is a tough town for black people. That's a fact. Now see, the difference is, I grew up here. I knew how to get by. But imagine a black kid coming to all this in 1963 from a little integrated town in Pennsylvania. Guy like that doesn't stand a chance."

It would be an understatement to say that Allen's initial run in Philadelphia, which lasted six full seasons before Allen demanded and was finally granted a trade to another team (the St. Louis Cardinals), was characterized by controversy, as he seemed to be a magnet for strife as well as for the vociferations of the boo birds. Whitaker does indeed allow Allen to address the most notable of these controversies: including his holdouts for bigger salaries; the charge that he got Gene Mauch fired by giving the team an "Either he goes or I go" ultimatum; the career-threatening injury he suffered when he pushed his right hand through the headlight of a car he was working on and the public's refusal to believe his story about how the accident happened; the 26 day/29 game suspension he received when he showed up late for a re-scheduled doubleheader in New York; and the messages (e.g., BOO) and names (e.g., MOM) he wrote in the infield dirt with his spikes when he knew that his days with the Phillies were numbered ("Dirt-doodling" he called it). Allen was undoubtedly involved in even more sticky situations, many of his own doing, and he admits that he gradually let the constant negativity surrounding him change him for the worse. "I'm no psychiatrist," he tells Whitaker, "but I believe that it was during those '67–'68 seasons that I first began to act the role that Philadelphia had carved out for me. I'd been hearing I was a bum for so long that I began to think maybe that's just what I was. I began to hit the sauce pretty good, and I didn't care who knew it." While many in the press and some fans wished him good riddance, ownership let him go only reluctantly, as they knew all too well how good a player they were giving up. And Allen did prove in his subsequent one-year stints with the Cardinals and Los Angeles Dodgers and his two-year run with the Chicago White Sox that he remained one of the best all-around players in the game. With the White Sox especially he made his case; winning the American League Most Valuable Player Award in 1972 for hitting .308 with 37 home runs and 113 RBI and leading the Sox to a second-place finish in the AL West Division. He even returned to Philadelphia for a year-and-a-half do-over, becoming a mentor and friend to Mike Schmidt and helping the Phillies capture the 1976 division championship. Yet, like Billy Martin and Bobby Bonds he had become a baseball vagabond who wore out his welcome all too quickly.

Whitaker does not shy away from asking tough questions, and in several of the conversations presented as interviews Allen provides candidly honest answers to questions about touchy topics, such as his drinking and marijuana use, his philandering and failed marriage, the drain his love of horses took on the family finances, the loss of his uninsured home to an electrical fire, the fate of the teams he played for (especially the infamous '64 Phillies), and racism in baseball. With Allen, the latter is the topic the story always seems to return to. On that account there is a great deal to digest, and the reader finally must answer for himself the key question Whitaker asks in the Preface, "Was Dick Allen a baseball martyr or merely his own worst enemy?" However, too much of a focus on that question would miss the more important point of the book, which is the discovery of what kind of a man Dick Allen was. After spending two years in the man's company, Whitaker realizes that Dick Allen, in addition to whatever else he may have been, was a gentle, compassionate soul who truly cared about other people. Small deeds done in private can speak louder than great public accomplishments, and Allen's saving uneaten dinner rolls to provide breakfast for the birds impresses the author and reminds him of what his mother had done when he was a boy. This scene is described in the Epilogue which opens with Whitaker renouncing all professional objectivity, declaring proudly that he not only now considers Allen a friend but a friend he loves. Fair-minded readers of *Crash* will likely reach a similar, vicarious destination, and the journey will have begun much earlier in the book when we are taken with our guides to visit the Wampum home, bought with baseball money, of Era Allen, the matriarch of the Allen family. A deeply religious woman, Era explains how she knew her son Dickie was put on the earth to do one thing: play baseball. She condoned Allen's spending thousands of hours playing "imaginary baseball," hitting small stones with a stick while pretending to be every batter in the Jackie Robinson–led Dodgers lineup, and she patiently paid for all the broken windows caused by stones that flew a bit too far. Mrs. Allen's influence was monumental in the lives of all her boys, and nothing would have made her prouder than Dick's response when Whitaker asks him about making the Baseball Hall of Fame. "Who elects guys to the Hall of Fame?" he asks. "Sportswriters. You think they're going to get behind Dick Allen? I don't care about the Hall of Fame. I do care about getting to heaven. Given the choice, I'll take heaven every time."

For all the turbulent moments it examines, *Crash* is a positive, uplifting book, yet it contains an element of wistful sadness too. It is Allen himself, who early in the book, gives voice to the emotion. "I wonder how good I could have been," he says. "It could have been a joy, a celebration. Instead, I played angry. In baseball, if a couple of things go wrong for you, and those things get misperceived, or distorted, you get a label. After a while, the label becomes you, and you become the label, whether that's really you or not. I was labeled an outlaw, and after a while that's what I became." Later in the book, Whitaker asks Allen if he wishes he had done things differently. Allen replies emphatically in the negative, suggesting that a different path would not have been possible for him to follow. Regrets are part of every human life; we all have at least a few. But those regrets and the failures and weaknesses they represent are also part of who we are or have been. Our imperfections are as important as the shining elements. *Crash* makes the case that as a ballplayer and as a person, Dick Allen was a rarity, an unforgettable beauty.

Cy Young: A Baseball Life

◆

REED BROWNING

◆

Amherst: University of Massachusetts Press, 2000. Cloth, 283 pages, ISBN: 1-55849-262–3. Preface. Appendix One: Cy Young's Salary History, Appendix Two: Cy Young's Greatest Games, Appendix Three: 511 Wins? Notes, Bibliography, Index, 29 black & white photos between pages 144 and 145.

Comments: *Cy Young* won the 18th CASEY Award in 2000.

Warren Goldstein, author of *Playing for Keeps: A History of Early Baseball*: "The most in-depth study to date of one of baseball's greatest pitchers, a name known by all, but a man known to very few. Young's career spanned an incredibly long period in baseball history, one in which the game was transformed several times. Browning's biography illuminates those changes. I think it will be the authoritative book on Cy Young."

If there was ever unassailable justification for a historian to embark on a baseball biography, Reed Browning recognized it when he considered the literary standing of baseball's top three immortals: Babe Ruth, Ty Cobb, and Cy Young. While the former two giants had been served by small armies of chroniclers, the latter had been by comparison virtually ignored. Yet, because Ruth's and Cobb's most prestigious records had been surpassed, Browning perceived Young's monumental 511 wins to be standing alone as the most astounding and most unbreakable career record. Thus, in publishing *Cy Young: A Baseball Life*, Reed not only closed a major gap in the literature of the game, but he also reanimated a practically faceless baseball icon most worthy of knowing well and finally demonstrated the wisdom in the annual award for pitching excellence having been named after the subject.

For his efforts Reed Browning won the 2000 CASEY Award for Best Baseball Book of the Year, and at this distance it seems hardly surprising; as his study of the great pitcher, as previously mentioned, filled in a gaping baseball biographical hole. That Browning did the job to perfection is evident in the fact that no one since has felt the need to follow in his footsteps in an effort to add relevant material or to dispute any of his conclusions. There is something else though which adds to the book's supremacy: the author's approach to his subject and his method of dealing with the challenges presented by his task.

There is, first of all, an important element to *Cy Young: A Baseball Life* that rarely informs biography of any kind so directly, and that is the willingness of the author to admit that not everything that one would like to know about the subject and his career is, in fact, knowable. A laconic, completely non-controversial person who left very little correspondence, Cy Young, in fact, was for a biographer something of a sphinx or perhaps a *tabula rasa*. Throughout the book, the reader encounters Browning using phrasing, such as "I suspect," "As far as I can tell," "and I admit I am fleshing it out from somewhat fragmentary remarks," and "Or am I missing something?" *I suspect* that the reader regards these qualifications, not as failures of due research diligence, but as indications of an admirable honesty and humility that cause him to trust the author *more* not less. It starts in the Preface where Browning clearly states his goal: "And so I'm moved to conclude that if Cy Young was cast as a salt-of-the-earth farmer, it was because the picture was in significant measure true. My task, therefore, is not to discredit the received view of Cy Young but, by scrutinizing contemporary press coverage and other kinds of testimony from those who knew him well, to add detail and nuance to it."

One example of Browning doing exactly what he says he sees as his main task is recording Young's post-season activities. With very few exceptions, throughout his long career Young eschewed barnstorming and intra-city-series money-making opportunities to return home to the peace, quiet, and restful duties of his farm in Tuscarawas County, Ohio. Descending from a line of farmers, Young, whose formal education ended after the sixth grade, was proud of his heritage and non-baseball station, and he was prepared all along to live out his life on the farm. Prior to his first major league start with the Cleveland Spiders on August 6, 1890, against the Chicago Colts, the modest Young said, "Well, I'll pitch a game. And if I win I'll stay; if I lose, I'll go home this evening." Colts' player-manager Cap Anson declared he wasn't worried about facing the rookie, calling Young "just another big farmer." However, after Young shut down Chicago on a three-hitter, Anson tried to buy his contract for $1,000. Young always called this victory, among all his other glorious moments, the most satisfying win of his career. In an incisive summation of the meaning of the event typical of the book, Browning writes: "Pride alloyed with realism: that was a yoking of attitudes that would accompany Cy Young throughout his life."

Secondly, Browning loves lists and uses them often to help the reader keep straight multi-faceted issues. Two such lists: the three reasons for Young's worst season in 1897 "since he became an established star" and the four reasons he was willing to risk jumping from the older National League to the Boston club in Ban Johnson's upstart American League in 1901. Thirdly, Browning intersperses the narrative chapters with those which focus on some specific topic which requires special attention: the effects on Young and other standout pitchers of the rule change which moved the pitching mound back five feet to sixty feet/six inches; a brilliant recitation of Young's physical appearance, personality, and predilections; the effects of the birth of the American League and the adoption of the rule which made the first two foul balls count as strikes; Young's adding an improved curve ball, a devastating change of pace, and even an occasional spitball to his repertoire to offset a slight decline in the speed of his blazing fastball as he got older; and his third no-hitter enshrining him in the eyes of many contemporary baseball writers as "the enduring symbol of the American game."

While all are important, the most affecting of these interludes is Chapter Seven, "Snapshot of a Private Man," which brings the subject vividly to life. Browning tells us that the blue-eyed, sandy-haired Young at 6'2" was tall for the day, barrel-chested, and prone to put on weight. He sported a mustache during the first part of his big league career and was considered handsome by the ladies (he was also devoted to his wife Robba, probably a second cousin). He was frugal, an early riser, a hard worker, and intelligent but "only marginally literate." A quiet, shy man, he avoided the limelight but liked to have fun, had a good sense of humor, and loved to chat with and tell stories to close friends. He disliked brawling and violence and stayed out of pubs yet occasionally enjoyed a beer or whiskey. A moral, honest man, he had a commitment to moderation and believed that "Common sense is all a man needs." Above all, Cy Young valued his good name and highly resented any attack on his reputation; such as the off-season letter sent by St. Louis Perfectos owner Frank Robison to his players, including Young, accusing them of "indifference, drunkenness, gambling, and what the press gently termed 'kindred vices.'" The letter maligned most of the players but especially Young, about whom Browning says, "Amid the shifting sands of baseball excesses Cy Young was a rock."

And what of Cy Young's accomplishments from the mound? Well, they were numerous and spectacular. Aside from those monolithic 511 wins, his three no-hitters, including a perfect game; his record 15 20-win seasons; his 24 consecutive hitless innings streak; and his three consecutive 1–0 shutouts comprise just the highlights. Throughout the narrative Browning provides the particulars of Young's performance, and in an effort to put his yearly pitching statistics into perspective he notes the numerous times Young's total in a category either led the league or came close to doing so. It's a dizzying record, made all the more impressive when one takes into account Young's sedulousness and adaptability. Young got his nickname because of the tremendous speed of his fastball, but he rose to an entirely higher plane when, through persistent hard work, he mastered his control. Young, who didn't even wear a glove until his sixth year in the major leagues, also better than any other hurler of the time successfully made the transition from pitching's formative days to its modern era.

At the end of the book Browning asks, "Was Cy Young the greatest pitcher of all time?" Dependent as it is on definitions and numerous factors impossible to determine with complete accuracy, the answer, according to the author, is, "We don't know, of course." Perhaps, but given what we learn about the pitcher in this book, his amazing accomplishments over a very long career and the admiration we come to have for him as a person, he will certainly have as strong a claim to the title as anyone else as long as people care to raise the question.

Dalko: The Untold Story of Baseball's Fastest Pitcher

◆

Bill Dembski, Alex Thomas, and Brian Vikander

◆

Nashville: Influence Publishers, 2020. Cloth, 304 pages, ISBN: 978-1-64542-710-0. Foreword by "Sudden" Sam McDowell. Acknowledgments, Authors' Note, Notes, Bibliography, Index, 34 color and black & white photos between pages 176 and 177.

Comments: In 2009 Dalkowski was inducted into the Baseball Reliquary's Shrine of the Eternals, along with Roger Maris and Jim Eisenreich, in a ceremony which took place at the Pasadena, California, Public Library.

For a career minor leaguer who never played even one game in the major leagues to warrant a full-length biography, and a biography years in the making which involved countless hours of research, there would have to be something pretty special about him and his story. And such is the case with the legendary Steve Dalkowki, the subject of *Dalko: The Untold Story of Baseball's Fastest Pitcher* by Bill Dembski, Alex Thomas, and Brian Vikander. Bits and pieces of the Dalkowski story had been published in the past and continued to circulate for years as reverential gossip and seemingly exaggerated tall tales throughout the baseball community, yet no one until the authors came along had done the heavy lifting of starting from the beginning, tracing the many stops along the subject's promising but frustrating career in minor league baseball, and detailing the subject's sad decline once his final chance to harness his spectacular gift had expired. In the eyes of the results-oriented public, Steve Dalkowski was a failure. This humane, stirringly empathetic biography proves otherwise.

The legend of Steve Dalkowski came into being in New Britain, Connecticut, a city of blue collar, working class people, many employed in the town's thriving auto parts industry. High school sports in the region were important, and Steve became not only a big star of both the baseball and football teams but a hero of the community; a status he enjoyed for the rest of his life. His spectacular pitching attracted huge crowds, including scouts from virtually every major league organization.

That's what happens when you strike out 150 batters in 69 2/3 innings, which is what Steve did as a high school senior. The Baltimore Orioles won the Dalkowski sweepstakes, giving him $12,000 and a new Pontiac. That technically made him a "bonus baby" and required the Orioles to keep him on the major league roster for two years; something they had no intention of doing because, as blindingly fast as Dalkowski was, they knew he was nowhere near ready to pitch winning baseball in the big time.

That's because for Dalkowski the astonishing speed of his fastball was as much a curse as a blessing. Simply put, he had severe control problems. A typical Dalkowski performance resulted in an amazing number of strikeouts but also an excessive number of walks and wild pitches. He opened his senior year in high school by throwing back-to-back no hitters but in the next two games he struck out 18 and walked 14 and struck out 20 while walking 13, respectively. The Orioles knew that Dalkowski was wild, as young fast ballers often are, but they believed he was worth the gamble. In the summer of 1957, the 6'1" 175-pound 18-year-old lefthander began his pro career in the rookie classification Appalachian League with Kingsport, and he was immediately plagued with control problems, sometimes not even making it out of the first inning. He was summoned to Baltimore where manager Paul Richards and pitching coach Harry Brecheen worked with him on his control. After he returned to Kingsport, he beat Bluefield 7–5 on August 31; the game establishing a frustrating pattern that hindered his advancement and spread awe and fear of his pitching throughout baseball. Dalkowski set a league record with 24 strikeouts in that game, but he also issued an astonishing 18 free passes. His record for the season was 1–8 with 115 strikeouts and 129 walks in 63 innings.

The great understanding of the authors for Dalkowski's dilemma is evident in the following passage:

> What did Steve Dalkowski learn from his first season in professional baseball? What sort of progress had he made as a pitcher as opposed to simply a thrower? Who around him understood that throwing strikes begins in the head, not in the arm? The answers: nothing, none, and nobody. Steve had confirmed that he could throw very hard, that fans and players alike knew of his reputation, and that the strike zone remained lost in some nebulous haze sixty feet, six inches away. He must have at least subconsciously sensed that no one understood the process required to convert him into a pitcher. He must have begun to realize that, no matter how well intentioned those around him might be, he was on his own.

This is a sad but accurate and predictive assessment, which the authors demonstrate in carefully documenting the rest of Dalkowski's professional career; an eight-year odyssey spent moving up and down the low minor league ladder. Dalko suited up for Knoxville, Wilson (NC), Aberdeen (SD) twice, Pensacola, Stockton (CA) twice, Elmira (NY) three times, Kennewick (WA) twice, and San Jose. He got as high as Triple A twice but briefly, pitching a total of 15 games for Rochester and Columbus. His lifetime record, according to *Baseball Reference*, was 46–80 in 236 games, 152 of then started. He pitched 38 complete games with 12 shutouts, gave up only 664 hits, and racked up 1,324 strikeouts and issued an equally amazing 1,236 base on balls in 956 innings.

Dalkowski had his moments, of course, those days when he was able to get the ball over the plate enough to be effective … and at times, unhittable. But such moments never happened often enough. As indicated, many of his coaches and managers, who were not close to being sports psychologists, were at a loss on how to help him, especially because on the sidelines or in the bullpen Dalkowski was able to throw strikes. It was only when he toed the rubber in a game that his control deserted him. One strategy was to have him throw on the sidelines for up to an hour before a game in the hope that tiring him out would help his control … a ridiculous waste of hundreds of pitches that would never be countenanced today. Others tinkered with various aspects of his delivery … some telling him to do this, others to do that, which only served to confuse him. Dalkowski actually had a good curveball and was encouraged to throw it, but when he did and his curve was hit, he angrily, and it might be said, "arrogantly" resorted to relying on his overpowering fastball. Again, that fastest of all fastballs and Dalkowski's awareness of it actually hampered him. Earl Weaver, Dalko's manager at Aberdeen and Elmira who went on to a Hall of Fame career as the manager of the Orioles, helped Dalkowski the most; by teaching him to throw a slider but mostly by simply trying to show confidence in the young man. Yet even Weaver's encouragement was insufficient. As the authors say about Dalko's lack of progress,

> There was a lot of hype to live up to. Steve was so eager to please that his natural reaction was to overreach, try too hard, throw too hard, worry about the game ahead, and thus slip back into old habits and old results. He had no support to help him reconcile the three people each of us has inside: the one others see. The one you know you want to be, and the one you know you are.

In addition to a lack of confidence, excessive nervousness, an inability to concentrate properly, or whatever other undefined, non-physical problems thwarted Dalkowski's ability to master the strike zone, other recognized problems contributed to his difficulties: namely, alcoholism. The authors speculate that Dalkowski's father introduced him to drinking as a New Britain rite of passage, and while it is impossible to say how much his habitual drunkenness hampered his efforts, it is a certainty that the drinking, which helped Dalkowski feel like one of the boys, did not benefit his pitching; nor did his befriending infamous playboy and late-night partier Bo Belinsky. Largely because of his immoderate imbibing, Dalkowski also frequently ran out of money and borrowed from teammates. The authors, who characterize their subject as a generous, loveable soul, emphasize the integrity evident in Dalkowski's having always repaid every penny on payday, never questioning his teammates' assessment of how much money he owed. They acknowledge that he unfortunately, all too often, re-borrowed money the same day from his buddies. While there is no proof, they also raise the possibility that Steve accepted payments from mobsters, betting like the Orioles that one day he might become a star.

The great irony of the book and the subject's life is that in the spring of 1963 Steve Dalkowski had finally become a pitcher the Orioles wanted to take north to start the regular major league season. Steve had apparently turned a corner pitching over the winter in Venezuela under Weaver. Observers believed he had learned to quit trying to strike everybody out and accept help from his defense, and his confidence had never been higher. Then, in the final spring exhibition he felt something pop in his arm while throwing a breaking ball. He was sent to Rochester to rest and recover but never received a proper diagnosis of or treatment for his injury. When he returned to action, he was erratic and soon demoted, never to get as close to the big leagues again. Eventually, his drinking got the best of him, and the Orioles finally gave up on him. After a couple of unsuccessful comeback attempts, he found himself out of baseball with no marketable skills or career prospects. He lived a vagabond life for decades afterwards, working mostly as a farm laborer. Surprisingly, he found conjugal happiness twice, and the authors' accounts of his years with the two women who loved him deeply assuage somewhat the pity readers are inclined to feel for the great disappointment he suffered as a pitcher. Even in the final years of his life during which he suffered from dementia, Dalkowski benefited from the love and support of many people, such as his old high school coach and teammates, New Britain residents, and especially his sister Pat.

Many myths grew up around Steve Dalkowski and the speed of his fastball, such as the stories about one of his pitches tearing the ear off a minor league batter, Ted Williams being afraid to take BP against him, and Steve having a low IQ. The authors dispel all these myths, and in addition competently explain why the results of the tests to measure the speed of the Dalkowski fastball taken at the army's Aberdeen Proving Ground in Maryland in June of 1958 were inadequate. So, how fast was Steve Dalkowski? Could he really bring it up to the plate at 115 mph? And how did he throw so fast? We will never know the answer to that latter question because there exists no film of Dalkowski throwing, a matter of great disappointment to the authors, two of whom are experts on the mechanics of pitching. We will never know the exact answers to the former questions either, but it hardly matters. We have the testimony of reliable, expert witnesses throughout this book … that of at least one minor leaguer who refused to play if Dalkowski was slated to pitch; that of another opponent who said that if Dalkowski had been wild in and out instead of up and down, "there would have been dead guys everywhere"; and what Branch Rickey, GM of the Pittsburgh Pirates, told the Grand Forks Chiefs after Steve no-hit them while striking out 21. "Boys," he said, "the way he was throwing tonight, he would have no-hit the Big Club. Remember, we have Groat, Big Klu, Maz, Smokey, and Bobby. So, don't worry."

Thus, as *Dalko* proves, while Steve Dalkowski never pitched an inning of major league baseball, he is a bona fide legend of the game who will never be forgotten. As the authors say in the book's final words: "Steve Dalkowski was the fastest pitcher who ever played the game. Rewind the video of his life, stop it anywhere, and ask anyone who saw him in action on the mound. Nobody claims otherwise. We don't have to allow him a place in history. He's there. He earned it."

Diz: The Story of Dizzy Dean and Baseball During the Great Depression

◆

ROBERT GREGORY

◆

New York: Viking Penguin, 1992. Cloth, 402 pages, ISBN: 0-670-82141-1. Acknowledgments, Prologue: Who's Afraid of the Deans? Index, 14 black & white photos between pages 84 and 85 and 11 black & white photos between pages 244 and 245.

Few baseball biographies are as engaging and just plain fun to read as Robert Gregory's brilliant account of the life and career of St. Louis Cardinals pitcher Dizzy Dean, entitled *Diz: The Story of Dizzy Dean and Baseball During the Great Depression*. Dean was already widely recognized as one of baseball's true originals, but no one previously had brought him to life so vividly and masterfully as Gregory; who in addition to revivifying the legend, effortlessly delineates the subject's greatness as a pitcher, as well as his stature as the preeminent drawing card of his day. Gregory understands his subject as if he'd invented him, and the genius of his biography is that he is able to convey that understanding to the reader through flawless, economical prose and a narrative that speeds by like the ceaselessly fascinating view from a Pullman club car.

While Gregory did not invent his subject, he gives us a portrait of Dizzy Dean as someone who strutted through life as if he were a living and breathing Ring Lardner character. Dean grew up in the midst of the great depression in an America which no longer exists today. His mother died early, and his sharecropping father, moving the family from one small farming community to another, provided a minimum of parental support and guidance (The Deans once lost Dizzy's elder, mentally challenged brother Elmer on a road trip and didn't recover him until four years later. "He'll show up," said Pa Dean). Completely unsupervised, Dean and younger brother Paul went to school once a week, if that, and benefited little from the experience. Yet, Dean grew up unharmed by such normally debilitating circumstances, protected by his sunny disposition, irresistible likability, off-the-charts self-confidence, and innate happiness. An underaged Dizzy joined the Army, attracted mostly by the promise of three squares a day, and naturally became the worst solider in history: an incompetent Gomer Pyle with one glaring talent: a God-given ability, not to plant seeds, but to throw them tirelessly from the slab of a pitcher's mound. It was, in fact, a drill sergeant who also managed a baseball team on the base at Fort Sam Houston, James K. Brought, who turned Dean from a thrower into a pitcher.

As Gregory's rich narrative unfolds, it dawns on the reader that the Dizzy Dean who seems like a fictional character in *Diz* would not be possible today. For example, Dean wasn't the first enlistee to regret his decision to join the armed forces, but he was allowed to buy his way out of it after he somehow scraped up the cash to do so. He was almost immediately signed by the St. Louis Cardinals, and after dominating hitters in both the Western and Texas Leagues, he was promoted to the big leagues at the end of his rookie year in pro ball (he sat on the bench for a month as the Cards were in a pennant fight, but he started, and won the last game of the regular season, 3–1). During his first stop in the minors at St. Joseph, Missouri, Dean went around town splurging on whatever goods and services he fancied and then insouciantly charged everything to the Cardinals organization (St. Louis GM Branch Rickey nearly had a stroke over this one and curtailed Dean's profligacy by deducting the expenses from his current and future salaries). Part of Dean's success was due to his fearlessness and his willingness to throw his high hard one as often as necessary. He was a Don Drysdale before Drysdale. Once in a pique of anger, he knocked down almost every hitter in the Giants lineup, repeatedly, and was never even cautioned by the home plate umpire. After he'd established himself in the big leagues, Dean constantly risked everything by throwing countless innings during meaningless barnstorming exhibitions in two-bit towns, often without warming up properly or taking care of his arm afterwards. Off the diamond, he did even crazier things, like instigate and find himself in the middle of a riot over a "wrassler" named Bulldog Mallory he decided to root against. And then, there was Dean's epic verbiage, a never-ending stream of corn-pone sayings, boasts, demands, insults, challenges, and predictions which tickled folks sometimes but annoyed and even enraged them at other times: all of it issued with the fractured grammar that was his trademark and a good part of his charm. And, while all players want as much money as they can make, Dean raised his constant demands for salary increases to a galling and irritating art form, especially when wife Pat (a party girl Diz had taken a liking to in the minors) took control of his finances and the negotiations.

Perhaps the most amazing thing about Dizzy Dean was the brevity of his career. He basically pitched ten seasons in the major leagues, and four of those were partial, injury-plagued ones that came with the Chicago Cubs after he'd hurt his arm, the result of his coming back too soon from a broken toe suffered in the 1937 All-Star Game. Nevertheless, for his first five seasons with St. Louis he was unquestionably the best pitcher in baseball, with the possible exception of the New York Giants' Card Hubbell, with whom he had many heralded duels. He won 18, 20, 30, 28, and 24 games those years, averaging almost 50 appearances and more than 300 innings per year. Deprived of his blazing, intimidating fastball, Dean still fashioned a winning record (16–8) over a three-year period for the Cubs, getting by on guile, "pitching smarts," and superb control. The reader is almost shocked when Gregory says that Dean retired having won a total of 150 major league games.

Readers often skip a book's "Prologue," but that would be a big mistake with *Diz* because it is there that the author begins his tale with a mesmerizing account of the Cardinals and Dean's arrival in Detroit, on the day before the start of the 1934 World Series, the highlight of Dean's career. Gregory follows Dean's movements throughout the day … from his last-off-the-train, regal exit from the Wabash Special to breakfast at the Book-Cadillac Hotel with Will Rogers and Damon Runyon to his walk at the head of a procession of fans and well wishes out to Navin Field for the Cards' final practice to Dizzy and his brother Paul hitting the hay at nine o'clock and dreaming "not of Tigers, as Diz said later, but of 'pussycats'" … with Gregory all the while providing amazing details about the scene, recording Dean's humorous remarks and pronouncements, and explaining how it all came to be. It is a narrative tour de force unlike anything else in baseball biography, and it guarantees the commitment of the reader to the rest of the book.

Inevitably, there are a lot of game accounts in any baseball biography, but no one has made them more palatable and less tiring than Gregory does in *Diz* (a good example of this is Gregory's treatment of the Dean-Hubbell "game of the century" 1937 matchup when King Carl was going for his 23rd consecutive victory and Dizzy's aforementioned headhunting resulted in a real brawl. No one would want any of the detail Gregory supplies left out). Gregory sets the record straight about Dean's true names (he was Jay Hanna, not Jerome Herman) and his date and place of birth; explains the origin of his nickname (Sgt. Brought heard him throwing peeled potatoes at garbage can lids and yelled, "You dizzy son of a bitch!"); and he dispels myths (there is no evidence that Dean said, "They x-rayed my head and found nothin'"). Finally, Gregory employs a deceptively simply style that makes use of language as disparate as "caterwauling" and "Augustinian habits," and sentences that are spare yet pregnant with meaning. For example, at the end of a passage about the Cardinals sending a raw Dean back down to Houston for more work with Branch Rickey hoping that he would mature some and quit running his mouth so much, Gregory writes: "The Cardinals would get back what they were sending down, a pitcher who knew he was good and wanted the whole world to know it." The final chapters covering Dean's post-playing life and his extensive broadcasting career are brief, but they are sufficient; especially when Gregory is able to rely on Dean himself to explain a lot in a few words. In discussing some teachers' disapproval of Dizzy Dean's employment as a professional on-air word mangler, Gregory writes:

> In giving his side, Diz confessed to "butcherin'" the language but wondered if his accusers might not do the same if they had spent their childhoods in the cotton fields instead of the schoolhouse. Anyway, he'd learned enough to get by in radio. "I know what's a ball and what's a strike," he said, "and 'vice-uh-veeda.'"

Anyone who can read that, the kind of Dean utterings found throughout the book, and not laugh, needs to have his funny bone checked.

Dynastic, Bombastic, Fantastic: Reggie, Rollie, Catfish, and Charlie Finley's Swingin' A's

Jason Turbow

Boston: Houghton Mifflin Harcourt, 2017. Cloth, 386 pages, ISBN: 978-0-544-30317-1. Introduction. Epilogue, Cast of Characters, Acknowledgments, Notes, Index, 27 black & white photos between pages 146 and 147 and 36 black & white photos in the Cast of Characters section (pages 327–344). Front and rear end papers are photos of victorious A's players dousing themselves with champagne. Other baseball books by the author: The Baseball Codes: Beanballs, Sign Stealing, and Bench-Clearing Brawls. The Unwritten Rules of America's Pastime *(Anchor, 2011) and* They Bled Blue: Fernandomania, Strike-Season Mayhem, and the Weirdest Championship Baseball Had Ever Seen: The 1981 Los Angeles Dodgers *(Houghton Mifflin Harcourt, 2019).*

For the first half of the 1970s, there was no better team in baseball than the Oakland A's: a combative, colorful, and controversial band of warriors who won five consecutive divisional titles and three straight American League pennants and World Championships (1972–74). Built around a core of dedicated and talented players, led by future Hall of Famers Catfish Hunter, Rollie Fingers, and Reggie Jackson, and continually united by a vehement dislike of owner Charlie Finley, the A's overcame the indifference of their fan base and the local media, a lack of support by a persistently undermanned front office, and the galling cheapness and overbearing egotism of the megalomaniacal Finley, to put together a run of success worthy of the title "dynasty." Theirs is a head-shaking story of audacity, mendacity, infighting, betrayal, excellence, desire, professionalism, and grace under pressure that can hardly be believed, and nobody has ever told the story better than Jason Turbow in *Dynastic, Bombastic, Fantastic*.

The A's story begins and ends with Charles O. Finley, a Chicago business man whose lifelong dream of owning a major league baseball team was fulfilled after the 1960 season when he wrested controlling interest of the woeful Kansas City Athletics away from the wife of Arnold Johnson in a distressed sale. A man of ideas, Finley had made a fortune with the innovation of selling group insurance plans to surgeons and doctors, and he carried his unshakeable faith in the superiority of his creativity into baseball; sometimes to positive but often to disastrous effect. For instance, he invented the colorful baseball uniform, dressing the A's in splashy gold and kelly green hues; and he advocated the adoption of the DH, night World Series and All-Star games, and interleague play. On the other hand, his experiments with orange baseballs and a player (Herb Washington) as a pinch-running specialist were failures. And, like another owner infamous for dictating lineups and strategy to a musical chairs list of dugout managers, George Steinbrenner, Finley grossly over-estimated his understanding of the subtler aspects of the game.

Despite putting on a good show in the beginning, Finley had no intention of keeping the A's in Kansas City and was determined to get League permission to move to what he assumed would be a larger and more lucrative market. Lawsuits and threats of more law suits became a standard Finley tactic which enabled him to eventually get his way, as the A's moved to Oakland after the 1968 season, but such behavior made him anathema to his fellow owners and a virtual enemy of Commissioner Bowie Kuhn. Finley did know baseball talent when he saw it though, and through brilliant draft choices and shrewd trades (particularly getting Ken Holtzman from the Cubs for Rick Monday), he quickly assembled a powerhouse of a ball club in Oakland, one built upon pitching, defense, speed, and power hitting. The A's of the early '70s were simply the best-balanced team in the majors.

As Turbow notes, Finley adopted a personal motto of *Sweat plus sacrifice equals success* (the short version of which was S + S = S), and it served him well in his insurance and real estate businesses; yet that success deluded him into thinking he could achieve similar results in baseball through the sheer force of his will and authority. Attendance in Oakland was poor for several reasons beyond the team's control, but Finley needlessly exacerbated the situation by never moving to the city and becoming involved in the community, by serving (from his Chicago office) as his own general manager and doing virtually nothing to promote the ballclub, by doing nothing to quash rumors that he wanted to move the team again to another city, and by disrespecting the media. As second baseman Dick Green said, "The reason Finley got a lot of bad press was because he treated the press terribly."

What it boiled down to was that Finley was his and his team's own worst enemy. The book is rife with examples of Finley doing something stupid, selfish, and/or mean … sometimes to save money but all too often just to prove a point or to show that he was the boss. The most incomprehensible example of this penchant for counter-productiveness is the appalling way he handled Vida Blue's demand for a salary bump after the youngster's sensational rookie season. Blue took baseball by storm in 1971, going 24–8 and striking out 301 batters with a blazing fastball he could control while leading the American League in ERA with a mark of 1.82. His pay for that extraordinary performance was $14,500. Blue had been a huge drawing card, responsible for an estimated $1,500,000 in gate receipts, and his agent, Bob Gerst, asked that his salary be increased to the average for the best pitchers in the game, $115,000. Finley ridiculed the figure, countering with his first and last offer of $50,000. Holding all the cards, Finley arrogantly informed Blue, "I don't have to pay you." As Turbow adroitly chronicles, Gerst proposed all kinds of compromises and resorted to various strategies intent on pressuring Finley, but the owner never budged, even as Blue glumly sat out spring training. In the end, Blue caved and through the intervention of Kuhn actually received a little more than the $50,000, but the process soured him on the game. Worse, his holdout and Finley's assault on his psyche resulted in him slumping to a 6–10 record for 1972. As a rookie, Blue had pitched like the reincarnation of a mature Sandy Koufax! But it was more important to Finley to put the pitcher in his place as a mere employee than to make him happy and to accelerate his development into a true superstar and the team into champions.

Turbow duly recounts other instances of Finley's counter-productive moves, many of them stinking of vindictiveness: unceremoniously cutting Tommy Davis for introducing Blue to Gerst; trading first baseman Mike Epstein for brawling with Reggie Jackson (a fight instigated by Jackson); and, worst of all, attempting to expunge second baseman Mike Andrews from the roster by putting him on the Disabled List after Andrews made a pair of errors in Game Two of the 1973 World Series.

It is astonishing that the A's dynasty unfolded in the midst of such circumstances. Remarkably, as Turbow points out, the A's were never given much respect by their National League World Series opponents, but the Reds, Mets, and Dodgers were all dispatched in turn with surgical precision. Unsurprisingly, their triumphs were also adulterated by their negative feelings towards Finley. After the A's beat the Mets in the '73 Series, a reporter asked Jackson how much credit Finley should get. Jackson said, "Please don't give that man the credit…. He spoiled what should have been a beautiful thing." Fed up with Finley's constant interference and disgusted by the way he treated the players, Dick Williams felt no joy in having led the A's to consecutive World Championships and resigned as team manager as a subdued clubhouse celebration unfolded.

After a slow start under retread manager Alvin Dark, who had particular difficulty in handling the pitching staff, the A's pulled themselves together to win a third straight AL pennant and World Series championship in 1974. By that time, tax problems, a messy divorce, and a penny-pinching contract snafu which led to the A's losing the rights to Catfish Hunter all began to unravel Finley's control over his baseball business. The onset of free agency which came on the heels of the Hunter case made Finley's ouster from the game inevitable. Turbow delineates two great ironies in covering this downfall. One, many of Finley's stars offered to sign multi-year contracts for what turned out to be modest amounts before much higher market values were set. Finley, of course, turned down such offers; in retrospect, one of the worst mistakes he made. And two, Finley suggested to his fellow owners that they stop free agency (and the escalation of higher and higher salaries) in its tracks by making all players free agents at the end of every season. This was a brilliant idea, the only one feared by labor leader Marvin Miller, yet by then Finley had alienated the other owners who were in no mood to listen to anything he had to say. One more divisional championship in 1975 was the team's last hurrah; and the A's sank to embarrassing competitive depths as Finley, totally opposed to and incapable of operating in the new free agency era, held fire sales of all marketable players to recoup what monies he could. It was an ignominious end that could have been avoided.

Turbow points out how young the mainstays of the A's ballclub were when it all fell apart, and he ponders how many more championships the team might have won if they had stayed together. They did, he notes, do something no other dynastic baseball team has done; i.e., win six championship series in a row (three American League Championship Series victories over the Tigers, the Orioles, and the Orioles again, in addition to the three World Series wins). As for Finley, he faded from the scene quickly after he sold the A's to the heirs of the Levi Strauss clothing business, and only three people from baseball attended his funeral in 1996. At the press conference announcing the sale of the ballclub, AL President Lee MacPhail kindly acknowledged Finley's contributions to the game, saying that "Baseball has lost its number one innovator." Yet more likely to stay with readers of this unforgettable, highly affecting account is the author's concluding assessment of the force behind the dynasty: "At his core, Finley equated power with importance and importance with love, even in the empiric absence of actual affection. As it turned out, fear and enmity did not equal respect, a fact borne out by the lack of representatives at his funeral from a sport he helped shape more than any other during his time in it.

For Charley Finley, it was lonely at the top. In the end he discovered that it was even lonelier at the bottom."

Fenway 1912: The Birth of a Ballpark, a Championship Season, and Fenway's Remarkable First Year

◆

GLENN STOUT

◆

Boston: Houghton, Mifflin, Harcourt, 2011. Cloth, 392 pages, ISBN: 978-0-547-19562-9. Introduction, Prologue. Epilogue, Acknowledgments, Bibliographic Notes and Sources, Notes, Appendix: Boston Red Sox 1912 Statistics, Index, 12 black & white photos between pages 106 and 107 and 12 black & white photos between pages 202 and 203. Other baseball books by the author: Ted Williams: A Portrait in Words and Pictures *(Walker and Company, 1991),* Jackie Robinson: Between the Baselines *(Woodford, 1997),* Red Sox Century: The Definitive History of Baseball's Most Storied Franchise *(Houghton Mifflin, 2000),* Yankees Century: 100 Years of New York Yankees Baseball *(Houghton Mifflin, 2002),* The Dodgers: 120 Years of Dodgers Baseball *(Houghton Mifflin, 2004),* The Cubs: The Complete Story of Chicago Cubs Baseball *(Houghton Mifflin, 2007), and* The Selling of the Babe: The Deal That Changed Baseball and Created a Legend *(Thomas Dunne Books, 2016).*
Comments: *Fenway 1912* won the 2012 Seymour Medal and was a Finalist for the 2011 CASEY Award.
"In the capable hands of Stout, *Fenway 1912* promises to make all other books about Fenway's construction and first season obsolete."—*SportsIllustrated.com*

Expert on all things Red Sox, Glenn Stout had a brilliant idea for what would become his magnum opus on Boston baseball. Instead of writing a book only about the Sox's best season in history when they won a team record 105[*] regular season games and then defeated the powerful New York Giants in a thrilling, chaotic World Series; or writing a book devoted to the origins, design, construction, quirky playing characteristics, malleability, and history of the team's famous home, Fenway Park; he combined the two stories into one fascinating narrative, entitled *Fenway 1912: The Birth of a Ballpark, a Championship Season, and Fenway's Remarkable First Year.* The result is a unique achievement that places the work among

---

[*]The 105 wins were eventually bested by the 2018 Red Sox, who went 108–54, but the .691 winning percentage of the 1912 contingent has never been eclipsed.

the very best of both kinds of books: seasonal accounts and treatises on a single ballpark.

Stout opens the book with a Prologue that is notable for two key concepts, certain to contradict the assumptions of all but the most knowledgeable of Red Sox and Fenway Park fans. First, the idea that Fenway has survived not because it was preserved but because it was *not* preserved. As Stout ably demonstrates, the ballpark has been, from the very beginning, subject to continual changes and modifications in order to serve the competitive needs of the team and the financial needs of the organization. And, second, that Fenway's original shape and dimensions, which by and large remain in effect today, were not determined by the closeness of adjacent streets and buildings but simply by the designs of architect, James McLaughlin. Fenway may appear today to have been wedged into a cramped neighborhood parcel, but when it was built it was surrounded by empty lots and wide-open spaces. These two astonishing revelations prime the reader's curiosity and prep the stage for the rollicking account to follow.

Another amazing disclosure presented in Chapter One concerns the reason Fenway Park was built in the first place. Contrary to any belief that Fenway was erected as part of the concrete-and-steel modernization movement to replace wooden ballparks (in this case, Boston's Huntington Grounds), Fenway came into being strictly as an attempt by the owners of the team to lessen their headaches of running the team in favor of maximizing their profits by building a ballpark which they could rent to the team. Thus, General Charles Taylor and son John I. Taylor, with major real estate holdings in Boston, sold half their stake in the ballclub to Jimmy McAleer (a former outfielder with the Cleveland club) and Robert McRoy (the personal assistant of American League President Ban Johnson) and then used the proceeds to pay for the construction of Fenway. With the new half owners attending to the day-by-day affairs of the ballclub, the Taylors were positioned, as passive, part owners of the team, to benefit from increased profits generated by the new ballpark, as well as from the rental income.

Chapter One, mostly about the 1911 season and prior Red Sox history, also does a remarkable job of setting the scene for the team's championship year. After years of mediocrity, the team was on the rise, but it was hampered by the existence of two cliques which "divided the squad by age, geography, heritage, and most notably, by religion." The Catholic group of players became known as the "KCs" (for the Catholic service organization the Knights of Columbus), and the protestant group as the "Masons." Winning kept the lid on this simmering pot of antagonism for most of the season, but things eventually boiled over during the hard-fought World Series and resulted in fist fights among Sox teammates. Many of the team's key players are profiled here, and we acquire fascinating information about them. We learn, for instance, that budding superstar Tris Speaker played with a chip on his shoulder because the Red Sox had previously released him before realizing his potential; that veteran first baseman and savvy first-year player-manager Jake Stahl won over his new team by ceding some authority, making shortstop Charlie Wagner team captain; and that the raw fireballer and matinee idol Joe Wood was not exactly a choir boy (Stout later describes him as "cocksure and arrogant and occasionally even cruel").

Fenway was constructed over the winter of 1911–1912, and the book duly recounts the heroic efforts of McLaughlin, general contractor Charles Logue, and groundskeeper Jerome Kelley, who had to battle not only the calendar but pretty nasty northeastern weather as well in a race to have the new ballpark ready by spring. Detailing the technical issues involved might have proved boring were they not handled as artfully as Stout does. Under his spell, we visualize McLaughlin peering over architectural drawings, making a change here and another there; we hear the constant hammering of Logue's men and smell the mounds of sawdust they produce; and we feel the anxiety of Kelley trying to smooth out the diamond and get grass to take hold while workers and equipment are constantly on the move all over the site. In *Fenway 1912*, the reader roots just as hard for these experts in their fields as he later does for players wearing the Red Sox colors.

The Red Sox opened the 1912 season on the road and finished the trip with a 4–1 record with a rain out in the finale in Philadelphia. Opening Day in Boston was rained out not once, but twice. The new ballpark was finally christened before an overflow crowd on April 20 with an extra-inning win over New York on an infield single by the speedy Speaker. Official capacity was 24,400, consisting of 11,400 Grandstand seats, 8,000 pavilion seats (down the first base line), and another 5,000 in the distant center field bleachers; but Stout explains that management squeezed another 6,000 SRO patrons into the park, more than half of them ringing the far edges of the outfield behind hastily erected ropes. Surprisingly, there were no bleachers in right field or along the third base line. They were added later in September, in addition to seven rows of bleachers in front of the left field wall, to increase seating and profits for the upcoming World Series.

Everyone was thrilled with the new ballpark, and it did not take long for the peculiar dimensions of the place to manifest themselves. The closeness of the left field wall enabled left fielder Duffy Lewis to play "deep shortstop," as Carl Yastrzemski would later put it, and would enable him to take away numerous hits on flares that would normally have dropped in safely. Many a reader will also be surprised to learn that, like Cincinnati's Crosley Field, Fenway originally had an incline in front of the left field wall. In the fifth game ever played in the ballpark, Lewis stumbled on the embankment, fell down, and, while flat on his back, caught the fly ball he'd been chasing. He continually practiced going up and down the hill until his expertise doing so gave the Red Sox a notable home field advantage. By mid-summer, the incline was known as "Duffy's Cliff." Even though no one was worried about left field presenting too easy a target for long ball hitter—it was the Deadball era after all—quite a stir was created when Hugh Bradley, subbing for the injured Stahl, hit the first homer over the left field wall in the sixth game played at Fenway. As Stout says, home runs remained uncommon at Fenway for years afterwards. In a delicious bit of historical edification, he also explains how the term "Green Monster" for that left field wall did not come into common usage until the early 1970s.

When the ballpark itself is not the focus, Stout's recitation of the Red Sox's fortunes on the diamond is equally gripping. By May 30 at the end of the team's longest home stand of the year (21 games), Stahl had established a dependable starting rotation to complement his potent batting attack. In second place, only two games behind the surprising White Sox, the team then embarked on the longest road trip of the season. When that 27-day, 25-game marathon was over, so was the American League pennant race. The team came back to Fenway in first place, five games in front of Chicago and Washington, and they were never headed again.

The defending National League champion New York Giants got off to a blistering start in 1912 as well, and while John McGraw's men slumped in the middle of the season, it was a foregone conclusion that they would meet the Red Sox in the Fall Classic. It was the Giants' Rube Marquard who, by setting a "modern" major league record of 19 straight wins (from April 11 to July 3), provided the impetus for the interest in the second half of the season. Joe Wood, in the midst of a 34–5 season, was finally pitching like the ace everyone had expected him to become. He was, in fact, challenging Walter Johnson for the laurels of best and fastest moundsman in the game, and both pitchers (Johnson and Wood) went on winning streaks, challenging Marquard's just-established record. Johnson dropped out at 16 wins, losing a game in relief under a scoring decision that would be invalid today; setting up a re-match with Wood on September 6 that drove Boston fans bonkers in anticipation. To boost the gate as much as possible, McAleer and McRoy sold thousands of tickets for which there were no seats. Fans were everywhere: lying down underneath the grandstands, hanging on to a 30-foot ladder leaning against the outfield wall in foul ground, standing not just in front of the outfield wall but ringing the entire playing field, and even occupying both dugouts so that the players could not use them. Stout's conclusion: "Fenway Park, less than a season old, was already too small." Wood won the pitcher's duel for the ages 1–0, and he won another two games before his streak also ended at 16, but his ascendance was brief; as Stahl's overuse of him in the box during the 1912 season led to arm problems which prematurely ended his career.

The World Series was simply one of the craziest ever player: characterized as it was by ticket-selling snafus on the part of the Red Sox front office; widespread gambling by the fans and even some of the players; a tied third game called on account of darkness; the players' dissatisfaction with their split of the proceeds and their unsuccessful attempts to increase their share; the antics of the Sox's rabid fan club, the Royal Rooters, led by famous bar owner "Nuf Ced" McGreevy; the impact the enlargement of the seating areas had on the outcomes of games at Fenway, including ground rules that turned former fly ball outs into doubles and doubles that bounced over or through a temporary low outfield fence into home runs; the aforementioned intersquad squabbling; sensational performances; and devastating mistakes, both of the sloppy and boneheaded variety. It's can't-put-down reading to the end; the most amazing thing being the way the momentum shifted and then shifted again. Ahead three games to one (with the one tie), the Red Sox and their fans expected to wrap the Series up in Game Six at the Polo Grounds. But errors, cheap hits, and a costly balk gave that game to New York, and before anyone knew it, it came down to a final, Game Eight back in Fenway. By then, all of Boston, including the Red Sox themselves, were resigned to a Giants' triumph. Only 17,000 fans showed up to witness Boston's victory, coming in the eleventh inning on a sac fly against the immortal Christy Mathewson.

Stout concludes his masterpiece with an Epilogue that recounts what happened afterwards to the key players in the drama, including Fenway Park itself. In a book replete with delightful discoveries, he ends with one of the most striking: his assertion that, after all the changes it has seen, Fenway Park today ironically resembles modern retro parks designed to resemble it more than it resembles itself! Whether one agrees with that statement or not, at the end of the book the reader will realize that Stout had no choice but to write the story as he did, for the birth of Fenway Park and the Red Sox's championship season of 1912 were and always will be inseparable. And gloriously so.

Fifty-Nine in '84: Old Hoss Radbourn, Barehanded Baseball, and the Greatest Season a Pitcher Ever Had

◆

Edward Achorn

◆

New York: HarperCollins, 2010. Cloth, 366 pages, ISBN: 978-0-06-182586-6. Preface, Prologue. Epilogue, Appendix: Radbourn in 1884, Game by Game; 1884 Providence Grays Statistic, Sources & Notes, Index, 15 black & white photos between pages 176 and 177. Other baseball books by the author: The Summer of Beer and Whiskey: How Brewers, Barkeeps, Rowdies, Immigrants, and a Wild Pennant Fight Made Baseball America's Game *(Public Affairs, 2013).*

Comments: "First-class narrative history that can stand with everything Stephen Ambrose wrote.... Achorn's description of the utter insanity that was barehanded baseball is vivid and alive"—Charles P. Pierce, *Boston Globe*

"It's the vibrancy of his story that resonates, the sense of Radbourn and these others not as historical figures but as human beings. The game they played was brutal, with no gloves or protective gear, and no substitutions except in the case of catastrophic injury.... With *Fifty-nine in '84*, Achorn returns this remarkable season—and this remarkable pitcher—to something close to life"—*Los Angeles Times*

Some great books are great for one good reason. Others are so for multiple reasons, and *Fifty-Nine in '84: Old Hoss Radbourn, Barehanded Baseball, and the Greatest Season a Pitcher Ever Had* by Edward Achorn is a perfect example of the latter definition. As Achorn says, after taking us through the 1884 National League season, Charles "Old Hoss" Radbourn's winning 59 games for the Providence Grays against only 12 defeats amounted to "a towering achievement that has never been matched–and surely never will be." While the author's scintillating account of this remarkable feat creates the skeleton of the narrative, the book is gloriously fleshed out with a penetrating analysis of Radbourn's character and personality; vivid examples of the dangers inherent in playing glove-less baseball; and subplots of a hotly-contested pennant race and a touching love story.

Besides providing an unmatched portrayal of not only the way baseball was played but also of the way life in general was lived in America (and particularly in Providence, Rhode Island) in the waning years of the nineteenth century, Achorn was most intent on convincing readers, familiar with the modern game, that Radbourn's astonishing win total was not merely or even primarily a function of the pitching practices of the era. Yes, it was common for major league teams back then to rely basically on two pitchers, an ace and a number two man as competent and affordable as the team could find; and pitchers were expected to finish what they started ... so much so that being relieved was regarded as an insult to one's masculinity. And yearly win totals of between 25 and 35 games for pitchers were nothing special; yet what Radbourn did in 1884 was clearly an off-the-charts anomaly that could have been pulled off only by a master moundsman, impervious to pain and injury and driven monomaniacally by a cluster of fervent motivations.

As for Radbourn the man, he was admittedly not the type of person who would be universally admired today, especially by the media. He was reticent, surly, and even openly hostile: a hard-drinking, introverted grump who, in more than one surviving photo (including the one on the cover of the book), stares belligerently at the camera and nonchalantly gives the viewer the finger. These traits hardly held him back in his chosen profession though, and in fact they actually complemented and enhanced the ones he most needed to succeed on the diamond: an intense desire to win and to prove himself the best, an obstinate refusal to allow pain or injury to stop him, and his insistence on being paid what he believed he deserved. Of all these characteristics, Achorn most emphasizes the physical toll taken on Radbourn by his taking the ball, game after game after game during the 112-game season. Old Hoss pitched in 75 games, starting 73 and completing 73 of them. He wound up pitching 678.2 innings (with an ERA of 1.38) and dealt almost constantly with a sore arm and exhaustion: the latter condition exacerbated by the rough travel teams endured (similar to that endured later by Negro Leaguers) and the fact that "Rad" played another 12 games for the Grays as a position player, usually in the outfield (substitutions were illegal so managers often deployed a second pitcher in the day's lineup). Readers, like Radbourn's contemporaries, quickly come to admire him for his grit and dogged determination; especially given the fact that he was not a large or physically gifted man. Radbourn was fast enough but he was really a thinking pitcher, and his effectiveness came less from sheer speed and more from control, placement, unpredictability, and "an indomitable will."

Of course, there was more to the 1884 National League season than Radbourn's historic win total and iron-man performance, and Achorn's incorporation of these factors into the narrative is beautifully done and reliant to a delightful degree on the newspaper reporting of the day. First of all, *Fifty-Nine in '84* is an "underdog prevails" story. Providence was the smallest city in the National League but also the greatest rival, because of geographic proximity, of Boston, whose mighty Red Stockings club were defending champions. Boston had also won pennants in 1877 and '78 while Providence, league runners-up in 1880, '81, and '82, was still looking for its first pennant. The press in both cities routinely lambasted and mocked the players and fans of the other; and the desperation of Grays fans and everyone connected to the team was greatly increased by the knowledge that Radbourn, who'd won 49 games for third-place Providence in 1883, was itching to move to a better team that might help him finally win a championship.

Secondly, the Grays' pennant hopes were almost undone in 1884 by the sudden development of fire-balling 21-year-old San Franciscan Charles W. Sweeney, who at the beginning of his second season with the team threatened to unseat "Old Hoss" as Providence's unquestioned numero uno. Because Radbourn was still recovering from the overwork of the previous season, Sweeney did almost all the Grays pitching during the extensive pre-season schedule, and he did it so well (turning in a 19–0 ledger) that it appeared he had supplanted the older Radbourn. Sweeney was given the honor of starting on Opening Day and pitched effectively albeit in a Grays loss. Although he still suffered from a sore arm, a seething Radbourn roused himself and pitched Providence to a 5–2 win the next day; setting up the competitive dynamic that flavors the first half of the book and the Grays season. "The fight for the role of club ace was on," writes Achorn.

This inter-club rivalry intensified when Radbourn pitched 16 innings against Boston in a game that ended in a 1–1 tie but was one-upped the next day (June 7) by Sweeney, who struck out 19 Boston batters (a record not broken until 1986 by Red Sox pitcher Roger Clemens). The adulation accorded to the cocky young buck then was so over-the-top that Achorn describes his admirers as a cult. Grays fans made things worse by asking, for weeks, when Radbourn would strike out more than 19 batters in one game.

Just when it appeared that Providence had two aces in the fold, Sweeney hurt his arm and went on the shelf for weeks. Grays manager Frank Bancroft expected Radbourn to pick up the slack, which Radbourn was reluctantly willing to do but only if he were paid extra money, as Sweeney had been paid in the spring when he did all the pitching. Bancroft, a tight-fisted precursor of Branch Rickey refused. Consumed by jealousy of Sweeney and furious about not being compensated for his extra work, Radbourn soldiered on, pitching nearly every game until he was on the verge of a nervous breakdown. He appeared to give less than his best in a couple of games; and then on July 16 in the continuation of the earlier 1–1 tie game with Boston he became unhinged over terrible umpiring and sloppy defense behind him. Firing the ball with all his power with no concern for where it went, Radbourn subjected his poor catcher Barney Gilligan to a punishing pounding and gave the game away with walks and wild pitches; a dismal performance which resulted in his being suspended by the team's board of directors. Speculation abounded that the unhappy Radbourn would "jump" to the St. Louis Union Association outfit that had been trying to lure him away all season. Things then went from bad to worse when Sweeney, after returning and pitching well in a couple of games, became more interested in drinking and consorting with prostitutes than baseball. On July 22 a hung-over Sweeney pitched well for seven innings but quit the team rather than submit to being relieved. At this point, with Radbourn suspended and Sweeney now blacklisted for insubordination, the Grays were almost disbanded, but cooler heads prevailed and Bancroft found a solution to the desperate situation. It was decided that Radbourn would be given Sweeney's salary as well as his own and, as a pot-sweetener, his release after the season so that he could sign for more money with any team he wanted ... if he would give an all-out effort the rest of the season to win the pennant for Providence. And that's exactly what happened. From August 7 through September 18, Radbourn won 26 of 27 games, the highlight of the string being four consecutive wins over Boston during which he permitted a grand total of one run. The Grays won their first pennant by 10½ games and then beat the New York Metropolitans, champions of the American Association, in three straight, with Old Hoss "in the box" all three contests, to win the game's first World Series.

The love story of the book revolves around the relationship between Radbourn and Carrie Stanhope, a beautiful, charming "madam" who, abandoned by her husband, successfully ran the most respectable brothel in Providence. While much of what Achorn says about this relationship is conjecture, it is clear that Radbourn and Carrie loved each other. Achorn puts the two of them together, possibly, throughout the 1884 season. With greater assurance, he believes that Radbourn tried so hard to triumph in order to win the love and admiration of his beloved. Old Hoss and Carrie later lived together and eventually got married. In Bloomington, Illinois (Rad's home town), Carrie nursed Radbourn through his demise to his death, caused primarily by syphilis; and he saw to it that she benefited from his will. As it turned out, Radbourn, while free to sign with any other team, remained in Providence for another season after the crowning year of his career. Only a reader as curmudgeonly as Radbourn himself would opine that Carrie Stanhope had nothing to do with that decision.

The Final Season: Fathers, Sons, and One Last Season in a Classic American Ballpark

◆

Tom Stanton

◆

New York: Thomas Dunne Books, 2001. Cloth, 245 pages, ISBN: 0-312-27288-X. Preface. Acknowledgments, 36 black & white photos scattered throughout the book. Other baseball books by the author: The Road to Cooperstown: A Father, Two Sons, and the Journey of a Lifetime *(Thomas Dunne Books, 2003),* Hank Aaron and the Home Run That Changed America *(William Morrow, 2004), editor:* The Detroit Tigers Reader *(University of Michigan Press, 2005),* Ty and the Babe: Baseball's Fiercest Rivals: A Surprising Friendship and the 1941 Has-Beens Golf Championship *(Thomas Dunne Books, 2007), and* Terror in the City of Champions: Murder, Baseball, and the Secret Society That Shocked Depression-Era Detroit *(Lyons Press, 2016).*

Comments: The Final Season *won the 19th CASEY Award for the Best Baseball Book of 2001. The* Duke of Havana: Baseball, Cuba, and the Search for the American Dream *by Steve Fainaru and Ray Sanchez finished second, while* Hal Chase: The Defiant Life and Turbulent Times of Baseball's Biggest Crook *by Martin Donell Kahout ran third.*

Unfortunately, we Americans live in a society of planned obsolescence, ruled far too often by people who consider everything disposable, including our most venerable baseball ballparks. Even when major league ballparks have outlived their usefulness, their razing is seldom unaccompanied by regret on the part of untold fans who feel as if they are losing an important part of themselves. In the case of an aged, worn, but beloved ballpark such as Detroit's Tiger Stadium, which could have been saved, its relegation to the trash heap out of dubious economic necessity is a cultural tragedy. *The Final Season* by Tom Stanton, a chronicle of the last 81 home games played (in 1999) on the corner of Michigan and Trumbull Avenues, is a loving send-off to a classic American ballpark and a touching exploration of the meaning, in human, familial terms, of our most important architectural structures. Few who read the book will close it without a sense of bereavement.

As *The Final Season* is not about a pennant race, Stanton provides the barest bones of a game recap at the end of each diary entry. The comment about Game 65

"A beautiful gem of a book: tender, perceptive, compassionate, funny, and wise. I devoured it in one sitting and am still banging my tin cup on the dining room table wanting more."
— LAWRENCE S. RITTER, author of *The Glory of Their Times*

FATHERS, SONS, AND
ONE LAST SEASON IN A CLASSIC
AMERICAN BALLPARK

THE FINAL SEASON

TOM STANTON

is a good example of this brevity and indicative of the team's woeful performance: "Dave Mlicki wins his fifth straight, raising his record to 10–10, best on the team." Stanton was, it seems, the perfect person to discourse on the book's actual subject.

Besides being an experienced journalist, Stanton was a member of a large Polish Catholic family, originally named the Stankiewicz's, whose allegiance to the Detroit Tigers had spanned, with Stanton's three boys, four generations of grandfathers, fathers, and sons. Much of the book is a family history, replete with loving portraits and stories, passed down by Stanton's father Joe and Joe's brothers (and sisters), of the trials and tribulations "Pa" (Ted) and "Ma" (Anna) Stankiewicz faced in trying to raise ten children on an auto worker's salary when Detroit was a successful, livable city, the fifth most populated in the country. According to Stanton's telling, nothing, other than their faith and Polish heritage, held the males of the family together and connected them to prior and succeeding generations as securely as their love of baseball; and that love of course found its highest expression in a devotion to the Tigers and their ancestral home, Tiger Stadium.

Herein lies the essence of the book, the theme that the family history is inextricably bound to and entwined with the team history. While "Pa" Stankiewicz had never played baseball, he was a big fan of and identified with Tigers pitcher Elden Aucker, an unorthodox under-hander who made the most of limited ability. Most of "Pa's" sons did play ball and became even bigger Tigers fans. Joe, for example, was once handed a city league championship trophy by Tigers star Jo Jo White; and his having managed two bloop hits in a sandlot game off future Tigers Hall of Fame Hal Newhouser had become the stuff of family legend. Stanton does not claim that his family's connection to the Tigers is unique; in fact, he implies that his is merely one example of a ubiquitous experience, which explains as well as any other theory the hold baseball has long held over the American populace. And one of the joys of his experience was meeting other people throughout the season who shared a similar relationship with the game, the team, and the ballpark: fans such as Michael Bozymowski whose son is given a black baseball bat by current Tigers star Bobby Higginson; entrepreneurs such as parking lot owner Howard Stone, running his business for the 47th consecutive year; vendors such as Art Witkosky, who makes good money but doesn't do it anymore for the money; celebrities such as rocker Alice Cooper who like Stanton is in awe of former Tigers great Al Kaline; and even beloved team employees such as radio broadcaster Ernie Harwell who takes a friendly interest in Stanton's project.

There is also a second theme, the importance of place, which raises the book almost to the level of philosophical discourse. In the Preface, Stanton recounts a very important drive he took with his father before the start of the 1999 season. He says they "left the security of the freeway and ventured past boarded storefronts" to get to Montlieu Avenue. The once bustling neighborhood is unrecognizable, and the father looks sadly at the vacant lot where the family home used to sit. "But without the walls," Stanton writes, "without the French doors, without the roses in the yard, without something to touch, the bond had frayed the threads.

I kept driving."

This scene subtly sets the stage for the whole book, connecting as it does the destruction of the family home and neighborhood to the larger tragedy of the overall decline of the once great city of Detroit. Stanton never dwells on the latter–a subject for a different book (and the book is hardly a polemic as the replacement for Tiger Stadium, Comerica Park, was already under construction)–but the implication is clear: losing Tiger Stadium is akin to losing the house on Montlieu. Stanton is speaking of both structures when he writes: "Old buildings bring life to stories. They put a foundation to memories. They link you to the past and help you feel rooted."

Make no mistake, in the beginning Stanton is angry about the team's decision to abandon Tiger Stadium. His many sympathizers include John Lee David, the developer of the rejected Cochrane Plan that would have renovated the ballpark, who speaks eloquently of what is being lost:

> This stadium was built in Detroit, a workingman's town, for workingmen. The richest person and the poorest person sit next to each other. As an architect the greatest thing you can do is create a significant place for people. I don't think there's another place that means as much to the people of Michigan.

Nevertheless, as the season progresses Stanton is able to purge his anger and gracefully accept the inevitable. Near the end of the season (Game 72), while musing about the experience of Marty Taft, a native New Yorker who was a teenager when the Dodgers left Brooklyn, the author realizes that there's something even worse than losing a beloved ballpark.

While there was no saving Tiger Stadium, Stanton deeply desired to re-unite his family, to bring the estranged uncles, Tom and Herb, back into the fold. On one level the highlight of the book and Stanton's final season experience is arranging for his father Joe and Uncle Tom to attend Game 60 (August 15) together. In the Epilogue ("A Year Later") the author also clarifies his relationship with oldest son, Zach, which turns out to be fine, although Stanton had imagined the teenager was trying to distance himself from his father based on a couple of misinterpreted circumstances. Ironically, this causes the reader to wonder if Stanton's depiction of Kaline, presumably brooding nostalgically over times past when the right field pasture was his domain, is another miscalculation.

In any event, *The Final Season* preserves the beauty, the dignity, and the importance of what was the oldest major league ballpark at the time of its demise. Tiger Stadium lives on in its pages and in the memories of the fans lucky enough to have been there. It's appropriate that the author's final words, a description of a look backwards from the upper deck in Comerica Park, are joyful and celebratory:

> And on the horizon you can see the top of Tiger Stadium, its darkened light towers silhouetted by the setting sun. And if you listen beyond the silence, if you listen with your heart, you can hear all sorts of things. You can hear your childhood, you can hear your dad and your uncles, you can hear Kaline connecting, you can hear the muted cheers of distant, ghost crowds, and you can hear your grandpa calling out from the bleachers. It's a beautiful sound, and it echoes across the decades.

The Further Adventures of Slugger McBatt: Baseball Stories by W.P. Kinsella

◆

W.P. KINSELLA

◆

Boston: Houghton Mifflin, 1988. Cloth, 179 pages, ISBN: 0-395-47592-9. Other baseball books by the author: Shoeless Joe *(Houghton Mifflin, 1982),* The Thrill of the Grass *(Penguin, 1984),* The Iowa Baseball Confederacy *(Houghton Mifflin, 1986),* Box Socials *(Ballantine Books, 1991),* The Dixon Cornbelt League *(Harper Collins, 1993),* Butterfly Winter *(Enfield & Wizenty, 2011), and* Magic Time *(Voyager Press, 2001).*

Comment: The drawing of Slugger McBatt on the cover of the book was produced by famous cartoonist Arnold Roth.

In 1988, four years after the release of his highly acclaimed first baseball short story collection, *The Thrill of the Grass*, W.P. Kinsella published a worthy successor entitled *The Further Adventures of Slugger McBatt*; a volume of ten stories that solidified his status as a master of the genre. While the stories of *The Further Adventures* vary in theme, point of view, and setting, they all benefit from the trademarks of the author's craft: his fertile imagination and powerful narrative sense; his playful inventiveness and occasional use of fantasy; and, above all, his love of baseball and his confidence that the game can be used to plumb the depths of the human heart.

Kinsella's brand of fantasy, often referred to as "magic realism," is what most characterizes the two novels which brought him to the attention of literate baseball fans everywhere: *Shoeless Joe* and *The Iowa Baseball Confederacy*. As he said in *Baseball: the Writers' Game* (Diamond Communications, 1992), Kinsella believed he is so successful in getting the reader to "believe in the transition from realism to something outside of or on the edge of the realms of possibility" because "I do it in a straightforward manner. I don't beat around the bush with it at all." Readers enchanted by this approach will not be disappointed with *The Further Adventures* as two stories in the collection rely on it. *Reports Concerning the Death of the Seattle Albatross Are Somewhat Exaggerated* is a story about the mascot of the Seattle Mariners actually being an intelligent bird-like creature from a distant planet, sent to earth to collect information on human beings and our civilization. As the story opens, the alien (who adopted the name Mike Street) has been found out, involved in the accidental death of a woman who becomes infatuated with the person she assumes inhabits the Albatross costume, arrested, and interrogated and is being held in a cell, "somewhere inside Fort Lewis military base outside of Tacoma" ... although we only learn all this as the story unfolds. We are eight paragraphs into "Mike Street's" narrative before we realize that he is not a human being wearing a costume but an alien from outer space. "The first thing I have to admit," he says, "is that our people did not understand the civilization of Earth very well. I'm afraid the bureaucrats on our planet aren't very bright, which shouldn't come as any surprise, except that everyone here on Earth accepts the fact that other civilizations are far more intelligent. About the only advantage I have over people on Earth is a built-in ability to engage, with considerable help, in teleportative space travel. If our politicians and military bureaucrats had been smarter, they would have investigated conditions much more thoroughly before packing me off to Earth."

In addition to accomplishing the suspension of disbelief in the reader, this paragraph is the beginning of an inside joke by which Kinsella mocks the incompetence of our own "intelligence," law enforcement, and military bureaucrats; the punchline being the "unmasked" narrator imagining our incompetents investigating the mascots of every other sports team and consumer product (Mr. Peanut, e.g.) as potential aliens. On the one hand, the story can be seen as one long joke, the first laughs coming when the narrator, as an explanation of why his people thought the mission might succeed, shares the reaction of his prime minister to their intercepting television signals of the San Diego Chicken. "Look! Look!" he exclaims. "They have an integrated society. It appears that fifty thousand people on Earth are gathered together to worship one of our own." On the other hand, the tragedy of the story is oddly affective, and the loneliness of the alien which is its cause is all too relatable.

The second fantasy, *Frank Pierce, Iowa*, is a story about the disappearance, all at once, of an entire small town named after the 14th president of the United States. According to an unnamed narrator repeating a story he heard from Marylyle Baron, the unofficial historian of Johnson County, years ago Ezra, the village handyman charged with mowing the grass of the baseball diamond across the street from Saint Zacharias in time for a game to be played right after Sunday church services were over, sat in the grandstands refusing to budge because the night before a 10-year-old boy appearing to him in a dream said that the world would end at exactly twelve noon. And that is exactly what happened, at least for the town and its residents. At noon the boy from the dream emerged from the corn field edging the outfield (shades of *Shoeless Joe*!), the townspeople became weightless spirits flying around effortlessly, and they entered an ethereal dimension where people of the past exist happily and enjoy ghostly baseball games. Kinsella cushions this impossibility by having the narrator say, "Such events were accepted in the early days of Johnson County, a time when the presence of magic was taken for granted. Marylyle's favorite expression was, 'Things are out of kilter in Johnson County.' And indeed, up to and including the present day, they are."

This statement is as close to an explanation for the impossible as we ever get in Kinsella who is too clever by far to allow the demands of rationality to ruin a good story. In fact, this story employs another bit of legerdemain that Kinsella uses to bolster his fiction's believability: basing the story on an odd bit of actual history. Here, the narrator concludes by returning to the present to explain that the town got its name due to a train wreck near where the town was founded. Tragically, that wreck killed one person in a horrible accident: the 11-year-old son of Franklin Pierce. Naturally, the reader can only assume that the angelic boy of Ezra's dream was the son of the President. The narrator ends with another fact (or supposed fact) meant to lend credibility to the story: an entry about Abandoned Post Offices in the archives of the University of Iowa Library, stating that the town's post office opened in 1895 and closed in 1901. Reason: "Unknown." Iowa as the setting of the story is also very important. The earthy solidness and the palpable fecundity of the endless Iowan crop fields that always seem to stretch to the horizon provide a sense of reality that combined with the fantastic occurrences of Kinsella's fiction produce a world both comfortingly familiar and hauntingly strange.

Kinsella once said that he tried to avoid outfitting his stories with themes, yet love (mostly unrequited or dashed) and sex abound in these stories. *K Mart*, for example, is a tale of betrayal, in which the protagonist did not have the guts to declare his feelings for or to defend the honor of the love of his life, a young girl who loyally watched him and his buddies play sandlot ball for several summers. When he returns as an adult to the scene of his crimes of the heart, he and his buddies find that a huge variety store and its parking lot now cover the diamond of their youth. In a grand gesture of despair, the protagonist takes BP inside the store, trying, by bashing the pitches of one of his buddies, to assuage the guilt he feels over the suicide of his should-have-been lover. Death too, if not at the heart of every story, lurks around the corner. *Diehard*, as an obvious example, is the touching story of the widow of an ex-major league ball player and his best friend's attempts to find the perfect resting place for his ashes. The widow and friend dump the ashes into concrete being poured at the site of Minneapolis' new ballpark, symbolically giving the deceased a long-lasting front row seat. More subtle, but no less pertinent, is the symbolic death which takes place in the title story. Protagonist and narrator Artie is an unathletic boy who is befriended and protected by the bully Freddie MacLeish, who takes a liking to Artie's ability to draw cartoons. Artie flatters Freddie by making him the crime-fighting hero of a comic strip called "Slugger McBatt"; but when Freddie humiliates Artie by pulling Artie's pants down with Freddie's sister Marjorie nearby (for whom Artie secretly carries a torch), Artie violently kills Slugger McBatt in an act of vengeance that is also self-immolating. If death has any purpose in these stories, it is probably to remind us that life is precious because it is so fragile and so temporary.

As straightforward as Kinsella generally is, it is also necessary to read these stories carefully so as not to miss their meanings, not always so obvious. In *Punchlines* a talented Triple A player, "the team bad boy. A troublemaker," can't himself understand why he is such a pain in the ass, until at the end of the story his noticing a young man hanging around outside a gay bar forces him to confront his own repressed sexual urgings. And in *The Valley of the Schmoon* an aging coach for the Mariners named "Bookie" DeMarco, driving himself and the team's Rookie-of-the-Year prospect from training camp to Seattle for the start of the season, subjects the young man to a sad, sometimes tearful monologue of "woe-is-me" reminiscences, suggesting that he just might end it all by driving the car off an overpass and into the valley below. When the coach begins to pull over to ostensibly fix a problem with the car's steering, the rookie bails out of the car and stars running away even before it comes to a complete stop. At first, it seems as though the coach is puzzled by what seems to be the rookie's over-reaction, but then we remember his fond remembrances about the hazing of rookies in the good old days. Then looking back though the monologue we realize what an artful set-up the whole thing has been and how funny is his rhetorical question, "Geez, was it somethin' I said?"

Each story in this collection is deserving of a careful reading, and few short story collections about any subject are as entertaining and rewarding as *The Further Adventures of Slugger McBatt*.

Gil Hodges: The Brooklyn Bums, the Miracle Mets, and the Extraordinary Life of a Baseball Legend

◆

Tom Clavin *and* Danny Peary

◆

New York: New American Library, 2012. Cloth, 403 pages, ISBN: 978-0-451-23586-2. Prelude. Acknowledgments, Selected Bibliography, Index, 35 black & white photos between pages 216 and 217. Other baseball books by the authors: Roger Maris: Baseball's Reluctant Hero *(Touchstone, 2010).* We Played the Game: 65 Players Remember Baseball's Greatest Era *(Hyperion, 1994),* 1,001 Reasons to Love Baseball *(Harry N. Abrams, 2004),* Baseball Immortal Derek Jeter: A Career in Quotes *(Page Street, 2015), and* Jackie Robinson in Quotes: The Remarkable Life of Baseball's Most Significant Player *(Page Street, 2016) by Danny Peary.* The Perfect Season: Why 1998 Was Baseball's Greatest Year *(Villard, 1999) by Danny Peary and Tim McCarver.* We Played the Game: Memories of Baseball's Greatest Era *(Black Dog & Leventhal, 2002) by Danny Peary and Lawrence S. Ritter.* Baseball Forever: Reflections on 60 Years in the Game *(Triumph Books, 2004) by Ralph Kiner with Danny Peary.*

Sometimes the most important thing about a baseball biography is not the baseball ... the player's feats, achievements, and records ... but the character of the man whose story is being told. And such a book is *Gil Hodges: The Brooklyn Bums, the Miracle Mets, and the Extraordinary Life of a Baseball Legend* by Tom Clavin and Danny Peary. When the authors released their book in 2012, it was high time for a re-evaluation of Gil Hodges, as his failure to gain election to the National Baseball Hall of Fame had resulted in a sort of mass amnesia among the public, not only about his accomplishments but also about the extremely high regard in which he was held by everyone who knew him because of the way he played the game and lived his life. As few other books have been able to do, *Gil Hodges* brought about a total re-appreciation of its subject and proved that the great Brooklyn-L.A. Dodgers first baseman's case for being worthy of baseball's highest honor was not closed at all.

The first chapters of *Gil Hodges* are unusually significant in that they do much more than merely chronicle the youth of the subject in a perfunctory manner. What these chapters do is demonstrate that the facets of Hodges' admirable character were established early in his life, and as the book unfolds the reader perceives Hodges never deviating from the principles he adopted from the beginning. In short, by growing up in Princeton and Petersburg, Indiana, Gil Hodges experienced a small-town, Midwestern, blue-collar, Catholic upbringing that instilled in him a strong, unbending sense of morality and personal responsibility that formed the core of his being. The authors interviewed numerous family members, neighbors, and classmates of Hodges who knew him well in his formative years (and referred to him as "Bud"), and they all remember him as a laconic, confident, humble, and unselfish person who could always be counted on to do the right thing. Extremely strong and gifted with huge hands, Hodges was also an exceptional athlete. He and his brother, Bob, one year older and a talented pitcher himself, were inseparable as youngsters and remained close all their lives.

Ironically, basketball was Hodges' favorite sport by far, and he played it on scholarship with Bob for St. Joseph's College in Rensselaer for two years (and later for Oakland City College after he'd become a major leaguer) before fate and the times intervened. In the late summer of 1943, Brooklyn scout Stan Feezle watched Hodges play for an industrial team and, dazzled by the young Hossier's explosive swing which sent baseballs soaring into the distance (as well as his powerful arm at shortstop), he talked him into attending a three-day tryout in Olean, New York ... at the Dodgers' expense. Although raw, Hodges was so impressive that veteran coach Jake Pitler told farm director Branch Rickey, Jr., "He's one in a million, that big kid. Don't let him get away." Junior sent Hodges to New York, where Rickey Sr., taking no chances, signed him to a major league contract and decided that he would become a catcher. Hodges spent the last month of the season in the Dodgers' bullpen being tutored by Mickey Owen, but World War II put his baseball career on hold just as it was getting started. A couple of weeks after the end of the season, he reported to San Diego for duty with the Marine Corps.

Hodges spent more than two years in the Corps and saw action in Okinawa, the final big battle in the Pacific in which one in five Marines was either killed or wounded. Afterwards, Hodges refused to talk about the war, but the authors make it clear that the war affected him deeply: "For years, family and friends sensed that something was troubling him, whether it be the deaths of friends, his own actions during combat, or guilt that he'd survived while so many died around him." Hodges' reticence about the war, while common among veterans, was characteristic of him, and the authors go on to portray him as a stoic figure constantly burying within himself his worries, disappointments, and frustrations as a player and manager in order to spare others.

After the war, Hodges spent one year in the minors, the next season on the Dodgers' bench, and the year after that playing semi-regularly before becoming the team's regular first baseman in 1949. For the next decade the Dodgers were the National League's dominant team, and the authors carefully chronicle Hodges' contributions to their success. Typically a slow starter and prone to slumps, Hodges invariably recovered to lead (or come close to leading) the team in homers and runs batted in. He hit 20 or more home runs eleven years in a row (with highs of 40 and 42) and drove in 100 or more runs seven consecutive seasons. Hodges' 370 career homers may not impress today's statistics-obsessed cognoscenti, but at the time of his retirement Gil was the National League's all-time righthanded leader in homers. Furthermore, with his soft hands and matchless footwork, he was the League's best fielding first sacker and won the League's first three Gold Glove Awards for first basemen ... at the end of his career! Hodges was such an agile fielder that Dodgers shortstop Pee Wee Reese said with two weeks practice Gil could take any player's job away, including his own.

As necessary as it was for the authors to chronicle Hodges' play, their focus on the other dimensions of his story are much more interesting and important. First, Hodges was perhaps the most popular player on a team packed with stars, each possessing unique talents and appealing attributes. Marrying a local Catholic girl (Joan Lombardi) and making Brooklyn his home endeared him to the Bums' diehards, and their love for him never wavered throughout his dismal 0–26 performance in the 1952 World Series. No Dodger interacted more with the fans than Hodges, and his greatest satisfaction in helping the Dodgers finally beat the Yankees in 1955 to cop Brooklyn's first (and only) World Championship was the knowledge of how happy it made the entire borough. Second, despite his taciturn nature, Hodges was the unacknowledged leader of the team. As emotionally steady as they come, he never alibied, sulked, complained about the umpiring, or gave any indication that he was worried or felt the pressure. He broke up numerous fights, sometimes with nothing more than the sound of his voice, and had no trouble restraining the toughest guys in the league. Most significant of all, the authors contend that Hodges helped Jackie Robinson survive his famous ordeal as much as the player who usually gets the credit, Pee Wee Reese. Certainly, Hodges was loved by Robinson, who said about Hodges' premature death in 1972 at the age of 47 that "Next to my son's death, this is the worst day of my life."

Hodges was a loving husband and father but also an "old school" disciplinarian who believed in order and obedience to legitimate authority, beliefs which prompted him to unquestionably accept the Dodgers' move to Los Angeles after the 1957 season and which later characterized his managerial career, first with the Washington Senators (1963–67) and then with the New York Mets (1968–71). While some of his players in Washington disliked his refusal to explain his moves and decisions, he was universally respected, and by all accounts he got as much out of sub-par rosters as could have been expected. Mets players loved him and gave him the lion's share of the credit for the team's miraculous ascent from ninth place in 1968 to the World Championship the following year. It has been assumed that Hodges' death in the spring of 1972 was caused by his second heart attack, but Clavin and Peary suggest that he may have suffered a stroke, brought on by the years of excessive smoking and his habit of keeping all the negative stuff of life bottled up inside him. In any event, his death devastated and saddened everyone who knew him, inside the game and out. In the last chapter, the authors address what Hodges' many fans considered to be baseball's unjustified lack of appreciation for his contributions to the game, offering several plausible if not fair explanations for it. It took another ten years, but a Veteran's Committee finally agreed with them and made Hodges a member of Cooperstown's Class of 2022, a recognition completely in line with the fact that Rule 4 on the Hall of Fame ballots states: "Candidates shall be chosen on the basis of playing ability, integrity, sportsmanship, character, their contributions to the team on which they played and to baseball in general." Even acerbic sportswriter Dick Young admired Hodges and campaigned on his behalf. As he said in the *Daily News* back in 1980 in reference to Rule 4, "No man more qualifies on all counts than Gil Hodges."

Gods of Wood and Stone

Mark Di Ionna

New York: Touchstone, 2018. Cloth, 388 pages, ISBN: 978-1-5011-7890-0. Acknowledgments, About the Author.

    Comments: Di Ionna worked on this novel for fourteen years. The novel's very unusual, unlikely title, especially for a baseball book, was suggested by the book's editor, David Falk, and recognized as perfect by the author.

    A common left-handed compliment made by critics of baseball novels is that the book in question is not really about baseball; rather, it is about something more important, some controversial subject or popular cultural meme such as … well, pick a topic. The suggestion behind this comment, of course, is that baseball is *not* important; at least not important enough to deserve the attention of any serious writer. It's a silly contention, given the lie by many outstanding baseball novels, and none more emphatically than the stunning *Gods of Wood and Stone* by Mark Di Ionna. *Gods* does examine some of the type of big ideas the critics insist on emphasizing, but the book is also indisputably about baseball and the iron grip it holds on its fans, despite there being not a single inning of a game played in the course of the narrative. Stunningly inventive yet extremely close to reality, *Gods* is that rare fiction which reflects the world and at the same time forces the reader to question many of his most treasured assumptions about it.

    The book opens with the most explosive scene in all of baseball fiction. Former Boston Red Sox catcher Joe Grudeck, being inducted into the National Baseball Hall of Fame, is standing at the podium about to address the crowd, when a huge and powerful madman appears out of nowhere to clamber onto the stage and destroy Grudeck's bronze plaque with two devastating sledgehammer blows. Instinctively, Grudeck attempts to tackle the assailant but slips and is beaten nearly unconscious by him. Police subdue the madman and lead him off to jail through a gauntlet of outraged fans while the barely conscious Grudeck is rushed to the hospital. With no explanation for what has happened, the reader is hooked so immediately and securely that it is impossible for him not to finish the rest of the book: a months-long flashback through three seasons (Winter, Spring, and Summer) and a final fateful seven days (Induction Week) which enables him to understand how the lives of these two protagonists inevitably sped headlong towards such a catastrophic confrontation.

In somewhat alternating chapters, the narration follows the lives of Grudeck and the spoiler of his party, a man named Horace Mueller, whom we learn works at another Cooperstown, New York, museum, the far less renowned, less popular, and underfunded Farmers Museum. Technically, Horace works as an historical re-enactor, yet he takes his role as a village blacksmith seriously, and his punishing labors have turned him into a muscular mountain of a man while simultaneously wearing out parts of his body simultaneously, especially his over-worked hands.

At first glance, the two men seem to be polar opposites, but as the story unfolds we grasp their surface differences are far out-weighed by the thing they have in common: their unhappiness. Financially secure, famous, and fawned over by a legion of fans, Grudeck has never married and has no family other than an elderly mother whom he loves but is not particularly close to. His numerous sexual encounters with prostitutes and baseball Annies leave him emotionally unfulfilled, and he is haunted by memories of having sexually abused a pair of star-struck teen-aged girls when he was an up-and-coming prospect in the Red Sox minor league system (He is also terrified that the horrific episode might somehow become public knowledge). It all adds up to an emptiness at the core of his being and the unshakeable feeling that his celebrity is a sham.

Horace, on the other hand, is not disturbed by self-doubts. A graduate of Cornell's Agricultural College, he envisions himself as an heroic preservationist of a rural agricultural way of life superior to the hollow pursuit of money and ease which he believes dominates present-day America. His talks at the Farmers' Museum "were a continuous update on the loss of small-town country life and character." Horace's problem is that his dedication and Herculean efforts are unrecognized which makes him feel unappreciated ... by his corporate-centric boss, the public, and, most hurtfully, by his wife and son, Michael: a talented baseball player himself who loves and respects his father but who is also more interested in the diversions of the typical 14-year-old (playing video games, watching ESPN) than engaging in manual labor, especially if the point is to illustrate something about ancient history or to prove one's toughness.

Developing events raise the anxiety levels of both men. Grudeck agonizes over his upcoming Induction Day acceptance speech and seems determined, against the advice of his agent and confidant, to use it as an opportunity to unburden himself by telling the truth, for once, that he is unworthy of the fans' "worship." Joe turns to the still beautiful Stacey, a divorcee from his high school days, for help with his speech; and as their relationship slowly deepens, it becomes less about the speech and more about helping the desperate ex-ballplayer discover exactly who superstar Joe Grudeck really is.

Horace's anger and dissatisfaction with the world and his inability to change it finally becomes too much for Sally. She tires of walking on egg shells in their mortgaged-to-the-hilt, ramshackle New York farm house and hiding from Horace a stack of unpaid bills. She plots an escape from Horace's stifling obsessions by using a baseball scholarship offer for Michael to attend a prestigious high school in Cincinnati as her ticket out. Realizing that he no longer loves Sally and having discovered the true, hopeless family financial situation, Horace allows himself to fantasize about an attractive young co-worker, Natalia, even as he sets into motion his own, scorched-earth retreat from Cooperstown and the land of his ancestors. Despite his disdain for all the fuss being made over Grudeck, Horace can hardly escape notice of it, and his attack on the catcher's Hall of Fame plaque is his parting and ultimate protest against everything it represents and which he detests.

The contrasting yet parallel lives of Joe and Horace introduce important themes, such as the shallowness of celebrity culture, the inadequacy of anchoring one's identity in one's occupation, and the essence of manhood. Referencing the art of Fritz Vogt and Thomas Cole and the novels of James Fenimore Cooper, Horace tells Michael, "Cooperstown may not be the birthplace of baseball, but it is the birthplace of something bigger. It is the birthplace of American manhood." Thus, Cooperstown is absolutely critical for the book's setting, as its fraudulence mirrors the concerns disturbing the protagonists. In addition, few books articulate as poignantly as *Gods* the doomed yearnings of the male heart. When Michael's infatuation with June, the young woman who has been his summer boss at the Cooperstown souvenir shop called "Gone Batty," is crushed by his accidentally seeing her practically force herself on Joe Grudeck (of all people), Horace wants to tell his son:

> …that all those adolescent emotions, that optimistic, romantic tachycardia Michael was now experiencing, were something to cherish and enjoy, but to never, ever hold on to as real expectations. Even strong men, like Horace, were weakened by those fantasies. He wanted to warn Michael that June, the Gone Batty girl, like life itself would show him unintended but nonetheless painful cruelty. Because June, Sally, Natalia, no woman from Ann to Zoe, ever cured the inherent ache of a man's loneliness. They soothed it for a while, but in the end made you realize you were never too far from being alone.

Yet, the genius of *Gods* cannot be appreciated without recognizing the symbolic importance of the Cardiff Giant, an actual nineteenth-century hoax and national sensation which the author uses for his thematic purposes. The historical truth is that an atheist from Binghamton, New York, named George Hull had a crude statue carved out of gypsum to resemble a "fossilized biblical goliath"; had it buried on a farm in Cardiff, New York; and a year later had it "accidentally" discovered. All this to prove the gullibility of those who accept everything in the Bible literally. The Giant excited heated debate, drew streams of the curious who paid to behold it, and inspired P.T. Barnum to attempt to purchase it, even after it was discredited; and, when rebuffed, to shamelessly make his own freak show giant. Eventually, the Cardiff Giant found a home in Cooperstown at the Farmers' Museum, where it was displayed respectfully as a historical curiosity. In the novel, Horace is asked to take over the task of talking to tourist groups about the Giant. It is a terrible idea, given his state of mind. As Horace's personal world falls apart, the lack of respect shown towards the Giant, especially in a tense scene involving unruly Little Leaguers and their indulgent fathers, increases his bitterness and exemplifies for him the spiritual poverty of a society which makes gods of men merely because they are adroit at playing a game.

The title of the book comes from a manuscript which the author imagines George Hull to have written. It is owned by the Museum and Horace re-reads it upon getting his new assignment. In a key passage of the manuscript, Hull randomly opens a Bible to the Book of Deuteronomy and reads, "And the LORD shall scatter thee among all people from the one end of the earth even to the other; and there thou shalt serve other gods, which neither thou nor thy fathers have known, even wood and stone." This warning to unbelievers not only supposedly supplied Hull with the idea of making his Cardiff Giant, a god of stone; but it also gives the reader insight into what lies at the heart of the unhappiness of both Joe Grudeck and Horace Mueller: the tendency of men to make false gods of many things, such as strength, sexual prowess, wealth, fame, power, pride, etc. The Cardiff Giant also figures in the book's dramatic denouement, but I leave that and the revelations about the post-confrontation lives of the protagonists for you to discover for yourself. Surely, enough has been said to convince you of the need to read for yourself this masterpiece of fiction: a brilliant novel of consummate artistry about baseball and so much more.

Heart of a Tiger: Growing Up with My Grandfather, Ty Cobb

Herschel Cobb

Toronto: ECW Press, 2012. Cloth, 279 pages, ISBN: 978-1-77041-130-2. Preface. No index.

Comments: *Heart of a Tiger* won the 2012 CASEY Award, finishing ahead of runner-up *Mr. Wrigley's Ball Club: Chicago and the Cubs during the Jazz Age* by Roberts Ehrgott and *Color Blind: The Forgotten Team that Broke Baseball's Color Line* by Tom Dunkel, which placed third.

When Herschel Cobb signed copies of his book at the CASEY Awards in Cincinnati, Ohio, on March 9, 2014, he used a fountain pen with green ink … carrying on the practice his grandfather had made famous.

No player in major league baseball history has been misrepresented as badly as Ty Cobb, the twelve-time American League batting champion and the holder of the highest lifetime major league batting average. No one has ever disputed his unique greatness as a batsman and base runner, but for decades after his retirement Cobb was maligned as a person: depicted as a dirty player who intentionally injured opponents, as a vicious racist and murderer, and as a generally despicable human being, guilty of cruelty even towards his wife and children. In recent years a correction of this flawed and unfair portrayal has taken place and been greatly aided by the astonishing memoir *Heart of a Tiger*, authored by a person eminently qualified to share with the world a previously unknown side of the subject: grandson Herschel Roswell Cobb, Jr.

For a long time the author never had any intention of writing a book about his famous grandfather. In fact, he guarded his memories of the man he knew and loved as treasures that might be spoiled if openly shared with others. An innocent moment with his daughter Madelyn changed that. When the curious young girl asked her father to tell her a story about his own childhood, the shaken Cobb realized that "I could not think of one single time with my father that was not filled with dread and terror." Cobb quickly recovered and related an amusing story about donning a bear skin rug (with bear head attached) and scaring his older sister Susan at the Lake Tahoe cabin owned by their grandfather, Ty Cobb. Madelyn and Cobb's son, also

HERSCHEL COBB

HEART of a TIGER

GROWING UP WITH MY GRANDFATHER, TY COBB

named Ty, wanted more such stories, and so Herschel began, with his wife's encouragement, to write them down before they were forgotten. It wasn't long before the exercise became a cathartic experience that would turn into the riveting true tale of an abusive childhood, salvaged only by the love and concern of a man believed to be incapable of such kindness.

Herschel Cobb begins this story of his childhood with an account of a pre-dawn duck hunting trip on the Snake River (Idaho) when he was six years old. It was the first time he had spent any appreciable time with his grandfather, and it is our first glimpse of the elderly Ty Cobb and the author's father, who is immediately depicted as an irritable, violent bully. The scene reaches its climax when Herschel Sr. forces his son to shoot a shotgun he has no ability to control. The knocked-down, blubbering Herschel is dazed, bruised, and bleeding from a cut on his finger, yet his father insists that he shoot the gun again, as an exercise in growing up, in "becoming a man." This is when Herschel's grandfather, still a strong man, steps in, physically restrains his son, and forces an end to the ridiculous training session. The next day when Herschel awakens in his bedroom at home, his grandfather is gone but a note (written in Cobb's trademark green ink) from him remains. It says, "Hersch, Remember I love you, Your Grandfather."

As disturbing as this scene is, it is only a prelude to the horrifying abuse which the author chronicles in the following chapter. Here we witness Herschel Sr. subjecting the author and his sister during bath time to whippings with a twisted wet towel, a "game" the father calls "Rat Tail" which nevertheless leaves painful welts on the frightened children. We see the father, a huge man, while wrestling with his son practically squeeze the life out of him with leg scissors and snap a bullwhip at him as the son is forced to jump back and forth over a sidewalk. The sadistic father terrifies his son with gruesome stories about the "bogeyman" and takes him on a harrowing upside-down ride in his prop airplane. All of these tortures are perpetrated in the name of fun or supposedly to help toughen up young Herschel. Perhaps the most sickening incident the author shares is the account of his father making him dance by shooting him in the legs with a new bb pistol. Herschel's mother comes out of the house, but instead of stopping the abuse as Herschel silently hopes she will, she puts her arm around her husband and merely watches the show. When the father stops to re-load the pistol Herschel finally runs away to temporary safety. Devastated not only by his father's attack but by his mother's insouciance, Herschel recalls that "I was stunned. Only my heart screamed, not in words but in feeling, screamed so loudly that it felt like a white lightning bolt piercing my bones, my muscles, my veins, every bit of my being: *I will never, ever need or trust anybody ever, ever again!*"

The author attributes his father's behavior mainly to his unhappiness with his marriage, caused mainly by the infidelity of Herschel's mother, her dissatisfaction with Herschel Sr.'s inability to provide the big city social life she desires, and her generally sour outlook on life. According to the author the two parents warred continually, and the father all too often took out his anger on his children. The emotional abuse that the mother heaped on the author and his siblings may have been worse than the father's physical abuse, and it culminated when Herschel overheard his mother tell a friend that she never wanted her children in the first place. After Herschel Sr. dies from a heart attack at 33, his wife moves the family to Santa Monica where she lives a life of drunken and promiscuous dissipation. One night she abandons Herschel in a bar to go party elsewhere, leaving car fare and a home address with the bartender. As Herschel rides home he realizes "how expendable I was."

Against this terrible backdrop, the second half of the story begins to unfold: Ty Cobb's crucial role in the lives of his grandchildren. As their mother moves the family around, every summer Herschel and his siblings visit Palo Alto, California, to stay with their grandmother, estranged from her famous husband, who gives them unconditional love. They also begin to spend afternoons with their grandfather at his regal home in nearby Atherton and weeks at a time at his cabin on Lake Tahoe. Slowly, the three grandchildren get close to their grandfather, while Herschel and Susan begin to piece together much of the Cobb family history, especially with information they gleam from the conversations of Cobb's oldest daughter, their Aunt Beverly.

Cobb dotes on Susan but loves all three of his grandkids. He takes a sincere interest in their lives, tries to give them the sense of safety and security he knows they've previously been denied, and spoils them with ice cream orgies. Herschel and his siblings reciprocate the love of their grandfather and, ironically, even try to comfort him at times. Shortly after Herschel Sr. died, Cobb's eldest son, Ty, passed away from brain cancer, and Cobb grieved terribly over the loss of his boys, with whom he was never able to reconcile. The author views his grandfather with compassion rather than criticism, writing, "He was emotionally devastated, isolated from his family, alone, and unable to right what had gone so tragically wrong."

As Herschel moves into adolescence, he witnesses his grandfather trying to make amends, trying do a better job with him and his siblings than he did with his children. For instance, Herschel witnesses Cobb keeping his identity a secret from those who don't recognize him in an effort to protect his grandchildren from the burden of heightened expectations, and he recounts numerous episodes of Cobb patiently trying to teach his grandchildren life lessons he had learned the hard way. As part of his effort to protect his grandchildren, Cobb never even tells them about his baseball career until he is forced to. After Herschel asks him to explain why everybody expects him to perform like a superstar during his Middle League baseball games, Cobb takes Herschel for the first time into his baseball "man cave" where the boy is astounded by the trappings of his grandfather's fame and greatness. The only humor in the book comes from Herschel's reaction to this bombshell ("Now, what was I supposed to do?") and his still-incomplete understanding of what his grandfather had accomplished ("Could an old guy really do that?"). Herschel gets a further education about his grandfather's storied past when he passes Cobb in the hallway on the way to the bathroom. Cobb's partially-opened bathrobe reveals horribly disfigured legs, which Herschel learns are the result of the abuse that Cobb endured as a player, as well as the price he paid to be the best in the game.

The most touching moment in the book comes when a remorseful Cobb tries to take the blame for Herschel Sr.'s failures as a parent. Herschel Jr. says he wouldn't hear of it, writing, "I'd lost my father. I was not going to lose my grandfather." In a very real sense, the author and his brother Kit took the place of Ty and Herschel Sr., and there is no doubt that the love of Cobb's grandsons and his granddaughter for him were an inestimable comfort to him as he navigated the final years of his life. Herschel became rightly proud of his heritage and, even before he became an adult, sought to protect his grandfather; as he did when he foiled the machinations of ghost writer Al Stump who tried to pump him for dirt he could insert into the autobiography Cobb came to regret he agreed to let Stump write.

Cobb, who died a wealthy man, remembered his beloved grandchildren in his will. Using the money set aside by his grandfather, Herschel got a first-class education, became a successful businessman, married happily, and fathered two wonderful well-adjusted children. In other words, he overcame one of the worst beginnings one can imagine. He found a way to heal all the undeserved hurts he experienced and even became capable of heroic forgiveness. All credit is due him, but this beautiful transformation would not have been possible without the love of Ty Cobb, his grandfather. This inspirational account is also the story of the transformation of Ty Cobb, and it shows that people can and do change for the better. The title encapsulates this idea, as there clearly was room for both ferocity and love in the heart of Cobb.

How Baseball Happened: Outrageous Lies Exposed! The True Story Revealed

◆

THOMAS W. GILBERT

◆

Boston: David R. Godine, Publisher, 2020. Cloth, 381 pages, ISBN: 9781567926774. Introduction by John Thorn, Early Baseball Timeline. Afterword, Acknowledgments, Bibliography, Index, bottom-of-the-page citations throughout the book, 29 black & white photos scattered throughout the book. Other baseball books by the author: Roberto Clemente *(Chelsea House, 1989),* Pete Rose *(Chelsea House, 1994),* Baseball and the Color Line *(Franklin Watts, 1995),* Elysian Fields: The Birth of Baseball *(Franklin Watts, 1995),* Superstars and Monopoly Wars: Nineteenth-Century Major League Baseball *(Franklin Watts, 1995),* Dead Ball: Major League Baseball Before Babe Ruth *(Franklin Watts, 1996),* The Good Old Days: Baseball in the 1930s *(Franklin Watts, 1996),* The Soaring Twenties: Babe Ruth and the Home-Run Decade *(Franklin Watts, 1996),* Baseball at War: World War II and the Fall of the Color Line *(Franklin Watts, 1997), and* Playing First: Early Baseball Lives at Brooklyn's Green-Wood Cemetery *(Green-Wood Cemetery, 2015).*

Comments: *How Baseball Happened* won the 2020 CASEY Award, beating out second-place *Bouton: The Life of a Baseball Original* by Mitchell Nathanson and *The Wax Pack: On the Open Road in Search of Baseball's Afterlife* by Brad Balukjian (third). CASEY Award Judge Lorine Parks wrote: "*How Baseball Happened* does for baseball what David McCullough did for U.S. history: places baseball firmly in the mainstream of American culture. Great gift for anyone who loves Americana. By far the best—brilliant, stimulating, funny. Made me start taking notes to look up. 'Debunking the myths' is just a ploy to tell the story."

Of all the books examined in this sequel, the most iconoclastic, most fearlessly myth-battering work is *How Baseball Happened: Outrageous Lies Exposed! The True Story Revealed* by Tom Gilbert. Like the bulldozers that mowed down the shacks of Chavez Ravine for the Los Angeles Dodgers, Gilbert razes and buries all the fables and canards of baseball's early years, especially those put forward as the game's origin story. More than a demolition expert though, Gilbert proceeds like a skilled Egyptologist. After clearing away the rubble, he unearths the facts which constitute actual evidence and then erects out of that information a detailed and sensible edifice representing early baseball history that should, like the pyramids, stand

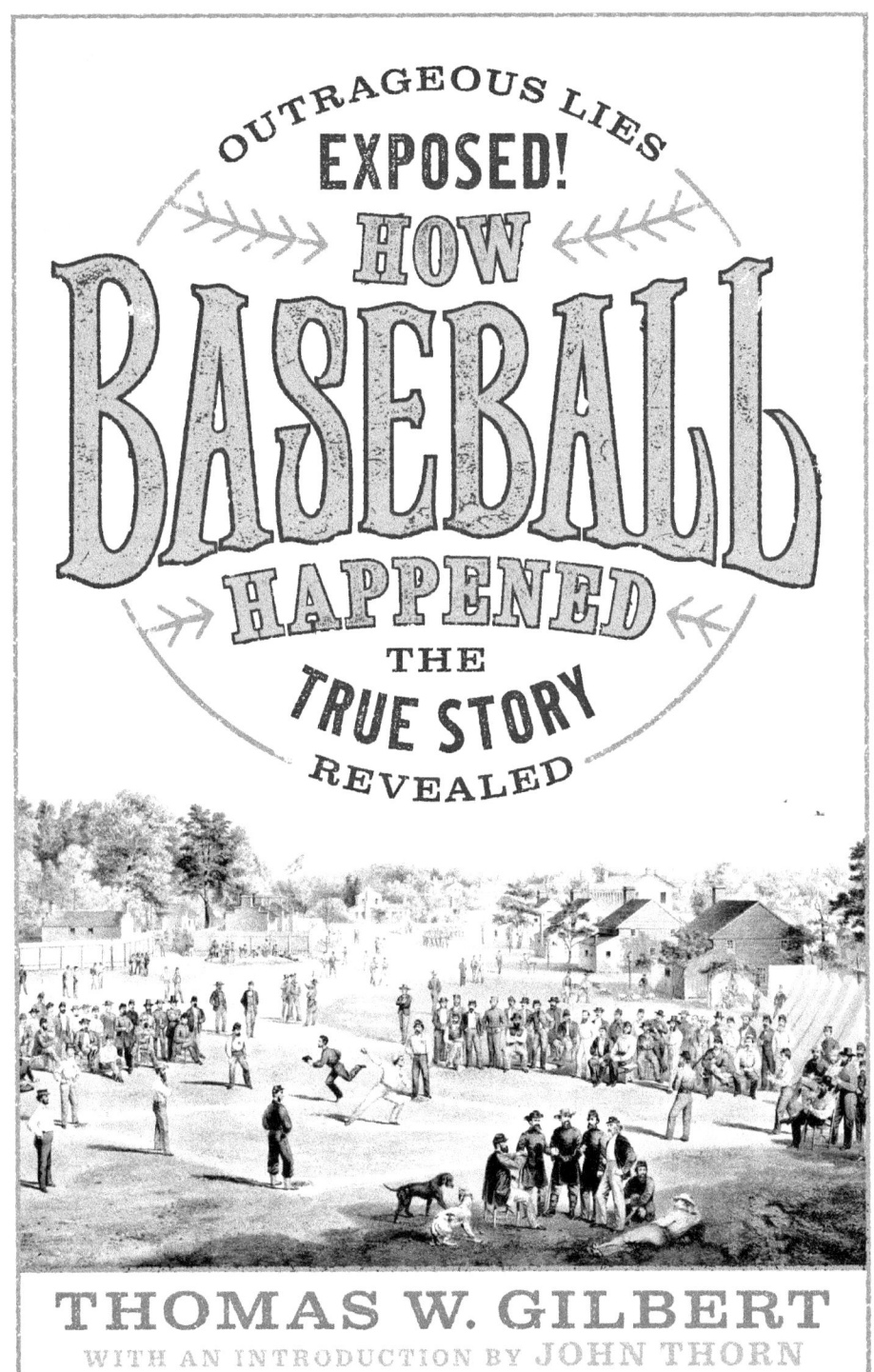

the test of time. Along with other corrective works on the subject, such as David Block's *Baseball before We Knew It: A Search for the Roots of the Game* (Nebraska, 2005), William J. Ryczek's *Baseball's First Inning: A History of the National Pastime Through the Civil War* (McFarland, 2009), and John Thorn's *Baseball in the Garden of Eden: The Secret History of the Early Game* (Simon & Schuster, 2011), *How Baseball Happened* has radically changed our views of the seminal period that converted America into a country in love with baseball, as a sport and not just a mere game.

Gilbert begins the book by not only dismantling the two most common baseball origin stories, those crediting Abner Doubleday and Alexander Cartwright as founding fathers, but also the very idea that baseball was invented at all. Displaying the playful wit he employs throughout the book, he states that "...no one invented baseball, just as no one invented other cultural phenomena like rock and roll, bachelor parties, or brunch." He points out that there is a long list of supposed founding fathers and says of the founding-father idea, "It is a historiographical zombie, beaten and bloodied but impossible to kill." (Later, in Chapter Seven, he includes the list of 13 "Dads" to whom the invention of baseball has been attributed in print: Robert Ferguson, John Joyce, Abner Doubleday, Doc Adams, Harry Wright, William Wheaton, Billy McMahon, Henry Chadwick, Alexander Cartwright, Duncan Curry, T G Van Cott, Albert Spalding, and Louis Wadsworth.) The myth that Civil War general Abner Doubleday invented baseball in Cooperstown, New York, had already been definitively discredited, but Gilbert has fun tamping down its grave even further, explaining that Albert Spalding at least had two understandable reasons for establishing the Mills Commission which invented the Doubleday myth: Spalding's nativist proclivities that caused him, like many Americans at the time, to eschew any British influence (in this case, the idea that baseball descended from rounders) and his desire to increase his sporting goods company's sales of baseball equipment.

The rejection of Alexander Cartwright as the inventor of baseball takes more effort (a good part of Chapter Two), as he became through the efforts of his ancestors the face of the famous New York Knickerbocker club; which has been given credit, erroneously, for establishing many basic elements of the game as we know it today. According to Gilbert, the 1845 Knickerbockers were *not* the first organized baseball club; the match they played against a team called the New York Nine on June 19, 1946, in Hoboken, New Jersey, was *not* the first game; they did *not* draw up the first set of rules; they did *not* spin off numerous other clubs; and they did *not* organize the first convention of baseball clubs. Although they were picky, even "exclusionary," about membership, the Knickerbockers were also *not* gentlemen of inherited wealth in the English sense, but simply professional men who liked belonging to a club and playing ball. The Knickerbockers not only had no interest in ever paying players, they were also an intramural club which rarely played other clubs. Their main contribution turned out to be their marketing value; they were a good story used to sell the game to the rest of the country.

So how *did* baseball happen? According to Mr. Gilbert, it came about through the efforts of the "emerging urban bourgeoisie (EUB)": professionals, entrepreneurs, and businessmen involved in the 1840s and 1850s in all sorts of new industries. Out of necessity, huge numbers of these men, many of whom eventually fought in the

Civil War, joined local militias (or "target companies") and volunteer fire companies. As baseball began to be viewed as a popular form of exercise and a means of enjoying fresh air, the EUB also formed amateur baseball clubs as offshoots of the other two types of clubs. Many of these amateur baseball clubs were formed by members of the same profession (such as men in the printing business), and much fraternal drinking and eating took place after the matches. As the author points out, it was not uncommon for a man to belong to all three types of clubs. This is the gist of the book, along with the key point that ground zero for the establishment of the early amateur baseball clubs was New York City and Brooklyn.

In fact, the latter idea is probably more important than the former; it is certainly emphasized as such by the author who points out over and over that when the first baseball clubs were formed in cities around the country, these founding fathers were almost without exception visiting or transplanted New Yorkers. In addition, a number of first clubs around the country "grew out of" New York or Brooklyn clubs as "satellite" clubs; while others, such as the famous 1869–70 Cincinnati Red Stockings who may not have been founded by New Yorkers, stocked their initial rosters with players with New York pedigrees. A two-page map in Chapter Seven illustrating this phenomenon shows arrows emanating from New York stretching towards far flung cities where clubs were formed during the early amateur era (including Hamilton, Ontario, in 1854).

Gilbert takes this idea even further by positing that Brooklyn eventually became even more important to the adoption, growth, and spread of what was called the New York Game than New York itself. By 1858, Brooklyn's top four clubs (the Excelsiors, Atlantics, Eckfords, and Putnams) achieved parity with New York's big four (the Knickerbockers, Gothams, Eagles, and Empires). That year Brooklyn politicians challenged their New York counterparts to a best-of-three series contested by all-star teams from the two cities. Although the New Yorkers won the series, Brooklyn teams dominated play the next two years, with the Excelsiors becoming recognized as the best team in the country. More important historically, the games were played for the first time in an enclosed venue, the Fashion Race Course in Queens, and fans were charged an admission fee to attend, also for the first time. Gilbert calls the rivalry between New York and Brooklyn clubs as represented by the Fashion Course series "the oldest, longest, and most important of any sports rivalry in American history" … "the watershed event to which we can trace the triumph of the American sports movement and baseball's arrival as a national sport."

Gilbert hails the little-known Dr. Joseph B. Jones of Brooklyn as a most important figure of these years (make it 14 baseball "Dads"). It was he who assembled the great Excelsiors teams, with the explicit goal of playing winning baseball. Jones' Excelsiors were the first to go on the road in an effort to popularize the game outside of New York and Brooklyn; they started junior teams which functioned as farm clubs to supply the main club with young talent; and they employed the game's first national superstar, James Creighton, who revolutionized pitching. It is these credentials, along with Brooklyn's producing the game's most important early writer, Henry Chadwick, as well as the first enclosed baseball park, Union Grounds, that gives Gilbert the confidence to declare Brooklyn as "the real birthplace of baseball."

As startling and as important as these big ideas are, they are paralleled and supported by a mound of other minor ones ... "the hundred stories [of the author] you haven't heard before" that John Thorn alludes to on the back of the book's dust jacket: stories such as the irresistible attraction of the Elysian Fields and other "pleasure grounds" as an escape from the unpleasant conditions of the city; the importance of canals and railroads to the spread of baseball; the inevitable abandonment of Philadelphia's "town ball" and Boston's "Massachusetts game" in favor of the New York Game; the rise and sad demise of the 21-year-old Creighton who died of an undiagnosed strangulated intestine; the role of the Knickerbockers' James Whyte Davis in erecting the color barrier; the fascinating origins of the names of the baseball clubs of the early amateur era (at least 28 clubs had literary names! ... including Waverly, Irving, and Hiawatha); and the wholesale involvement of amateur baseball players in the Civil War (the chapter devoted to baseball in the Civil War, Chapter 8, may be the best summary of the subject in the literature). It's a dazzling array of untold tales by a master raconteur who clearly delights in telling us what we didn't know before.

This lively, crucial amateur era was succeeded, of course, by the rise of the professional game; a phenomenon which calls to mind the famous Cincinnati Red Stockings team of 1869. Gilbert takes up the topic in the final chapter and begins, as far as proud Cincinnatians are concerned, by throwing down the gauntlet: "This book ends the way it begins, with a bogus origin story." Gilbert challenges many aspects of the Red Stockings' claim to fame as the first openly professional baseball team; noting, first of all, that five other teams (the New York Mutuals, Brooklyn Atlantics, Philadelphia Athletics, Washington Nationals, and Troy Haymakers) went pro at the same time as the Red Stockings; and secondly, that these five teams "have a closer connection to professional baseball" because they all went on to play in the National Association, the first professional league (founded in 1871), while the Reds, who disbanded after the 1870 season, did not. Agree or disagree with Gilbert's contrary views on the "firsts" traditionally attributed to the Red Stockings, they make for fascinating reading that simply cannot be ignored. The same is true for every page of this irreverent, original work, a gold mine of a baseball history.

Jackie Robinson: A Biography

◆

Arnold Rampersad

◆

New York: Alfred A. Knopf, 1997. Cloth, 512 pages, ISBN: 0-679-44495-5. Prologue (1962). Epilogue (1997), Notes, Acknowledgments, Index, Photographic Credits, A Note About the Author, 40 black & white photos between pages 180 and 181.

   Comments: The author dedicated the book to Luke Rampersad, for the best of reasons, for his being a person "who loves baseball—and books."

As befitting his status as one of baseball's most iconic, important figures, Jackie Robinson has been one of baseball literature's most popular subjects. Indeed, the number of words written about him rivals that devoted to other cynosures, such as Babe Ruth, Ted Williams, and Mickey Mantle. Still, it was not until 1997 with the publication of Arnold Rampersad's *Jackie Robinson: A Biography* that the man's life finally received the comprehensive, empathetic treatment it long deserved. Robinson remains such an attractive personage that writers have continued to examine and re-examine various aspects of his story; Michael Lee Lanning's *The Court-Martial of Jackie Robinson* (Stackpole Books, 2020) is an excellent example of a book devoted to one small but important part of the life. Yet, a fuller, more well-rounded portrait, as well as a more detailed accounting of Robinson's extremely busy and accomplished life in one volume than the one presented by Rampersad is unimaginable.

   Nowhere is Rampersad's perspicacity in regard to Robinson's character more in evidence than in his account of the subject's upbringing in Pasadena, California. Robinson's mother, Mallie, who had led a family exodus from a hardscrabble life of sharecropping in Cairo, Georgia, was the greatest influence in Robinson's life, we learn. As Robinson grew up, he witnessed his mother continually doing all she could to provide for the needs of others (and not just family members), and he thought she was too giving, a victim being taken advantage of. As he grew older, he changed his mind, instilled his mother's values of Christian forgiveness and generosity, and took the view that his mother was living a heroic life of self-sacrifice. Robinson also keenly felt the lack of a father, Jerry, who had left Mallie and the family for another woman; and it is not an exaggeration at all to describe, as many writers have, Branch Rickey later serving as a father-figure for Jack (Roger Kahn's *Rickey & Robinson*, published in 2014 by Rodale, is a superb account of the special relationship between the two men.)

Rampersad, who looked for signs of the man in the boy, describes the adolescent Robinson as shy, quiet, and non-confrontational but also as a person already more than willing, when necessary, to stand up for himself and whatever deserved defending. To the surprise of some readers no doubt, Rampersad characterizes the Pasadena Robinson grew up in as a place that was mostly segregated and more racist than not. According to the author, Robinson accepted the fact early in life that much of his acceptance by whites was the result of his value as an athlete. It is a bit surprising to learn that Robinson (born in 1919) was older than UCLA as a four-year college; as happened throughout Robinson's life, many of the friends he made at the school became friends for life.

Robinson's stint in the U.S. Army was notable for his growth as a person and his growing awareness of institutionalized racial inequality, his first public racial confrontation (his court martial trial ended in an acquittal), and an ankle injury which plagued him the rest of his life. Most importantly, the three-year tour solidified the man's "contempt for Jim Crow." With no clear career path in view, Robinson joined the Negro Leagues by default. Rampersad says that somehow everyone seemed to know that he would be the player selected to integrate the white major leagues, and teammates and opponents alike tutored him, especially helping him to overcome his physical weaknesses (his arm) and his lack of proficiency in the finer points (like how to properly apply the tag to a skillful slider). Rampersad points out that Robinson's career as a Kansas City Monarch was brief not only because Branch Rickey came calling, but also because Jackie despised the segregation and ramshackle conditions under which Negro League games were played. According to the author, had Robinson not been chosen for the great experiment, he would have quit the Negro Leagues to become a high school coach, but of course it never came to that. Rampersad says that Robinson believed in Divine Providence ... believed that God had a plan for his life, that he was destined to fulfill a special purpose; and so it came to pass.

Robinson's career in "organized" baseball is covered deftly and economically; with Rampersad focusing less on the games and Robinson's playing heroics and more on his meeting the challenges offered by those opposed to integration (he describes Robinson's debut with the Triple A Montreal Royals as a "brilliant personal triumph"). Rampersad's handling of two such incidents are prime examples of his skill as a biographer. Concerning the legendary story about Pee Wee Reese defying a redneck's threat to gun down Robinson by draping an arm around his shoulders while the two stood together in the infield, Rampersad says there is no evidence that the gesture happened in Cincinnati or anywhere else for that matter. And then, there is no doubt that Enos Slaughter, one of the reputed ringleaders of the Cardinals' ultimately unsuccessful attempt to boycott games played in by Robinson, stomped on Jackie's ankle while he stretched for a throw at first base; barely missing Jack's Achilles tendon. Robinson insisted the act was intentional; Slaughter vehemently denied it. (Joe Garagiola also stepped on Robinson's ankle and also denied doing it intentionally). Rampersad leaves it to the reader to determine for himself the intentions of Slaughter and Garagiola, while quoting the comment of Dodgers Traveling Secretary Harold Parrott, who later wrote of the incident: "Hate was running high in that first Robinson year." Robinson loved baseball, and his first priority was always helping the Dodgers win, but Rampersad points out that money was also important; no one was more aware than Jackie of how much his late start was going to limit his earning power from the game. Rampersad also presents numerous instances of Robinson turning the tables on his adversaries once he had proved himself and Rickey allowed him to fight back. He especially had trouble with umpires, convinced as he was that certain ones had it in for him.

One of the most important threads running throughout the book is the importance of Rachel Robinson. Jack not only loved her dearly and faithfully, but he also continually leaned on her for strength and understanding. Rachel was crucial to the success of the great experiment in ways no other person was, and the Robinson marriage was a true partnership in every way. Rampersad follows Rachel's comings and goings and documents her many contributions to such an extent that it is fair to say that no other spouse assumes equal treatment in the history of baseball biography.

Jackie Robinson: A Biography is also unique in its extensive coverage of the life after the spikes and glove were hung up. Readers narrowly focused on the baseball may soon tire of the long, in-depth recitation of the events of Robinson's life after his retirement from the game, but to undervalue this part of the story is to miss the meaning of the famous epitaph on his tombstone: "A life is not important except for the impact it has on other lives." As far as Robinson was concerned, his breaking the baseball color barrier was just the first part of the job. He spent the rest of his life trying to help the members of his race achieve full integration into American society and equality. He did this by continually traveling around the country to speak and support the cause; by lending his name and presence to fund-raising events (he and Rachel even hosted numerous such events); and especially by involving himself in electoral politics (he worked on Nelson Rockefeller campaigns, e.g.). His preferences were not always approved of or understood by others–he supported Richard Nixon, Hubert Humphrey, and Robert Kennedy but not JFK–and he often clashed with civil rights groups such as the NAACP; but the touchstone of his support was always his view of whether or not the candidate was willing to fight for the goals of the movement, not just provide lip service. Robinson simply could not say no to requests to support the cause. He barely slowed down even after the onset of the diabetes and heart disease which eventually killed him, and while Rampersad does not say so, the man's unceasing efforts on behalf of racial equality probably took years off his life.

Also given their due along the way: Robinson's career as an executive for Chock Full of Nuts; the building of the Robinson's dream home in Connecticut; the raising of the three Robinson children; the drug abuse of son Jackie Jr. and his death in an auto accident at the age of twenty-four, just 16 months before his father's demise; and Robinson's ground-breaking careers as a newspaper columnist and a radio program host. It was in the latter two capacities that Robinson was often able to disseminate his political opinions and to call out those with whom he took umbrage over civil rights issues.

The effect of Rampersad's accounting of Robinson's tireless political efforts is to raise the reader's admiration of the man to a whole new level. Jackie Robinson, we conclude, was a great baseball player, but he was also a great American who selflessly did as much as anyone else to further the ideals of racial equality. In the end he is properly recognized for helping not just his own race but the white race as well. It is difficult to conceive of a greater legacy than that ... or of a book which better captures the character and spirit of the man behind such a legacy than *Jackie Robinson: A Biography*.

Joe DiMaggio: The Hero's Life

◆

Richard Ben Cramer

◆

New York: Simon & Schuster, 2000. Cloth, 546 Pages, ISBN: 0-684-85391-4. Prologue. Epilogue, Letter from the law firm of Engelberg, Cantor & Milgrim to the author, Author's Note and Acknowledgments, Index, 69 black & white photos throughout the book, mostly before each chapter. Other baseball books by the author: What Do You Think of Ted Williams Now? A Remembrance *(Simon & Schuster, 2002).*

In undertaking to write the first complete, definitive, and honest biography of Joe DiMaggio, Richard Ben Cramer understood that he faced two daunting challenges. First, a massive amount of information about the New York Yankees center fielder and American icon was already in print; and second, the monolithically, intimidatingly private DiMaggio would not cooperate with Cramer (or any other would-be biographer, for that matter). The resulting unauthorized biography entitled *Joe DiMaggio: The Hero's Life* is astounding proof that Cramer not only overcame the twin obstacles, but that in doing so he produced a life story as fascinating, iconoclastic, and as empathetic as any writer could hope to achieve. In addition to presenting the first complete portrait of the subject, warts and all, the book broaches the very idea of the hero, tacitly questioning several aspects of the notion which are seldom examined.

From the very beginning of the book, via the Prologue, the reader realizes that Cramer's book is not going to be another laudatory, gee-whiz piece of "Yankee Clipper" hagiography. The scene is Yankee Stadium on Joe DiMaggio Day, September 27, 1998, only months before DiMaggio's death, and Cramer describes the great man as being a physical wreck, old and suffering from a litany of illnesses. Entering the Stadium in a classic convertible, DiMaggio waves like the Pope so that "a whiff of his chrism, some glint of his godhood" might fly from him to the adoring crowd. The glorious purported purpose of the ceremony is for the Yankees to present DiMaggio with nine replica World Series rings that were stolen from a hotel room long ago; but no, that story is a myth, says Cramer. Joe almost certainly sold the rings. The real reason the decrepit DiMaggio wanted this day and made a grueling trip to get to it was so that he would receive fifteen thousand free "Joe DiMaggio Day" baseballs from the Rawlings sporting goods company, like the ones they had made for Mickey Mantle on his day; baseballs that the jealous DiMaggio planned to autograph and sell at a higher price than the Mantle balls commanded. And there we have it: the "want" that Creamer says was the essence of the man. The cheap, crass, overriding desire for money that ruled DiMaggio's being and motivated him to endure anything. "That was why he'd hauled himself out of bed at four in the morning, coughing up blood from the cancer he wouldn't speak about … to get to the airport, to fly to New York in time for his day. That was want. That was DiMaggio. If you lost track of that hunger, that toughness, you lost his core," writes Cramer. This three-page cameo is devastating–even the praise in it seems a left-handed compliment–yet it gives us more reality than virtually all of the previous writing on the subject. It effectively sets the stage for the point of view that informs the rest of the book which in the end seems justified.

According to Cramer, the essence of DiMaggio's character was evident at an early age. As a youngster in San Francisco Joe liked baseball okay, but he needed to get something, some pocket change perhaps, for playing even sandlot ball. It was older brother Vince, the first DiMaggio to make the major leagues, who really loved baseball. However, it was Joe who was extraordinarily baseball gifted. It was Joe the sportswriters immediately began to mythologize about: the poor immigrant Joe learned to hit using a broken oar, and he rebelled against his old-school Papa who wanted him to fish for a living. And it was Joe, even as a teenaged star for the hometown Seals of the PCL, who instinctively knew the value of letting the press turn him into a hero, as well as how to further their efforts. Later while covering DiMaggio's early years with the Yankees, Cramer uses a comparison between DiMaggio and the great and beloved Lou Gehrig to illustrate this talent. "But Joe was as shy–and just as silent–as Gehrig," he writes. "The difference was that Joe was aware from the first moment, aware at every moment, of the hero game. He was alive to the power of the camera: he made himself available, he could smile, and he knew when to smile. With writers he was as alert, as poised and pent as he was in center field. Positioning was the edge in both games."

From the beginning of his career as a professional baseball player, DiMaggio knew his value and fought to receive it. He chaffed at the Yankees' dilatoriness in rewarding him for his outstanding play and routinely held out. When the team, holding all the cards and using the press to turn the public against him, forced him into a humiliating surrender early on, DiMaggio swore to himself that he would eventually get his due and many times over. The Yankees did eventually make DiMaggio the highest paid player in baseball, but along the way the desire for money became an obsession for DiMaggio and it turned him, in so many words, into the tightest of cheap-ass tight wads. In Cramer's telling, DiMaggio became an entitled hero, who always expected somebody else to pick up the tab. And there was never any shortage of infatuated hangers-on, sycophants, and starry-eyed fans, including several prominent mobsters, ready to do just that, over and over again, just to convince themselves that they were friends with the great DiMaggio.

DiMaggio cultivated a mystique of personality that helped him guard his privacy and made others, even teammates, feel honored just to be in his presence or be recognized by a remark directed at them. The mystique, readily supported by newsmen, was also central to the elevation of DiMaggio from mere great player to hero status. Everyone it seemed was happy to go along with this apotheosis, with few exceptions, such as DiMaggio's first wife (starlet Dorothy Arnold) who divorced him and his only child, Joe Jr. (Dorothy's son), who never felt loved by his father. Being catered to like this (to put it mildly) helped turn DiMaggio into a "sufferable" egomaniac (a word Cramer never uses), and friends (Toots Shor and Frank Sinatra, e.g.) were often abruptly cast out of the hero's inner circle for the slightest infraction. Despite his peevish, often boorish behavior and his never-ending obsession with lucre, DiMaggio always managed to maintain the facade of dignity that the public came to expect of someone so superior to themselves. And only DiMaggio could have gotten away with all the demands he made on the rest of the world, such as his insistence that he always be introduced as "Baseball's greatest living player."

This is not to say that Cramer does not give DiMaggio his due. He does; and in fact, because of the author's deft way of framing the baseball achievements, many readers will come away from the book with a new appreciation of just how great a player DiMaggio was. For instance, although there was no Rookie of the Year Award in 1936, Cramer says DiMaggio would have won such a prize hands-down. "The only question," writes Cramer, "was whether Joe D. (.323, 29 HRs, 125 RBIs) was the best rookie *in history*." Cramer brilliantly describes things DiMaggio did to win important games and emphasizes that his monomaniac desire to win was the key to his greatness as a player. DiMaggio did in fact lead the Yankees to ten pennants in his 13-year career (often playing hurt), a record that Joe was rightfully extremely proud of. (Although it is seldom mentioned as it is with other players, DiMaggio also lost two prime years of his career to World War II.)

Perhaps the most amazing thing about DiMaggio, which is reflected in the length of the book, is that his life after he retired from the game was so interesting and a whirlwind of activity … in large part because of his marriage to Marilyn Monroe but also because of his need, paradoxically, to suck psychic sustenance from the adoration of the public he disdained in general and his pathological need to squeeze one more big memorabilia sale or paid appearance payday from his fame and the continually pumped up value of his signature.

Cramer never got a word out of DiMaggio, but he successfully interviewed hundreds of people who knew the man well; and only by doing so could the author have produced a work so detailed, so rich, and so revealing as *Joe DiMaggio: The Hero's Life*. Knowing the man as we do now, should Joe DiMaggio have been regarded as a hero? Do sports heroes have certain obligations beyond performing at a high level? And if so, did DiMaggio meet those obligations?

These are questions beyond the scope of this essay; however, they will occur to anyone who reads this great biography, and each reader will have to come to his own conclusions. What is certain is that no one will look at DiMaggio in all his guises–the consecutive game-hitting record holder, the model that Hemingway's heroic fisherman looked up to, Mr. Coffee–the same way ever again.

Johnny Evers: A Baseball Life

♦

Dennis Snelling

♦

Jefferson, NC: McFarland, 2014. Paper, 229 pages, ISBN: 978-0-7864-7591-9. Preface. Notes, Bibliography, Index, 34 black & white photos scattered throughout the book. Other baseball books by the author: A Glimpse of Fame: Brilliant but Fleeting Major League Careers *(McFarland, 1993),* The Pacific Coast League: A Statistical History, 1903–1957 *(McFarland, 1995),* The Greatest Minor League: A History of the Pacific Coast League, 1903–1957 *(McFarland, 2012),* Lefty O'Doul: Baseball's Forgotten Ambassador *(University of Nebraska Press, 2017), and* The Whiz Kids: How the 1950 Phillies Took the Pennant, Lost the World Series, and Changed Philadelphia Baseball Forever *(University of Nebraska Press, 2025).*

Few baseball biographies have been as important as *Johnny Evers: A Baseball Life* by Dennis Snelling, because seldom has an author penned a reappraisal as desperately needed as Snelling's. If it is possible to be a member of the National Baseball Hall of Fame and, at the same time, be *underrated*, then Evers has been the red-headed, bleacher-gate crasher of that august institution for some time. Unimpressed by Evers' seemingly modest batting averages and his Dead ball-era lack of power, many contemporary fans have concluded that the skinny Irish second sacker owes his plaque in Cooperstown not to his record or prowess on the diamond but to the famous "Tinker to Evers to Chance" bit of verse. Such critics have even maligned the fielding abilities alluded to in "Baseball's Sad Lexicon," pointing out that the number of double plays actually turned by Chicago's "trio of bear cubs" pales in comparison to that of many modern combos. All of which is misleading and irrelevant when weighed against the player Johnny Evers actually was. As Snelling so ably demonstrates, Evers was not just a good player but a great one; and this biography, a spectacular reminder of the value of the historical endeavor, firmly re-establishes the unquestioned credentials for which his contemporaries gladly and confidently conferred on him the ultimate baseball honor for posterity.

The case for Evers' greatness is lengthy and manifold. As a defensive player he was without peer, and he practically wrote the book on how to play second base (he did, in fact, in 1920 author *How to Play Second Base*, a book not to be confused with the more general *Touching Second: The Science of Baseball*, written with the help of

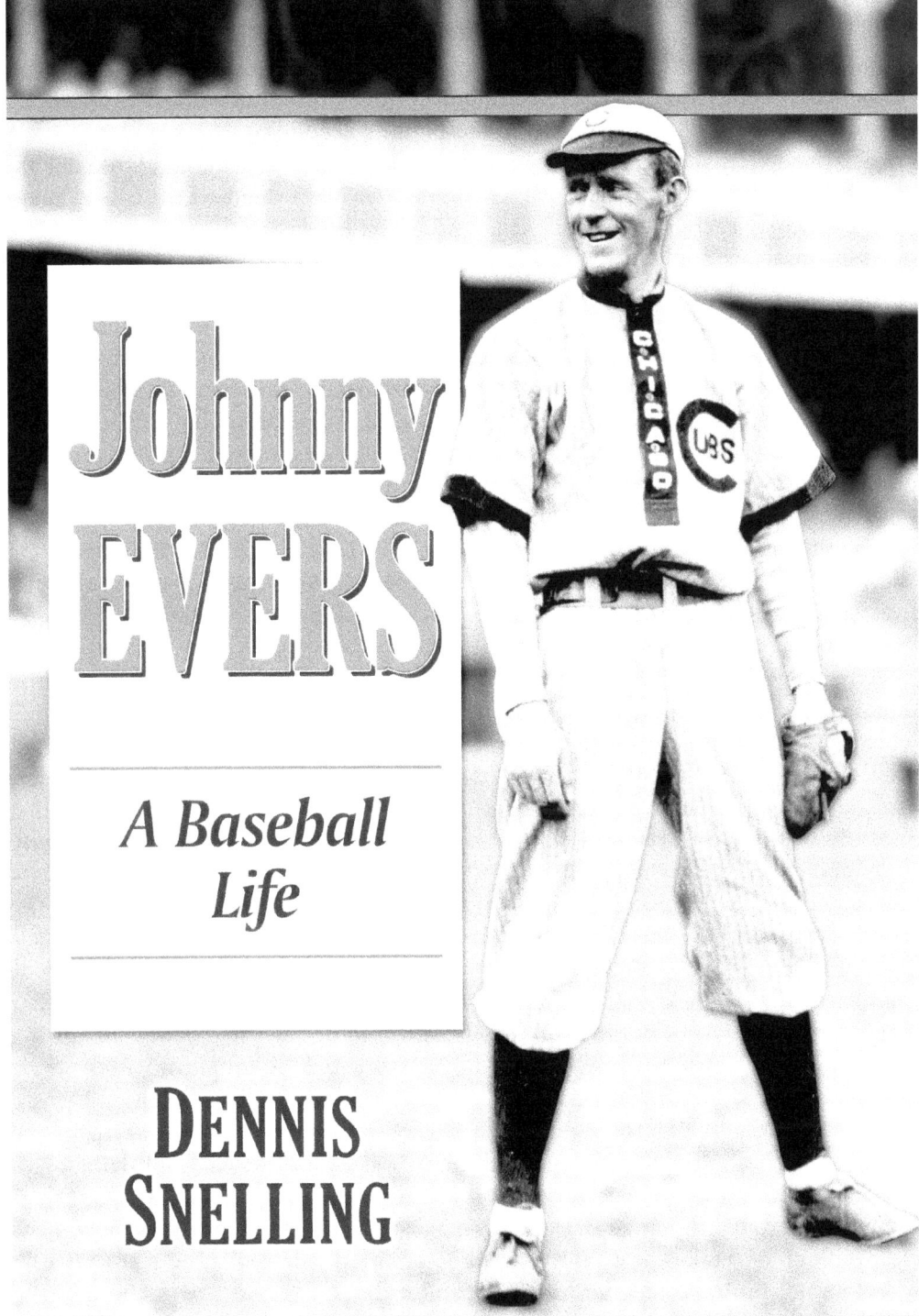

Hugh Fullerton and published in 1910). Evers pioneered one-handed catches (a difficult and risky technique considering the tiny gloves in use at the time), sweep tags (ditto), sidearm snap throws, and moving across the bag on double plays to avoid runners barreling into the base. Snelling describes these innovations as "nothing less than the birth of the modern style of playing second base." Evers was such a guru of the defensive side of the game that it was he, not shortstop Joe Tinker, team captain Frank Chance, or the Cubs' catchers, who positioned all the others players according to each batter's tendencies and where he was going to be pitched. The most dramatic example of this genius occurred during the second part of Evers' playing career when he was a member of the Boston Braves playing in the second game of the 1914 World Series. With the Braves clinging to a 1–0 lead in the bottom of the ninth, the Philadelphia A's batted with one out and a runner on first. Evers called time and shifted the Braves' infield, instructing shortstop Rabbit Maranville to play right next to the second base bag and third baseman Charlie Dean to move towards short. On the next pitch the A's Eddie Murphy hit a grounder right up the middle, exactly where Evers expected him to. Maranville fielded it, stepped on second and fired to first for a nifty game-ending twin killing. "They all cheered for Rabbit," Maranville said, "but it was Evers' generalship that won the game. If he hadn't called time, the Athletics could have won." As Snelling's narration reveals, Evers also made exceptional catches and plays with amazing regularity, often saving games with his glove.

The game that defined Evers' defensive greatness more than any other was the famous "Merkle" game that occurred on September 23, 1908, at the Polo Grounds when the Cubs faced off against their nemesis, the Giants, with whom they had moved into a tie for first place the day before by sweeping them in a doubleheader. The Giants appeared to win the game in the bottom of the ninth when, with two outs, Al Bridwell singled Harry McCormick home from third base. Except that Johnny Evers had other ideas when he saw Giants rookie Fred Merkle, who had moments before singled McCormick to third, stop running towards second and peel off for the safety of the clubhouse, away from the New York partisans storming the field in celebration. A chaotic scene ensued, but Evers eventually stood atop second base, holding a baseball (no one knows if it was the actual game ball) and demonstrating that he was applying a force out of Merkle, which would be the third out of the inning and invalidate the run seemingly scored by McCormick. A couple of weeks previously, the same situation had occurred but umpire Hank O'Day had ignored Evers' claim of a force out. As fate would have it O'Day was the home plate umpire for the Merkle game, and this time he enforced the rule as Evers and the Cubs demanded. The game was ruled a tie, with a replay scheduled for the end of the season if necessary. The two teams ended the season in a dead heat, and the Cubs then won the replayed game to take the National League pennant, their third in a row. While Merkle was haunted thereafter for his infamous bone-headed play or "boner," the play made Evers' reputation as the savviest player in the game and "elevated him to stardom." Prior to the decisive ninth inning of the Merkle game, Evers had twice made outstanding plays to rob Bridwell of base hits; Snelling adroitly points out that the force out on Merkle at second amounted to the third time in the game that Evers robbed the Giants shortstop of a hit (with Merkle forced out at second, Bridwell was credited with a fielder's choice, not a single).

Something else contributed to Evers' greatness, something that Snelling goes to great pains to make the reader aware of: his off-the-charts competitiveness. A quiet friendly man away from the game, in uniform Evers was a high-strung ferocity of an opponent, one who neither gave nor asked for any quarter. While he lacked Ty Cobb's batting skill, he was the National League's version of Cobb as a competitor, and one thing drove him like an obsession: his unrelenting desire to win. Evers' desire to win was so great that it often led him to criticize teammates for their failures and lapses, a habit that did not endear him to his colleagues. It was probably this habit which led to the quarrel between Evers and Joe Tinker and their resulting refusal to speak to each other off the diamond for a few years; and even Frank Chance, whom Evers revered, was not immune from his tongue lashings. Of course, the most frequent targets of the volatile Evers' eruptions were the umpires, who were almost guaranteed to be in for a rough time whenever they made a close call against Evers' team. Evers, who said, "My favorite umpire is a dead one," seemed to have a real hostility for the authority represented by umpires, and the latter fought back using the sharpest weapon in their limited arsenal by often throwing Evers out of the game. It was umpire Billy Evans, who in a magazine article, hung the most unflattering of his several nicknames upon the high-strung second baseman, calling him a "warm and generous person" off the diamond but an "awful *crab*" on it. Evers was also often suspended, and after one such occasion National League President John Tener said, "I don't know what I can do with him. I don't think he is civilized." Evers' all-consuming desire to win is what made him such an attractive candidate to coach and manage, and he was given numerous opportunities to do both; yet, ironically, the same inherent trait that made him a great player hampered him in the fulfilling of such duties. After being traded to the Pirates during the 1913 season, Mike Mitchell said of his former player-manager with the Cubs, "It is impossible for anyone to get along with Evers. I never had a word with any manager I ever worked for, but I couldn't please Johnny." Mitchell claimed many other players still with the club felt the same way.

Evers' hyper-competitiveness was accentuated by his general constitution. He was a nervous insomniac, so full of electric energy that, according to Giants pitching star Christy Mathewson, he was unable to wear a wrist watch because watches on his wrist wouldn't work properly. Constantly burning so brightly, of course, wore Evers down like a candle, and he did suffer a nervous breakdown at the beginning of the 1911 season. It was a lost season for him, as he played in only 46 games. The breakdown was caused in part by the stress of a fatal automobile accident, which happened the year before when Evers was driving in downtown Chicago and resulted in the gruesome death of Evers' best friend, sportswriter George McDonald. Just as Merkle could never escape the notoriety of his boner, Evers was never able to escape the feeling that he was to blame for the death of McDonald. He never again drove an automobile, not even the brand new Chalmers he received for being named NL MVP in 1914. As consequential as the auto accident was, it was merely one of a string of tragedies and misfortunes which plagued Evers throughout his adult life.

His equilibrium was also assaulted over the years by the death from scarlet fever of his 2-year-old daughter; his suffering a compound fracture of his leg right before the start of the 1910 World Series; his bankruptcy due to the embezzling of the friend who managed his shoe store in his hometown of Troy, New York; the burglarizing of his home in Troy; and the ultimate failure of his marriage to Helen Fitzgibbon. In a real sense, his life unwound in an amazing balance: success and triumph on the diamond, "the slings and arrows of outrageous fortune" off it.

If Evers infuriated and exasperated a lot of people, he impressed and gained the respect of virtually everyone who saw him play. And that's because, above everything else, Johnny Evers was a winner. Snelling never omits an opportunity to remind the reader of that, emphasizing the salient facts: during Evers' prime as a player the Cubs won four NL pennants and two World Series in a five-year period (1906–1910), and they averaged 106 wins per year (the equivalent of 112 wins over a modern 162-game schedule). It was Evers who led the lowly Boston Braves to their "miracle" NL pennant and stunning World Series sweep of the highly-favored Philadelphia A's in 1914 (the Braves did not vacate the NL cellar until July 19 on the way to a 61–17 finish). And during Evers' 18-year career as a player and player-manager, his teams never finished lower than third place. In the minds of the people who competed against Evers, there was never any doubt about who was the most important player on the teams he suited up for. One of Evers' biggest adversaries was Giants manager John McGraw, another unflinching competitor, who while despising Evers as an opponent couldn't help admiring him and giving him his due. "You only find a man of his natural ability and brains about once in ten years," said McGraw. And as the Braves began their climb into contention during the second half of the 1914 season and the sporting world began to take notice, McGraw said, "Stallings is a great manager, but Johnny is a pepper shaker. He makes men play ball whether they want to or not while he's alongside them."

And what of Evers as a hitter? Should he be defined by his .270 lifetime batting average? Not when one looks a little closer at the facts and then takes into consideration all of the above. In 1908 Evers turned in one of his best offensive seasons. None of his stats are impressive until they are compared, as Snelling does, to those turned in by the other players in the league. Evers batted an even .300 but it was the fifth highest mark in the league and by far the highest on the Cubs. "His .402 on-base percentage trailed only Honus Wagner's. He was fourth in the league in runs scored, third in bases on balls, fifth in stolen bases and was the league's second toughest batter to strike out." Hardly the record of an automatic out. No, the induction of Johnny Evers into the National Baseball Hall of Fame was no mistake. Years after his retirement as a player, Evers appeared on the radio quiz show *Information Please* and met for the first time Franklin P. Adams, who was one of the guest panelists. Evers told the sportswriter, "I owe you a debt of lasting gratitude for keeping my name before the public all these years. I'd have been forgotten long ago if it wasn't for 'Baseball's Sad Lexicon.'" For the biography that has set the record straight and rejuvenated his image, foibles and all, Evers now owes an even greater debt to Dennis Snelling.

Judge and Jury: The Life and Times of Judge Kenesaw Mountain Landis

◆

DAVID PIETRUSZA

◆

South Bend, IN: Diamond Communications, 1998. Cloth, 564 pages, ISBN: 1-888698-09-8. Foreword by Dick Thornburg, Acknowledgments, Introduction. Notes, Bibliography, Index, About the Author, 18 black & white photos between pages 432 and 433. Other baseball books by the author: Baseball's Can-Am League: A History of Its Inception, Franchises, Participating Locales, Demise and Legacy, 1936–1951 *(McFarland, 1990);* Major Leagues: The Formation, Sometimes Absorption, and Mostly Inevitable Demise of 18 Professional Baseball Organizations, 1871 to Present *(McFarland, 1991);* Minor Miracles: The Legend and Lure of Minor League Baseball *(Diamond Communications, 1995);* Total Indians: The 1995 American League Champions, *ed. with John Thorn, et al.;* Lights On! The Wild Century-Long Saga of Night Baseball *(Scarecrow Press, 1997);* Baseball: The Biographical Encyclopedia, *ed. with Matthew Silverman and Michael Gershman (Total Sports Illustrated, 2000);* Ted Williams: My Life in Pictures *(Total Sports Publishing, 2001);* Rothstein: The Life, Times, and Murder of the Criminal Genius Who Fixed the 1919 World Series *(Carrol & Graf, 2003);* Teddy Ballgame: My Life in Pictures with Ted Williams *(Sports Media Publishing, 2003); and* Total Baseball: The Ultimate Baseball Encyclopedia, *ed. with John Thorn (Sport Classic Books, 2004).*

Comments: While "Kennesaw" is the recognized spelling today, at the time of Landis' birth, both "Kennesaw" and "Kenesaw" were accepted as correct.

Morey Berger, *Library Journal*: "Pietrusza portrays a harsh if occasionally lenient baseball czar who banned the 1919 Black Sox, among others, for gambling but spared some players. Unlike Jerome Holtzman who recently blasted Landis 'a bigoted curmudgeon' in his *The Commissioners* (Total Sports, 1998) Pietrusza says that owners, not Landis, blocked the game's integration.'"

Unnamed for months after birth, he was finally christened after one of the bloodiest battles of the Civil War; a scrawny adult (and bad golfer with a foul mouth) weighing a little more than a couple of bags of concrete mix, he was feared by giants; and having never played anything but sandlot baseball, he became the symbol of the integrity of the game for more than two decades. Of whom do we speak? Why, the autocratic, imperious, fiercely independent first commissioner of baseball, of course, the subject of David Pietrusza's important, definitive biography entitled *Judge and Jury: The Life and Times of Judge Kenesaw Mountain Landis*.

Because there is little about the game in the first third of the book, impatient readers may wonder if *Judge and Jury* is a baseball book at all. But Pietrusza could hardly have ignored Landis' life and career prior to his becoming commissioner, especially as a proper examination of that period explains why the Judge was viewed as the right, perhaps only, man for the job. In the first place, we learn that Landis came into the world in Millville, Ohio, as part of a clan of tough and talented high achievers. His father, Abraham, was a Union doctor who suffered a gruesome and crippling leg injury in the Civil War at the bloody battle of Kennesaw Mountain, Georgia (hence, the subject's unusual name). Landis's three older brothers and his younger brother all became successful journalists or politicians, yet it was Kenesaw who seemed destined for great things and who displayed from an early age the desire to exercise his powers to the fullest. "I do remember that when I was a youngster" he once remarked, "I had an ambition to become the head of something. I mean the man who was responsible to nothing except his own conscience."

Second, after a couple of false career starts, Landis set his destiny into motion by opting for the legal profession. Due to his intelligence and diligence, as well as the minimum standards of the time, he became a lawyer and set up practice in Chicago without having graduated high school. His big break came when Walter Q. Gresham, appointed U.S. Secretary of State by President Grover Cleveland, took him along to Washington as his personal secretary. Gresham had been Abraham Landis' commanding officer in the Civil War, but Pietrusza rejects the notion that Kenesaw's hiring was an act of nepotism. Indeed, Landis proved extremely capable at his job, offered judicious advice that saved Gresham's hide several times, and made himself an attractive candidate for other significant positions. (Landis declined an offer to become minister to Venezuela, and years later his name would come up in discussions about possible presidential and VP candidates.) Upon Gresham's death in 1895, Landis returned to Chicago to marry Winifred Reed, daughter of the Ottawa, Illinois, postmaster, John H. Reed, and to resume his private law practice. Here again, the author rejects the standard impression (put forth by J.G. Taylor Spink in his *Judge Landis and 25 Years of Baseball*, Thomas Y. Crowell Company, 1947) that Landis's practice was of limited importance; arguing instead that "he resided at the center of a web of political connections that featured extremely useful ties to both parties. Ultimately, he would use them to win a federal judgeship."

Appointed by Theodore Roosevelt to the U.S. District Court for the Northern District of Illinois in 1905, Landis quickly gained a reputation for being a no-nonsense jurist who nevertheless conducted trials as if they were performance art. With his shock of white hair, perpetually grim expression, the bony finger he often used as a pointer, and his intimidating manner of questioning, he cut an impressive figure despite his modest size. Despite favoring the Republican party, he was seen as a champion of the little guy. And, while not an activist judge who felt entitled to make law (instead of simply applying it), his sentences often ran to extremes: being seen as charitably merciful or almost vindictively harsh.

Landis' fame was assured when he handled a 1907 case against Standard Oil of

Indiana. After a grand jury found the company guilty of violating federal laws forbidding rebates on railroad freight tariffs, Landis not only managed to drag the evasive John D. Rockefeller into his Chicago courtroom, he also slapped the maximum fine of $29 million (equivalent to $937 million in 2025 money) on the defendant. It was the largest fine ever handed down by an American court. Although the fine was overturned on appeal, it sealed Landis' image as a man of the people determined to rein in big business. The Standard Oil case may have made Landis' reputation as a Federal Judge, but he presided over a number of other sensational cases (involving lurid murders, audacious con men and women, socialist war protesters, etc.); all of them covered by Pietrusza in sufficient enough detail for the reader to get a firm grasp of the public's perception of the Judge by the time major league baseball came knocking at his chambers door.

The crisis which brought the owners, hats in hand, to Landis' domain, of course, was the 1919 Black Sox scandal which was threatening to destroy the public's confidence in the honesty of major league baseball competition. The owners' offer was akin to asking a fireman to save a building already engulfed in flames, so there was little resistance to Landis' demand for complete power. The owners actually signed an oath of fealty that concluded: "…and we assure him [Commissioner Landis] that each of us will acquiesce in his decisions even when we believe them mistaken and that we will not discredit the sport by public criticism of him and of one another." Landis exercised his absolute power immediately. Despite a jury finding the dirty White Sox players innocent, the Judge banned eight of them from organized baseball for life. His famous statement to that effect, a minor rhetorical masterpiece, has the sound of biblical doom and works well as a found poem:

> Regardless of the verdict of juries,
> No player who throws a game,
> No player that undertakes or promises to throw a game,
> No player that sits in conference
> > With a bunch of crooked players and gamblers
> > Where the ways and means of throwing games
> > Are discussed
> > And does not promptly
> > Tell his club about it,
> Will ever play professional baseball.

While the longball mashing Babe Ruth did much to re-energize fans disgusted by the treachery of the Black Sox, there can be no doubt that Landis' severe punishment did as much or more to "save" baseball. In fact, Landis had already saved baseball once before, in his handling of the Federal League lawsuit against major league baseball. Wary of the potential for a lengthy trial to abrogate baseball's reserve clause (which bound players to their teams in perpetuity), Landis delayed making a decision until the plaintiffs ran out of money and sued for peace. The delaying gambit was a favorite and effective tactic of the Judge. It is worth noting that Pietrusza credits Landis' banning of Sox third baseman Buck Weaver, who did not join the cabal of dirty players but knew about the plot and kept quiet, as a key to the effectiveness of the Judge's decision going forward. Ironically, because Landis put the fear of God into players throughout the game, a succession of accusations involving games fixed or attempted to be fixed by gamblers came to light in the following years and caused Landis no end of headaches and made the total eradication of gambling his number one priority. (The Cobb-Speaker affair was especially sensational and worrisome.) Other controversies the Judge had to deal with during his tenure as commissioner were Babe Ruth's flouting of rules against barnstorming, Branch Rickey's efforts to institute a farm system, illegal player signings, and the fiasco of Game Seven of the 1925 World Series: Landis' refusal to allow a rainout despite a torrential downpour (this because Landis was "still smarting from the uproar over [umpire] George Hildebrant's calling off Game Two of the 1922 World Series"). In the many fights over which ballclub a player belonged to, Landis invariably ruled in favor of emancipating the player.

To be sure, Landis had enemies in baseball, particularly American League President Ban Johnson, St. Louis Browns owner Phil Ball, Rickey, and to some degree even his first biographer *The Sporting News'* Spink; but he was universally respected and feared for the unassailability of his moral character.

Today, Landis is criticized mostly for his do-nothing stance on integration, a topic Pietrusza covers thoroughly and fairly; cautioning against condemning the man if not exactly exonerating him. And Landis, who repeatedly stated that there was no rule against integration, may have done more about the problem had he not died in office on November 25, 1944; having served baseball honorably for 25 years. Readers might well conclude after reading it that *Judge and Jury*, more than any other book discussed in these pages, may serve as an indictment of our times. Whatever his faults and questionable opinions (such as his idea that voting should be mandatory), Kenesaw Mountain Landis was a man of integrity who followed his own conscience. He was a patriot and saw it as his duty to do whatever he could to make the United States of America a better country; and perhaps, even to make the people who came before him as a Federal Judge and as the Commissioner of baseball better people. No one had to wonder who was pulling his strings, blackmailing him, or bribing him. He took the job that made him famous because he loved baseball and wanted to restore it to something young boys (and now girls) could believe in and be inspired by. As Pietrusza so ably demonstrates, Landis accomplished his goal, and surely no non-player deserves his plaque in the Baseball Hall of Fame more than the Judge.

The Last Innocents:
The Collision of the Turbulent Sixties and the Los Angeles Dodgers

Michael Leahy

New York: HarperCollins, 2016. Cloth, 473 pages, ISBN: 978-0-06-236056-4. Genesis. Acknowledgments, Appendix: (The Principals and Interviews Conducted with Other Dodger Players, Rival Players, Baseball Officials, Family Members of the Players, Prominent Observers, and Fans), Sources, About the Author, 18 black & white photos between pages 204 and 205.

Comments: *The Last Innocents* won the 34th CASEY Award in 2016, earning two first-place votes and a third-place vote from the three Judges. *The Arm: Inside the Billion-Dollar Mystery of the Most Valuable Commodity in Sports* by Jeff Passan and *The Selling of the Babe: The Deal that Changed Baseball and Created a Legend* by Glenn Stout finished second and third, respectively.

Leahy's work has been selected four times for the annual Best American Sports Writing anthologies. *GQ* magazine described *When Nothing Else Matters: Michael Jordan's Last Comeback* as "the best sports book of the year … easily the most fully formed portrait of Jordan ever written and one of the best sports books in recent memory."

Leahy's son, Cameron, is a talented musician and singer and the founder of the successful rock band The Downtown Fiction.

The great baseball historian Charles Alexander once opined that the reason many academics in his field approach baseball (and other sports) from socio-economic and cultural perspectives is that they actually do not like the game. Critics with the same starting point believe that the highest praise they can lavish on a book about the national pastime is to claim that the book in question is really not a book about baseball at all but a book about something else, something *more important* than a mere game. Unfortunately, authors who share this philosophy or who are influenced by it more often than not wind up writing books that, whatever their value as treatises on class, race, or gender (for example), are not very good baseball books. The eminent exception to this rule is Michael Leahy's *The Last Innocents: The Collision of the Turbulent Sixties and the Los Angeles Dodgers*, a book which seamlessly interweaves two fascinating stories: the rise and fall of a great ballclub and the external non-sport societal forces that affected the members of that great team.

There is no question that in the case of *The Last Innocents* we have a properly credentialed author, as his love of the game, manifested by his penetrating analyses and lyrical descriptions based on hundreds of hours of interviews with key personages, shines through on every page of the book. The Dodgers that the author writes about were, in fact, the heroes of his youth; a fact he strategically keeps under wraps until he reaches one of the climaxes of the action. Michael Leahy, as a 12-year-old boy, was one of the lucky fans to witness in person what a 1995 panel of SABR members deemed to be the "greatest pitched game in history": Sandy Koufax's 1–0 perfect game of September 9, 1965, during which Bob Hendley, the Cubs' losing pitcher, himself allowed only one hit (a bloop double by Lou Johnson). Leahy does not put himself on the scene in order to prove his chops but, as an eye witness, he is able to provide invaluable perspectives on crucial elements of Koufax's masterpiece: the lefthander's early control problems and the seemingly sure base hit off the bat of Byron Browne that center fielder Willie Davis ran down and caught with surprising ease. Every facet of Leahy's account of this game is brilliant, including his poetic explanation of the kind of ball Browne hit: "It was a rope, as ballplayers commonly call such a shot, a tribute to the quality of contact made and to its beautiful look, a ghostly white blur that stays at the same height for a considerable distance, as straight as a taut rope."

In a prologue-like first chapter ("Genesis") Leahy outlines baseball's supremacy among American sports in the mid–1950s and says that this status continued into the 1960s, even as other professional team sports began to rise. At the dawn of the decade, the '60s seemed to be full of promise, yet there were unimaginable troubles ahead which would threaten to tear the nation apart. The author's hinting at these troubles is made the more ominous by his sketching the contented outlook of a typical sports fan of the era, a fella named Bob Oswald, the innocent brother of a man who would be accused of being at the heart of one of the most tragic and notorious events in the country's history. In due course, amidst the excitement and drama of the baseball action, Leahy deals with these wrenching, epochal events: the assassinations of JFK, RFK, and MLK; racial tensions and the civil rights movements; and the Vietnam War.

Nevertheless, it is the baseball which most interests Leahy and us, the readers, and the game on the field never gets sublimated to other concerns, as important as they were. The same was true for the black Dodgers players themselves. E.g., as emotionally engaged as they were by the Watts race riots raging nearby, black Dodgers exhibited the utmost professionalism by keeping their focus on their jobs. Likewise, while most players embraced the changes ... like Tommy Davis who tells Leahy that "It was nothing but change going on everywhere you looked" ... it was too late for others. After hotels opened their dining rooms to blacks, catcher John Roseboro would still not join roommate Maury Wills in the restaurants and preferred to keep taking his meals in their room.

Behind great pitching and defense, the Dodgers dominated the National League in the early 1960s, taking flags in '63, '65, and '66, while losing the '62 pennant on the last day of the season in a playoff with the San Francisco Giants. To bring the struggles and triumphs of these years to life, Leahy focuses on seven key players: Maury Wills, Wes Parker, Sandy Koufax, Tommy Davis, Jeff Torborg, Dick Tracewski, and Lou Johnson. Each, in turn, adds something critical to the overall story. Utility infielder Tracewski, as the best friend and confidant of the reserved and highly private Koufax, supplies many insights into the great pitcher's mindset and his reactions to various controversies. Torborg, the light-hitting but outstanding receiver, recalls his naivete about racial discrimination when he was a young player struggling to establish himself. Davis, the only big bat in the Dodgers' lineup, spearheads the drive to get the Dodgers to integrate the stands at the team's Vero Beach ballpark; yet upon hearing of the death of JFK, he expresses the hope that the murderer was not a black man. And, outfielder Lou Johnson, the journeyman buried for a decade in the Dodgers farm system, finally gets his shot when Davis suffers a broken ankle … and makes the most of it, carrying the Dodgers to the 1965 pennant, imagining that the baseball he swings at in BP is the face of a white person.

Other than Koufax who spoke sparingly to Leahy for the book, Wills and Parker are the two most important and revelatory figures. The story of Parker's path to the big time is surely the most unlikely such tale in the history of modern baseball. An undrafted former small-college player, the purposeless Parker was bouncing aimlessly around Europe on his wealthy family's money when he suddenly had an epiphany that he was destined to play major league baseball. Less than two years later he *was* a member of the Dodgers, and the details of his incredible ascension are almost beyond belief. Along the way, Parker constantly and secretly battled self-confidence and self-esteem issues, which were by-products of an unhappy and abusive childhood. Through endless practice which began in boyhood, a helpful familial connection to the Dodgers front office, and his substantial natural talent, Parker willed himself a successful career in the major leagues; an achievement that meant far more than usual. As he explains, "I had one shot to make it in life—not in baseball—in *life*. I was fighting for my life. Baseball was just the means."

Will's backstory is equally heart-breaking, if not quite as dramatic. Like Lou Johnson, Wills lingered far too long in the minors before he got a chance in the major leagues. Some of the L.A. brass had no faith in him, offensively or defensively; but Bobby Bragan (who taught him to switch hit) and Pete Reiser (who taught him to hit the ball where it was pitched) saved his career. Once given the shortstop position, Wills almost immediately became such an unstoppable offensive weapon that he was regarded as someone who was changing the game. He exhibited a maniacal need to win, and he routinely sacrificed his body to help the Dodgers do just that; often through his small ball tactics (bunting, hitting to the opposite field, stealing bases, taking extra bases, etc.) enabling the weak-hitting Dodgers to score runs without the benefit of a hit. Yet as dynamic and as important a player as he was, Wills had crosses to bear too. Like Koufax, he faced racial prejudice, and to illustrate the point Leahy paints a sad scene during which the two players screen each other's hate mail. Some fans did not want to see Wills break Ty Cobb's record for stolen bases in a season, and the Dodgers themselves cautioned him about dating white women (namely, Doris Day). Like Parker, Wills never felt as if he had truly made it, and this insecurity was preyed upon by the Dodgers GM Buzzie Bavasi in order to annually underpay him. Other than Koufax, there was no more important player on these Dodgers teams, and former colleagues of Wills express shock to learn that he is not already in the Hall of Fame. After reading *The Last Innocents*, readers will understand their reaction.

Baseball itself was not immune from the sea changes underway in the decade, particularly on the economic and labor fronts. Walter O'Malley epitomized the "Lords of baseball" breed of owner who was used to holding all the cards in salary negotiations, and his hatchet man, Bavasi, was ruthless in manipulating players into accepting much lower compensation than they deserved. The double holdout of Koufax and Drysdale was one of the first player shots across the bow that instigated the labor war between the owners and players and led to the formation of the players union and ultimately to free agency, but it drove a wedge between Koufax and O'Malley that was a long time in being removed. While he lost that wage battle to the two pitchers, O'Malley continued to act imperiously, spitefully trading Wills to Pittsburgh for the exhausted shortstop having left an exhibition tour of games in Japan, commenced right after the 1966 World Series.

Leahy calls 1964 the pivotal year in the Dodgers dynasty because that's when Koufax's fate was determined. Diving back into second base, he injured his priceless left arm; causing the onset of traumatic arthritis, a condition that would only get worse. The author later adds that while it took years to build, the Dodgers dynasty was demolished in 13 days after the 1966 season, when Koufax announced his premature retirement and the trades of Wills and Tommy Davis (to the New York Mets) were executed. There is a definite sense of denouement in the post–1966 part of the book, with the cultural and societal changes taking precedence over baseball, even as Leahy follows the participants' fortunes in the face of the Dodgers decline. Yet, the significant moments on the field, such as Drysdale's scoreless innings streak, are not neglected.

In the end, it is Koufax who looms largest in the reader's mind. The reader is struck not just by his prodigious feats on the mound, but by how much his teammates loved him and felt added pressure to do their best in support of his efforts. Eight years after Koufax's masterpiece, Willie Davis told Leahy, then a young man, "I had to make that catch for Sandy—what if I didn't?"

Decades after that conversation, Michael Leahy would deliver his own masterpiece in the form of *The Last Innocents*, which time and again elevates the achievements of a mere baseball team and its players to a higher plane through prose the likes of which is seldom found in any book. Summing up the greatest pitched game in history he writes: "It remains to baseball chroniclers what the Gettysburg Address is to Lincoln scholars, a transcendent event that, though tracked by a prodigious paper trail and deeply chronicled by journalists and historians, stubbornly eludes efforts to picture and feel it.… The game marked the apotheosis of Koufax."

The League of Outsider Baseball: An Illustrated History of Baseball's Forgotten Heroes

◆

GARY CIERADKOWSKI

◆

New York: Touchstone, 2015. Cloth, 233 pages, ISBN: 978-1-4767-7523-4. Introduction. Acknowledgments.

Comments: Cieradkowski was responsible for many of the decorative design elements of Oriole Park at Camden Yards in Baltimore. He also created the logo for the 1993 MLB All-Star Game, illustrated a triptych mural of Negro Leagues legend Buck O'Neil for the Orioles' spring training facility in Sarasota, Florida, and produced a series of 15 seven-foot-tall drawings of Chicago Cubs legends which hang in a bleacher section of Wrigley Field. Gary was the recipient of the 2015 Tony Salin Award for Contributions to Baseball History, presented by the Baseball Reliquary.

The League of Outsider Baseball, written and illustrated by Gary Cieradkowski, is that rarest of baseball art books for offering a text that is as interesting and arresting as its beautiful images. The perfect marriage of history and illustration, the book is the author's tribute to a host of characters whose participation in the great game of baseball occurred, for the most part and in most cases, outside the narrow parameters of major league baseball. These one-year wonders, unrecognized pioneers, pretenders and blowhards, outcasts, could-have-beens, criminals and murderers, "barnstormers, journeymen, rogues, and odd balls" … who played on college and town ball teams, in the minors and in the Negro Leagues, on teams in the armed forces, in outlaw leagues, and in leagues in foreign countries … these are the players whose obscure and never-before-told stories Cieradkowski revels in telling with pen and paint brush.

Most of the illustrations in the book are full-size reproductions of the baseball cards created by Cieradkowski, part of a never-ending set of cards he has named "The Infinite Baseball Card Set." Similar in size to the typical business card, as well as the old Tobacco cards the author is fond of, the cards are boldly colorful, the graphic images of the players pleasingly suggestive of the most riveting poster art. A number of full-page illustrations done in the same inimitable style are also included;

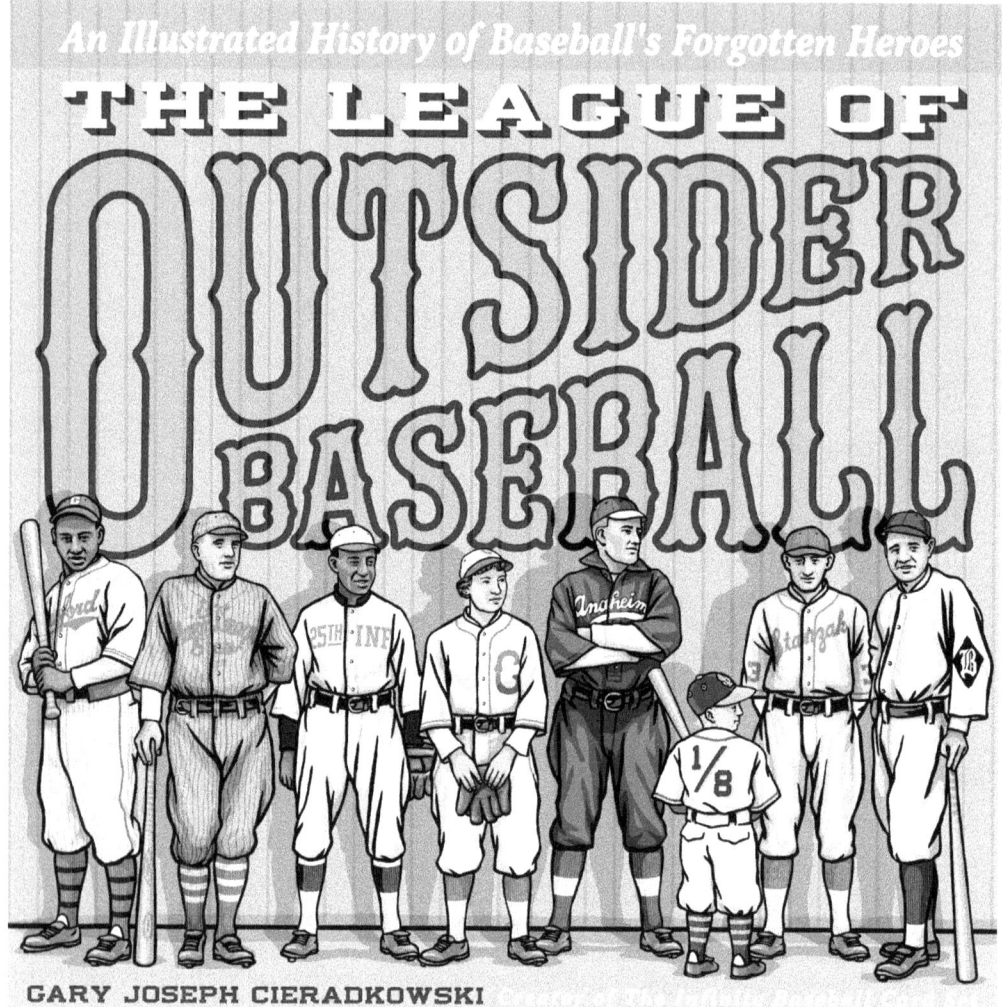

sometimes accompanied by a Cieradkowski baseball card and sometimes not. The consistent style of these images and of the design of the cards themselves provides a look for the book that is unique, immediately identifiable, and unforgettable. (The card design consists of the player image framed by pillars down each side of the card, with icons of crossed bats behind a baseball in each top corner spanned by a curved cornice for the team name, and across the bottom a banner bearing the player name and his position or identity, such as "Mascot," or "Manager" for writer Jack Kerouac, who played a table-top baseball game of his own invention all his life.)

The illustrations are so good they threaten to overshadow the text they illustrate; yet it is the research into so many forgotten corners of baseball history that is the point and the true delight of the book. A perfect example of the type of player to pique the author's interest might be Ray White, a pitcher who toiled for a number of seasons in the farm system of the New York Yankees. White's professional baseball career would not be worth much remembering were it not for the grudge he apparently bore all-time Yankees great Lou Gehrig. According to the author, Gehrig was introduced to White when the star-struck young man was the captain of the baseball team at Columbia University, the same school Gehrig had attended. Supposedly, Gehrig's indifference to the meeting greatly offended White who never forgave the slight. Years later, White buzzed Gehrig with a brush back pitch after Gehrig twice homered off him in an intrasquad spring training game in 1934. When asked about the close shave, Gehrig said, "That guy can go to hell!" A few months later White faced off against his nemesis again when the pitcher's Class B Norfolk Tars played an exhibition game against the parent Yankees. Gehrig homered against White in his first at bat but was seriously beaned by White in his second plate appearance. The injury did not keep Gehrig out of the lineup once the Yankees resumed championship season play, and this fact is the lead-in for Cieradkowski's rumination about the meaning of Gehrig's highly-lauded consecutive-games playing streak. Gehrig suffered several other bean-ball concussions during the setting of his streak and never rested after them either, which leads the author to write "...recently doctors have suggested that Gehrig may not have died from the disease that bears his name but been the victim of gradual brain degeneration that occurs after numerous head injuries." While Cieradkowski makes it clear he's not claiming that Ray White killed Lou Gehrig, he does raise the possibility that Gehrig's "pursuit of a record that ultimately meant nothing to his team" (in terms of winning championships) may have resulted in his premature death. The author concludes, as he always does, by giving us the rest of the story: not only White's continual denial that he meant to hurt Gehrig and his later success as the president of the Royal Crown Cola soft drink company, but also his doing what he felt Gehrig should have done for him: giving an alumnus a break. By 1938 when White was manager of the Tars, the Yankees wanted him to play a fellow named Claude Corbitt at shortstop. White showed faith in a player who'd attended the same high school as himself: a kid named Phil Rizzuto.

Many of the players in the book are even more obscure than White, such as Arnold Preedin, who never even played minor league baseball. Preedin was a socialist dreamer, part of the "little-known exodus" of Americans to the Soviet Union in the early 1930s. Preedin formed the first baseball team in the vast country, the Moscow Foreign Workers' Club; and the game started to grow in popularity (even the KGB planned to start not one but two teams!). That is, until Stalin's purges which murdered millions, including "almost every member of the large American expatriate population. Simply holding on to American magazines or visiting the U.S. embassy brought swift arrest by the secret police and a trip to the Gulag—or worse." Baseball didn't save Preedin or his brother Walter. Both were arrested and shot in an apple orchard outside Moscow.

The League of Outsider Baseball's roster is filled with such fascinating characters and include (as a few more examples): Nemesio Guillo (who, after studying at Alabama's Springhill College, introduced baseball to Cuba and founded the Habana Base Ball Club in 1868), Frederick Benteen (a rival of George Armstrong Custer and the founding member of a baseball team of soldiers from their Seventh Calvary Regiment), Canadian Will "Hippo" Galloway (the first black man to play professional hockey and the last man to play professional baseball before Jackie Robinson integrated the game in 1946), Jimmy Claxton (thought to be an American Indian by the 1916 Oakland

Oaks, the first black player to appear on an American baseball card), and Eddie Bennett (the mascot and batboy of three straight, different World Series teams: the 1919 White Sox, the 1920 Brooklyn Dodgers, and the 1921 New York Yankees).

Not all the players in the book are obscure. Many, in fact, played major league baseball, at least briefly, and a number are Hall of Famers: such as Christy Mathewson (Cieradkowski explains the genesis of Matty's out pitch, the fadeaway), Lefty Grove (the story is how the famous minor league Baltimore Orioles bought him for the price of a new outfield fence), Joe Medwick (the wonderful full-page illustration shows Medwick sitting in the Houston Buffaloes dugout next to a stack of the confectionary treat named after him, the "Joe Medwick Ducky-Wucky Chocolate Candy Bars"), a host of Negro Leaguers (everybody from Satchel Paige and Josh Gibson to Jud Wilson and Biz Mackey), and Willie Mays. The Mays story about the Say-Hey Kid's integration of the Interstate League in particular exhibits Cieradkowski's skill as a writer. The title of the story, "Willie Mays: The Late-Night Visitors," seems to promise an ugly tale; an impression reinforced by the story's pull quote set off in the middle of the second page: "Fueled by anger, they climbed the hotel's fire escape and huddled in the darkness." But the author is only teasing us. The visitors to the flea bag hotel in the "colored" part of Hagerstown were his Trenton Giants teammates (not KKK members), and they were not unhappy about Mays' presence on the team but angry and worried about Willie's having been "forced to accept different accommodations from the rest of the club."

Finally, as the book shows, nothing delights the author more than myth busting. When Yankees outfielder Jake Powell was asked in a radio interview how he stayed in shape during the winter, he said, "Oh, that's easy. I'm a policeman in Dayton, Ohio. I spend the off-season clubbing niggers over the head." Not only was the comment a morally offensive insult which triggered Powell's decline (he eventually committed suicide in a police station after being arrested for passing bad checks), it wasn't even true. Powell just made up the business about being a cop. Cuba was not nearly saved from the predations of revolutionary Fidel Castro because he was scouted and almost signed to a contract by the Washington Senators; he wasn't a good enough pitcher to even make the University of Havana's JV team. And Pete Gray ... while the courageous one-armed outfielder's batting .218 in 1945 was an amazing accomplishment, the feat may have cost the St. Louis Browns a chance at a second pennant. As teammate Ellis Clary said, "He screwed up the whole team. If he's playing, one of them two-armed guys is sitting in the dugout pissed off."

All in all, few baseball books cover the ground that *The League of Outsider Baseball* does, and no other book does so as beautifully, as artistically as Gary Cieradkowski's tribute to "Baseball's Forgotten Heroes."

The Legendary Harry Caray: Baseball's Greatest Salesman

◆

Don Zminda

◆

Lanham, MD: Rowman & Littlefield, 2019. Cloth, 317 pages, ISBN: 9781538112946. Acknowledgments, Introduction. Notes, Bibliography, Index, About the Author, 13 black & white photos between pages 141 and 142. Other baseball books by the author: From Abba-Dabba to Zorro: The World of Baseball Nicknames *(Stats Inc., 1999),* The Best Book of Baseball Facts and Stats Ever! With Luke Friend *(Carlton Books, 2000),* Go-Go to Glory: The 1959 Chicago White Sox *(Acta Publications, 2009),* Double Plays and Double Crosses: The Black Sox and Baseball in 1920 *(Rowman & Littlefield, 2021), and co-ed.* Stats Scouting Notebook *annual for several years.*

Of all the superb broadcasters baseball fans have enjoyed listening to over the decades, none has been as nationally popular, as much of a magnet for both unstinting praise and legitimate criticism, and as much in need of a judicious biography as Harry Caray. Happily, in *The Legendary Harry Caray: Baseball's Greatest Salesman* by Don Zminda we have such a book; a riveting read that not only chronicles Caray's long, tumultuous career, but also captures the essence of the man himself and his massive appeal. It is a book which makes the reader understand how much poorer the game of baseball has been without Harry Caray (who died in 1998) behind the microphone.

The first order of business for Zminda was straightening out, as much as possible, the details of the Caray origin story. Caray, whom Zminda says was born of Albanian, not Italian and Romanian, stock in 1914 in St. Louis, Missouri, provided different answers for the year of his birth ala kindred yarn spinners Satchel Paige and Dizzy Dean. This he did probably out of sheer mischievous insouciance. His carelessness with other key dates, also corrected by Zminda, was more a factor of the unhappiness he experienced growing up. He never met his father, his remarried mother died when he was fourteen, and he spent his high school years living as a fifth wheel with the family of a maternal uncle. The uncle abandoned the family, leaving Caray's aunt to fend by herself for her four children (all younger than Harry) and her nephew. This Dickensian upbringing goes a long way towards explaining

Caray's later reluctance to discuss his childhood, the marital difficulties that led to two divorces, his uncomfortableness in family situations even when he was among people he loved, and a sorrow at the core of his being; a melancholy that caused Caray, as he admitted in his autobiography (*Holy Cow!* With Bob Verdi) to always want to spend Christmas alone, by himself. Zminda does not dwell on this sadness, but the sensitive reader cannot help picking up on it and regarding as psychic compensation Caray's later infamous all-night convivial drinking sessions, for which he was nicknamed the "Mayor of Rush Street," as well as his total immersion in the adoration of his legion of fans. It was baseball, of course, which saved him.

Many fans, introduced to Harry Caray through superstation WGN's national cable TV broadcasts of Chicago Cubs games, probably believe to this day that Caray was always a Cubs announcer. In fact, while Caray enjoyed a long run with the team and while he reached legendary status with them, his stint with the Cubs came at the end of his career. He broke into the major leagues as a play-by-play man with the St. Louis Cardinals and the St. Louis Browns in 1945 after less than a five-year apprenticeship working in smaller markets (it was in Joliet, Illinois, that the station manager convinced him to change his name from Carrabina to Caray), and he spent the next quarter of a century solidifying much of the Midwest and most of the South as Cardinals territory. Most likely, the Cardinals fired Caray because of a rumored affair between him and the wife of the team owner's son, August Busch III. (Both Caray and Susan Hornibrook Busch denied the allegation.) After a single season toiling for Charlie Finley's Oakland A's, he jumped at the chance to ply his trade in the baseball-obsessed Windy City market, calling Chicago White Sox games with the controversial Jimmy Piersall as his partner for eleven years before the Cubs came calling. Zminda covers all this personal history admirably, sedulously chronicling all the deals, Caray's many partners and competitors, the changes in industry practices, the reactions to Caray's performances, the plights of the teams whose games he described, and the increased attendance figures for home games which he certainly had a major role in producing.

The epicenter of the book is Caray's broadcasting itself. Caray got into baseball broadcasting for the simplest of reasons: he loved baseball with a passion and thought he could do better than the guys he was listening to; in particular, France Laux, a respected but low-key announcer of St. Louis Cardinals games. By this he meant that he could make the games sound more exciting than Laux did. Indeed, he could, and this ability to inject drama and interest into even the most sluggish contest became a hallmark of his MO. Harry Caray broadcasts were must-listen-to performances because he identified so strongly with the fans and because he was honest to a fault. He prided himself on "telling it like it is," and he never shied away from criticizing players, managers, and even owners he felt had screwed up. He made life miserable for some of them, especially for Cardinals third baseman Ken Boyer, White Sox slugger Bill Melton, and Sox manager Chuck Tanner. Pitcher Jim Brosnan, who'd felt the sting of Caray's tongue, once asked Harry why he couldn't be more like Red Barber and Vin Scully. "I'm the fan," said Caray. "I talk like a fan." Brosnan countered that Barber and Scully didn't talk like fans. Rather, they spoke like poets. "That's true," admitted Caray. "I ain't no poet."

Speaking like Everyman, Caray nevertheless developed rhetorical devices that he used to great effect. Zminda says he didn't invent his favorite exclamation, "Holy Cow!," but that he was the first to use it while broadcasting a major league game. His home run call ("It might be ... it could be ... it is! ... a home run!") and his punctuation of a win by the home team ("Cubs win! Cubs win! Cubs win!") were original and became his signature calls. Then there was his incessant mentioning of fans by name during the broadcasts and his leading the crowd in the signing of "Take Me Out to the Ballgame" during the seventh inning stretch of every game; two other habits which stamped the broadcasts as uniquely his. Finally, Caray's gravelly voice, his almost full head of silver hair, and his over-sized black glasses made him more recognizable than the players he talked about, and his "hail fellow-well met" attitude endeared him to fans wherever he went.

As much as Caray was idolized, especially during his final go round with the Cubs, he had plenty of critics, not only players but also ordinary fans and other members of the media, many of whom accused him of being a "homer." Caray never denied it, never apologized for it, and thought it should be accepted as just part of his makeup. He also never apologized for always insisting that he be recognized as the number one man on any broadcast team he was a part of. As Zminda recounts, most broadcasters willingly deferred to this demand, but a few resented it and disliked working with Caray. Milo Hamilton, in particular, despised Caray, thought him unprofessional, and turned his back on the proceedings when Caray would lean out of the booth in the middle of the seventh to get the crowd started by screaming, "Lemme hear ya ... a-one ... a-two ... a-three ... 'Take Me Out to the Ballgame...'" The Hamilton-Caray feud lasted the rest of Caray's life and wasn't put to bed until Hamilton took a final posthumous shot at his nemesis.

The negative stuff never bothered Caray much though because he simply loved his job and never tired of doing it. His third marriage to Delores "Dutchie" Goldman was charmed, and he was handsomely paid for his services; not only as a play-by-play broadcaster but as a salesman. Surely, no other broadcaster in history has sold more beer than Harry Caray. Caray mellowed a bit as he got older and toned down his player critiques, and he became more popular than ever, even after a stroke in 1987 caused him to mispronounce names more badly and more frequently than in the past. A second stroke killed him in the spring of 1998, right before he was set to fulfill the dream of teaming up with grandson Chip Caray to become the first such team to regularly share a major league broadcasting booth (Caray's son Skip also became a top notch baseball broadcaster, but the circumstances were never right for them to join up as a team).

In the final chapters of the book, the author surmises that Caray would not find a place in the industry today, reflecting as it does the politically correct and easily offended "snowflake" society in which we live. Which is beside the point considering Zminda's summary of the many ways that Caray's legacy has lived on after his death. It is an amazing roll call of assessments, testimonials, and, recognitions; including Caray's having a statue of himself erected outside Wrigley Field before any Cubs player received a similar honor and sound bites of his broadcasts being pieced together to make it sound as if he were present calling the final outs of the Cubs long-awaited World Series victory in 2016. Of the numerous appreciations Zminda cites, we conclude with two that get closest to the heart of the matter. First, according to Bob Verdi, "Twenty years after Harry's death, he's remembered like it happened yesterday.... People still talk about him on the radio. People still imitate him. I think he is so beloved 20 years later not because he was great at what he did, but because as the years go by we realize how unique, how different he was. You will not replace him." And second, former major league catcher and broadcaster Tim McCarver who grew up listening to Caray broadcast Cardinals games, said, "There is a saying in our {sports broadcasting} business that people don't tune in to hear a broadcaster. If anyone came close to defying that, it was Harry."

Let's Play Two: The Legend of Mr. Cub, the Life of Ernie Banks

◆

RON RAPOPORT

◆

New York: Hachette Books, 2019. Cloth, 454 pages, ISBN: 9780316318631. Prologue. Epilogue, Acknowledgments, Sources, Index, 27 black & white photos between pages 246 and 247.

Every great biography consists of two complimentary elements: the external record of what the subject did and an internal assessment of who the subject was. No baseball biography does a better job of combining these dual requirements than *Let's Play Two: The Legend of Mr. Cub, The Life of Ernie Banks* by long-time *Chicago Sun-Times* sports columnist Ron Rapoport. The author clearly recognized the necessity of dealing with this dichotomy in regard to his famous subject and even used Bank's well-known catch-phrase in the title of the book to indicate both his imposing task and the nature of the superb work he has produced.

To his fans–and they were legion–Ernie Banks was not only a great player, but also the easiest superstar in all of sports to root for. Uncommonly accessible, preternaturally friendly, and eternally optimistic about a team that disappointed its fan base with the regularly of the changing of the seasons, Banks was too good to be true … except that, apparently, his sanguineness was authentic and indefatigable. It seemed that nothing was able to upset or disturb him, not even the Cubs' apparent willingness to trade him early in his career or the belief by some that he was too big to play shortstop and conversely (and ironically) that he was too slender to be the slugger that he proved himself to be. The greatest challenge to Banks' equanimity came from Leo Durocher, hired to manage the Cubs during the autumn of Banks' career in 1966, four years after Banks had shifted from short to first base because of bad knees. Despite, or perhaps because of, Mr. Cub's immense popularity, the tyrannical Durocher made life miserable for Banks; openly criticizing and demeaning him as over-the-hill, embarrassing him by pinch-hitting for him, and continually trying to find a replacement first baseman for him. To the amazement of all who witnessed such abuse, Banks, as the author painstakingly delineates, took it all in stride. The one possible instance of Banks defending himself came about when he supposedly warned his tormentor that it would be Durocher, not himself, who would be run out of town if their relationship did not improve.

In an amazing litany of examples of the Banks personality covered previously in the book, Rapoport explains that, unfortunately, the story of Banks warning Durocher was almost certainly apocryphal:

> In all probability, though, the story is only wishful thinking on the part of Cubs who heard and repeated it.
>
> Banks was, after all, the boy who never complained about the poverty and segregation in which he was raised.
>
> He was the dutiful son who, rather than argue with his mother, gave up playing football.
>
> He was the teenager whose friends called him Casper the Ghost because of his ability to melt away at the first sign of trouble.
>
> He was the batter who never questioned, or even looked back at, an umpire after a questionable call.
>
> He was the father who said, "I'm gone," got in his car, and drove away at the first sign of family discord.
>
> He was the black man who refused to engage in the great public struggle over race during the time of his greatest celebrity.
>
> He was the player who never once complained about wasting his finest seasons with a team that had no hope of winning a pennant.
>
> So it seems unlikely that Banks would change the habits of a lifetime, the very essence of who he was, at this stage of his life.

And, indeed, because Banks never did change in any appreciable way, one must conclude that what he presented to the public was not so much a winsome persona that could be put on and off but "the very essence" of the human being he instinctively willed himself to be.

Durocher turned out to be a major part of the Banks story, figuring so heavily as he did in Chicago's disastrous 1969 season, the year it all finally came together for a Cubs team loaded with talent but which still failed to produce a long-awaited pennant. Rapoport's analysis of the season is brilliant, and he lays the ultimate blame for the team's failure squarely on Durocher's shoulders; positing that the East Division Champion New York Mets' biggest advantage over the Cubs was having the beloved Gil Hodges, a calming inspirational father-figure of a manager in the dugout, rather than the bombastic dictatorial Durocher. Banks knew that the lost season was the team's best chance to win, and Rapoport describes him as being haunted for the rest of his life by his never having played in a World Series.

There were other crosses for Banks to bear, crosses which were beyond the ken of the vast majority of his adoring public. Although Banks was generous, requests for financial assistance from friends and family members kept him away from his home town of Dallas, Texas. Five of his brothers died "at an early age." He was married four times, each union ending in divorce, and the dissolutions drained him of his fortune. (Banks, whose rookie year was 1954, missed out on the explosion of values in the memorabilia market, and the relatively modest windfall resulting from the sale of most of his treasures went to Eloyce, his financially shrewd second wife.) Although he loved his three children, twins Joey and Jerry and daughter Jan, they were never as integral a part of his life as they could have been. He never prepared for life beyond baseball, and once his playing career ended, he became lost. Proposed business deals seemed to always fall through, and he never lasted long at a succession of sinecures.

Yet, he remained Mr. Cub, the face of the franchise, the upbeat Cubbie everyone wanted to meet, the guy with the photographic memory who never forgot a name, the humble celebrity who always deflected questions about himself and wanted to know about your family, your wife, your kids; and the somewhat sad picture of his final lonely years is brightened by the love and admiration showered on him by everyone who came into contact with him.

This focus on Ernie Banks as a person is not to suggest that Rapoport ignores Banks the Hall of Fame player. It's all there: Banks' stint with the Kansas City Monarchs, his fine rookie year integrating the Cubs with his double-play partner Gene Baker, his stupendous MVP seasons in 1957 and '58, and his 513 home runs (officially 512, but a bad call cheated him of one he clearly hit); not to mention Rapoport's riveting exploration of topics important to Banks' career, such as the Cubs ownership by W.P. Wrigley; the Cubs' ill-fated "College of Coaches" experiment; the origin, membership, and shenanigans of the original Bleacher Bums; and Banks' being awarded the Presidential Medal of Freedom. The game heroics and impressive personal statistics are all there, but they can also be found in other Banks biographies. Rapoport wanted to go deeper and get beyond the "one simplistic dimension" that has been the commonplace image of Ernie Banks and to deal with the "joyful, melancholy, humble, complicated, companionable, lonely man" who inhabited uniform number 14 of the Chicago Cubs for nineteen wonderful years. This, *Let's Play Two* does with empathy and panache and in so doing should stand as fittingly a tribute to its subject as the statue which graces the sidewalk outside the "Friendly Confines" … a nickname, by the way, bestowed on Wrigley Field by none other than Ernie Banks himself.

Lords of the Realm:
The Real History of Baseball

◆

John Helyar

◆

New York: Villard Books, 1994. Cloth, 576 pages, ISBN: 0-679-41197-6. Acknowledgments. Epilogue, Index, About the Author.

Comments: *Lords of the Realm* won the 12th CASEY Award in 1994, receiving two first-place votes and one second-place vote for a near-perfect score of 4, making it one of only five CASEY Award winners to receive such a score.

"This book is all you'll ever want to know about baseball the business, maybe a bit more than you'll want to know. It is the ultimate chronicle of the games behind the game, and John Helyar, an admitted fan, has a sure touch as play-by-play commentator" —Alan Abelson, *The New York Times Book Review*.

Helyar co-authored *Barbarians at the Gate: The Fall of RJR Nabisco*, which originated as a series of stories in the *Wall Street Journal*, for which Helyar and co-author Bryan Burrough won the Gerald Loeb Award for distinguished business journalism.

Of all the terrific books about baseball as a business, and there are, surprisingly, many of them to spend a contemplative afternoon or two reading; the clearly indispensable one is *Lords of the Realm: The Real History of Baseball* by *Wall Street Journal* reporter and co-author of the best-selling account of the hostile takeover of RJR Nabisco, *Barbarians at the Gate*, John Helyar. Thematically speaking, *Lords of the Realm* is an update of a similar Diamond Classic whose title it echoes, Harold Parrott's *The Lords of Baseball* (published in 1976), but it is also an expansion of the topic, as it covers the foibles, arrogance, and ineptitude of baseball ownership as a whole, instead of focusing on the ownership of one team, the Brooklyn-Los Angeles Dodgers, as in Parrott's book. More importantly, *Lords of the Realm* is a fascinating, most entertaining account of a watershed period in baseball history, the beginning of the free agency era when the balance of power shifted in favor of the players. The owners did not distinguish themselves in their attempts to prevent free agency and afterwards to accommodate themselves and their businesses to it when it was a fait accompli, and it is their maddening, self-destructive, and sometimes comic failures which form the heart of Helyar's hypnotic narrative.

The book begins with a brief history of the players' previous attempts to unionize and negotiate for better pay, benefits, and working conditions (beginning in 1885 with the formation of the Brotherhood of Professional Base Ball Players), and the meager gains they managed to eke out over the decades illustrate exactly the extent to which they operated basically as indentured servants. Two seemingly invincible things continually thwarted the players: the so-called "reserve clause," which as the owners interpreted it, bound every player to his team for one additional year after the expiration of his current contract for infinity, and the owners' paternalistic attitude towards the players. The owners typically believed that they took good care of the help and, furthermore, that the players should be grateful for getting paid anything at all for playing a children's game. The players could have been excused for not agreeing with the owners' views when they had to fight for every nickel. After Mickey Mantle won the AL Triple Crown in 1956, the club offered him the same salary as the year before (Mantle settled for a raise of $5,000).

Although no one foresaw the game-changing effects it would produce, the hiring in 1965 of Marvin Miller by the player's fairly irrelevant union, the Players Association, was the key event in the history of baseball labor relations.

If any one actor looms in importance above all the rest of the striking dramatis persona in the play Helyar reviews it is Miller. At first, the owners underestimated the soft-spoken, slightly-built Miller, as the advantages they held were numerous and the challenges he faced were daunting. But Miller was an experienced and tenacious labor negotiator with a biblical faith in the righteousness of the players' cause. In the brilliant way of neatly summarizing complex matters in a few words which he displays throughout the book, Helyar describes how Miller gradually won over the skeptical players and turned them into one of the most powerful unions in the country: "He listened to them. He educated them. And slowly he radicalized them."

As the players' union grew stronger, the response of the owners in their meetings was to rage against what they saw as Miller's and the players' audacity and ungratefulness and to insult Miller, often in racist terms (Walter O'Malley told the player relations committee's lead negotiator John Gaherin, "Tell that Jewish boy to go on back to Brooklyn"). Neither reaction, of course, was helpful or effective. Miller's first major victory came in 1969 when, at new Commissioner Bowie Kuhn's urging in order to prevent a players' strike, Gaherin caved on proposed improvements to the players' pension plan and gave Miller everything he'd asked for. As Gaherin, a seasoned labor negotiator who always favored compromise, knew it would, the surrender emboldened the opposition and forever changed the dynamics of power. In retrospect, from that point on, it was only a matter of time before an arbitrator (Peter Seitz, as it turned out) found that the reserve clause was invalid; meaning that the language in the basic agreement meant exactly what it said: that a team could renew the contract of a player who refused to sign his contract for one year and one year only, after which he would become free to sign with any other team. A number of contributing developments led to this decisive moment, of course, and Helyar covers them all in appropriate detail and with great understanding of the issues involved. The "test case" the owners' representatives knew was coming turned out to be Los Angeles Dodgers pitcher Andy Messersmith's playing the 1975 season without a signed contract. Nothing else in the book signals more clearly the litany of arrogance and inflexibility the owners as a group continually displayed than their position at this moment. Gaherin and Ed Fitzgerald, the Milwaukee Brewers chairman who would later replace Gaherin as PRC chief, were aware of the inevitability of the demise of the reserve clause and tried to get the owners to agree to negotiate its acceptance on terms favorable to them, but their appeals fell on deaf ears.

Seitz's decision shocked everyone. As expected, biding for free agents, such as pitcher Catfish Hunter, reached unheard of levels, player salaries across the board skyrocketed, and Cassandras such as the Cincinnati Reds GM Bob Howsam predicted the bankruptcy of baseball. The game survived, of course, and mostly because as salaries rose, so did revenue from broadcasting rights. Nevertheless, the owners, dead-set against revenue sharing which worked so well for the NBA and incapable of marketing their product as brilliantly as the NFL marketed its product, continued to be their own worst enemies. In addition to often ignoring the sensible advice of their own labor negotiators, they often butted heads with every Commissioner they hired (save one) and let their desire to field a championship team override any possibility of working for the common good of the industry. Atlanta Braves magnate Ted Turner squared up a BP straight ball when he said, "Gentlemen, we have the only legal monopoly in the country, and we're f**king it up."

In addition to Miller and the other chief negotiators (on both sides), it is the Commissioners who hold center stage. Helyar does a superb job of conveying the character of each man and of evaluating his effectiveness (or lack thereof) in steering baseball through the minefield of labor relations in the free agency era. His affectionate portrait of the learned, fair-minded Bart Giamatti is a stark contrast to that of his successor, the imperious Fay Vincent; yet, as presented by the author, the most significant successor to Judge Landis was Peter Ueberroth; a leader, as described by Helyar, as "pushing to get the maximum effort from people and maximum command for himself." The former head of the L.A. Olympics Committee, Ueberroth was actually not much of a baseball fan, and he lorded it over the lords, often berating them in meetings, to their faces, as "dumb" and "stupid." The owners put up with it because Ueberroth, who repeatedly insisted that the owners not be afraid to put a high value on what they had, was able to also maximize baseball profits; particularly by finally arranging highly lucrative deals for broadcasting rights. Most tellingly, he implemented collusion, the agreement among the owners not to sign free agents, under the guise of "fiscal responsibility." Other than the demise of the reserve clause by the Seitz ruling and the player strike of 1981, collusion is the most important event covered in the book. The owners stuck together for a while, but eventually collusion was struck down by arbitrators, and the illegal tactic wound up costing them dearly ($280 million in back salaries to unsigned players). And, true to form, the lords, unable to help themselves, went right back to their drunken sailor spending ways on free agents, lavishing huge sums of money on signing bonuses and long-term contracts; practices that have continued by and large to the present day

Helyar's chops as a first-rate reporter are constantly on display in *Lords of the Realm*, as he re-creates a long string of revealing phone conversations, meetings, and strategy sessions by both sides of the baseball industry; so that coupled with his expert analyses and ability to make complex issues understandable (such as the riff between large and small market teams), the book proves what insiders have known all along: that major league baseball is first and foremost a business. That the business has survived the people who "own" it, proves once again how great the business is also as a most entertaining game. The great irony of the book is that it debuted in the spring of 1994, the very year when baseball endured its eighth, longest, and most costly strike; a 232-day "play" stoppage which saw the cancellation of the final 50 regular-season games and, for the first time in history, the World Series. Everyone in the game, had they the desire to do so, had plenty of time to read Helyar's book.

Luckiest Man: The Life and Death of Lou Gehrig

Jonathan Eig

New York: Simon & Schuster, 2005. Cloth, 420 pages, ISBN: 0-7432-4591-1. Prologue. Epilogue, Appendix: Lou Gehrig's Career Statistics, Notes, Index, 37 black & white photos between pages 182 and 183. Other baseball books by the author: Opening Day: The Story of Jackie Robinson's First Season *(Simon & Schuster, 2007).*

Comments: *Luckiest Man* won the 23rd CASEY Award for Best Baseball Book of 2005. Eig won the 2024 Pulitzer Prize for Biography for *King: A Life*, his biography of Martin Luther King (Farrar, Straus and Giroux).

Cal Ripken, Jr.: "As my consecutive games streak grew, my curiosity about Lou Gehrig also grew and I wanted to learn more about him and what kind of person he was. Jonathan Eig's book, *Luckiest Man*, really helped me put all of the pieces together and gain a solid understanding of Lou, both on and off the field. I thought it was a wonderful book that provided insights about Lou, his amazing life and career."

Lou Gehrig, long considered to be an automatic choice for any all-time all-star team, could hardly have been described as an unsung or neglected historical figure. He played on baseball's most dominating team and formed, with Babe Ruth, the most potent, most feared one-two punch to ever unnerve pitchers. In the midst of dealing with the crippling disease (amyotrophic lateral sclerosis: ALS) that killed him and came to bear his name, he delivered the game's most famous speech. After his death, several fine writers penned biographies of him, including Paul Gallico, Frank Graham, and Ray Robinson, and he was the subject of what most fans regard as the greatest baseball movie ever filmed. Yet, until Jonathan Eig penned *Luckiest Man*, a huge part, perhaps the most important part, of the man's story remained basically untold.

The surpassing irony of the Gehrig story derives from Gehrig's status as the "Iron Horse," a nickname that captured his Adonis-like physique and exceptional strength and a testament to the spirit, work ethic, and endurance that enabled him to set the consecutive games-played record which once seemed unbreakable. Gehrig was the last ballplayer anyone thought would be brought low by disease, especially one like ALS which attacks the muscles and slowly renders one unable to perform even the simplest of motor tasks; including, eventually, involuntary ones, such as breathing. It seemed the height of cruelty for Gehrig to be afflicted by such a devastating malady which not only prematurely ended his playing career, but also snuffed out his very existence in the prime of life. In covering the events of the subject's heyday, Eig does such a marvelous job of portraying the aptness of the Iron Horse nickname that the reader effortlessly grasps the piteous physical degradation that Gehrig underwent, in addition to the immense waste and loss his death represented to so many people.

Eig opens the book with a "Prologue" that briefly presents the most important event in Gehrig's life: the moment when he is about to say a few words on Lou Gehrig Appreciation Day at Yankee Stadium, when the thousands of fans in attendance realize the great man is saying farewell. Eig sets the dramatic scene and then stops to begin the story at the beginning. This ploy is a common enough writing device but one especially effective here since the reader knows that all of the following pages will lead back to this moment, when Gehrig reveals more plainly than at any other time in his life his admirable character and courage by delivering "one of the saddest and strongest messages an American audience had ever heard." An indication of the most important contribution that *Luckiest Man* makes to the Gehrig canon is embedded in the book's subtitle, "The Life and Death of Lou Gehrig."

One of the most surprising elements of Eig's account of Gehrig's sad demise is the fact that, when he was stricken with it, ALS was not a well-known disease, even among those in the medical community. That's the main reason everyone, and especially Gehrig himself, was so baffled by his sudden physical decline. It was in 1938, when Gehrig was not quite 35 years old, that he began to show symptoms of the disease. He tired easily, his hands blistered quickly, and he became clumsy, once tripping while rounding first base and being tagged out before he could regain his feet. One doctor thought he had gall bladder problems. Many people concluded that he was simply showing the natural signs of slowing down due to age. Some even criticized the big first baseman for maintaining his playing streak, interpreting exhaustion as the culprit. Gehrig chalked up his dismal early season batting merely to a slump which all hitters are susceptible to, and his response was to work harder. He constantly changed bats and stances as the season wore on and somehow recovered enough to have a decent year (.295 with 29 homers and 114 RBI) but one considerably less spectacular than fans were accustomed to him producing.

Even after it became clear the next spring that something was very seriously wrong with Gehrig, even after he took himself out of the starting lineup in Detroit after having played 2,130 consecutive games—something that Yankees manager Joe McCarthy who loved and revered Gehrig refused to do unilaterally—his condition remained undiagnosed. Although he was not in any pain, Gehrig was losing weight and strength and coordination, especially is his extremities; and he remained with the team but on the bench. The last game Gehrig played was an exhibition against the Yankees farm club in Kansas City on June 12, 1939, and he turned in a pitiful performance: grounding out weakly to second, making two unassigned errors, and literally being knocked down while fielding a line drive. The next day he flew to Rochester, Minnesota, to be examined by specialists at the Mayo Clinic.

It didn't take long for the neurological experts there, particularly Dr. Henry W.

Woltman, to diagnose ALS, but this knowledge hardly cleared up the situation; and as Eig explains, it's not certain that the Mayo doctors were completely honest with him about the diagnosis being a virtual death sentence. If Gehrig was aware of the truth, he choose, as Eig's account of his activities and public statements during the remainder of his life reveal ... to ignore it, to strictly follow all doctors' orders, to try any and every suggested remedy, to live as normal and as productive a life as possible, to cherish every moment with his loved ones (especially his wife Eleanor), to reject pity and expressions of sympathy, and, above all, to hope against hope. For an amazingly long time the public and the press as well were in the dark. Jimmy Powers of the *Daily News* created a furor and inspired the ire of Gehrig when he blamed the Yankees' mid-summer tailspin on Gehrig's having possibly transmitted poliomyelitis to teammates; a not unreasonable supposition except for the fact that Gehrig had ALS (not contagious), not the infantile form of polio. (Gehrig sued, and the newspaper settled out of court for $17,500). For a time, only Eleanor, Yankees GM Ed Barrow, and family friend Fred Lieb knew that Gehrig's days were numbered. By the time Lou made the famous speech on July 4, 1939, everyone knew. Eig draws such an admirable portrait of Gehrig that any reader with the slightest feeling for humanity will get a lump in his throat as he vicariously experiences the conclusion of that scene: Gehrig's recitation of all the blessings he has to be thankful for in the face of his impending doom.

While the detailed, highly nuanced account of Gehrig's demise is the major contribution of *Luckiest Man*, the book also supersedes all previous biographies in its treatment of other facets of the story. Eig demonstrates a keen understanding of the elements that combined to make Gehrig the special individual he was: Gehrig's love of and reliance on physicality from boyhood onwards (a pudgy kid called "Fatty," he learned early that success in games brings acceptance); his almost excessive devotion to his doting German mother, Christina, whose jealousy served to prolong his bachelorhood (before he could marry Eleanor Twitchell he had to first divorce his mother!); his counter-intuitive lack of confidence which allowed the Yankees to consistently underpay him; and his lack of "color": a euphemism for the basic decency of a humble superstar who had no serious vices despite manifold opportunities to develop and exercise them.

There was also Gehrig's relationship with Babe Ruth, to whom Gehrig was compared from the beginning. Before the mythical national championship game between Gehrig's NY City Commerce High and Chicago's Lane Tech, the press referred to him as the "Babe Ruth of the high schools." Paul Krichell, the scout who signed Gehrig out of Columbia University, told the Yankees brass that he'd discovered "the next Babe Ruth." And Eig himself ... he calls Gehrig "Babe Ruth without the bad habits." True to his character, Gehrig was content to play second fiddle to the Bambino. He knew Ruth was king of the majestic, soaring home run (his own were usually line drives), so he made driving in runs his trademark. A true if subdued friendship existed between the two greats until something happened to ruin it. Eig speculates that it may have been a one-night stand, or something close to it, between Ruth and Eleanor on a barnstorming voyage to Japan. It's as good a guess as any other.

The alert reader is also surprised to discern just how often fate intervened to keep Gehrig's cap from becoming too small for his head, as if there was really any danger of that happening. Before he was signed by the Yankees, the Giants gave him a tryout but the venerable John McGraw was unimpressed. The day after a serious beaning in a 1934 exhibition game, Gehrig tripled three times against Washington in five innings, but the game was rained out. That same year he won the American League Triple Crown yet finished *fifth* in the MVP Award voting! The day he hit four home runs in one game and had a chance at a fifth, his feat was relegated to "also happened" status in the papers because the announcement of McGraw's retirement captured all the headlines. He was rejected by Hollywood for the role of Tarzan because he was too muscular. And after the Yankees' cynosure, Babe Ruth, retired, Gehrig reigned as the team's kingpin for one year before a glamorous rookie sensation named Joe DiMaggio arrived to soak up all the attention and adulation.

There was never any dispute concerning the player's greatness on the diamond. What Eig does in *Luckiest Man* is present the man in all his depth and essential goodness and show, as sports supposedly do, how the "bad break" he alluded to in his famous speech did not develop so much as reveal his character. The story, in Eig's telling, amounts to baseball's equivalent of the most affecting Elizabethan tragedy; a tale of genuine heroism and cathartic triumph over great adversity sans the ugliness of jealousy, revenge, and murder.

Mr. Wrigley's Ball Club: Chicago and the Cubs During the Jazz Age

Roberts Ehrgott

Lincoln: University of Nebraska Press, 2013. Cloth, 485 pages, ISBN: 978-0-8032-6478-6. Acknowledgments. Notes, Additional Source Comments, Bibliography, Index, 24 black & white photos between pages 226 and 227.

    Comments: The cover photo depicts the Cubs' version of "Murderers' Row," from left: Rogers Hornsby, Hack Wilson, Kiki Cuyler, and Riggs Stephenson.

    Most appearances to the contrary, and despite an excruciatingly long period of their having wandered as forlorn also-rans in the baseball wasteland, the Chicago Cubs have not always been losers. As winners of four pennants and two World Championships in five years (1906–1910), the Tinker-to-Evers-to Chance Cubs were, in fact, the National League's first dynasty. And more to the point of this essay, they rose again in the late 1920s under the ownership of chewing gum magnate William Wrigley, Jr., to establish themselves, if not as a second dynasty, as a highly competitive and exceedingly mesmerizing force to be reckoned with. As heavy drinkers, carousers, gamblers, and fierce battlers between the lines, the Cubs reflected the chaotic city they represented; one growing like an adolescent bursting out of recently-purchased jeans, combatting rampant crime and corruption on a daily basis, and straining always to overcome its inferiority complex as the nation's "Second City." Few baseball books can equal the fascinating depiction of the social, political, and cultural backdrop against which these Cubs struggled, and Roberts Ehrgott captures it all brilliantly in *Mr. Wrigley's Ball Club: Chicago & the Cubs during the Jazz Age*.

    Wrigley bought the Chicago Cubs because he was a baseball fan, not because he wanted or needed to make money on the team. What he wanted from the Cubs was personal and civic satisfaction in the form of championship teams. To that end he spent freely; laying out whatever sums were needed to acquire desired talent and paying his beloved players handsomely. (Acquiring Rogers Hornsby under his watch cost the Cubs five players and $135,000, more cash than it took for the Yankees to wrench Babe Ruth away from the Boston Red Sox; making it, as Ehrgott points out,

the biggest deal in baseball history). The Cubs enjoyed the best of everything (in uniforms, travel, etc.), and Wrigley even bought and developed an island off the coast of California to serve as the team's spring training tropical paradise.

The smartest move Wrigley made in the pursuit of his goal was the hiring of Bill Veeck, Sr., to serve as his General Manager and then getting and pretty much staying out of the way to allow Veeck an unfettered hand in running the ballclub. Bill Veeck, Jr., of midget-at-the-bat and exploding scoreboards notoriety, became far more famous than his father, so one of the biggest contributions of Ehrgott's history is its demonstration that the father was just as capable and innovative a baseball executive as the son, if not as flashy a showman. Veeck pere was responsible for numerous improvements and advances. Under his leadership the competing groups of low lifes and thugs who ran an anarchic, shake-down ushering system were replaced by the exquisitely uniformed Andy Frain professionals; Ladies Days, conferring free admission, were taken to a whole new level, swelled team attendance figures, and resulted in the installation of Wrigley Field's upper deck; and the Cubs not only committed to radio broadcasts of their home games when most teams were still suspicious of the practice, they allowed multiple stations the privilege. More importantly, Veeck recognized the managerial abilities of Joe McCarthy, a man with no major league experience when Veeck brought him to Chicago for the 1926 season from Louisville, where he had been wielding the reins of the American Association Colonels. It didn't take long for the hard-drinking Grover Cleveland Alexander, nearing the end of his great pitching career, to wear out his welcome with McCarthy, a no-nonsense manager of unassailable integrity. The released Alexander's parting shot was to call McCarthy "a busher," but Wrigley breathed a sigh of relief, telegramming Marse Joe, "Congratulations. For years I've been looking for a manager with the nerve to do this."

Wrigley's finally scratching his itch to acquire Hornsby, his most intrusive meddling into the affairs of the team, turned out to be a mixed blessing. The winner of six consecutive batting titles with the St. Louis Cardinals (three of them produced with averages over .400), Hornsby had the reputation of being a troublemaker. No player of his stature had ever been such a rolling stone as he, as the Cubs were his fourth different team in four years. Nevertheless, as Ehrgott says repeatedly, Hornsby gave the Cubs a "Murderer's Row" batting lineup of Hornsby, Hack Wilson, Kiki Cuyler, and Riggs Stephenson. (This core was ably supplemented by other sweet swingers, such as first baseman Charlie Grimm, infielder Woody English, and catcher Gabby Hartnett, the "original Mr. Cub.") Hornsby immediately had his last great year, batting .380 with 39 homers and 149 RBI to win the NL MVP Award and help lead the Cubs to the 1929 NL pennant, and he was a model citizen that year. Ehrgott sums up Hornsby's honeymoon with the team by writing, "The Rajah was having a hard time doing anything wrong." The problems started the next year, with Hornsby, who had World Series-winning managerial experience with the Cards, lurking in the background as Wrigley's favorite to succeed McCarthy.

While McCarthy did a great job in turning the Cubs into pennant winners in three short years, nothing short of a World Championship was going to save his job. He was out-managed by the venerable Connie Mack in the 1929 Series, as the Philadelphia

A's won in five game. The fourth game, in particular, was a historic disaster, the Cubs blowing an 8–0 lead when the A' scored 10 times in the seventh inning; aided by two fly balls lost in the sun by Hack Wilson. McCarthy's fate was sealed, when the Cubs, decimated with injuries, failed to defend their pennant the next year, after leading the league for most of the summer. McCarthy resigned with four games left in the season and moved to the New York Yankees where he won eight pennants and seven World Series. Hornsby replaced him but could not deliver Mr. Wrigley even a NL pennant. Ninety-seven games into the 1932 season, Charlie Grimm took over from Hornsby and guided the team to their second pennant in four years. Worse, Hornsby, an inveterate bettor on the horses, became embroiled in a gambling contretemps involving loans from his own players. Here again, Veeck was more than up to the task, and his shrewd handling of the matter not only greased Hornsby's non-costly departure, but also protected the Cubs, still operating in the shadows of the Black Sox scandal, from the potentially-disastrous inquiries of the sometimes severe Judge Landis. Ehrgott's low-key but subtly penetrating explanation of the sticky mess is a joy to read. As is other sensational matters covered in the book, such as the hi-jinks of White Sox braggart and publicity hound Art Shires, the Southsiders only answer to the glittering Cubs cynosures absorbing all the public's attention during this period; the ire of Babe Ruth directed at the Cubs during the 1932 World Series over the Cubs' voting former Yankee Mark Koenig only a half share of their Series money; and the hotel room shooting of shortstop Billy Jurges by a female fan. Not nearly as well-known as the Eddie Waikus shooting, the Jurges assault is a more salacious and mysterious affair, involving a cache of purloined love letters, black mail attempts, and indications that outfielder Cuyler, a married man, was also, perhaps primarily, involved.

Among the players, Hack Wilson is the star of stars in *Mr. Wrigley's Ball Club*. His heroics, more often than those of any of the other players, were what repeatedly launched the flights of cheap straw boaters onto the diamond of Wrigley Field and inspired the hordes of street urchins to chase Wilson to the closest watering hole after Cubs' victories. Wilson's monolithic 56-homer, 190-RBI season in 1930 was not realistically repeatable, and it was his infatuation with the bottle and his love of the night life, more than the decline of his game, that caused a parting of the ways. He was only one of several traded or released Cubbies who came back to haunt the team. Ehrgott does not neglect the lesser but still important role players either; men such as Hack's equally thirsty running mate, pitcher Perce "Pat" Malone; matinee idol outfielder Cliff Heathcote, doted on by the Ladies Days' mobs who often made up large parts of the SRO roped-off outfield crowds; and the banjo-playing, master mimic, German-accented (and self-styled "Der Kaptink") Charlie Grimm. (Ehrgott especially delights in drawing an amusing portrait of the multi-faceted Grimm.)

Above all, readers will enjoy the writing here, always lively and frequently inventive–Ehrgott refers to "the stockyard cheer," Chicago's equivalent of the Bronx cheer–as well as the author's painstaking efforts to re-create the times and local color aspects of the great city the Cubs called home. No incident better characterizes the tenor of the prohibition era in Chicago than Gabby Hartnett's socializing with gangster Al Capone and son, seated in Comiskey Park box seats, prior to a Cubs-White Sox inter-city post-season exhibition game. Questioned about this breech of baseball decorum by Landis, Hartnett supposedly replied, "I go to his place of business, Judge; why shouldn't he come to mine?" Ehrgott calls it "the least of the controversies that dogged the Cub franchise in the early 1930s."

The Cubs never won a World Championship for Mr. Wrigley, who died in his sleep near the end of January 1932. Nor did they win one for his son, Philip K. Wrigley, who retained ownership of the team solely out of "filial respect." Whether the family provided more pleasure to the public via the Cubs or its line of chewing gums may be a debatable matter to some, but surely not to the author nor to those who read his magnificent history.

Moneyball: The Art of Winning an Unfair Game

◆

Michael Lewis

◆

New York: W.W. Norton, 2003. Cloth, 288 pages, ISBN: 0-393-05765-8. Preface. Epilogue: The Badger, Acknowledgments.

Comments: *Moneyball* won the CASEY Award for Best Baseball Book of 2003. Former L.A. Dodger Wes Parker, the first baseman on Rawlings' All-Time Gold Glove Team, was a CASEY Award judge who said: "I ranked *Moneyball* first even though I was prepared not to like it. I hate the title and I hate the cover. But I loved the writing and the information and it held me throughout. Every page had something of interest and was well presented so that you felt a story line leading to some conclusion. And I learned, as all readers of this book will, a lot about the inner workings of baseball at the big league level."

The book was the basis of a film of the same name made by Columbia Pictures and starring Brad Pitt as Oakland A's General Manager Billy Beane. It premiered at the 2011 Toronto International Film Festival and was released September 23, 2011. It was nominated for six Academy Awards, including Best Picture, Best Adapted Screenplay, Best Actor (Pitt), and Best Supporting Actor (Jonah Hill who portrays Peter Brand, a character partially based on Beane's Assistant GM Paul DePodesta). The film grossed $110.2 million on a budget of $50 million.

At the turn of the century, Major League Baseball Commissioner Bud Selig believed, as did most people, that the huge disparity in their war chests made it impossible for poorer teams to compete with their richer counterparts. This despite the fact that the Oakland Athletics, baseball's second-poorest team, was in the process of routinely winning far more games than teams which considerably outspent them on players. Former Wall Street insider and financial writer Michael Lewis didn't buy Selig's theory and set out to discover how the A's, an "aberration" in Selig's opinion, were capable on shoe-string budgets of making the playoffs three years in a row (2000–2002) while winning two divisional titles. What Lewis found was that Oakland's front office, under the outlier leadership of General Manager Billy Beane, were playing an entirely different game than everyone else; a game that relied on statistical facts instead of opinion in player evaluations

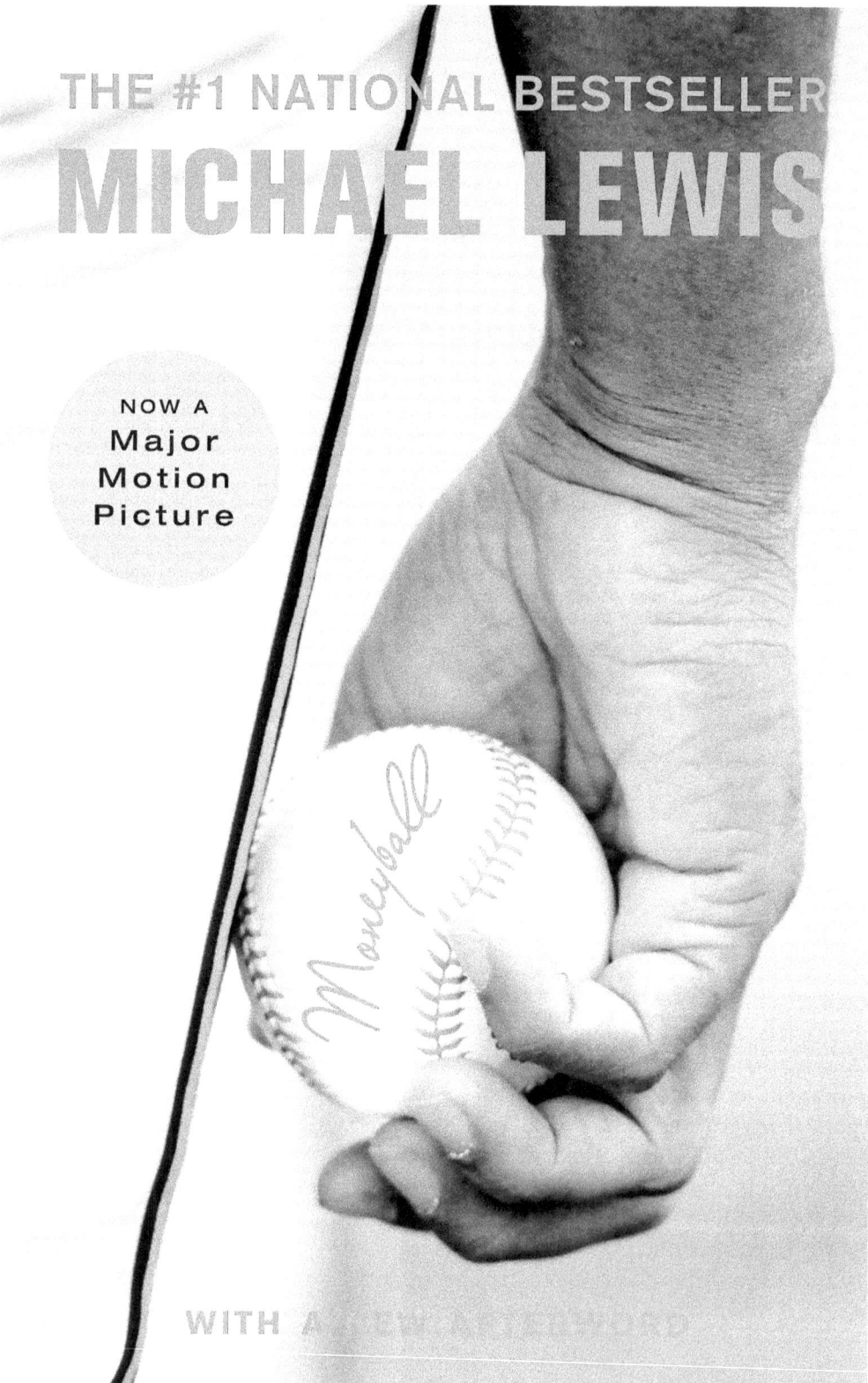

and which sought, out of necessity, to maximize the value of every dollar expended. Lewis named this radical approach "Moneyball," and his book under that title became not only the most interesting baseball book of 2003, but also the most influential baseball book in recent memory; eventually spinning off a major motion picture.

Moneyball begins with and centers around Billy Beane for at least three reasons: (1) he is the unquestioned leader of the A's organization whose trust Lewis needed in order to gain the total access the book demonstrates he enjoyed; (2) Beane is one of modern baseball's most original and unforgettable characters; and (3) Beane's own experience as a five-tool first-round draft pick of the New York Mets caused him to reject everything he thought he'd known about baseball and prepared him to accept the anti-establishment precepts encapsulated by the term "Moneyball." As Lewis explains in the riveting first chapter ("The Curse of Talent"), high school outfield sensation Billy Beane was universally considered to be a can't-miss prospect, one the Mets and other organizations favored over other well-thought-of prospects, such as Darryl Strawberry. Scouts were influenced by Beane's obvious talents, his statuesque physique, his charm, his foot speed which enabled him to outrace black first-round prospects, and his "good face" ... that square-jawed, chiseled look that scouts believe identifies a boy destined to become a star major leaguer.

This adherence to appearances and potentialities blinded many scouts to warning signs, such as a two hundred-point drop in Beane's senior year batting average from that of his junior year, his expressed preference for college over pro ball, and his violent intolerance of the slightest failure. Beane did play in the big leagues and he did on occasion display amazing physical ability, but his six-year four-team career which ended with a 37-game stint with the A's was a decided bust (his career average was .219 with an OPS of .247). Nevertheless, Beane did the unthinkable by quitting, voluntarily hanging up his spikes to take a job as a scout with the A's; a decision that reversed the course of his life, as he came under the tutelage of Oakland GM Sandy Alderson, a hard-nosed ex-Marine, who had already begun the process of overhauling the organization to operate under the principles of sabermetrics, as advanced by people such as Eric Walker and Bill James. Alderson perceived the incongruity of baseball teams' most important financial decisions (those involving player acquisitions) being made not by those at the top but by middle management (the manager in the dugout), and he was one of the first GMs to recognize the importance of walks and on-base percentage. Beane absorbed these views like a sponge and quickly became Alderson's heir apparent. As Alderson put it, "What Billy figured out at some point is that he wanted to be me more than he wanted to be Jose Canseco."

The entirety of *Moneyball* is an in-depth explanation of how Beane and the A's became the first team to make the philosophical transition to relying on statistical information instead of scouting opinion that shortly thereafter swept through the game and which continues to this day. Lewis explains that this transition was inevitable because of two things that happened in the late 1970s: the radical advances in computer technology which made analyzing vast amounts of baseball data easier and the huge increase in baseball salaries. As Beane put it, all of baseball but especially the poor A's could no longer afford to be satisfied with two successes out of 50 drafted players, not when the mistakes were becoming so expensive to make (the same rationale applied to the signing of free agents). However, the most dramatic playing out of the transition occurs in the multi-chapter account of the A's 2002 draft which Lewis was allowed to sit in on. The previous year's draft was the final one controlled by Oakland's scouts; through Lewis's superb reporting we witness Beane's wrenching control of the 2002 draft from the scouts who have traditionally been in charge. Supremely confident, passionate, and so intense that he cannot bear to watch his own team play the games, Beane is more dictator than teacher or facilitator, and the draft has the mood of a public execution for the scouts who cling to their old ways and viewpoints in contrast to those Beane has about lost patience in trying to get them to adopt. The discussions about players and prospects, much of it conducted in scouting and player evaluation jargon, is fascinating, and we witness a changing of the guard as it becomes clear that Beane, his assistant GM Paul DePodesta (a computer wizard), and their converts are fully committed to drafting a lineup of players not highly regarded at all by the veteran scouts in the room; the termination of some of whom, including head scout Grady Fusin, is imminent.

The player who best represents this brain change is University of Alabama catcher Jeremy Brown. The scouts laughingly disdain him because of his "bad body" (meaning he's overweight and fat-assed) and don't consider him a prospect at all, despite DePodesta pointing out that he holds the SEC career record for hits (300) and walks (200). They are incredulous when they realize that Beane not only intends to draft Brown but to take him with one of the A's' seven first-round picks, many accumulated in trades. Beane mockingly accuses the demurring scouts of wanting to "sell jeans" (i.e., draft players who *look* good in their uniforms), and he reminds them that none of them wanted to draft star pitcher Barry Zito either because he threw only 88 MPH. The A's do draft Brown and because the scouts of other teams also hold Brown in such low esteem, the A's sign him for a bonus ridiculously lower than the normal "slot price." Brown also represents another lesson that Beane and his ilk have learned by applying the laws of Moneyball: that college players are significantly better risks than high schoolers because the former have much more of a statistical record to go on.

Realizing that the education of Billy Beane and the success of the low budget Oakland A's is merely the climax of the story he'd fallen in love with, Lewis returns to the modern beginning of the search for provable baseball knowledge, to the great awakening inaugurated by the greatest of sabermetricians, Bill James.

His account of James' career and the way his insights have influenced the game and inspired others to follow him in the search for new ways to understand and measure baseball performance is brilliant and will elucidate the subject even for those familiar with the bearded Kansan wonder. This expounding of the sabermetrics evolution fans out in both directions; covering James predecessors such as Henry Chadwick, Allan Roth, and Earnshaw Cook, as well as the contributions of contemporaries and descendants, such as Carl Morris, Eddie Epstein, Dick Cramer, Pete Palmer, James J. Skipper, Craig Wright, Rob Neyer, and Voros McCracken. Many of Lewis' comments about James are typical of his uncanny ability to get at the heart of things in striking, memorable statements. While explaining James' humble beginnings and his dedication in the face of anonymity, exemplified by his selling 75 copies of the first, mimeographed, self-published *Baseball Abstract*, he writes: "No author has ever been so energized by so little."

As Lewis follows the A's through the 2002 season, he continues to explain other sabermetric advances, such as Range Factor (an attempt to measure fielding performance) and Defense Independent Pitching (an attempt to strip luck out of pitching performances) and to illustrate the basic goal of Moneyball: finding players grossly undervalued by other teams and acquiring them for grossly small amounts of mullah. Chapters on DH-1B Scott Hatteberg (an on-base machine) and physically unimposing pitcher Chad Bradford whose unorthodox delivery befuddles hitters function as amazing examples of how Beane and DePodesta employed their Moneyball strategies to perfection. Armed with the Moneyball advantage, a high stakes gambler's coolness, and a ruthless desire to win, Beane shows himself to be the shrewdest trader of baseball players since Branch Rickey. Somehow Lewis gives us the workings of several Beane trades ... the preliminary in-house discussions but also the actual phone conversations between Beane and the GMs he fleeces ... that help propel the A's toward a record-setting second half surge. These scenes also make the reader wonder why other GMs didn't slam the phone down as soon as they realized Billy Beane of the Oakland A's was the person on the other end of the call.

Moneyball ends with an Epilogue that catches up with Jeremy Brown. Lewis reports that after he turned in an outstanding rookie pro season at high Single-A Visalia of the California League, Brown received as a reward an invitation to play in the fall Arizona Instructional League. Lewis recounts one particular at bat there in great detail. The slow-footed Brown cracks a long one that he thinks even he can leg out for a triple, but he loses his balance and flops onto his back between first and second. He gets to his feet and scrambles back to first while his teammates laugh good-naturedly. He can jog around the bases; he's hit the ball out of the park. The scene is presented as a validation of Beane's vision for the player; the succeeding reality was a bit less triumphant. Brown did make the major leagues, and he batted .300. He knocked out three hits in ten at bats before retiring. No matter. The concepts of Moneyball have been adopted throughout major league baseball. The Oakland A's continue, to this day, to compete with less, and *Moneyball*: *The Art of Winning an Unfair Game* remains one of the most enlightening and engrossing reads in modern baseball literature.

Mover & Shaker: Walter O'Malley, the Dodgers, & Baseball's Westward Expansion

◆

ANDY MCCUE

◆

Lincoln: University of Nebraska Press, 2014. Cloth, 468 pages, ISBN: 978-0-8032-4508-2. Acknowledgments, Introduction: Hitler, Stalin, Walter O'Malley. Source Acknowledgments, Notes, Bibliography, Index, Illustrations: Table 1. Dodger attendance in the Walter O'Malley Years, Figure 1. Declining attendance as a percentage of league totals, Table 2. Dodgers versus Braves, Table 3. Negotiating with the Coliseum. Other baseball books by the author: Baseball by the Books: A Complete History and Bibliography of Baseball Fiction *(Wm. C. Brown, 1991) and* Stumbling Around the Bases: The American League's Mismanagement in the Expansion Era *(University of Nebraska Press, 2022).*

Comments: *Mover & Shaker* won the 2015 Seymour Medal and was a finalist for the CASEY Award. The striking portrait of O'Malley (cigar jutting from the corner of his mouth) on the book's cover is by Boris Chaliapin.

Walter F. O'Malley, the owner of the Brooklyn-Los Angeles Dodgers has been one of the most villainized figures in baseball history. To this day bar room pundits take perverse pleasure in repeating the story that two prominent Brooklyn writers found themselves in agreement that the three worst human beings to ever live were Hitler, Stalin, and O'Malley. Supposedly amusing and indicative of the angst felt by abandoned Brooklyn Dodgers fans, the simplistic postulation is absurd; as Andy McCue, author of *Mover & Shaker: Walter O'Malley, the Dodgers, & Baseball's Westward Expansion*, points out, writing in the book's Introduction: "By most recent accounting, Adolf Hitler killed 11 million people and Joseph Stalin murdered 6 million. O'Malley moved a baseball team." In this one sentence McCue sets an adult tone, indicating that in the following pages he would finally provide what the subject richly deserved and had long been bereft of: a balanced biography that with impressive intellectual dexterity deals with the extreme complexity, characteristic of both the subject himself and the momentous events which he greatly influenced.

Atypically, McCue devotes few words to O'Malley's NYC youth (spent in the

MOVER & SHAKER
Walter O'Malley, the Dodgers, & Baseball's Westward Expansion

Andy McCue

Bronx and Queens), described as "that of a pretty normal suburban boy." This short shrift is due perhaps to a lack of available information but more to the fact that O'Malley grew up fast. At the age of sixteen he was sent away to Culver Military Academy in Indiana to shield him from the charges of corruption dogging his father, Edwin, the Commissioner of Public Markets in New York City. While an average student, O'Malley began at Culver to demonstrate his ability to lead people. Not qualified for acceptance to Princeton or Cornell, he settled for admission to the University of Pennsylvania. There he increased his involvement in social and political activities and developed his ability "to bring people to his point of view" which colleagues and competitors would later describe as "legendary." Notably, it is in covering O'Malley's academic career that McCue first deals with the man's life-long "habit of improving on the facts"; e.g., O'Malley was not, as he claimed, the valedictorian of his class or an engineering major (in fact, he didn't even take one engineering class).

Despite his "mixed academic career," O'Malley was intelligent, persuasive, energetic, bold, and ambitious, and these traits practically leap off the page in the course of McCue's narration. After graduating from Penn, O'Malley entered Columbia Law School but withdrew because of his father's slide into bankruptcy. He instead obtained his law degree by taking night classes at Fordham. Thereafter, he engaged in a number of business ventures, even opening for a short time the W.F. O'Malley Engineering Company, but he eventually resigned himself to a career as a lawyer. His big break came when he was taken under the wing of George V. McLaughlin, former police commissioner and president of the Brooklyn Trust Company. McLaughlin hired O'Malley to deal with many of the bank's problem loans, and O'Malley obtained partial ownership in several businesses by shrewdly waiving his fees for stock in those companies. Thus, it was McLaughlin who helped O'Malley "go from struggling young lawyer to Brooklyn pillar and financial success." McCue covers all of this, the first part of O'Malley's life, in the brief first chapter (25 pages); spending the remaining 332 pages of the book on the subject's involvement with the Dodgers.

McLaughlin was also the conduit through which O'Malley became involved with the Dodgers. In the 1930s the Dodgers were heavily in debt to McLaughlin's bank and, worse, not a profitable business. To help rectify this situation, capable baseball executives were lured to run the team, first Larry McPhail and then Branch Rickey. Through McLaughlin, O'Malley became the team's legal counsel and an inside man to watch over the bank's interests. For years a 50/50 ownership split between the Ebbets and McKeever families had ensured deadlock and stymied resolutions of any problems facing the ballclub; a situation which, combined with the team's money problems, necessitated a sale of the club. Many offers were made, but Rickey, O'Malley, and John L. Smith, president of the Pfizer Chemical Company, formed a partnership to buy the ballclub with Rickey obtaining majority ownership. Rickey ran the team, handling all baseball matters; Smith watched over the finances and tried to keep expenses down; and O'Malley headed business operations. This partnership not only turned the Dodgers into a winning team but a profitable business as well. Within a decade, O'Malley bought out Rickey so that by the end of 1950 he was in complete control of the Brooklyn Dodgers (it was not until 1957 that he owned the team outright). The maneuvers and transactions involved in this dramatic transition were quite complicated, but fortunately McCue is able to convey the complexity involved without burying the reader under a mountain of detail.

Unlike most owners, O'Malley had only a mild interest in baseball. He viewed the Dodgers as a business and a winning ballclub as the means to profitability. To that end, he hired the best people he could find, notably GM Buzzie Bavasi, and let them run the baseball side of the operation; while he focused on the business side, especially the marketing of the product. The volcano in the backyard was always Ebbets Field and its increasing inadequacy. Even while he was still a partner of Rickey's, O'Malley recognized the problem and began to look for possible solutions. Thus, the efforts to find a new home for the Dodgers in New York (if not Brooklyn) and the move to Los Angeles, which turned out to be the solution to the problem, make up the bulk of the book, as they represent the two critical periods in the life of the subject.

As Neil Sullivan demonstrated in his excellent book *The Dodgers Move West* (which McCue gratefully acknowledges), O'Malley really did have a huge problem on his hands, and he really did make every effort to keep the Dodgers in New York. Small and expensive to maintain, Ebbets Field itself was obsolete. The neighborhood, the borough itself, and attendance were all in decline. Contributing to the latter was the advent of television and a lack of parking exacerbated by the increasing reliance of Americans on travel by auto. An even bigger obstacle was the indifference of the NY City political class and the hostility of Robert Moses, the NYC Planning Commissioner (among other positions of power he held) without whose support practically no projects as big as a major league ballpark ever broke ground. O'Malley needed help acquiring land through the public domain process, and Moses, who at best suggested sites that he knew O'Malley would reject, was not interested in using public tax money for a project he believed would benefit mostly private interests (O'Malley's). As McCue points out, not only did O'Malley do his best to work with Moses, he gave anyone paying attention clear signs that he felt he was being forced to take his business elsewhere: by initiating discussions with Los Angeles city officials as early as 1953 about a move to the West Coast; by announcing in August of 1955 that the Dodgers would play seven games in 1956 at Roosevelt Stadium in Jersey City, New Jersey; by selling Ebbets Field in October of 1956 to a developer; by purchasing in early 1957 the PCL Los Angeles franchise and the ballpark the Angels played in, the L.A. Wrigley Field, from the Chicago Cubs; and by announcing that 1957 would be the last season the Dodgers would play at Ebbets.

McCue acknowledges that there was an element in all of this of playing one side against the other in order to get a better deal; yet it's reasonable to conclude that, whether or not it was fair, it was a necessary ploy for O'Malley to use, as he could not get a solid commitment from either New York or Los Angeles until the last minute. While Moses stonewalled him in New York, O'Malley learned much to his dismay that he was facing some serious opposition in L.A. as well and that several pro–Dodgers Los Angeles officials had made him promises which they were not able to keep. The commitment he desperately needed finally came on October 7, 1957, when the L.A. city council approved a deal acceptable to both parties. O'Malley immediately sent city councilman Norris Poulson a telegram, saying, "Get your wheel barrow and shovel. Will see you at Chavez Ravine."

O'Malley's troubles were far from over though, as the battle to overcome an almost endless series of roadblocks made the acquisition of Chavez Ravine and the construction of Dodger Stadium the greatest challenges of his life. For some time the Dodgers didn't even know where they would play before the new ballpark was ready. Their four-year run (1958–61) at the Coliseum was a mixed bag. As a jerry-rigged baseball park, the mammoth football stadium was a joke; yet Angelenos, ecstatic to finally have a big league team to call their own, set attendance records there. Again, the negotiations, the fits and starts, and the various forces and parties involved in these events were legion, and only McCue's adroit narrative powers enable the reader to follow them with pleasure.

During that get-acquainted period, O'Malley kept his eye on the ball. He wanted a ballpark that would be a legacy to his vision, and when Dodger Stadium opened in 1962, despite some problems, it was a triumph. Under his reign and the sunny skies of southern California, the Dodgers became one of the most successful and most profitable franchises in all of professional sports, and in retrospect there is no question that their relocation was a bold, transformative move, not just for Los Angeles but for baseball and the country as a whole. McCue does not ignore his subject's faults (e.g., O'Malley often underpaid his employees, and he could hold a grudge; after he bought the team, any employee who mentioned the name Rickey was fined a dollar), nor does he exaggerate the man's virtues. There is, after all, no need to do so. *Mover & Shaker* treats the reader to a portrait of a man who was not the greedy, rapacious monster some have made him out to be, but a talented businessman, willing to take huge risks and driven to accomplish something great that has been of tremendous value to millions of people besides himself and his family. Surely, that is enough to win the admiration of fair-minded fans.

The Numbers Game: Baseball's Lifelong Fascination with Statistics

ALAN SCHWARZ

New York: Thomas Dunne Books, 2004. Cloth, 270 pages, ISBN: 0-312-32222-4. Foreword by Peter Gammons, Introduction. Acknowledgments, Index, 28 black & white photos scattered throughout the book.

The Numbers Game: Baseball's Lifelong Fascination with Statistics by Alan Schwarz is the best pure history of its subject ever published. It differs from its excellent predecessor, *The Hidden Game of Baseball* (1984) by John Thorn and Pete Palmer, by eschewing the application of weighted stats to perform functions, such as the compilation of lists of the greatest hitters and pitchers, in order to keep its eye on the ball: the presentation of a scintillating narrative that chronicles and elucidates every significant advance in the field of statistical analysis as applied to baseball up to the time of its publication in 2004. Many excellent baseball statistical analysis books, most of them focusing on the latest innovations, have been published since; yet *The Numbers Game* continues to provide the most in-depth and comprehensive treatment of the subject between two covers.

While the point of the book is the various ways statistical analysis has led to an ever-growing understanding of the things that increase or decrease the odds of winning baseball games, the author takes a great man approach to his history; and rightfully so, for as with every field of knowledge, each addition to the edifice is made upon the foundations laid by predecessors. Thus, it is impossible for Shwarz to begin with anyone other than Henry Chadwick, "The Father of Baseball," who might also be characterized as the "Father of Baseball Statistics." Chadwick not only reported on scads of early contests played under constantly evolving rules, but he also devised the first box score and obsessed over statistics, urging the adoption of new ones and the abandonment of ones he believed had outlasted their usefulness. He was the first person of note to stress the importance of stats in the evaluation of players, and as the book progresses the author continually points out how later statisticians introduced new statistics that were refinements of ones originated by Chadwick.

From there we are treated to a long list of notables; ranging from well-known

The Numbers Game
Baseball's Lifelong Fascination with Statistics

Foreword by Peter Gammons, ESPN

Alan Schwarz

"*The Numbers Game* is a riveting history of the search for new baseball knowledge." —MICHAEL LEWIS, author of *Moneyball* contributors, such as Ernie Lanigan (a newspaper man and later the first official historian at the Baseball Hall of Fame who was responsible for RBI becoming an accepted part of box scores), F.C. Lane (editor of *Baseball Magazine* and as author of *Batting*, a critic of batting average as a near useless stat), and the Brooklyn Dodgers' Allan Roth (the first statistician to be hired by a major league ballclub) to lesser-known ones, such as Ted Oliver (who presented a "Weighted Rating System" for pitchers in his self-published *Kings of the Mound*), Lt. Colonel Charles Lindsey and son George (Canadian Department of Defense employees who scored thousands of games by radio in order to study baseball strategic questions), and brothers Harlan and Eldon Mills who used first generation main frame computers to analyze not just what players did but *when* they did it. Schwarz, of course, brings all of these men to life by providing key biographical detail, and he expertly discusses their work, summarizing exactly what their main contributions were, usually in one pregnant sentence. In regard to the book encapsulating the work of the Mills brothers, for instance, he writes: "Though it received little acclaim in its day, *Player Win Averages* rates as perhaps the largest leap toward quantifying something baseball fans have debated since the games' birth: Who has performed best with the game on the line, and how can that he measured."

Chadwick, Lane, and their ilk were hardly the only pioneers to produce foundational work that influenced later generations of baseball statisticians. There were many such notables in the chain of progress, such as Earnshaw Cook, a metallurgist, who in 1964 published *Percentage Baseball*: a "hopelessly inaccessible" and flawed work, but one which nonetheless drew later statistical pilgrims to his doorstep, literally. Like most of the pioneers Schwarz discusses in the first half of the book, Cook was way ahead of his time; particularly in his case by emphasizing the importance of not making outs, a concept which "didn't become understood by a majority of baseball executives for 35 years, and continues to baffle more than a few franchises." As an aside: it is interesting to note how many of the great baseball statistical analysts cited by the author worked for the military or defense contractors and how many of them as youngsters in the second half of the twentieth century cut their statistical teeth playing table-top baseball games, such as Ethan Allen's All-Star Baseball, Hal Richman's Strat-O-Matic, or APBA. For nearly all of them baseball statistical analysis was a labor of love, and the monetization of statistics into big business came much later (with the exception of Al and Walter Elias and Irwin Howe who formed eponymous firms to supply stats to the National and American Leagues).

Coming late in the game though it did, the popularization of stats occurred like an unforeseen land mine exploding. The creation of *The Baseball Encyclopedia* in 1969 and the ascension of Bill James into statistical analysis-guru status in the early 1980s did more than just about anything else to turn baseball records and statistics into a national obsession, as well as, for some, a source of profits previously undreamed of. Each of these events receive entire-chapter treatment, as well they should, considering the challenges involved in their coming to fruition and the fact that both eventually became embroiled in bitter controversy; all covered in fascinating detail. The founding of SABR (the Society for American Baseball Research) was another momentous event, as members of the organization discovered one error after another in the record book that was supposed to be "The Bible of Baseball" (*The Baseball Encyclopedia*). When it finally accepted the fact that Hack Wilson had a record 191 RBI in 1930 rather than the historically promulgated 190, MLB admitted that the game had entered a new era. "After 25 years of fighting with baseball to be taken seriously," Schwarz writes, "SABR's sensibilities, valuing fact over fiction and accuracy over myths, had won out."

Baseball itself, represented by the men in the dugouts and in the front offices, was slow to accept the importance of statistical analysis, with the exception of willing mavericks, such as Earl Weaver, Tal Smith, Davey Johnson, and Steve Boros. Gradually things changed though. More and more arbitration cases forced teams to rely on statistics, and the fantasy league baseball craze suddenly produced millions of fans hungry for as much accurate data on player performance as possible. The publication of *Total Baseball* (by Pete Palmer and John Thorn), incorporating corrected records and advanced metrics, obviated the problems associated with *TBE*; and STATS (Sports Teams Analysis and Tracking Systems Incorporated) made co-founder John Dewan a wealthy man by selling to MLB teams, newspapers (especially *USA Today*), and individual fans information and analysis never before available to them. (Dewan, who wrested sole control of STATS via somewhat Machiavellian means, was the former Executive Director of Project Scoresheet, the volunteer organization started by Bill James to score every MLB game. Project Scoresheet was James' response to Seymour Siwoff's refusal to freely share with James Elias Sports Bureau's score sheets.)

By the 1990s, ubiquitous and relatively cheap computers had "changed the face of statistical analysis," and scholars at top universities specializing in all sorts of esoteric fields, such as Carl Morris, Stephen Jay Gould, and Ed Purcell (all Harvard men), were gaining traction for radical ideas … for instance, that luck "plays far more of a role in baseball than anyone before had cared to understand or admit" and that stat splits (how a player did in day vs. night games, home vs. away games, etc.) "were little more than trivia."

It was all leading inevitably towards a greater acceptance of the importance and usefulness of statistical analysis where it matters most: inside MLB dugouts and front offices. Influenced by Eric Walker (the author of *The Sinister First Baseman*), Oakland A's GM Sandy Alderson made on-base percentage the team's guiding principle of player procurement. Alderson's successor, Billy Beane, took the concept and ran with it, and when Michael Lewis in the CASEY Award-winning book *Moneyball* shone the spotlight on the reasons behind the small market A's seemingly unexplainable success, it was pretty much game over for skeptics and cynics.

Schwarz dedicates the final chapter to a demonstration of how contemporary MLB clubs use statistical analysis to improve their teams (in this case, Theo Epstein and the Boston Red Sox) and to the story of the latest significant organizations in the field: Ron Antinoja's commercial service providing immensely detailed data on players' tendencies to do things (hence, the company name, Tendu) and Dave Smith's Retrosheet, an attempt to compile box scores and play-by-play score sheets for every major league baseball game back to 1871. It is the latter endeavor which is the most fitting conclusion for the book, as Smith's decision to make Retrosheet's invaluable information free to all users is in keeping with the spirit which had motivated so many researchers, scientists, and fans to dedicate substantial portions of their lives to the search for real baseball knowledge. In the end, then, we may say that this great book (to echo the words of the world's greatest writer) is an engrossing tale told by a savant signifying, not "nothing," but almost everything knowable about the percentages ruling the great game of baseball.

October 1964

♦

DAVID HALBERSTAM

♦

New York: Villard Books, 1994. Cloth, 380 pages, ISBN: 0-679-41560-2. Prologue. Epilogue, Interviewees, Bibliography, Acknowledgments, 36 black & white photos between pages 178 and 179. Other baseball books by the author: Summer of '49 *(William Morrow, 1989) and* The Teammates: A Portrait of Friendship *(Hyperion, 2003).*

    Comments: One of America's most distinguished historians, Halberstam published thirteen consecutive national bestsellers. He won a Pulitzer Prize for his reporting on the Vietnam War, and *Summer of '49* about the Yankee–Red Sox pennant race went to number one on the *New York Times* bestseller list.

    Many a baseball book attempts to characterize a particular season as a watershed year in the game's history, and none more brilliantly and convincingly than *October 1964* by David Halberstam. While not apparent beforehand, the 1964 World Series presented a stark contrast, pitting one dynasty running out of steam, the New York Yankees, against a former powerhouse once again coming into its own, the St. Louis Cardinals. More importantly, the Cardinals' upset victory over the favored Yankees in an exciting seven-game series represented a changing of the guard: an elevation of the National League over its American League counterpart in the overall quality of play due to the former's prompter and more complete embracing of integration. As important as this thesis is though, Halberstam never belabors it; deftly illustrating it instead through backstory, anecdote, a plethora of incisive portraits, and increasingly dramatic narration.

    Halberstam immediately draws the reader into the vortex that was the 1964 major league baseball season by reviewing the pre-season state of affairs of the two teams that would meet six months later in the World Series. Both teams were under enormous pressure to win. The Yankees, who had won 13 pennants and nine World Championships since 1949, were in the habit of re-loading, not rebuilding. Keys to their success were a deep farm system and recurring pick-pocketing trades with "some hapless have-not franchise." Their players were indomitable because of all the big games they had played in, and they believed in their own invincibility. The Cardinals, on the other hand, were immensely talented but underachieving. Their owner, Gussie Busch, was embarrassed that he was regarded as being incapable of running a baseball team as successfully as he ran his beer empire, and his patience with GM Bing Devine, who had been hired in 1957, and manager Johnny Keane was wearing thin.

Halberstam identifies three main reasons for the approaching Yankees' demise: improved management by other American League teams, decreased spending on the Yankee farm system, and a reluctance to sign black players. Chiefly responsible for the two self-inflicted failures was George Weiss, the Yankees' tight-fisted GM. Halberstam says Weiss quit spending money on the Yankees' minor league clubs because his bonus was based on the organization's yearly profit. His disdain for black players, whom he considered lazy, dull-witted, and inferior to whites, was far more damaging. One of the great ironies of this prejudice was the fact that the young, uber-determined blacks entering baseball at the time were exactly the type of hard-nosed stalwarts the Yankee organization had always looked for among the white population. As for the Cardinals organization, it not only welcomed integration, but four of the team's most important players were black, including the ace of the pitching staff and the player whose professionalism and give-no-quarter attitude best personified the team's group personality, Bob Gibson. And while Devine, undermined by announcer Harry Caray and "Special Consultant" Branch Rickey, was fired mid-season, it was his team, put together by shrewd trades (particularly for shortstop Dick Groat and outfielder Lou Brock) and faith in veteran players (like Ken Boyer), that rallied to win the National League pennant on the last day of the season.

Once Halberstam outlines the contrasting starting points of each team, he turns his attention to the regular season. And it is here that his artful approach becomes apparent. Following (for the most part) the two teams in alternating chapters, he eschews game-by-game or even series-by-series reporting to focus on key moments and the players who found themselves in the middle of these moments. A perfect example of this selective game reporting occurs in Chapter 24 when Halberstam goes into some detail to explain how Lou Brock, acquired from the Chicago Cubs a third of the way into the season, used his speed and daring to help the on-coming Cardinals win a crucial game on September 9 against the Philadelphia Phillies, whose once huge lead had started dwindling. In the top of the ninth inning with St. Louis trailing 5–3, Brock, first, simply ran out of a rundown safely back to first and then a couple of pitches later stole second to take an inning-and-game-ending double play out of order. When Bill White hit a routine grounder to second, Curt Flood scored a run that cut the lead to one. The Cardinals then tied the game and later won it in extra innings. Halberstam cites Ken Boyer's view of the play to sum up the moment's significance. "They win the game, maybe they break the whole thing open," he says. "I think they may be peeking back at us now." As for Brock himself, he later said it was the most important base he ever stole.

The stars, such as Gibson and Mickey Mantle, get plenty of attention from the author, but virtually every player on both teams of any significance also is vividly profiled: career minor league reliever Barney Schultz, suddenly getting his chance, smug youngster Ray Sadecki who blossoms into a 20-game winner, ex-Philadelphia starter Curt Simmons who becomes a Phillies-killer, and Mike Shannon, called up from Triple A halfway through the season to solidify the outfield and batting order, for the Cardinals; and for the Yankees, rookie reliever Pete Mikkelsen who nabs the only open spot on the roster out of spring training; Elston Howard, the dignified black who accepted a position change to catcher (against the wishes of his enraged wife who wanted him to demand a trade) because he realized "The Yankees are special"; super-sub Phil Linz who helps blunt the frequent absence of oft-injured Tony Kubek; and the dominating closer the Yankees trade for to help sew up the pennant, Pedro Ramos.

Halberstam's understanding of the people involved in his story is astonishing to say the least, and it is what elevates the narrative so far above the efforts of less talented writers. His insights into Mickey Mantle, for example, illustrate this ability to uncover things about even the most familiar players that were previously not noted or expressed nearly as cogently. Yankees pitcher Al Downing, for example, recalls noticing the habit of the worn-down Mantle pausing on the top step of the dugout before running onto the field to start a game, gathering himself, mustering up the strength that he used to call forth effortlessly. Halberstam himself explains that this older, debilitated Mantle takes indirect routes toward fly balls because he no longer has the agility and speed to cut sharply. He also points out Mantle's obsession with tape measure home runs as the quality which sets him apart from all other sluggers (in the same way that the speed of their fastballs is used to separate pitchers from one another). And he finds a quote which sums up Mantle's greatness about as well as one statement can. "He is," Clete Boyer says, "the only baseball player I know who is a bigger hero to his teammates than he is to the fans."

On top of this, the author's keen understanding of events is equal to his insight into his subjects. As it happened, the Phillies blew a huge lead, which set up the real possibility of the season ending in a three-way tie among the Phillies, the Cardinals, and the Cincinnati Reds. St. Louis' win against the New York Mets coupled with Philadelphia's victory over Cincinnati gave the Cardinals the National League pennant on the last day of the season. Phillies' manager Gene Mauch, who lost confidence in three of his starting pitchers and used Jim Bunning and Chris Short six times on only two days' rest during the final weeks of the campaign, has been routinely blamed for his team's collapse; but Halberstam talked to Bunning who basically told him, "Don't blame Gene. I wanted the ball, and I thought I could win those games. It's the way elite athletes think." Halberstam also shrewdly notes something overlooked about the power-hitting Yankees, noting that their "secret strength had always been their superior infield play." He characterizes the hiring of Yogi Berra for the 1964 season as a mistake in the eyes of the players, quoting Mantle who says, "We can win in spite of it." And then, once his narration of the World Series begins to unfold, he explains that the racial prejudice of the Yankees' organization hurt the team once again, as their scouts failed to convey how fast, how tough, and how talented their opponents actually were. As Downing says, the Yankees "were betrayed by the arrogance of its own scouting reports."

Appropriately, when he gets to the Fall Classic, Halberstam does review the Series game by game. The thing to note is the deep appreciation the reader has for all the participants at this point, the author having laid such incisive biographical groundwork in the preceding chapters. Halberstam's analysis and description of

Gibson's heroic Game Seven performance is simply not to be missed. The Epilogue which follows recounts a number of fascinating events, including the farcical presser at which Busch's attempt to rehire his manager was undermined by Keane's having already agreed to manage the Yankees in 1965; yet it is not the typical "what happened to them afterwards" survey. Instead, it demonstrates the validity of the book's thesis, as it cites the paths of the two teams in the following years: one towards two more pennants and another World Championship, the other into a morass of mediocrity that lasted for more than a decade.

Odd Man Out: A Year on the Mound with a Minor League Misfit

◆

Matt McCarthy

◆

New York: Viking, 2009. Cloth, 294 pages, ISBN: 978-0-670-02070-6. Acknowledgments.

Comments: Despite positive early reviews, a couple of people mentioned in the book disputed its accuracy. After fact checking the book, Benjamin Hill and Alan Schwarz published an article in the *New York Times* titled "Errors Cast Doubt on a Baseball Memoir" which concludes that "many portions of the book are incorrect, embellished, or impossible."

The claims of Hill and Schwartz were rebutted by Jon Greenberg, a contributor to the *HuffPost* blog: "While the aggregation of erroneous detail is lamentable, none of the mistakes seem to be malicious, and in the context of the book, they're almost invisible.... *Odd Man Out* isn't a masterpiece of the game, like Jim Bouton's *Ball Four*, but it is an enjoyable, intellectual, and unsentimental look at the minor leagues, a diverse splinter of the professional sports landscape that is all too often sanitized or ignored. This is a universal story, a coming-of-age narrative that focuses on how people come to find their place in the world. When you read a book like this, you don't look at every quote and wonder if it's spot-on. An author is allowed some creative license for dialogue and situations. If they [sic] weren't, David Sedaris would still be cleaning kitchens in New York."

McCarthy himself stands by what he wrote. Most recently he is a professor of medicine at Weill Cornell and a staff physician at New York-Presbyterian Hospital. He is also the author of two other books: *The Real Doctor Will See You Shortly: A Physician's First Year* (Crown, 2015) and *Superbugs: The Race to Stop an Epidemic* (Avery, 2019). Both *Odd Man Out* and *Superbugs* were national bestsellers.

Some of the most unforgettable reads in the canon of baseball literature are the memoirs in which the authors lay bare their souls, honestly sharing their thoughts and reactions and thus providing a powerful sense of what it was like to be there and have the same experiences as the author. Such a book is *Odd Man Out: A Year on the Mound with a Minor League Misfit*, Matt McCarthy's riveting account of his season pitching for the Provo Angels of the Pioneer League, the now defunct rookie league that in 2002 fielded teams in Utah (Provo and Ogden), Wyoming (Casper), Idaho (Idaho Falls), Montana (Billings, Great Falls, and Missoula), and Alberta,

Canada (Medicine Hat). While providing an unmatched, inside look at the realities of contemporary minor league baseball in the mode of Jim Bouton and Pat Jordan, the book is at heart a bildungsroman in which the author is on a journey of self-discovery as a human being more than a professional athlete. As brief as it was, the author's career in minor league baseball amounted to a crucible that tested him constantly and ultimately rewarded him handsomely (though not monetarily).

Making it in professional baseball is difficult enough, especially for a player like Matt McCarthy, who was an average-sized left-handed pitcher with below-average velocity and inconsistent breaking stuff, coming out of a downtrodden college program (Yale University never posted a winning record in the four years the author played for them). As explained early in the book, McCarthy knew that the odds of his being drafted were low, and he recounts asking his coach, former St. Louis Cardinals pitcher John Stuper, to pull a few strings for him. (Stuper tries but is not any help.) McCarthy receives a "Don't call us; we'll call you" response to an invitation-only tryout with the New York Yankees, and as draft day drags on and on without his name being called, he resigns himself to the apparent end of his dream of playing major league baseball. But then the Anaheim Angels select him in the 21st round, and the dream is revived. The Angels offer him a non-negotiable bonus of $1,000, but he is too elated to much care about the paltry amount.

At this point, the stage is set for a typical story about a lightly-regarded player heroically overcoming adversity and his physical limitations, but the situation that McCarthy walks into amounts to nothing less than culture shock; and his describing his attempts to deal with the inherent challenges is what electrifies the narration and elevates the book above one merely about balls and strikes.

First of all, McCarthy immediately discovers that his Yale pedigree is an albatross, not a badge of prestige. As the Provo strength coach drives him and two other players from the airport to Anaheim's spring training facility in Mesa, Arizona, the coach asks Matt if he is "one of those goddamn Ivy League know-it-alls." This is a seminal moment which will determine how McCarthy will handle all summer long the attitudes of others suspicious of his high falutin' background and resentful of his attractive options should he fail at baseball, and he chooses to downplay his scholastic accomplishments. His reply to the coach is so mendacious it's comical. "No, definitely not. I barely graduated," he lies. "I didn't go to class and didn't do any work. I just played baseball."

Second, according to second-year pitcher Blake Allen who immediately befriends him, McCarthy discovers that the Provo Angels are a team strictly divided by language and culture according to national origin. As Allen, a good old boy from Alabama with a sore arm, explains: "You've got your Dominicans and you've got everybody else. You don't want nuthin' to do with the Dominicans. They're loud, they don't speak English, they don't have no respect for nobody, and for God's sake, don't ever go in the shower when they are in there." "Dominicans," it turns out, is a term encompassing all Latin players, whether they hail from Mexico, Puerto Rico, or the Dominican Republic; and Blake's insensitive if not racist attitude pretty much prevails throughout the summer.

And then there is the fact that Provo, the home of Brigham Young University, is overwhelmingly Mormon country where religious belief is taken very seriously. Such an environment is diametrically opposed to the proclivities and pastimes of the typical young professional ballplayer, and McCarthy's American teammates continually complain about the restrictions the community places on them (such as watered-down beer). They mock the mores of the true believers, and they do their best to corrupt the weak links ("Jack Mormons," those females who profess belief in chastity but are willing to engage in illicit sex nonetheless). Halfway through the season, Matt himself breaks up with his girlfriend, visiting from Minnesota, when she tells him that she's decided to be a "born again virgin." It's an honest portrayal but not McCarthy's finest moment.

As if this is not enough to deal with, the manager of the Angels is 48-year-old Tom Kotchman, a skinny, bald-headed, foul-mouthed drill sergeant of a baseball lifer who, on the surface, is the complete opposite of the avuncular John Stuper, who would innocently quiz his players about female Yale professors he might want to work up the courage to ask out. Kotchman is demanding, tempestuous, and maniacal about winning—contrary to the normal emphasis in the minors on player development. He is also as crude as any of his players. In desperate circumstances, he brings out a two-foot black dildo dubbed the "Rally Penis"; and his third rule, after "Be on time" and "Play hard," is "Don't fart on the bus." "We've got some fifteen-hour bus rides," he tells the players, "and I don't want to be smelling your ass all the way to Montana." All in all, Kotchman is one of the most vividly drawn personages in baseball literature.

It's quite a lot to take in all at once, and to deal with it McCarthy tries to lay low and blend in with his teammates. He adopts the guarded persona of an aloof observer and as much as possible keeps his opinions to himself, allowing others, such as Blake Allen, to frame controversial topics. Yet, inevitably, he is drawn into conflicts and situations when he reveals more of himself than he wants to. For example, southern redneck Heath Luther, another pitcher, takes a dislike to McCarthy and berates him for not encouraging catcher Alex Dvorsky to take steroids, which Heath and others believe Dvorsky needs to do to increase his power. Later, at Heath's insistence, Matt takes a dip of tobacco to save face and is unable to prevent his teammates from hearing him vomit in the bathroom of his motel room. Matt takes a "live and let live" attitude towards the Latin players but does express astonishment at how far talented prospects Erick Aybar and Alberto Callaspo (both of whom eventually make the major leagues) are willing to go for a joke in pantomiming homosexual acts in the nude. More significantly, he kindly attempts to comfort pitcher Hector Astacio who draws Kotchman's wrath for not beaning an opposing player; telling Astacio the lie that "everyone will understand" his position of not being willing to risk permanently injuring another player. This is the one scene in the book where we get the viewpoint of the Latin players (spoken in perfect English, by the way, according to the author's narration), and it's not a pretty picture. "I know what you guys think of us," says Hector, whom McCarthy guesses correctly is more worried about displeasing God than Tom Kotchman. "We're the Dominicans and you're the Americans. I know what it means to be a second-class citizen. But you guys don't know anything about me. You think we're a bunch of idiots with gold chains who only care about ourselves." When Matt replies, "That's not true," he is speaking of himself, at least.

As for the Mormons, although McCarthy disdains religion, he extends to them the same respect he gives the Latin players. He even accepts a generous invitation to live rent-free with an affluent Mormon family, that of Sarah and Jeff Glynn. While he is curious about the Glynn's religious beliefs, he never gets a chance to discuss them, and his relationship with the family (of four kids) is characterized by gratitude for their hospitality.

Against this backdrop of cultural and philosophical differences, the short Pioneer League season unfolds, 76 games played in 80 days, and Matt struggles to prove himself. Initially, he is given a spot in the rotation, but the competition is so stiff that a bad performance in his first start results in a demotion to the bullpen. At one point, Kotchman questions his manhood, accusing him of being afraid to pitch to Prince Fielder, and pitching coach Kernan Ronan later decides it advisable for Matt to start throwing side-armed, the proverbial pitching "kiss of death." Nothing much seems to work. McCarthy can never seem to attain any consistency, and he agonizes over every poor outing. He throws two good innings in relief in the last game of the season but declines to go back out for a third inning, a decision he says he regrets "to this day." "I wasn't playing to win; I was playing not to fail," he admits. In all, he appears in only 15 games and compiles an ERA of 6.92. The Angels finish 38–38 and are knocked out of the playoffs by a clearly superior Great Falls Dodgers team.

Despite his own and the team's lack of success, as well as his emotional and physical exhaustion, McCarthy is clearly sad to see the season end. He has come to respect Tom Kotchman as a man who actually cares about his players, despite all appearances to the contrary; and he has begun to re-think his studied indifference, if not outright hostility, towards religious belief. Early in the book McCarthy portrays himself as an accidental Catholic who is contentedly ignorant about the faith, but at the end of his rookie season in pro baseball, the teammate who most affects him is late-season roommate and fellow pitcher Randy Burden, a Bible-reading evangelical out of Chowan (NC) College. Although Matt earlier declines the offer to borrow Randy's Good Book and later rudely cuts off a story of faith Randy tries to share, he is touched when Burden gives him a new King James Bible as a going-away present. A few months later McCarthy learns that Burden has died in his sleep.

Despite his mediocre rookie year, McCarthy is not cut by the parent club and goes to spring training the following spring. However, it's only a stay of execution as he's gotten no better over the winter. When other players tell him that he is tipping his pitches, as well as his move to first base, he wonders if the coaches have given up on him. A bad omen occurs when he is called upon to pitch an inning for the Angels' Triple A ballclub against the Giants' Triple A affiliate, after not pitching at all for the Low A Cedar Rapids club to which he had been assigned six days before. He throws a four-pitch scoreless inning against the Fresno Grizzlies but gives up the three hardest hit balls of his life, two towering warning track fly balls and a rocket of a line drive, all caught. "I don't belong out here," he confides to himself. After the game he finally gets the dreaded pink slip; and the scene in which Matt consoles the weeping "Grim Reaper," the Angels' Director of Player Personnel Tony Reagins … instead of the other way around … is amusing and indicative of what Matt McCarthy has been all along: somebody different, a person out of place, the misfit of the subtitle. "Mr.

Reagins," he says, "I want to let you know something. I'm going to be fine. I appreciate all that you and the Angels have done for me, but I'm going to be okay. I realize this is a numbers game and that this time, I'm the odd man out."

It is not until his flight home along with another player cut by the organization that McCarthy dispenses with his practiced cool and stoicism. When the other player ponders the uncertainty of his future and then asks about Matt, McCarthy writes, " 'I don't know,' I said as a tear rolled down my cheek." This may be at last the first overtly emotional indication of what the game has meant to the author, but Matt McCarthy's love of baseball is evident right from the start, and especially when he tells us that he needed "five years of distance" in order to write the book.

In the Epilogue McCarthy, who eventually becomes a doctor, reveals that baseball haunted him so strongly that he took jobs in exotic places to get as far away from the game as possible. He details what has become of numerous people important in the book, and he ends by revealing that the person he thinks of the most is Randy Burden. The tribute to Burden is representative of the transformation that one season as a Provo Angel effected on the author:

> *As I respond to the pages about my octogenarian patients who are slowly losing their grip on life, I think about the young man from Virginia who just wanted to be close with God and play baseball. I think of him being in his baseball uniform and I imagine him in heaven, having his own conversation with God, undoubtedly trying to find out the best way to throw a fastball.*

Oscar Charleston: The Life and Legend of Baseball's Greatest Forgotten Player

◆

Jeremy Beer

◆

Lincoln: University of Nebraska Press, 2019. Cloth, 417 pages, ISBN: 9781 496217110. Preface, Introduction: Craftsman. Epilogue, Acknowledgments, Appendix: Statistical Record, Notes, Bibliography, Index, 32 black & white photos between pages 182 and 183.

Comments: *Oscar Charleston* won the 38th CASEY Award and the 2020 Seymour Medal. In posting a near-unanimous score of 4 (1 + 1 + 2), *Oscar Charleston* bested a strong lineup of other CASEY Award Finalists, including *Let's Play Two: The Legend of Mr. Cub, The Life of Ernie Banks* by Ron Rapoport, *The Legend of Harry Caray: Baseball's Greatest Salesman* by Don Zminda, *Ballpark: Baseball in the American City* by Paul Goldberger, *K: A History of Baseball in Ten Pitches* by Tyler Kepner, *They Bled Blue: Fernandomania, Strike-Season Mayhem, and the Weirdest Championship Baseball Had Ever Seen: The 1981 Los Angeles Dodgers* by Jason Turbow, *Homegrown: How the Red Sox Built a Champion from the Ground Up* by Alex Speier, *Inside the Empire: The True Power Behind the New York Yankees* by Bob Klapisch and Paul Solotaroff, and *Chumps to Champs: How the Worst Teams in Yankees History Led to the 90s Dynasty* by Bill Pennington.

Poor contemporary media coverage and the lack of proper record keeping has plagued the writing of Negro League history from the very beginning, and no player has suffered more from these inadequacies than the greatest Negro Leaguer of them all: Oscar Charleston, a five-tool player who exhibited exceptional power, speed, and fielding ability for decades. Charleston's preeminence would still be an undocumented rumor were it not for the Ruthian efforts of Jeremy Beer, who was immensely aided in his research by gaining access to Charleston's personal scrapbook and photo album; providentially saved by Oscar's estranged second wife, Janie; passed on to his sister, Katherine; handed down to a niece, Anna Bradley; and finally donated to the Negro Leagues Museum and Hall of Fame in Kansas City, Missouri, where Beer was able to access them. The result of Beer's exhaustive study, *Oscar Charleston: The Life and Legend of Baseball's Greatest Forgotten Player*, not only represents the fortuitous rescue of the reputation of one of the game's top five players (in the opinion of Bill James, as well as Mr. Beer), but it also offers a spectacular tour through the entire history of the Negro Leagues.

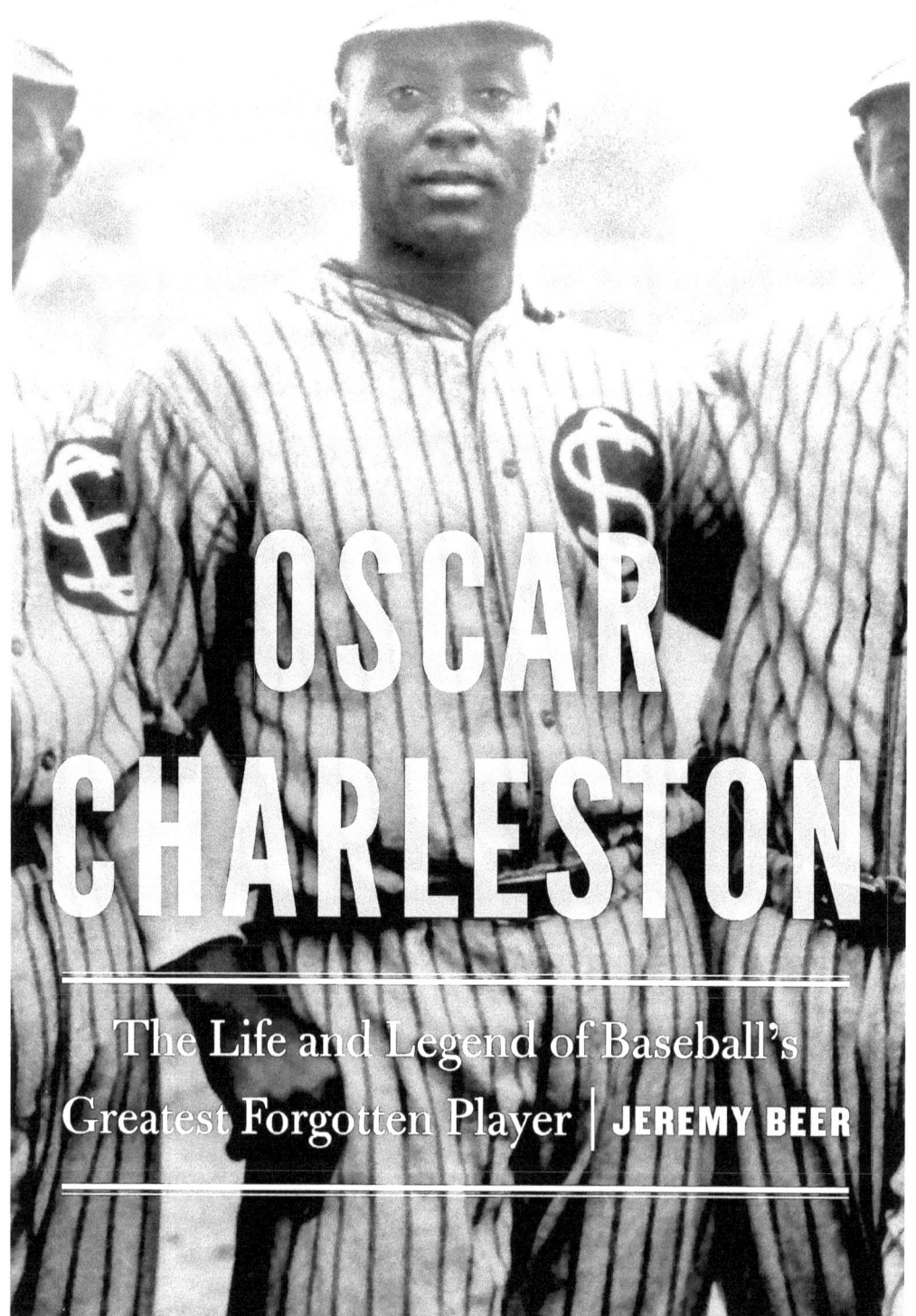

We can say that the book is as much a history as a biography because Oscar Charleston was there, right in the middle of so much of it. He started his Negro League career as an 18-year-old in 1915, playing for his hometown and independent (like all NL teams at the time) Indianapolis ABC's, and then headed, as numerous Negro Leaguers did, to Cuba, to play winter ball: a trek that became an annual event. He participated at times in the two-team Florida Hotel League in Palm Beach, and he played countless barnstorming games against amateur and semi-pro ball clubs, as well as numerous exhibition contests against all-star teams made up of white minor and major league players. He was there when Rube Foster organized the first league for blacks, the Negro National League; and he was also on hand for the formation of the Eastern Colored League and the Negro American League. In 1932 he was named player-manager of the famous Pittsburgh Crawfords, beginning a long second career as "The Man in the Dugout" (to use Leonard Koppett's moniker); and at 36 years of age, he played in the first East-West All-Star Game in 1933 as the leading vote-getter for the exhibition. After retiring as a player (except for sporadic appearances for another five seasons) at the end of the 1936 season, he continued managing through the 1941 season. Too old to integrate baseball himself, he organized and briefly managed the Brooklyn Brown Dodgers at the behest of Branch Rickey and assisted Rickey in identifying Jackie Robinson and Roy Campanella as the best candidates for the momentous task. He was still there as the post-integration Negro Leagues slowly wound down, managing the Philadelphia Stars (1948–52) and guiding the Indianapolis Clowns to a NAL championship shortly before his death on October 5, 1954, at the age of 57.

Charleston's vagabond-like record looks like the career of a journeyman player, but he played for so many different teams not because he was a marginal performer but because he was constantly in such high demand ... and because "jumping" from one team to another offering higher pay was a commonplace practice in the Negro Leagues. Fortunately, Beer's great organizational skills keep the reader from becoming overwhelmed by the incessant moving around. One thing is clear: right from the beginning and wherever Charleston went, his exceptional abilities and inherent aptitude for the game were easily recognized and highly praised. By the end of Oscar's rookie season, veteran pitcher William "Dizzy" Dismukes and the ABC's manager and co-owner C.I. Taylor agreed that Charleston was the "best defensive outfielder" either of them had ever seen. Beer himself opines that the Santa Clara Leopardos outfield of Alejandro Oms and Pablo Mesa flanking Charleston in center field made up the best outfield in Cuban baseball history and that "by the time he [Oscar] said his final goodbye to Cuba, he had become the nation's most famous and respected American player." Charleston became known, before the nickname was passed on to Josh Gibson, as the "Black Babe Ruth," and years after Oscar's death Buck O'Neil described him as "Ty Cobb, Babe Ruth, and Tris Speaker rolled into one." He was "the greatest player I have ever seen in eight-and-a-third decades," said O'Neil.

The litany of opinion-based superlatives rolls on throughout the book, and Beer can be excused for leaning heavily on them since the statistical record is "radically" incomplete. In a note prefacing Charleston's batting record, Beer points out that the stats represent those compiled in "games versus major competition only," and he estimates that Charleston had "at least three times as many plate appearances as reported here" in professional games. The insufficiency of the statistical record, as well as the random number of games played by Negro League teams in any particular season, also requires Beer at times to extrapolate Charleston's numbers over the length of a 162-game major league schedule. For instance, in regard to Oscar's 1924 season with the Harrisburg (PA) Giants which produced extrapolated stats of 45 home runs, 15 triples, 66 doubles, and 60 stolen bases, Beer asks rhetorically, "Has anyone ever had a better year?"

While Charleston clearly has a champion in the author, Beer does not write like a partisan homer. He notes the subject's failings, particularly the eagerness Oscar showed to participate in on-field brawls and his puzzling, usually unexplainable conflicts with some managers and owners. And he is particularly unflinchingly honest about some of the Negro League team owners, whom he calls racketeers. "No matter what social good they achieved with their profits," he writes, "no matter how magnanimously they distributed their largess, their numbers lotteries were inherently predatory, a fact a little too easily passed over by many Negro Leagues historians–not to mention the even less pleasant fact that many of the numbers men, including Greenlee [Gus, owner of the Pittsburgh Crawfords], also profited from the sex trade." Beer, well versed in the literature and an adept borrower, is careful to withhold certainty when it is appropriate to do so, as when he says that during late May and early June of 1930 the Homestead Grays *reportedly* won 19 games in a row. He also does his share of myth debunking: rejecting the story about Charleston snatching the hood off the head of a Klan member and correcting the apocryphal "debut" story of the Grays grabbing youngster Josh Gibson out of the stands to replace a catcher who was injured and unable to continue playing the game. On the other hand, the author includes many sensational stories which enliven the narrative, such as black Negro League umpires routinely packing heat; *both* automobiles carrying Grays players on one road trip flipping over without a single injury to anybody; and Ted Page and George Scales sleeping in the same bed after a terrible fight, a knife under one pillow and a gun under the other!

It is all one long fascinating feast for lovers of baseball history and particularly for those mesmerized by the romance of the Negro Leagues. And long before the final page, most every reader will be persuaded that Charleston does indeed deserve the high regard in which the author holds him. But one should not overlook the fact that equally important for Beer was the mission to convey what kind of person Oscar Charleston was. Very little of what Charleston said has been saved for posterity, but Beer deduces from the scrapbook that Oscar was interested in many of the issues of the day, particularly those directly affecting his race. The reader can deduce from Oscar's running off to enlist in the army at age 15 that he was adventure-some, patriotic, and fearless. And probably most important of all, what was Charleston's long career as a manger and his being the first black hired to scout for a major league team all about if not his desire to help others, to pay it forward, so to speak? If Beer uncovered criticisms of Charleston as a person (or a ballplayer or a manager), he left them out of the book. In the end we are left with a portrait of a man who was totally dedicated to one thing: the game of baseball. This outstanding biography does much to rectify the neglect this great player has suffered from; a neglect summed up perfectly by Beer noting in the Introduction that when Charleston died, "few outside the rapidly shrinking world of the Negro Leagues noticed.

The occupation given on his death certificate was baggage handler."

Pete Rose: An American Dilemma

◆

Kostya Kennedy

◆

New York: Sports Illustrated Books, 2014. Cloth, 341 pages, ISBN: 978-1-61893-096-5. Introduction. Footnotes at bottom of pages, Acknowledgments, Selected Bibliography, Index, About the Author, six black & white photos. Other baseball books by the author: 56: Joe DiMaggio and the Last Magic Number in Sports *(Sports Illustrated Books, 2011) and* True: The Four Seasons of Jackie Robinson *(St. Martin's Press, 2022).*

Comments: Kennedy won the 32nd CASEY Award in 2014 for *Pete Rose*, making him the first three-time winner of the Award. He also won the 29th CASEY in 2011 for *56* and the 40th CASEY in 2022 for *True*. *Pete Rose* beat out a slew of outstanding books, including *The Chalmers Race: Ty Cobb, Napoleon Lajoie, and the Controversial 1910 Batting Title That Became a National Obsession* by Rick Huhn and *Mover and Shaker: Walter O'Malley, the Dodgers, and Baseball's Westward Expansion* by Andy McCue which finished in a tie for second place.

Richard Ford: "Kennedy's book on the tarnished and enigmatic Rose is exceptional. Like the best writing about sport—Liebling, Angell—it qualifies as stirring literature. I'd read Kennedy no matter what he writes about."

Pete Rose. The most controversial player in baseball history. A name which, even today, long after Rose's last at bat, immediately arouses strong reactions, ranging from admiration and sympathy to disgust and condemnation. Whatever one's view of the man, everyone can agree that his story is a complicated one, and some highly respected and very talented writers have attempted to tell it; writers, such as Roger Kahn (*Pete Rose: My Story*), Michael Y. Sokolove (*Hustle: The Myth, Life, and Lies of Pete Rose*), and James Reston, Jr. (*Collision at Home Plate: The Lives of Pete Rose and Bart Giamatti*), who released their books in three successive years (1989–1991), at the height of the scandal which led to Rose's banishment from baseball. Yet, the Rose saga never went away, nor did we get a truly satisfactory picture of the man and his demons until the publication in 2014 of *Pete Rose: An American Dilemma* by Kostya Kennedy: one of the most probing and enlightening investigations of a major baseball figure ever published.

Kennedy's book about Pete Rose is a biography, true enough, but it is a biography in the same sense that the Sistine Chapel is a painting. It's not just that Kennedy had the benefit of being able to assess momentous events which transpired after the above-mentioned books were written; it's that he brought to the task transcendent gifts of curiosity, perception, understanding, explication, and expression. No matter what else is added in the future to the "wheel of fortune" soap opera that has been Pete Rose's life, it is highly unlikely that a more nuanced, more complete, or truer portrait of the man will be captured between two covers.

The book is also more than a biography, even perhaps not primarily a biography, but more of an implied polemic in the sense that three overriding questions undergird the book, while referencing the subtitle, as Pete Rose remains a highly disputed topic of conversation in this country. Once Rose finally admitted to having bet on baseball, the first and most obvious of those questions became "Was his offense egregious enough to justify his continued disqualification for the National Baseball Hall of Fame?" Kennedy acknowledges this by setting the first chapter of the book in Cooperstown, New York, dateline Induction Weekend 2012: the year Reds shortstop Barry Larkin, who broke into the major leagues under manager Pete Rose, was inducted. He also repeatedly returns to the scene in chapters 4, 7, 11, 22, and 25. And he does this not just because Cooperstown–a repository of living baseball history and the center of the baseball universe—is such a spectacular backdrop for the Pete Rose question, but because Rose's presence there, as tacky and unwelcome as some regard it, is a continual reminder that something is amiss, is not quite right. Many fans who make the Induction Weekend pilgrimage cannot shake the unsettling feeling of dinner guests who keep one eye on the front door hoping for the arrival of the favorite uncle who has incurred the displeasure of the host.

Kennedy writes brilliantly and with approbation about Rose's multifarious achievements (excepting his 44-game consecutive hit streak which he points out he covered in depth in *56: Joe DiMaggio and the Last Magic Number in Sports*). He also looks squarely at Rose's defects: his verbal crudeness, his womanizing and marital infidelity, his addiction to gambling and his greed, his implied shortcomings as a father. This balance is what primes the reader to agree with his position on whether or not Rose was treated fairly in regard to his eligibility for the Hall of Fame. As Kennedy explains, in January of 1991, a few days after Rose had finished serving his prison sentence for tax evasion, a special committee was formed to advise the Hall of Fame Board of Directors to adopt a rule that stated "Any person on baseball's ineligible list [for employment by a team] shall not be eligible for election to the Hall of Fame." This measure was obviously directed at Pete Rose and remains the only time the board has done something "designed specifically to keep a particular player *out*." To make sure he is not misunderstood, Kennedy concludes this section with a withering description of what was done to Rose:

> The Rose resolution was then and remains the greatest disservice to be inflicted upon the Hall of Fame induction process, an injustice not simply to the player and the voters but also to the fans, the people who sustain the institution. There have been other cases in which the voting has for one reason or another seemed compromised—mostly relating to the earliest years of the Hall or to matters of the Veterans Committee—but none other has so deeply stained the procedure nor delivered such a blow to the integrity of the process as a whole.

Calling them as he sees them, Kennedy also doubts ex–Commissioner Fay Vincent's claims that he had nothing to do with the Rose rule, characterizing such claims as "a tough pill to get down."

The irony of Rose's banishment from the ballot is that denying him the honor his playing career so clearly merited him has turned him into a sort of baseball martyr and ensured that he and his case annually upstage, at least to some degree, every Induction ceremony he is left on the outside looking in at. If he'd been given his shot, I have no doubt that he would have been elected (and probably on the first ballot) and, furthermore, that long ago he would have ceased to be the disruptive attraction so annoying to the powers that be.

The second question addressed by the book derives from the impact that Rose's father, Harry Rose, might have had on his son had he not died from an untimely heart attack early in Rose's career. Numerous writers have noted Rose's adoration of his father and, without recognizing the comparison to Mutt Mantle and his son, commented on Harry's molding of Pete into a ballplayer. But none of them have conveyed so thoroughly, as Kennedy does, the unrelenting, obsessive teaching of the father, whose lessons Rose absorbed, internalized, and transformed into the playing philosophy he lived by: a philosophy characterized by his total dedication and all-out/all-the-time hustle. More importantly, what was missed before Kennedy is the very real possibility that Harry Rose's enormous influence on his son may have been enough to forestall the bad behaviors which led to his downfall. Or barring that scenario, Harry might have successfully shamed Pete into immediately confessing his baseball sins, seeking forgiveness, and trying to make amends. Kennedy knows that a plethora of factors go into the makeup of every human being, and he provides numerous examples of such factors in the attempt to understand his subject. The day Rose received an ovation at Crosley Field after being caught running a red light at four in the morning in disreputable Newport, Kentucky, is a good example. The incident, says Kennedy, "was a suggestion to Rose that the things he did at the ballpark, his excellence there, could camouflage some of the other things he chose to do in life." Yet, more than anything else, it was the desire to please his father, on the one hand, and the fear of disappointing him, on the other, that might have saved Rose. After Harry's death, Kennedy says, "Rose would never again feel the demand for accountability the way he had felt it from Harry. He would never again feel that there was anyone else, a wife or child, not his brother or siblings, not the agents or the associates serving him, who could see through him or tell him what to do."

The final question raised by the book is the most important and fundamental one of all: namely, "Who is Pete Rose?" We know that he was, beyond the owner of the title he bestowed on himself of "Hit King," a great all-around ballplayer, a winning ballplayer who made All-Star teams at five different positions. In addition to covering the highlights and records set, Kennedy provides numerous examples of the way Rose played, of the things he did which amazed other players and set him apart from them: including, his kamikaze crash into Ray Fosse to win the 1970 All-Star Game (the "most iconic single play" in the history of the Game, according to Kennedy); his keeping the Reds alive in Game Seven of the 1975 World Series by breaking up a sure double play with a hard slide into second; and his dousing a Royals last-gasp rally in the 1980 World Series by catching a pop-up dropped by Philadelphia Phillies teammate Bob Boone. This is all well and good, but Rose's preeminence as a ballplayer does not provide the answer to the question of what kind of person he is and has been.

Is he the loyal, generous friend loved by teammates such as Joe Morgan, Tommy Harper, and Mike Schmidt; or is he the convicted felon who hangs out with low life's and who welshes on bets?

Is he the loving father idolized by his children, particularly son Petey who has spent his entire early manhood playing minor league baseball in an attempt to live up to his father's legacy; or is he a self-centered narcissist enslaved to mammon?

Is he the vulnerable figure humbled by the nine-minute ovation showered upon him after he broke Ty Cobb's record, a regular guy who remembers grade school classmates and treats them as equals; or is he the entitled liar who thinks himself above the laws of common decency, a bad guy with "no moral compass" (in the words of Fay Vincent)?

Kennedy's own view of this question comes into play with his discussing the famous fable of "The Scorpion and the Frog"; the point suggested being that Rose has acted, like the scorpion, according to his nature. This "character is destiny" view is not meant to absolve Rose of his sins but to offer an explanation for why he acted as he did even when his actions were self-destructive. Similarly, in a brilliant dissection of Rose's own book, *My Prison Without Bars*, Kennedy exhibits compassion for Rose, saying: "There remains something heart-breaking about the way Rose revealed himself at the time of his public confession—a man trapped like many men by his own pathology, trapped by his own delusions and denials. Indeed, a prison without bars."

The last chapter is one more look at Cooperstown and in particular the statue of *The Sand Lot Kid* near Doubleday Park. After running through all the things we don't know about the generic bronzed boy, Kennedy says, "All we know about the boy, true in 1944, in 1964, and in 2014, is that he is in his stance forever, his bat in hand and awaiting the pitch, and each person who looks at *The Sand Lot Kid* can make of him what they will." To conclude the book this way is a remarkable gesture of humility, given what Kennedy accomplishes in it. It may be true that, as Sparky Anderson says about Rose, "Nobody will ever know him completely." But because of *Pete Rose: An American Dilemma*, each of us knows what we need to know about Rose to fix him clearly in our own minds.

Pie Traynor: A Baseball Biography

◆

JAMES FORR *and* DAVID PROCTOR

◆

Jefferson, NC: McFarland, 2010. Paper, 265 pages, ISBN: 978-0-7864-4385-7. Acknowledgments, Preface. Appendix 1: Funeral Service; Appendix 2: Major League Statistics, Chapter Notes, Bibliography, Index, 34 black & white photos scattered throughout the book.

Comments: The authors began working on biographies of the subject independently at roughly the same time, completely unaware of the other's efforts: Proctor focusing on Traynor's early life in the Boston, Massachusetts, area; Forr, on Pie's retirement years in Pittsburgh, Pennsylvania. They decided to collaborate after John Garner, director of public relations and broadcasting for the Cape Cod League, put them in touch with each other.

In 1937 Harold Joseph "Pie" Traynor played the final game of his outstanding 17-year major league career, all with the Pittsburgh Pirates. Eleven years later he became the first third baseman elected to the Baseball Hall of Fame; and in 1969, as part of baseball's centennial celebration, he was voted both the greatest third baseman in baseball history and the greatest living third baseman. A humble man never much concerned with money, Traynor (who died in 1972) never sought in retirement to profit from his memoirs. As the years went by and the statistical analysis revolution dimmed the luster of his achievements, he slipped from the public consciousness, his nickname contributing significantly to what fame he retained. Fortunately, James Forr and David Proctor, realizing that Traynor had become the most prominent Hall of Famer never to have been the subject of a biography, published *Pie Traynor: A Baseball Biography* in 2012; and in so doing they gave us a lively, affectionate portrait of a man and athlete it would be a travesty not to remember properly.

While the authors lament the lack of "readily available background information" about Traynor, they present a wealth of information about their subject's early life and career that was not well known. Namely, that Traynor grew up in Massachusetts (Somerville), after his family migrated to America from Canada (Halifax, Nova Scotia); that his play on an amateur summer team on Cape Cod (before the famous collegiate Cape Cod League was officially established) enhanced his reputation and greased his way into pro baseball; that he had tryouts with both the Boston Braves and Red Sox, and that when they bought him for $10,000 from the Portsmouth

Truckers of the Virginia League, the Pirates practically stole him from the Red Sox and their shrewd general manager Ed Barrow, who thought he had an understanding with Portsmouth that would give the Red Sox first dibs on the youngster when he was ready for better competition; and that, despite his making lots of throwing errors as a shortstop, he was "wildly popular" while playing for the Birmingham Barons of the Southern Association in 1921 ... so popular that years later Barons owner Rick Woodward called him "the finest player in the history of the franchise."

Perhaps because Traynor spent his entire major league career in Pittsburgh and not in a more media-centric city such as New York or Chicago, many of the important highlights of his big league career as a player and as a manager, which the authors deftly weave into their narrative, may come to many readers as revelations as well. For instance, Traynor never hit a lot of home runs because he was basically a line drive hitter and because he played home games in cavernous Forbes Field; however, he hit a lot of triples, ranking in the National League top ten in the category ten times. He also legged out 18 inside-the-park home runs. Pie received the most votes for the NL third base position and the sixth highest number of votes among all players for the first All-Star Game in 1933, and in the 1934 Game he stole home, a feat that has never been duplicated. And, as a manager, he made the biggest blunder of his career when he rejected a trade that would have brought the great Carl Hubbell, still in his prime, to the Pirates.

Most surprising of all is the utterly stunning information about Traynor's development into one of the greatest fielders at his position. In the beginning the Pirates played Traynor at shortstop, his preferred position, in the hope that he could replace the recently retired Honus Wagner. Not even Pie's making 12 errors in a 17-game late-season call-up in 1920 dashed their hopes. When the errors persisted, the Pirates tried him at second base and then, in desperation to get his bat into the lineup, at third base after they acquired the slick-fielding shortstop Rabbit Maranville from the Boston Braves. As part of their keen analysis, the authors write, "He was not a natural third baseman and the position did not come to him easily; he had to strangle the position into submission.... He was a big man, pretty muscular for his day, with long arms and legs.... Traynor was very much a self-taught genius, and in April 1922 he was still working hard to match his raw physical gifts to the demands of this new and unfamiliar position." Eventually, it was manager Bill McKechnie who had the foresight to install Traynor at third base and leave him there, come what may.

Traynor mastered the position with amazing rapidity. He had a terrific year in 1925, batting .320 with 106 RBI, and led the Pirates to a dramatic seven-game victory in the World Series over the Washington Senators and an aging but courageous Walter Johnson. The *New York Times* called Pie "the greatest third baseman since Jimmy Collins," and the pontifical John McGraw said, "He will go down as one of the really great third basemen." Such praise amounted to an early coronation that the rest of Traynor's career did nothing to depose in the minds of the game's leading experts.

Traynor was so respected that by the time his playing career was winding down he became the obvious choice to manage the Pirates. He was hired as a player-manager in mid–June 1934, his last full season, and remained at the helm for five more seasons before resigning at the end of 1939 to avoid getting a pink slip.

The Pirates were moderately successful during his tenure; their best showing being a second-place finish in 1938 to the Cubs when Gabby Hartnett's famous "homer in the gloaming" at Wrigley Field knocked them out of first place for good. In retrospect, it was about as much as should have been expected, as according to the authors, "…in many ways Traynor–sensitive, neurotic, and averse to confrontation–was psychologically unsuited for the role of major league manager." Traynor had other faults too that hardly helped him. He was brutally honest with the press about his players and his teams, he held grudges, and, in the opinion of many observers, he was simply too much of a nice guy to demand nothing but the best from his players. Given all this, the authors ask the logical question: Why did Traynor want to manage? Their answer: Baseball was all that he had known, and the job provided financial security, as well as a continuing positive self-identity.

After scouting for the Pirates for a few years, Traynor finally moved on, but in essence baseball remained his life. After stints in Brookville, Indiana, and Cincinnati, he and his devoted wife Eve made Pittsburgh their permanent home (Traynor loved kids and was never known to refuse to sign autographs for them, but he and Eve never had children of their own.) Because he never obtained a driver's license, Traynor walked the streets of Pittsburgh like a postman, reveling in being gleefully recognized wherever he went. An enthusiastic and enthralling raconteur, he was a welcome guest in every sports hangout and office in town. He had a radio sports news show in Pittsburgh for years and later became a locally well-known pitchman for an HVC company which sponsored, of all things, an extremely popular pro wrestling television show. Generous to a fault, he made countless appearances at all manner of banquets, fund raisers, and speaking engagements, never accepting a penny for his time and trouble. The authors spend a good amount of time on these years, but nary a page is wasted as their efforts to define Traynor as a good and beloved human being (despite some of the flaws we all have) are richly executed and totally successful.

The one thing this book does not do is argue about Traynor's place in the baseball pantheon. It wasn't necessary. Traynor earned the lofty status he enjoyed his entire life by batting over .300 ten times (with a high of .366 in 1930), by driving in more than 100 runs seven times, and by fielding the hot corner like a magician. Despite the fact that his lifetime batting average of .320 was compiled in an era of inflated averages, he was a productive hitter who seldom struck out and who helped his team win two NL pennants and a World Championship. Those who saw him play had no doubts that he was the best ever at his position. More importantly, Pie Traynor was one of the finest human beings to play major league baseball, and no reassessment of his value as a player by comparing him to the greats who followed him will change that. Lastly, the authors were well aware going in of the old saw that books about nice guys are boring. To their and the publishers' credit, they recognized that in Pie Traynor's case, nothing could be further from the truth.

Pinstripe Empire: The New York Yankees from Babe Ruth to After the Boss

◆

MARTY APPEL

◆

New York: Bloomsbury, 2012. Cloth, 620 pages, ISBN: 978-1-60819-492-6. Foreword by Yogi Berra, Preface by Bernie Williams, Special Introduction by Frank Graham, Jr.: Growing Up Yankee, Author's Introduction and Acknowledgments. Information notes at bottom of pages, Appendix: Yankees Year-by-Year Results, Bibliography, Index, 32 black & white and color photos between pages 206 and 207 and 30 black & white and color photos between pages 494 and 495. Other baseball books by the author: Baseball's Best: The Hall of Fame Gallery with Burt Goldblatt *(McGraw-Hill, 1977)*, Thurman Munson: An Autobiography with Thurman Munson *(Tempo Books, 1978)*, Batting Secrets of the Major Leaguers *(Julian Messner, 1981)*, Tom Seaver's All-Time Baseball Greats with Tom Seaver *(Julian Messner, 1984)*, Hardball: The Education of a Baseball Commissioner with Bowie Kuhn *(Times Books, 1987)*, The First Book of Baseball *(Crown, 1988)*, Yesterday's Heroes *(Morrow, 1988)*, My Nine Innings with Lee MacPhail *(Meckler Books, 1989)*, Joe DiMaggio *(Chelsea House, 1990)*, Working the Plate with Eric Gregg *(Morrow, 1990)*, Yogi Berra *(Chelsea House, 1992)*, Great Moments in Baseball with Tom Seaver *(Citadel Press, 1992)*, Slide, Kelly, Slide: The Wild Life and Times of Mike "King" Kelly, Baseball's First Superstar *(Scarecrow Press, 1996)*, Baseball: 100 Classic Moments in the History of the Game with Joseph Wallace and Neil Hamilton *(Dorling Kindersley, 2000)*, Now Pitching for the Yankees *(Sports Illustrated Books, 2001)*, Munson: The Life and Death of a Yankee Captain *(Doubleday, 2009)*, 162–0: The Greatest Wins in Yankee History with Bucky Dent *(Triumph Books, 2010)*, Pinstripe Pride: The Inside Story of the New York Yankees *(Simon & Schuster, 2015)*, Casey Stengel: Baseball's Greatest Character *(Doubleday, 2017)*, Pinstripes by the Tale *(Triumph Books, 2023)*, and Thurm: Memories of a Former Yankee *(Diversion Books, 2023)*.

Comments: Appel is a two-time winner of the CASEY Award. *Slide, Kelly, Slide* won the 14th CASEY Award in 1996, and *Casey Stengel* won the 35th CASEY Award in 2017.

"*Pinstripe Empire* by Marty Appel is the mother of all narrative histories about the team from the Bronx.... At times serious, funny, insightful, dramatic, sad, inspiring and nostalgic, this is a book to take to the beach, to rummage through, to pick up again and again for all the grand nuggets inside of it. The sweep of Yankee legend and lore, facts and figures is here for all time..."—Harvey Frommer, *BleacherReport.com*

Every great story eventually finds its storyteller, and in regard to baseball and its rich history it is difficult to imagine a better pairing than Marty Appel and the New York Yankees. A native New Yorker, lifetime fan of the team, and a Public Relations Director of the team during the George Steinbrenner era, as well as a connoisseur of baseball literature who has tracked the appearances of baseball books on the *New York Time's* bestsellers lists, Appel was uniquely qualified to examine the team from both the insider's up-close and the historian's long-distance viewpoints. The resulting work, the massive 620-page tome entitled *Pinstripe Empire*, in effect replaces Frank Graham's Yankees history that was the first volume in the famous Putnam's series; a book first published in 1943 and then updated in 1958. Simply put, *Pinstripe Empire* set a new standard in team history. Covering 109 seasons of Yankees baseball (1903–2011), it was a challenge to write and it is a challenge to read, but a most pleasurable and rewarding one for those with the stamina to roll through to the end.

Including a "Special Introduction" by Franks Graham, Jr., and his own acknowledgment of the work of his distinguished predecessor was a classy thing to do, but Marty Appel no doubt felt obligated to make such recognitions; and similar ones, noting the contributions to Yankees history of hundreds of lesser-known lights, are seeded throughout the book. Appel's most obvious (and sensible) nod to Graham is his decision to follow Graham's chronological, year-by-year approach; which invariably involves identifying and discussing the basic building blocks and results of any season: owners, field managers, and general managers; key players added to or subtracted from the roster; notable individual and team performances and records set; the team's won-loss record and finish for the year; the gate attendance; and key games, particularly those played in the post-season and World Series.

And of course, no team has played and won more of those games than the New York Yankees, which is what all the fuss is about to begin with. Appel delights in chronicling all the milestone Yankees wins and achievements, none more impressive and definitive than the Yankees being named the "Team of the Century" at the end of 1999 for having won 25 World Championships in the previous 79 seasons. However, he also takes to heart the advice of a friend (mentioned in the introduction) not to rub in the Yankees' amazing record of success out of respect for the fans of other teams who were victims of the team's dominance. Thus, the periods of Yankees mediocrity are not shortchanged, including the first rather lengthy one which began with the team's hasty inception in 1903, as part of Ban Johnson's efforts to create a second major circuit, the American League. The original Yankees, known as the Highlanders or NY Americans or Greater New Yorks, spent the first 18 years of their existence in the also-ran wilderness. They finished last twice (in 1908 and 1912), drew poorly, and after leaving Hilltop Park spend a decade playing in the Polo Grounds and paying rent to their intra-city rivals, the New York Giants, before they moved into the original Yankee Stadium in 1923. Even after they found their first great manager, it took Miller Huggins four years to finally lead the team to a pennant in 1921. And then the Giants defeated them twice, in the 1921 and '22 World Series, before they claimed their first World Championship in 1923, finally besting those same pesky Giants. While that first one was the worst, the Yankees and their multitude of fans suffered through two other long stretches when the team could not buy a pennant (so to speak): 1965–1975 and 1982–1993.

The Yankees began to cement their legend by adding three more pennants and two more World Championships in the 1920s, and with the exception of the two periods noted above were seldom out of the pennant race on a yearly basis. They experienced only two more last-place finishes (1966 and 1990), and oddly enough through 2011 had finished .500 only once, in 1911.

Babe Ruth was the catalyst of those first pennants, establishing a line of superstar talent that the team continually built around, including Lou Gehrig, Joe DiMaggio, Yogi Berra, Whitey Ford, Mickey Mantle, Thurman Munson, Bobby Murcer, Chris Chambliss, Graig Nettles, Reggie Jackson, Goose Gossage, Don Mattingly, Dave Winfield, Derek Jeter, Mariano Rivera, Jorge Posada, Andy Pettitte, Alex Rodriguez, and C.C. Sabathia. The highly capable members of the supporting casts always surrounding the team's biggest stars were legion and far too numerous to mention here, but Appel makes sure to note and credit them all.

Appel may not address the question directly, but by a close reading of his text the reader can deduce the reasons for the franchise's unparalleled success. The team always began with good ownership. Beer baron Jacob Ruppert, the duo of construction magnate Del Webb and tin fortune heir Dan Topping, and ship-building super patriot George Steinbrenner all had deep pockets, a willingness to spend money, and a commitment to winning as if keeping the team on top were a civic duty. Proficient scouting, shrewd trades, and a productive farm system almost continually restocked the team with top talent. (About the Yankees signing of a teen-aged Joe DiMaggio despite concerns about an injury, Appel says: "DiMaggio was a tribute to good scouting, faith in scouts, and a commitment to keep signing the best players.") Finally, once the Yankees established themselves as ruthless baseball royalty in the largest and most important market in the country, a mystique attached itself to everything Yankees: the team name, the logo, the uniforms, the ballpark, the bigger-than-life heroes, and the many many traditions, from the team belting out its theme song after World Series victories ("The Beer Barrell Polka") to the staging of elaborate Old-Timers Games to the unveiling of new plaques in Yankee Stadium's Monument Park. There is no doubt that this mystique has been felt throughout the organization, encouraged by ownership, used by the marketing department to enhance the brand, and embraced not only by players but fans as well. The powerful sense of familial belonging engendered by this mystique is the reason Appel notes the contributions of so many Yankees who never put on the uniform: the groundskeepers, clubhouse men, broadcasters, public address announcers, traveling secretaries, equipment men, trainers, public relations guys, marketing men, stadium operations and construction supervisors, and so on. For the most part, Appel conveys this mindset subtly, although he does early in the book briefly elucidate the effect of the Yankees on the lives of their fans. As for what playing in pinstripes has meant to the players, he lets a statement by former infielder and later Yankees broadcaster Jerry Coleman speak for them all: "Being a Yankee was never a job. It was a religion."

With so many seasons and epochal events to cover, it was incumbent on Appel to be concise and judicious, as he is in summarizing the 1924 and 1925 seasons. About the team's second-place finish in '24 he says, "The Yankees had managed a strong season; it was just the Senators' turn." To explain the drop to seventh place the following year, he writes: "This was going to be just a horrible year in Yankee history, a year when their big stars got old all at once." While Appel did not have the luxury of devoting entire chapters to sensational stories, of which they are many in Yankees history, some moments demanded enhanced treatment; such as Thurman Munson's tragic death, about which the author writes compassionately and evocatively. Appel's conciseness is also much in evidence in his striking ability to get to the heart of personalities and the meaning of events with a few well-chosen words. In introducing Lou Gehrig, he writes: "He was Ruth without drama, Ruth without nightlife, Ruth without scandal." And his seemingly off-hand remark that the 1935 season was Gehrig's "only season in which he didn't share the spotlight with Ruth or Joe DiMaggio" speaks volumes about the peculiar nature of Gehrig's great but often overshadowed career.

Finally, in addition to its other numerous virtues, *Pinstripe Empire* is a trivia question maker's dream, as Appel is constantly alerting us to first and last occurrences and to the kind of statistical and historical oddities that fans consume like Jelly Bellies. The first player to homer in a World Series game in Yankee Stadium, Appel reminds us, was not Babe Ruth but an aging bow-legged Giants outfielder named Casey Stengel; he notes that over the course of his 193 regular and post-season starts in pinstripes, Roger Clemens pitched a total of four complete games; and he surprises all but the very best informed readers when he points out that the immortal moniker "Murderer's Row" did not come into being to describe the 1927 Yankees batting lineup but that of the 1918 team, which was populated by players named Gilhooley, Peckinpaugh, Baker, Pratt, Pipp, and Bodie.

Throughout the book one notices the author looking backwards and forwards. He foreshadows great periods ahead by dropping asides about the births of Mantle and Jeter; and when he covers the talent pipeline that the Kansas City A's provided for the Yankees in the 1950s, we can't help but recall that the same remarkable generosity was displayed by the Red Sox back in the 1920s (after the lop-sided trade that sent Boston third baseman Joe Dugan to the Yanks, Cleveland manager Tris Speaker said of the on-going pick-pocketing, "It's a crime"). Of the numerous times Appel injects his own experiences into the narrative, the most telling one is his account of his attending the last game in old Yankee Stadium with son Brian in tow. Father and son sit in the right field bleachers behind right fielder Bobby Abreu, just as Appel had sat with his dad when he witnessed his first major league game back in the 1950s with Hank Bauer manning the position. Unscrambling the letters in Abreu to produce Bauer causes Appel to state an important truth which undergirds the history he has been unraveling: "Everything connects."

After the Yankees became the first team to win three World Championships in a row in 1938, cries of "Break up the Yankees!" became the mantra throughout baseball. Later, with the fierce rivalry between the Red Sox and Yankees firmly established, opposing fans delighted in characterizing the team as the "evil empire." And today Yankee hating remains a lively pastime. Yet, after reading *Pinstripe Empire* one must accord respect and admiration to the franchise and its amazing history of excellence, as well as to the author whose efforts in writing this grandiose history were nothing short of heroic.

The Pitch That Killed:
Carl Mays, Ray Chapman
and the Pennant Race of 1920

◆

MIKE SOWELL

◆

New York: Macmillan, 1989. Cloth, 330 pages, ISBN: 0-02-612410-6. Prologue, Acknowledgments. Bibliography, Index, 19 black & white photos between pages 110 and 111. Other baseball books by the author: July 2, 1903: The Mysterious Death of Hall-of-Famer Big Ed Delahanty *(Macmillan, 1992) and* One Pitch Away: The Players' Stories of the 1986 League Championship and World Series *(Macmillan, 1995).*

Comments: *The Pitch That Killed* won the seventh CASEY Award for the Best Baseball Book of 1989.

While it was common knowledge that the beaning death of Cleveland Indians shortstop Ray Chapman was the only such event to ever occur in a major league baseball game, few people realized how much more there was to the story until the publication of *The Pitch that Killed* by Mike Sowell. Via Sowell's skillful telling, the rest of the story, involving a convenient villain, a torrid pennant race, a fateful adjustment of the rules of the game, the devastating effects of Chapman's death, and the heroic reaction of Chapman's teammates amounts to one of the most dramatic, affecting, and unforgettable chapters a fan of baseball history will ever read.

Sowell collects the factual material he unearthed into major sections, which focus on one aspect of the story at a time yet seamlessly move the narration forward without any sense of digression or irrelevance. He first spotlights the main participants: Boston Red Sox-New York Yankees pitcher Carl Mays and then Ray Chapman. He next delves into the major movements of the action: The Pennant Race, The Beaning, and the Boycott. And he then concludes with a focus on Chapman's replacement, rookie shortstop Joe Sewell, and the story's denouement, The Aftermath. This logical, orderly progression not only aids the author in controlling the pace and proper sequencing of events, but it also helps the reader understand the many nuances that make the Chapman beaning and death such a multi-faceted, unique happening.

Opening the book with brief biographies of Mays and Chapman was a stroke of

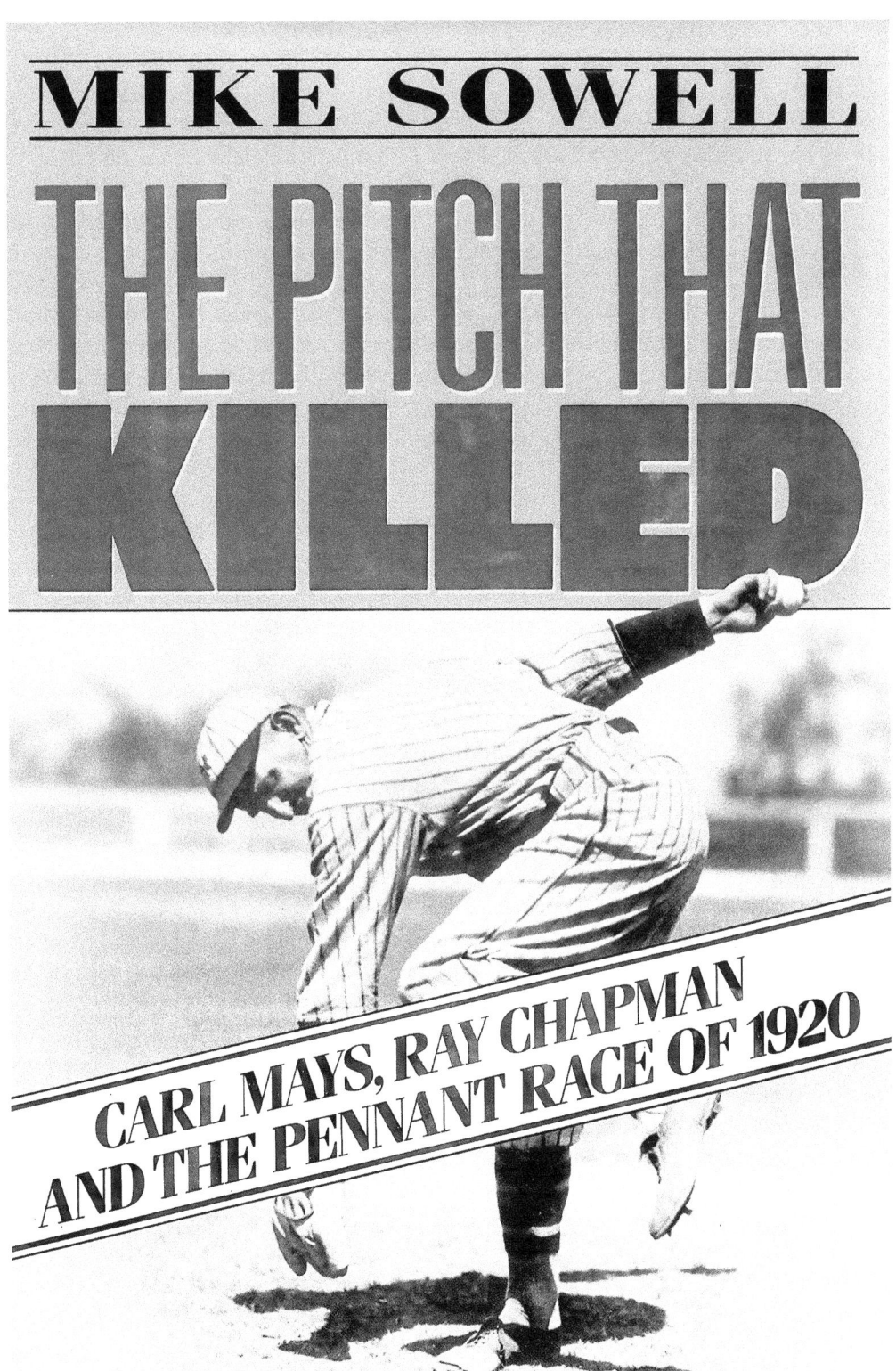

brilliance, as the differences between the two men, who seemed like polar opposites, could not have been more pronounced. Mays was quiet, even gloomy, and standoffish. He was a loner, almost universally disliked, had trouble getting along with his teammates, and was despised by many opponents for the aggressive way he pitched; asking nor granting any quarter in the heat of competition. Chapman was effusive, outgoing, and joyous. The best storyteller and singer on the Indians ballclub who actually caused his rough and tumble teammates to enjoy joining him in sing-alongs on train trips between American League cities, he was highly popular and even beloved, by teammates and fans alike.

As the two opening chapters demonstrate, the differences in personality and character between the two players manifested themselves in the events of their lives. Mays, as just the most egregious example, became embroiled in a huge controversy that had enormous consequences. Convinced that some of his Boston Red Sox teammates were intentionally playing poorly behind him, he quit the team in a huff and stayed home until he was signed by the New York Yankees. AL President Ban Johnson suspended Mays and tried to penalize the Yankees for signing a player who was Red Sox property, but the Yankees' fought back vigorously and won. The conflict, which ripped apart the American League, pitting groups of clubs against each other, led to a re-alignment of the League power structure and greatly diminished the authority of Johnson. In contrast, Chapman disappointed the bachelorettes of an entire region by marrying the aristocratic Kathleen Daly. Their wedding was described as the Cleveland area's "social event of the fall" of 1919, and the newlyweds soon commenced supervising the construction of their dream home, which they planned to fill with children. At the behest of his father-in-law, Chapman announced that the 1920 season would be his last, as he planned to enter the business world, helping run one of Mr. Daly's going concerns. Mays entered the 1920 season accompanied by grudges and score-settling agendas; Chapman with the burning desire to end his career on a high note by helping bring the city of Cleveland its first baseball World Championship.

As if the drama of the story needed any inflation, Sowell adroitly peppers instances of foreboding throughout the narration leading up to the fateful game of August 16, 1920, played in New York (the Yankees were a game out of first behind the Indians, and Mays was going for his 100th major league victory). Despite his unpopularity, Mays enjoyed a period of happiness after getting married, avoiding seeing action in World War I, surviving the flu epidemic, and establishing himself as a winning pitcher. Yet, in looking back on that time, Mays realized it was the calm before the storm: "I remember a conversation I had with my wife about this time in which I told her my baseball career had been singularly free from trouble. I said to her in a joking way that perhaps it would be necessary for me to do something out of the ordinary to get my name in the papers.

But I needn't have been impatient. For could I have looked into the future, I would have seen trouble enough headed in my direction to satisfy the most ambitious seeker who ever lived." Then during the spring training of 1920, Mays witnessed the terrible beaning of one of his few friends on the Yankees, scrawny second baseman Chick Fewster. The beaning, which almost killed Fewster, shook up Mays and the Brooklyn pitcher who threw the pitch, Jeff Pfeffer. The book contains even more descriptions of ominous events and utterances connected to Chapman. At his bachelor dinner, Sowell tells us, Chapman whistled one of his favorite songs, "Good-Bye, Boys, I'm Through." When the train-boarding, spring training-bound Chapman waved goodbye to his family, Sowell writes, "It was the last time they (family members) ever saw him alive." When a sportswriter asked Yankees manager Miller Huggins if he was worried about "howlers" who insinuated they would retaliate against Mays for throwing bean balls, Miller defended his pitcher, saying, "Mays wouldn't hurt anybody." While discussing the AL's best pitchers with his family, Chapman said that Mays "…throws it so he'll dust you off the plate. But I'll stand right up there. He doesn't bother me. He's not going to intimidate me." And on the very day that a pitch from Mays killed him, Chapman joked about the difficulty he had batting against the submariner, telling his teammates, "Mays is pitching for the Yankees today, so I'll do the fielding and you fellows do the hitting."

Apart from these forebodings which loom significant perhaps mostly in retrospect, a couple of actual factors combined to make the incident, or one like it on some other day involving some other player, fateful as well as fatal. First, there was Mays' unusual delivery, a kind of extreme submarine style, that made his tosses not only difficult to hit but difficult to catch as well. Prior to the 1920 season a host of trick pitches were outlawed, but nothing Mays did on the mound was banned, including his surreptitious habit of scrapping the baseball across the edge of the pitcher's rubber. Second, while Mays had excellent control, he did pitch inside and he did use the knock down as a key part of his arsenal. He led the league in HBP in 1917 and finished second in 1918. And, finally, in a cost-saving move, umpires for the 1920 season were ordered to keep baseballs in play as long as possible; increasing the odds of a ball being used that was hard for pitchers to control and for batters to see. It was this very thing that Mays afterwards blamed for the fateful pitch.

Sowell makes it clear that the beaning, which came in Chapman's leadoff at bat in the top of the fifth inning, was an accident, as the pitch was in the strike zone when it struck Chapman in the temple with a sickening report. Apparently, Chapman simply froze in place, perhaps because he did not pick up the flight of the ball as quickly as he needed to. Because of the pitch's location and the sound made when it struck Chapman, Mays believed at first that the ball hit the bat. He, in fact, picked up the carom which rolled out to the mound and threw the ball to first base as if it were in play. Several Indians players had to be held back from attacking Mays, who not immediately knowing the severity of Chapman's injury, remained in the game until he was pinch hit for in the bottom of the eighth. While Sowell recounts the tragic event dispassionately, it is heart-rending reading; especially the scene inside the visitors' clubhouse when the stricken Chapman recovers the power of speech just long enough to tell his close friend, John Henry, a former major league catcher: "John, for God's sake, don't call Kate. But if you do, tell her I'm all right." At 12:30 in the morning the 29-year-old Chapman underwent a brain operation for an hour and a half but died nevertheless a few hours later. The next day Kate Chapman arrived in New York and rushed to player-manager Tris Speaker's hotel room, where a group of players were assembled in shocked mourning. "He's dead, isn't he?" Kate asked. When Speaker nodded his head, she fainted.

As gripping as Sowell's account of the accident is, the rest of the story is equally riveting and involves: the massive grief felt by the entire city of Cleveland; the threats of boycotts, ultimately defused, by several teams of games scheduled to be pitched by Mays; the emergence of rookie shortstop Joe Sewell who vowed to become the reincarnation of his predecessor; the Indians' gutsy drive to outlast the Chicago White Sox and Yankees to win the pennant and then defeat the Brooklyn Dodgers in the World Series to indeed present Cleveland with its first World Championship; and the impact of the entire affair on the remaining career and life of Carl Mays. It is the latter part of the story which is most haunting. Mays expressed remorse for what happened to Chapman, and he always maintained that the beaning was accidental. Nevertheless, he was never able to shake the stigma of blame that attached itself to him, and he died an embittered man; certain that the fatal pitch he delivered was unfairly held against him and used to deny him his rightful place in the Baseball Hall of Fame. While his merits for that honor may be debatable, *The Pitch That Killed* convinces us that what happened to Ray Chapman was a tragedy for Carl Mays as well as for Chapman.

Play for a Kingdom

Thomas Dyja

New York: Harcourt Brace & Company, 1997. Cloth, 416 pages, ISBN: 0-15-10 0267-3. Prologue. Epilogue.
  Comments: The title of the novel is taken from Shakespeare, *Henry V*, Act III: "…for when lenity and cruelty play for a kingdom, the gentler gamester is the soonest winner."

One of the many fascinating auxiliary aspects of the American Civil War is the extent to which baseball was played by participants of the conflict. We know for a fact that baseball was played by Union army officers in the Confederate prison camp in Salisbury, North Carolina, as early as July 1962, and historian Tom Gilbert assures us that during the numerous, often boring, lulls in the fighting enlisted men on both sides engaged in games among themselves. What there is no credible evidence for is teams of Yankee and Rebel soldiers having played baseball against each other. Nevertheless, to the ever-lasting joy of lovers of great fiction, this most enticing, fantastic scenario was given life by Thomas Dyja when he published his CASEY-winning novel about this very idea, *Play for a Kingdom*.

The protagonists of Dyja's story are all fictional, the men of the 14th Brooklyn, Company L: a unit that Dyja places in the historical Colonel Jacob B. Switzer's brigade, part of the Grant and Meade Army of the Potomac. As the story begins, Grant has just assumed overall command of the Northern forces. He believes, as does his boss Abraham Lincoln, that the way to defeat the Confederate army is not to out-strategize the brilliant Robert E. Lee, but to win, no matter the cost, a war of attrition, wearing down the South through constant assaults, aided by superior numbers of men, materiel, and resources. Grant is about to launch on 5 May 1864 the Overland Campaign, which will consist of two of the bloodiest and costliest battles of the entire war: the Battle of the Wilderness followed almost immediately by the Battle of Spotsylvania Courthouse. Insiders view this Campaign as crucial, fearing that if the North loses, a "cooperhead" (a Democrat pacifist) will be elected president and sue for peace.

Company L has been fighting for three long years and is manned by only 20 of its original 100 members: "mostly the dregs of the company, save for a handful of brave men lucky enough to never have been hit or so unlucky that their injuries weren't bad enough to send them home." An example of the former is the inspiring Sargent Danny Anson, an undertaker back in Brooklyn who tells his fellow soldiers that "three years of burying brave men in shallow graves" has made him determined to give up his profession; while butcher Lyman Alder, who suffered a painful and potentially fatal bullet wound in his shoulder at Gettysburg represents the latter. (Typical of the novel's eloquent prose, Dyja writes "The hem of Death's robe had brushed his arm.") Several characters qualify as the "dregs" of the company, such as Oliver Stives, "a long, Scripture-spouting loner with wild hair and beard of Moses"; Felix Cathorne, an untrustworthy actor demoted after one month as a corporal; and grocer Newton "Newt" Fry, a coward who not only froze in an earlier battle when a Rebel was about to finish off Lyman but who lets Alder believe it was he, and not the steelier Tiger Quigley, who saved his life. These Irish, English, and German war-weary veterans have only 18 days left until the end of their three-year enlistment, and so their minds are focused more on staying alive than on fighting. Similarly, the predicament of these men hoping to run out the clock on death deepens the reader's vicarious involvement in their fates.

Baseball enters the picture in a surprising way. There is a traitorous spy in the Confederate army who wishes to help the Union, and Company L's unctuous Captain Schuyler Henry, who travels with all the luxuries and comforts of home, needs someone he can trust to meet with this spy. Henry bypasses his second-in-command and fellow lingerer in the rear, his calculating first lieutenant Linden Stewart, in favor of timorous second lieutenant John Burridge, a young Latin and Greek-loving lawyer in whom the soldiers have no confidence. Proud of being chosen, Burridge is so focused on seeking out the spy that he leads the men into combat during the Battle of the Wilderness with reckless abandonment for his own safety. Anson is killed as the unit performs miserably, and Alder basically assumes leadership. He even engineers a momentary cease-fire, with the help of a like-minded Rebel, Micah Breese, so that dying soldiers from both sides can be extracted from a conflagration of human flesh started by cannon fire. Company L performs no better the next day as the two sides fight to a bloody draw, and the soldiers believe that the army will, as in the past, withdraw from the field and head north to reorganize and resupply. But this time is different, as Grant is determined to keep fighting while Lee's army remains in the area; a decision which leads to the even more catastrophic (for both sides) Battle of Spotsylvania.

While resting from picket duty, Company L finds a clearing in the thick wooded forest, and Lyman Alder who has a baseball and Newt Fry who has a bat begin to toss the ball around. Then, in a scene reminiscent of *Shoeless Joe*, a rag tag group of gray and brown figures emerge from the woods: Rebel soldiers of the Twelfth Alabama, led by Captain Sydney Mink who turns out to be the spy Burridge has been looking for, who are willing to risk (along with the Northerners) court martial and either prison or death for the pleasure of engaging in a normal, spirit-lifting, soul-soothing activity like playing a game of ball. Nervously at first, but increasingly trusting, the soldiers play a nine-inning match—Lyman pitching to Newt—won by the Confederates 12–10. The close, surprising outcome (from the Union's point of view) results in the two sides agreeing to play a best-of-five series, with the lone baseball designated as the winner's trophy. Mink and Burridge both play first base so that Mink, speaking Latin in the First Match and drawing maps in the dirt with his foot in the Second, can pass on to Burridge sensitive information about Confederate losses, positions, and plans.

As risky and as difficult to be arranged as the matches are, they come to pass with some unforeseen consequences. From the beginning, some of the members of Company L have objected to risking their lives for blacks. Now the Union soldiers discover that the aristocratic Mink is the only Reb who owns slaves and that, furthermore, most of the Rebels don't care if the slaves are freed. In his mind Newt formulates the irony of this situation: "He was surrounded by Yankees who at best didn't care about Africans, fighting against abolitionist Rebs." In a similar vein, Tiger Quigley asks a Rebel named Deal, "So if none of ye wants to keep slavery, what the hell are ye fighting for?" " 'Cause yo' here. On our land," Deal replies; expressing the understandable opposition to an invasion of one's country, for whatever reason, that men have rallied for throughout the ages (something American policy makers should have understood about the "ungrateful" partisans in the Iraq war). As we learn later, Lyman signed up (and dragged his friend Newt along with him) for another reason other than the abolition of slavery: to enforce the rights of the Federal government over the states, including the forced preservation of the union, which was Lincoln's overriding concern. Lyman felt that ending slavery was a righteous cause but that "if the slaves had never been brought over from Africa … something else would have caused this crisis." Dyja's including such philosophical arguments brings his characters to life more vividly, conveys the complexity of the reasons for the war, and heightens both the tragedy of it and the respect we should have for the memory of all who had the courage and conviction to participate in it.

By the end of the Third Match, players on both sides are beginning to get suspicious and to wonder if they are being used. Lieutenant Stewart is all too ready to arrest his own men for treason if he can prove they are fraternizing with the enemy; Captain Henry is afraid that Burridge is inadvertently passing on Union secrets to Mink (which Burridge is); and Burridge begins to worry that he is endangering his own men, whom he used to despise but now cares for deeply.

And then the ferocious Battle of Spotsylvania begins, a seemingly never-ending mutual massacre which frightens even the bravest members of the 14th as they get close to the slaughter. As every honest war novel must, Dyja's highly imaginative description of the scene through the eyes of Lyman portrays the madness and horror of it all:

> In most battles, men screamed to exhilarate themselves, to relive tension and convince their eternal souls that they could kill. The noise of Spotsylvania was a churning, a steady buzz more like a building site than any battle Lyman had seen. He knew that this meant that those fighting were too tired to yell, though men still shrieked in death. Like drones, the men accomplished their individual murders methodically under the eyes of pitiless foremen; insanity was necessary to perform the job. Lyman, nearly folded by the cramping of fear, his balls shriveled into his guts, wondered how he'd get his men out alive.

Particularly in the long section devoted to this battle and its aftermath, the descriptions of the brutal fighting and killings; the horrific wounds; the pitiable moans and cries of the wounded and dying; and the unimaginable suffering of those operated on, especially the amputees are so graphic that at times the novel is difficult to read. Yet, *Play for a Kingdom* is a book about war, above all. (Like all good historical novels, the book is also rich in period detail and language. "Quickstep" means diarrhea, a malady so common and dangerous that one character dies from it.)

The meaning of the baseball in the story is less obvious. By the time the Fifth and deciding Match is played, the stakes have been raised considerably. Burridge admits to the men that Mink, in an attempt to save his own skin, has arranged for an ambush of the Confederates. Thus, the men of Company L, just days away from being mustered out, risk everything; playing the game not just to have at least one clear victory to take home with them but to try to save their new friends by convincing them to "take the oath" of allegiance; i.e., desert and join the Union army. The climax turns on one more act of heroic sacrifice and righteous men inevitably remaining true to their principles, providing a satisfying conclusion to the novel.

The end of the war did not, of course, resolve all the difficulties over which the war was fought. The reconstruction of the South was slow and painful, and life for American blacks remained difficult no matter on which side of the Mason-Dixon Line they lived. And baseball? Blacks were prohibited for a long time thereafter from playing in the white major leagues, on teams all located in supposedly more enlightened Northern cities, until Jackie Robinson finally broke the color line in 1947. After reading *Play for a Kingdom*, one cannot help but see Brooklyn, home of the 14th, Company L, as the perfect place for that great emancipation to have occurred.

The Pride of the Yankees: Lou Gehrig, Gary Cooper, and the Making of a Classic

Richard Sandomir

New York: Hachette Books, 2017. Cloth, 293 pages, ISBN: 978-0-316-35505-6. Foreword. Epilogue: Cooper Says Good-Bye, Acknowledgments, Bibliography, Source Notes, Index, 17 black & white photos between pages 150 and 151.

A surprising fact about books about a particular baseball movie is the counter intuitive truth that the book is often more interesting than the movie it celebrates. Granted, reading a book and watching a movie are disparate experiences, and given the production challenges and financial and time limitations of film, it may seem unfair to compare the two. Yet, despite outshining their counterparts, the best books about baseball movies also inevitably enhance our appreciation for the films, so that we are happily left with the proverbial win-win situation. Such is the case with *The Pride of the Yankees: Lou Gehrig, Gary Cooper, and the Making of a Classic* by Richard Sandomir.

As many others do, Sandomir considers *Pride* a great film, perhaps the best baseball movie ever made, and he writes about it lovingly. Because other authors had already dealt thoroughly with all facets of Gehrig's death from ALS, he covers the topic briefly and dives almost immediately into the story of how the movie came to be made. He states that within days of Gehrig's death, "Hollywood's pursuit of the Gehrig story began." This was not because baseball was a favored subject. In fact, the mogul who made the film, Samuel Goldwyn, knew practically nothing about baseball, reportedly had never even heard of Gehrig, and considered the game "box office poison." "If people want baseball," he said, "they go to the ballpark." The unsung hero in the story is Niven Busch, Jr., a writer and story editor for Goldwyn Studios, as well as a baseball fan, who convinced his boss to watch newsreels of Gehrig delivering his "luckiest man" speech. When the lights went up, Goldwyn's face was wet with tears, and he was suddenly determined to make a movie about the Yankees' tragic first baseman.

Another key figure whose contributions are duly chronicled by Sandomir was Christy Walsh, the "fixer, publicist, ad man, marketer, and agent" who represented

Gehrig's widow, Eleanor Twitchell Gehrig. Walsh had made a lot of money operating a ballplayer-ghostwriting syndicate; and while his partnership with the flamboyant Babe Ruth had been way more lucrative for both parties than the one with Gehrig, he did his best to protect the interests of Eleanor out of his deep respect for the humble "Iron Horse." In regard to Hollywood offers, the savvy Walsh told her to "Take your time and wear a poker face." Without much competition, he got her a contract for $30,000 from Goldwyn and continued to serve as a sounding board and to run interference for her throughout the movie-making process.

The studio ran a national contest to cast the leading male role, but, as Sandomir demonstrates, it was in reality a publicity stratagem as the fix was in. From the beginning Gary Cooper, who made his living playing men of quiet dignity such as Sergeant York, was slated to portray Gehrig because the role fell into his wheelhouse. Sandomir says that *Pride* represents "a near-perfect marriage of a modest heroic subject and an actor who specialized in modest, heroic characters." In addition, Cooper was under contract with Goldwyn for one more movie, and Goldwyn knew that no better role was on the horizon for his star than the Gehrig biopic.

During her visit to San Francisco to sign the Goldwyn contract, Eleanor met writer Paul Gallico who took 38 pages of notes of their conversations. Gallico was a talented writer, but his first script enraged Goldwyn for the simple fact that it contained too much baseball. Goldwyn envisioned a "romantic, heroic" film that would appeal as much, if not more, to women than to men, and that's what he got. While Gallico accepted Goldwyn's vision for the film and continued to have some influence on it, the mogul still brought on board two in-house screenwriters, Herman Mankiewicz and Jo Swerling, who became responsible for the final script. In the middle chapters of the book, there is much fascinating discussion about scenes that were cut, revised, proposed but not adopted, or added. And throughout the process, there was Eleanor, who at a distance, argued for historical accuracy and vigilantly attempted to protect her dead husband's image.

The role of Eleanor was given to Theresa Wright "whose screen persona was fixed as an intelligent, pretty, blue-eyed girl-next-door who could hold her own against Bette Davis, Greer Garson, and, as audiences would learn, Cooper." She was much younger than Cooper, a potential problem in terms of plausibility, but she and Cooper convinced audiences of their compatibility; so much so that Sandomir says that "Their chemistry is at the center of *Pride*."

The film had other obstacles to hurdle, including the need to make what baseball scenes do exist in it appear authentic. Several of Gehrig's Yankees teammates disqualified themselves due to outlandish monetary demands, and in the end four others made the cut, including Gehrig's best friend, catcher Bill Dickey who wound up bonding with Cooper over their mutual interest in hunting, and Babe Ruth, who finagled a stipend of $1,500 per week. Resentful of how Ruth had always overshadowed Lou in life, Eleanor feared that he might do so again in *Pride*, but the Bambino behaved himself; turning in a winning performance while never detracting from the focus on Cooper-Gehrig. (Eleanor surely approved of a contrived scene which puts Lou in a much better light than Ruth. After Ruth promises with great fanfare to hit a home run for a polio-stricken lad, Cooper remains behind in the hospital room, minus all the writers and photographers, to encourage the kid to get better by promising to hit two homers ... which of course he does in a dramatic way.) Then there was Cooper himself. His slender form was hardly reminiscent of Gehrig's heavily-muscled broad-shouldered physique; and at age 41, it took some special efforts by cinematographer Rudolph Mate to make the scenes of him playing a young Gehrig believable. The biggest problem of all was Cooper's total lack of baseball ability, a problem compounded by his righthandedness (the powerful Gehrig had swung the bat and thrown left-handed), so Goldwyn hired ex-major league batting champion Lefty O'Doul to train Cooper in the fine arts. O'Doul said Cooper threw a ball "like an old woman tossing a hot biscuit," but the actor improved just enough to passably perform the basics. Still, for some batting scenes Babe Herman was used as a stand-in. The author also presents the analysis of an expert to conclude that very little flipping of negatives occurred (to make it appear as if the right-handed Cooper was swinging the bat left-handed) and none at all during the critical New York Yankees scenes.

Given Goldwyn's determination to make *Pride* a love story rather than a baseball movie per se, it is hardly surprising that numerous liberties were taken with the narrative. A number of harmless fictional scenes were included to invest the staid Gehrig with more personality than he had been known to exhibit, and more than a few others were added as devices to simplify the story or to gloss over negative aspects of some of the film's personages. For instance, intent on becoming an engineer as his mother wants him to, Cooper-Gehrig signs with the Yankees mainly to pay for an operation needed by his mother which the family cannot afford. The date, place, and circumstances of the first meeting between Lou and Eleanor are all wrong, and Eleanor's father is presented as a genteel, successful businessman, when in reality he was a failure who abandoned his family. Most glaring of all, Ma Gehrig is depicted as what is today called a "helicopter" parent but not the jealous, vindictive mother-in-law from hell who totally alienated Eleanor and forced her son to choose between his mother and his wife.

Ultimately, the success of *Pride* hinged on the handling of the farewell speech Gehrig had delivered at Yankee Stadium on July 4, 1939. Amazingly, for being one of the most famous addresses in American history, there were unanswerable questions about it. For instance, we don't know for certain whether Gehrig wrote the speech himself or received help from Eleanor or perhaps from a sportswriter, such as their friend Fred Lieb. We also don't know if Gehrig practiced reciting it beforehand. Only four lines of the speech were recorded on newsreels, and various newspapers reported differing versions of it the next day. Eleanor composed a scintillating version of it for Goldwyn and insisted that it was accurate to the word. To her displeasure, the screenwriters shortened it, but they also shifted the two most memorable lines from the beginning to the end of the speech: "People all say that I've had a bad break. But today ... today, I consider myself the luckiest man on the face of the earth." It was a stroke of genius to conclude the speech with this sentiment of humility, optimism, and courage; as was the decision to end the movie here with Cooper slowly trudging off the field, awkwardly ducking into the Yankees' dugout, and walking down the tunnel to be reunited with a sobbing Theresa Wright. There was no need to dramatize Gehrig's inevitable and sad demise, a given. What the ending conveys is what was most important and what lasted: the love between husband and wife.

To everyone's relief, Eleanor was happy with the movie, which made a respectable profit and elicited warm praise from the critics. Also relieved was Goldwyn, who could return to making films he was more comfortable with. The role turned out to be one of the most important of Cooper's long and distinguished career; his performance so moving that he was repeatedly called upon to reprise the speech for American servicemen during a 24,000-mile USO tour of the South Pacific during World War II. In a final chapter recounting the rest of Eleanor's life and her reactions to succeeding treatments of the story, including parodies, Sandomir concludes the book with the effect the film had on the rest of Theresa Wright's life and career. Late in life, she became a rabid New York Yankees fan. The author sends her off with a sweet kiss of a last line: "She died in 2005, in rapturous love with Lou Gehrig's game."

Prophet of the Sandlots: Journeys with a Major League Scout

Mark Winegardner

New York: Atlantic Monthly Press, 1990. Cloth, 279 pages, ISBN: 0-87113-336-9. Acknowledgments. Epilogue: Edison's Drugstore, Appendix: Signed for the Chicago Cubs (player, position, major league debut), Signed for the Philadelphia Phillies. Other baseball books by the author: The 26th Man: One Minor Leaguer's Pursuit of a Dream with Steve Fireovid *(Macmillan, 1991) and* The Veracruz Blues *(Viking, 1996).*

In Kevin Kerrane's book on the art of scouting, Dodgers scout Reggie Otero says, "To *see* the talents is as much a gift as to *have* the talents. I do not say as great a gift, but is as much a gift." God blessed no baseball scout with the gift Otero speaks of more abundantly than Tony Lucadello, who signed more players (for the Chicago Cubs and Philadelphia Phillies) who eventually made the major leagues than any other scout: including Hall of Famers Ferguson Jenkins and Mike Schmidt. In his long career Lucadello drove leased cars nearly 2.5 million miles throughout nine states and three Canadian provinces and in the process became a legend among professional baseball insiders and the amateur and scholastic ranks which support the professional game. After reading a newspaper article about Lucadello, Mark Winegardner, still in the early stages of his own career as a writer, decided "on a whim" to write a book about him. Winegarder followed Lucadello around for a year and a half, and the resulting account of their travels together, *Prophet of the Sandlots*, takes the reader on one of the most enjoyable and poignant journeys in the canon of baseball literature.

As the book begins Lucadello is an old man, an octogenarian at the end of his long career. Nevertheless, the diminutive little man, who once played Class D minor league baseball for his hometown Fostoria (OH) Redbirds, maintains a high level of energy and enthusiasm for his job, as well as his appearance. Lucadello always wears a coat and tie, and his hat (a houndstooth fedora, not a ball cap) is his sartorial trademark. His formal but dated wardrobe lends him, in the words of Winegardner, "a particularly midwestern humility that made him seem like Everygrandpa…."

At first Lucadello is not sure he wants to do a book. Another writer had tried and failed, and Winegardner suspects that the manuscript having been roundly rejected has made Tony gun shy. While Lucadello later asks Winegardner several times if he still wants to proceed, during Winegardner's initial visit to the modest Lucadello home, Tony reveals why he does indeed want to participate in the book. Lucadello feels that baseball is in trouble. More and more often American boys are turning to other sports, and too often the boys who do play baseball are not playing it well due to a lack of training in the fundamentals. Tony, of course, has a remedy for this, and it is a four-foot wall that he wants to make as ubiquitous in every American backyard as basketball hoops are in the country's driveways. Lucadello believes that throwing a baseball against such a wall and fielding the caroms develops proper footwork, improved body positioning, and arm strength. He also advocates batters improving their swings by swatting buckets of plastic golf balls. In the very first chapter, before the two men set out on their first scouting trip together, they look for and find a couple of such walls erected in the nearby backyards of young Lucadello disciples. Lucadello reveals that his main interest in doing a book will be to spread the gospel of his walls as a means of saving baseball. As the pair's adventure unfolds, the wall remains a topic that Lucadello returns to repeatedly; when Mark's wife becomes pregnant with their first child, Tony even gets Mark to promise that he'll build a wall for the assumed-to-be boy.

During the narration of the scouting trips which Winegardner accompanies Lucadello on, a thoroughly endearing portrait of the man quickly begins to emerge. Tony Lucadello, we discover, is a gentleman. He is humble, repeatedly giving credit to his part-time scouts, but also confident of his worth and not above wondering aloud why, with his track record, the Phillies don't put more stock in his judgment. Respectful of others, he is careful never to criticize a player within earshot of that player or his family; he goes out of his way to pay his respects to coaches he knows have no current players worth scouting; and he leaves ballgames as unobtrusively as possible so as not to give anybody the idea he has seen nothing of value. He is extremely loyal: to his wife, to the players he takes an interest in and their families, to the Phillies organization, and even to the Knights Inn motel chain, because he is friends with the president of the company. He is also disciplined (his road diet consists of salads and fruit plates), kind (he scours parking lots and ball fields for loose change he donates to the first church he passes on September 15 of each year), and compassionate, always keeping a player's best interests in mind. Winegarder builds up this portrait so skillfully, mainly using Lucadello's own words, stories, and actions to do so, that before the reader has finished a quarter of the book he is in love himself with the subject.

This is not to say that Lucadello is a pushover. He is highly competitive, secretive, and paranoid, constantly fearful that other scouts will swoop in and start following one of his "sleepers": a player nobody else has yet to recognize as being a prospect. Borne out of his character and refined over decades of plying his trade, Lucadello's primary advantage over his competition is the relationship he slowly and carefully develops over years with each player and his parents. When it comes time for the player to decide whether or not to sign a contract with the Phillies, most of them have no chance. Tony Lucadello is a closer on the order of Mariano Rivera.

As we follow the two men on the backroads leading to sandlot, high school, municipal, and college diamonds all over northern Ohio and southern Michigan, we learn a tremendous amount about the actual nuts and bolts of scouting a la Tony Lucadello. For instance, Tony teaches Mark that 87 percent of a player's ability resides below the waist; that every player's body has eight "sides" to be evaluated and that a diamond has six different prime viewing spots (not one of which is behind home plate); and that there are four kinds of scouts: Poor (lazy guys who go to any game and hope to find the next Mickey Mantle), Pickers (those who focus so much on one flaw they overlook all the good), Performance (the easily impressed who judge a player by how well he plays), and Projectors (scouts who can accurately assess how much a player will develop, how good he will be in the future). Lucadello is obviously the latter, and there's no better evidence of his ability as a baseball seer than his belief in Mike Schmidt, who struggled in both the minors and major leagues before developing into a Hall of Famer. Lucadello cautioned the Phillies to be patient, insisting that Schmidt would be a late bloomer.

Highlighting the travels of the two men and the account of their patronizing a series of hotels and roadside restaurants are the wonderful stories told by Lucadello, both the whoppers that demand a bemused respect earned by Tony and the true stories that make up the amazing multi-colored cloth of his career. Lucadello, we learn, would do anything to see or sign a player: including watching a pitcher throw in a coal mine 400 feet below ground, arranging for another pitcher to throw from one barn into another during an unrelenting rain storm, and risking his life to sneak into a gang-ridden Chicago ghetto in the middle of the night to get a signature on a contract. Signings, in particular, provide insight into the man's character. In the story of Dick Drott, who went on to pitch for the Cubs, Tony was faced with an impossible situation. Because of the rules of the day, the Cubs who could not afford to keep a raw rookie on the major league roster were limited to offering a bonus of $4,000. Other teams were offering a $100,000. At the last minute, Lucadello left the family kitchen, went to his car, and rubbed onion juice on his little finger. Back inside, after rubbing that finger around his eyes, Tony began to weep, just thinking about how much it hurt to lose the boy he loved so much to another organization over money. Drott began crying, his parents who loved Tony just as much began crying, and Lucadello got the signature he wanted. One might debate the ethics of such a tactic, but only a mirthless reader would not want such a story in the book. (Besides, based on the success Drott later enjoyed, it can be argued that accepting less money and developing in the minors was best for the young man in the long run, no matter that it also benefited the scout who signed him.)

It's one long interesting and educational joy ride, climaxing in the days after the June draft when we witness the indefatigable old scout race around to sign all six of his draftees. Such a haul is the best harvest Lucadello has enjoyed in a number of years, as the Phillies in recent years ignored many of his painstakingly determined recommendations. The ride is so fun that readers are apt to ignore or underestimate the forebodings that portend a dark outcome to the story. From the beginning of their time together Lucadello shares his worries with the author that his eyesight might be failing him and that he might be getting too old to drive long distances anymore. The MLB Scouting Bureau is a bigger problem. The Phillies like most other teams are starting to rely on the centralized organization which supplies the same information on the same players to all major league teams; and the more influence the Scouting Bureau has the less that old-time scouts like Tony have. In regard to some years when the Phillies did not draft a single player Tony recommended, Winegardner writes: "He feels like a player who has hit .300 or won twenty games, only to find his season erased from *The Baseball Encyclopedia* by a cruel technicality."

In one of the final chapters, Winegarder describes a trip he and Tony take to Toledo's Ned Skeldon Stadium, home of the Ohio Baseball Hall of Fame, that catches us completely off guard. The writer and the old scout enjoy surveying the Hall of Fame, and, then as they watch the Mudhens take BP, Tony tells another of his baseball whoppers. Winegarder gives Tony a beautiful tribute and validates his penchant for telling tale tales by comparing him to novelists who "learn there are things in life more truthful that the facts." It's only then that he reveals that the purpose of the visit is Lucadello's own induction into the Ohio Baseball Hall of Fame.

In the following, penultimate chapter we see pitcher Scott Service get the call, Tony's highly anticipated 50th signing to reach the big time. This is followed by details of cost-cutting moves to scouting and player development made by the Phillies and a description of Tony dropping off at a randomly selected church another year's worth of found small change. Perhaps because of the way Winegardner surprises us with the Hall of Fame Induction, we never see coming in the final chapter the Hemingway-esque ending to the Tony Lucadello story. It's neutrally, artfully narrated, and readers have to decide for themselves its meaning. No such ambivalence is possible about the subject's greatness or the achievement of the author in conveying it to us.

Sal Maglie: Baseball's Demon Barber

◆

Judith Testa

◆

Dekalb: Northern Illinois University Press, 2007. Cloth, 468 pages, ISBN: 978-0-87580-367-8. List of Illustrations, Preface. Pitching Statistics for Sal Maglie, Acknowledgments, Notes, Bibliography, Index, 31 black & white photos scattered throughout the book.

    Comments: A former professor at Northern Illinois University, Testa served as a Judge for the 2024 CASEY Awards.

    William J. Marshall: "Testa writes well-at times with brilliance. The real value of this biography is its foray into social history. Few baseball biographies have dared to discuss the sexual or psychological aspects of players' marriages in the manner this work does."

    The 1950s was one of the most exciting decades in the history of major league baseball, and New York City was at the heart of all the drama. The Yankees, Giants, and Dodgers all called the City home, a proximity which engendered ferocious rivalries, aided and abetted by the rabid, unstintingly loyal fans of each team, the jousting players themselves, and the ubiquitous, highly competitive newspaper media which recorded every pregnant pitch. Of all the notable players on these teams, and there were many, few aroused the incendiary passions and made the indelible impressions on the memory as did pitcher Sal Maglie, who wound up playing for all three teams. While Maglie's major league career was not lengthy, it was highly significant and worthy of an empathetic, first-class biography, which is exactly what he received upon the publication of Judith Testa's Diamond Classic, entitled *Sal Maglie: Baseball's Demon Barber*.

    Testa's superbly constructed narrative is undergirded by three pillars: the drawn-out incubation of Maglie as a developing pitcher; his uncanny ability to find himself at "the Axis of Event," and the ultimate definition of him as (in Donald Honig's words) the "ultimate professional and a gentleman."

    To begin with, Maglie's ascension to star status was as unlikely as a perfect game in the World Series, as he was not only a late bloomer but a late starter. Because his high school in Niagara Falls did not sponsor a baseball program, Maglie first attracted attention playing semi-pro ball in the area. The manager of the Buffalo Bisons thought he had potential and was worth signing to a contract, as a local-boy gate draw if nothing else, so Sal went as a 21-year-old from a cut above the sandlots to the International League; one step below the major leagues. Totally outclassed, he turned in a 3–15 record over three seasons (1938–40) before being demoted to Class D Jamestown (NY). In 1941 with Elmira in the Single A Eastern League he made enough improvement (20–15, 2.57 ERA) to prompt the New York Giants to draft him and return him the following year to their Jersey City club in the International League, where he posted a 9–6 record and a 2.78 ERA. Sal spent the next two years performing war work for Union Carbide but kept his hand in the game by pitching on weekends for a semi-pro team in Welland, Ontario. As the war ended, Maglie rejoined the Jersey City club and soon thereafter, due to the manpower shortage which also affected the big leagues, found himself being called up to New York. Testa's well-crafted description of this seminal event in the subject's life is typical of her impressive ability to summarize and define in one fell stroke:

> Now 28 years old, with rusty skills and all the earmarks of a career minor leaguer, Sal registered yet another series of poor performances during a partial season at Jersey City, compiling a 3–7 record with an equally dismal 4.09 ERA. Incredible as it seems, in August of 1945 that was good enough to get him to the show.

Maglie pitched pretty well for a rookie, but his success came against inferior war-time competition. He realized that the Giants would not be counting on him when their bona fide major leaguers returned for the 1946 season, and so he readily accepted the offer to play Cuban Winter League ball for Dolf Luque, who had already worked with Sal as the Giants' pitching coach. The decision was the most important of Maglie's life, as it committed him to the intensive apprenticeship under Luque which would transform him "from an ordinary pitcher into one of the most feared and fearless moundsmen of his generation." Equally fateful was Maglie's financially-motivated decision to jump to the Mexican League the next spring. The move ostracized him and other jumpers from Major League Baseball, but for Maglie the tradeoff was worth it as his two seasons (1946 and 1947) toiling under Luque (who managed the Pueblo Parrots) put the finishing touches on his education. In polite terms, the demanding, pistol-brandishing Luque taught Maglie to pitch inside, but what he really did was teach him how to ruthlessly instill fear in the hitter by throwing knockdown pitches without ever worrying about the consequences. The Mexican League outlaws were eventually given reprieves, and the 33-year-old Maglie rejoined the Giants in the spring of 1950, with one final chance to prove himself. And prove himself he did, posting a League-best winning percentage of .818 via an 18–4 record and turning in the second-best ERA of 2.71. He pitched 45 consecutive scoreless innings (including four shutouts in a row) and beat the team's nemesis, the Brooklyn Dodgers, four times. Maglie would prove to be special poison to the Dodgers. He won his first ten decisions at Ebbets Field, Giants manager Leo Durocher routinely saved him to pitch against the Bums, and Sal compiled an overall record of 23–9 against Brooklyn. Dodgers fans hated him, but their venomous booing delighted him and only caused him to pitch better.

Which brings us to the second pillar: Maglie's uncanny ability to find himself in the middle of great events. Surviving the ban against jumpers to the Mexican League was merely a warmup. By winning 23 games, including a 3–0 shutout of

Boston in the team's penultimate contest, Maglie was instrumental in the Giants' comeback from a huge deficit to tie the Dodgers for the 1951 pennant. Durocher then saved him for the rubber game of the three-game playoff, won in the bottom of the ninth on Bobby Thomson's famous three-run home run. He won the Giants' pennant-clinching game (against the Dodgers) in 1954; helped the Dodgers (who'd acquired him for peanuts from the Cleveland Indians) win the 1956 National League pennant, pitching a no-hitter along the way; won Game One of the 1956 World Series; and then pitched well in Game Five but lost 2–0 as Don Larsen hurled the first and-to-date only perfect game in Series history. Even after he quit pitching, Maglie made significant contributions to the game; serving as a very effective and appreciated pitching coach for the "Impossible Dream" 1967 Red Sox and the ill-fated Seattle Pilots of 1969.

Testa covers Maglie's development and pitching performances with aplomb, but what especially sets her book apart from other baseball biographies is her deep understanding of the subject as a person and her ability to perfectly convey to the reader the many facets of his personality and character. Her book-wide emphasis on Luque's great influence on Maglie is completely justified because it produced everything that went into the making of Sal Maglie, the Barber: his intimidating glower (and perpetual five-o'clock shadow), his reputation, and his MO as a pitcher. But equally important, she points out that Maglie was pre-disposed to tolerate Luque's harsh methods; partially because he always had a deep-seated respect for authority but mainly because in Luque "He knew he had found the teacher he had been looking for all his life." Similarly, while Maglie was a fierce competitor who aroused volcanic responses from opposing players and fans, he was at heart a gentle person averse to violence and antipathy. Dodgers players and fans were shocked and apprehensive when they learned that The Barber, the pitcher they loved to hate, would become one of them, but Maglie joined the club without incident and even immediately put at ease fellow Italian Carl Furillo, who reportedly carried the biggest grudge against Sal for the way Maglie had made the Brooklyn right fielder hit the dirt in the batter's box so often. Testa explains that Maglie and Furillo quickly became best friends, and Brooklyn fans soon found themselves lavishing more affection on him than Giants fans ever had. The author brings this kind of keen analysis to bear throughout the book. She also corrects numerous myths, such as the apocryphal story about Maglie spitting a mouthful of water at Durocher; examines the somewhat racist contemporary newspaper/magazine coverage of Maglie's Italian heritage; and is careful to examine multiple versions of important stories, such as exactly how Sal got his colorful nickname. (Maglie did not like the nickname until he realized that it suited his purposes nicely.)

Nor does Testa neglect Maglie's family life, a huge part of his story. Maglie married his high school sweetheart, Kay Pileggi, and loved her deeply, if not always perfectly faithfully. The couple bore the sorrow of being unable to have children but adopted two boys, over whom they doted. Kay's succumbing to cancer at a fairly young age affected Maglie deeply and sent Sal Jr., the older of the two boys, into a drug-using tailspin from which he never recovered. With Kay gone, Sal, the boys, and Kay's mom, Mae, moved into the home of Kay's brother, John. Sal began staying out late, to which Mae took offense. Again, the understanding which Testa brings to this situation is amazing: "He had buried his grief over Kay's death deep inside him, but there was Mae, night after night, insisting he drag it out and dwell on it. The situation grew intolerable." Sal eventually remarried, happily.

There is a certain sadness to Maglie's last days, spent in a nursing home, suffering from dementia, but the reader is buoyed by all that comes before: the uplifting account of a humble, utterly decent baseball hero who off the field was the complete antithesis of the knockdown specialist who terrified batters and infuriated the fans of opposing teams from the pitching mound. Sal Maglie was a generous, devoted family man and loyal friend with simple tastes (other than a penchant for fine suits), who was loved by everybody who knew him. As author, Judith Testa is not blind to her subject's faults, but her acknowledgment of them will scarcely diminish the great admiration readers will acquire for him upon finishing this splendid biography.

A Season in the Sun: The Rise of Mickey Mantle

Randy Roberts *and* Johnny Smith

New York, NY: Basic Books, 2018. Cloth, 276 pages, ISBN 9780465094424. Introduction: The Blue-Eyed Boy. Acknowledgments, Abbreviations Used in Notes, Notes, Bibliography, Index, 15 black & white photos, scattered throughout. Other baseball books by the authors: War Fever: Boston, Baseball, and America in the Shadow of the Great War *(Basic Books, 2020).*

Comments: "Though the authors recount the 1956 season in detail that might bore those uninterested in baseball history, their narrative of off-field controversies should have no trouble holding the interest of all readers. Most sports journalists and other baseball insiders covered up for the naïve Mantle, feeling that dishonesty by omission served their audiences' desire for hero worship. After 1956, as Mantle's stardom peaked and then declined, revelations about his less-than-sterling behaviors seeped out. The publication of *Ball Four* (1970), the classic memoir by pitcher Jim Bouton, ended any remaining illusion of Mantle as a golden boy. When Mantle died relatively young in 1995, few who knew the real Mantle expressed shock." —*Kirkus*.

Of all the excellent books about Mickey Mantle (and there are more than a couple), the most memorable is *A Season in the Sun: The Rise of Mickey Mantle*, written by Randy Roberts and Johnny Smith and published by Basic Books. A trenchant examination of Mantle's Triple Crown performance in 1956, the book triumphantly combines scholarly research and insight with graceful, even at times poetic, exposition. The authors zeroed in on 1956 (as did Phil Pepe and Mantle himself in *My Favorite Summer 1956,* Doubleday, 1991) because that season was the best of Mantle's career and because it came at such a critical juncture for both Mantle and his team, and the country as well. That Triple Crown season officially enshrined Mantle in public opinion as a worthy successor in the New York Yankees' unique lineage of team-elevating superstars, and it stamped him as something more than the greatest player in the game. It made him a hero, a status that survives to this very day.

While *A Season in the Sun* is about Mantle's breakthrough year, the authors constantly supplement the seasonal narration with relevant historical precedent in order to convey the context in which the events of 1956 unfolded, and they go to great pains to establish the complex situation Mantle faced at that point in his career. To begin with, no other player ever began his major league career with expectations as high as those under which Mickey Mantle debuted. As the authors explain, it wasn't just the New York Yankees and their legions of fans who needed Mantle to pick up the gauntlet of greatness; it was baseball itself and the entire country as well that longed for a hero who could be counted on to perform exceptional deeds and serve as a national inspiration. From his very first spring training with the Yankees in 1951, it was manifest to all observers that Mantle was something special. He was not only the quintessential five-tool player but one whose blazing speed and awesome power were off the charts. Moreover, he was a switch-hitter, utilizing an unheard-of extra ability among players of his ilk that gave him further competitive advantages and caused him to stand out even more from his mere mortal colleagues. Add Mantle's Adonis-like physique, his cover-boy handsomeness, his Oklahoma small-town background, and, yes … his race, he was the complete package; one the voracious New York press was only too eager to gushingly promote.

There was only one problem. Mantle was not ready. He was still raw, unsure of himself, and uncomfortable having the bright lights of the biggest city in America constantly illuminating his every move. His demotion to the minors in the middle of his 1951 rookie season shook his confidence even more and led to the famous "I thought I raised a man" hotel room lecture by his disappointed father Mutt that woke him up and triggered the batting tear which hastened his return to New York. Just when things seemed to be falling into place, Mantle suffered a devastating injury, torn ligaments in his right knee during Game Two of the 1951 World Series. He was never again as fast or agile as he once had been, and thereafter he was taped like an Egyptian mummy from ankle to thigh before every game.

During the next few years Mantle had some good seasons, even excellent ones, but by 1955 he was considered a disappointment, and a surly uncooperative one at that. As the authors say, "The press wrote off Mickey as a lost cause, a player who had entered the big leagues with too much fanfare, failed to perform in the clutch, and proved incapable of getting through a season without debilitating injuries. Writers complained that he was a dull country bumpkin, moody and colorless. He lacked Babe Ruth's charisma, Lou Gehrig's fierce resolve, and DiMaggio's impeccable style. He had tried to live up to the hype, to be the star that New York desired, but the 'poor kid from the slag hills of Oklahoma' seemed out of place in the Big Apple." Hard as it is to imagine, Mantle was routinely booed in Yankee Stadium.

Entering the 1956 season it was clear that Mantle was approaching a crossroads in his career, and the authors explain that a little soul searching by Mantle was one of the keys to his turnaround. Although Mantle clearly had a better year at bat in 1955 than teammate Yogi Berra, the Yankees catcher won the American League Most Valuable Player Award for the third time in five years. When Mantle asked Yankees' assistant general manager Bill DeWitt what he had to do to win such an honor, Dewitt replied, "Maybe a ballplayer has to do more than have a good season on the field. Maybe he has to win a little personal popularity." Mantle took DeWitt's advice to heart and transformed his adversarial relationship with the press into a much more friendly one. The writers, in turn, were not only happy to resume extolling his greatness, but they also created a protective but false image of him as a loyal husband, doting father, and vice-free ingenue.

It was essentially a re-born Mickey Mantle who began the 1956 season; one with the extra incentive to recapture the World Championship the Brooklyn Dodgers had finally wrestled from the Yankees the previous fall and in the process atone for what he considered to have been his personal failure (his bad leg had limited Mickey to two hits in 10 at bats in three games). And 1956 turned out to be the perfect after-the-storm day for Mantle on the cusp of baseball greatness. The authors summarize the situation brilliantly:

> *In the mid–1950s, faced with plummeting attendance caused by demographic change and the rise of competing entertainment opportunities, baseball needed a little "Godding up" to bring spectators back to the ball parks. With DiMaggio retired, Ted Williams claiming he was washed up, and Jackie Robinson graying and overweight, the game sorely needed a young hero, a downy-cheeked, blue-eyed Lancelot. It needed someone who looked and hit like Mickey Mantle. And in April 1956, when Mantle started slugging homers from the first day of the season, the god-makers in the press box sharpened their pencils.*

Mantle's torrid home run pace as he chased after Ruth's vaunted record of 60 became the story of the season, until two late-season slumps ended any reasonable chance of his catching the Bambino. Readers may be surprised to learn that Mantle faced the pressures of chasing the beloved Ruth years before Roger Maris (the first player to actually best the Babe's single-season homer total) joined the Yankees. However, by the time Ruth's record was out of reach, Mantle had embarked on a different quest, the challenge to become only the seventh batter in baseball history to win the Triple Crown; a challenge made all the more difficult by his having, as always, to constantly battle injuries. For a while Ted Williams challenged Mantle for the batting title but he faded. Rookie Al Kaline's challenge for the league lead in RBI lasted longer, until the very last day of the season, but Mantle held him off too; with help from Casey Stengel, who, while playing his worn-out star sparingly the final week of the season, made sure to pinch hit him in RBI situations only. When the long season was over, Mickey's 52 home runs, .353 batting average, and 130 RBI not only earned him the AL Triple Crown, they represented the highest marks in each category in the National League as well. More importantly, after helping the Yankees beat the Dodgers in another seven-game World Series with a critical home run and a great running catch that preserved Don Larsen's perfect game, Mantle "only twenty-five years old, had transcended baseball. Sportswriters crowned him simply 'the Hero.'" It was a title Mantle bore uncomfortably, but as the years passed he grew to understand it better. With age and hindsight, he realized better what he had meant to people, and he came to terms with his own feelings that he had not fulfilled his promise. Injuries and alcoholism unquestionably diminished the Mick's final resume, but they also humanized him and made what he did accomplish all the more remarkable. In the end, Mantle remains a heroic figure simply because he inspired the love of so many people who watched him play and who read about his marvelous talents and feats. *A Season in the Sun* is a book which captures this Mantle, warts and all, and keeps alive the most glorious moments of a baseball hero who was kissed by the baseball gods.

Slouching Toward Fargo: A Two-Year Saga of Sinners and St. Paul Saints at the Bottom of the Bush Leagues with Bill Murray, Darryl Strawberry, Dakota Sadie and Me

◆

NEAL KARLEN

◆

New York: Avon Books, 1999. Cloth, 362 pages, ISBN: 0-380-97484-3. Cast of Characters, Map of the Northern League. Epilogue, Acknowledgments and Author's Note, Index, 70 black & white photos scattered throughout the book.

Comments: *Slouching Toward Fargo* won the 17th CASEY Award for Best Baseball Book of 1999.

Sports Illustrated called it "a fun-is-good book ... [with] enough oddballs to make Alice's Adventures in Wonderland seem like a straightforward account of a schoolgirl's visit to a theme park."

"Hilarious, insightful, touching, informative, Neal Karlen's baseball account delivers a world of vivid characters and ironic redemptions. Karlen is simply one of the best, most sophisticated, and literate practitioners of journalism we have. He goes out and gets the full story, while turning himself into a wonderfully self-mocking, truthful, and likeable narrator. I loved every page of his book"—Phillip Lopate

As independent league teams, who have no affiliation with major league baseball clubs, can do whatever they wish to please and entertain their fans, it is perhaps no surprise that they are the focus of some of the best books ever written about minor league baseball. The best of these books is a soul-searching first-hand account by veteran freelance writer Neal Karlen called *Slouching Toward Fargo: A Two-Year Saga of Sinners and St. Paul Saints at the Bottom of the Bush Leagues with Bill Murray, Darryl Strawberry, Dakota Sadie, and Me*. What sets the book apart from the competition, besides its wacky cast of characters and gonzo journalistic approach, is the transformative journey taken during the 1996 and '97 seasons by the author himself, which the reader finds irresistibly satisfying.

A native of cross-river Minneapolis, Neal Karlen was coming late to the St. Paul Saints' party. A founding member of the Northern League (1993), the Saints were highly profitable (every game was a sell-out), dominant in the standings, and true to their motto, "Fun Is Good": a motto epitomized by a pig which delivered fresh baseballs to the home plate umpire, the passing train whose engineer interacted with the fans each game, and a Hollywood celebrity who threw ceremonial first pitches over the backstop and grandstand, completely out of the ballpark. Burnt-out by the pressures of living and working in New York City and desperate for a paying gig, Karlen was on hand, not as an objective reporter, but as a paid assassin: his mission to write an expose of comedian Bill Murray for *Rolling Stone* magazine. Murray was on the scene because he was part of a Saints ownership group of four, which included lawyer and talent scout Van Schley, minor league operator Marv Goldklang, and Mike Veeck, the disgraced son of baseball promotional genius Bill Veeck: he of the inimitable autobiography *Veeck as in Wreck*. Karlen's assignment was given to him by editor Jann Wenner who wanted payback for Murray (playing writer Hunter S. Thompson) having "hilariously and accurately" savaged and ridiculed Wenner "as a cheap corporate bastard who wouldn't pay his writers their expense money" in the cult classic *Where the Buffalo Roam*. Karlen was thought to be the perfect man for the hatchet job because years before he had done a similar number, gaining the trust of and then trashing in print (also for *Rolling Stone*) the motley crew of the outcast San Jose Bees, in particular the oft-suspended drug abusing Steve Howe. Karlen says his role model is Hunter S. Thompson, but it is Joan Didion's tactics he plans to rely on as he quotes approvingly from her book of essays about the Haight-Ashbury district of San Francisco during the neighborhood's heyday as a countercultural center, *Slouching Towards Bethlehem*: "My only advantage as a reporter is that I am so physically small, so temperamentally unobtrusive, and so neurotically inarticulate that people tend to forget that my presence runs counter to their best interests. And it always does."

The cagey Murray sees through Karlen right from the beginning and repeatedly pleads with him to be fair. "Please don't hose me," Murray says. "And please don't hose the Saints. And most of all, don't hose Mike Veeck." And right from the beginning, Karlen has misgivings, doubts about whether he has the stomach to deliver what *Rolling Stone* wants. Because the outcomes of the games on the field are not the point of the book, the author's battle with his conscience provides what tension there is in the narrative.

Murray's concern for his buddy Veeck, while admirable, is hardly necessary, as Veeck was never the intended target of *Rolling Stone*. Veeck himself is portrayed as being immune from criticism by that point, as he had been thoroughly lambasted and ostracized from major league baseball for his role (as his father's employee) in organizing the most disastrous promotion in the game's history: Disco Demolition Night of 1979, which resulted in a riot on the field of Comiskey Park and the White Sox having to forfeit the second game of a scheduled doubleheader. Haunted by this epic failure, Veeck, as president and co-owner of the Saints, is in the midst of trying not to mess up a second chance and still dreams of returning to the major leagues. This desire for redemption is the theme of the book, and Mike Veeck is only the poster boy for the idea. He is surrounded by others also in need of the same thing. Indeed, the scarred Veeck can't seem to say no to such people.

The Saints have a chance to sign Darryl Strawberry, the former New York Mets star who once blasted Ruthian home runs, now on the outside because of his repeated drug abuse. With some misgivings, Veeck decides to give the slugger another chance, and the decision pays off brilliantly; as Straw hits 18 home runs in 29 games and successfully returns to the big leagues with the New York Yankees. (Karlen befriends Strawberry who refers to the author as "cigarette boy" for the smokes Neal slips Darryl in the dugout.) The Saints give Dave Stevens, a man born with no legs, a real tryout in spring training (the photo of Stevens in "full" Saints uniform standing in the outfield next to the 6'6"Strawberry is one of the most amazing to be found in any baseball book). The Saints nice-guy manager is Marty Scott, fired in 1994 from a position as the director of the Texas Rangers farm system. Wayne "Twig" Terwilliger, former major leaguer journeyman, coaches for the team; available because he was unceremoniously dumped by the Minnesota Twins who thought he was too old (Saints players love the encouraging old gent, who never tires of hitting them fungoes). Veeck gives Dave Wright the opportunity to live his dream of doing the radio play-by-play but only for two years after which he will return to his regular job as the Saints PR director; one of Wright's replacements is Don Wardlow, the first blind broadcaster in professional baseball history. Of course, the entire Saints roster is full of players who by definition are second-chancers: non-draftees, cuts from affiliated ball, guys who got labeled as bad attitudes ("head case" Marty Neff, e.g., who is nevertheless extremely popular with Saints fans), guys trying to recover from injuries or self-imposed impediments, such as drug or alcohol abuse. And finally, the city of St. Paul itself, suffering from feelings of inferiority and disdained by residents of the larger Minneapolis, receives an enormous confidence and happiness boost via the beloved Saints. The very real competition between the two cities runs as a theme-supporting motif throughout the book, and the villainous aspect of the larger metropolis is represented by the dull, unimaginative Twins major league club and Patrick Reusse, the mean sportswriter for the *Minneapolis Star Tribune*, who refuses to give Mike Veeck or the Saints even the slightest of credit.

The direction of the book begins to emerge when Karlen gets a massage from Sister Rosalind Gefre, a 74-year-old Benedictine nun who is a fixture at the Saints' ballpark. While "Sister Roz" works out the kinks in his back and shoulders, the conflicted Karlen breaks down. It is a precious scene: a Jewish boy "confessing" not to a Catholic priest but to a Catholic nun, that he no longer loves baseball because his heart has been broken in divorce by his former wife, the "Baddest baddest Girl in Minneapolis" whom Karlen wooed through their mutual interest in the game. Karlen, it turns out, is the perfect person to tell the Saints story but not for the reasons he originally thought.

In one of their first encounters Karlen asks Murray, "So what is this all about, you and the Saints? What's the connection?" Murray replies, "You have to find that out for yourself. I can't tell you." And, while Murray does open up episodically to Karlen and talk honestly about why he loves the Saints, St. Paul, and the entire Northern League so much, Karlen discovers that the answer to his question about Murray evolves from his own metamorphosis, compliments of the Saints and the spirit of the rest of the Northern League. Of course, the best evidence of the author's transformation is his decision to hang around for a second season; by the end of which he not only unabashedly loves baseball again, but another woman as well. While Karlen might have easily wrapped up his spiritual journey after the first season, the reader is treated to developments in the second season that no one would want to miss; such as the Saints signing of Ila Borders, the first woman to play professional baseball, and J.D. Drew, the first-round pick of the Phillies who played for the Saints while holding out for a better deal than the $3.1 million he was offered by Philadelphia.

In the end Karlen makes the right decisions. He portrays Murray and Veeck fairly, protects the players from the more embarrassing indiscretions he undoubtedly witnesses, and works up the courage to apologize to a grizzled Steve Howe, then a pitcher with the Sioux Falls Canaries (amusingly, Howe recognizes Karlen but does not remember his name. Howe addresses him as "Rolling Stone!"). The book also includes portraits of other interesting personages from around the league, such as Monica Toppen of the Madison Black Wolf, The Most Beloved Woman in the Northern League; "Singing Ed" Nottle, manager of the Sioux City Explorers; and Dakota Sadie, one of a pair of nubile female scoreboard workers in Fargo who make a sexy trek out to their station before every game. *Slouching*, which reads at times like a travel guide to the Upper Midwest, is a sprawling journey with numerous side trips but one that the reader is reluctant to end. That is proof enough that the author more than did his job.

The Soul of Baseball: A Road Trip Through Buck O'Neil's America

◆

Joe Posnanski

◆

New York: William Morrow, 2007. Cloth, 276 pages, ISBN: 978-0-06-08 5403-4. Afterword, Acknowledgments. Other baseball books by the author: The Machine: A Hot Team, a Legendary Season, and a Heart-Stopping World Series: The Story of the 1975 Cincinnati Reds *(William Morrow, 2009),* The Baseball 100 *(Avid Reader Press, 2021), and* Why We Love Baseball *(Dutton, 2023).*

 Comments: *The Soul of Baseball* won the 25th CASEY Award in 2007. Posnanski became the second writer to win three CASEY Awards when *The Baseball 100* won the 39th CASEY in 2021 and *Why We Love Baseball* won the 41st CASEY in 2023. At the CASEY Awards ceremony in Cincinnati, Ohio, in 2021, Joe thanked his editor at Avid Reader Press for having the courage to sign up an 869-page baseball book.

 Boston Sunday Globe: "In *The Soul of Baseball*, Joe Posnanski presents the most energetic and delightful ambassador baseball has ever had."

 Sports Illustrated: "Engaging and spirit-lifting…. Like Mitch Albom's *Morrie*, O'Neil possesses a relentless, infectious optimism…."

 Buck O'Neil finally did receive his day in the baseball spotlight when he was inducted into the National Baseball Hall of Fame in Cooperstown, New York, on July 24, 2002; along with Bud Fowler, Gil Hodges, Jim Kaat, Minnie Minoso, Tony Oliva, and David Ortiz.

 Because of his friendship with former Kansas City Monarchs player and manager John Jordan "Buck" O'Neil, Kansas City sportswriter Joe Posnanski committed himself to writing a book about the long gone Negro Leagues, those historically-alluring all-black professional baseball circuits that had been born out of racial exclusion and which were doomed once Jackie Robinson broke the color barrier in 1947. O'Neil trusted Posnanski to tell the story correctly: meaning, to properly convey the high quality of play and professionalism exhibited by Negro Leagues players. The task seemed impossibly daunting until the author realized that O'Neil himself represented the best testament to all that was good and admirable about the Negro Leagues; and so Posnanski accompanied the peripatetic 94-year-old O'Neil around the country for a year to compose a rich and deeply affecting portrait of a beautiful soul and one of the greatest ambassadors, white or black, that the game has ever seen.

Denied and disappointed professionally as he'd been, Buck O'Neil had every right to be an embittered man; but, as Posnanski quickly discovered, Buck had risen above the injustices he had endured and, more than that, he'd made it a habit of spreading the happiness he felt and of always leaving others feeling better about themselves. The author shows us this in the first couple of pages when he and Buck are watching the Astros play in Houston. Posnanski becomes angry, highly indignant, when he sees a grown man out-maneuver a boy to snatch a baseball thrown into the stands by an Astros player ... and then not even consider giving the souvenir to the clearly disappointed youngster. Asked for a reaction, Buck says, "Don't be so hard on him. He might have a kid of his own at home." This extension of the benefit-of-the-doubt catches the author off guard and he begins to imagine a scenario that corresponds with Buck's suggestion; until it dawns on him to say, "Wait a minute. If this jerk has a kid, why didn't he bring the kid to the ballgame?" "Maybe," says Buck without a pause, "his child is sick." And with that Posnanski realizes, as we do, that he is dealing with a person of exceptionally high character, someone who always tries to see the good in everyone else.

Throughout the period covered by the book, Buck O'Neil was on a mission to win recognition and support for the budding Negro League Museum at 18th Street and Vine in Kansas City. Used to making more than 200 public appearances a year, O'Neil was willing to go anywhere to spread the word, and Posnanski says that the two of them (accompanied by Bob Kendrick, a sort of chaperone and traveling secretary) traveled 30,000 miles by air and a couple of thousand more by car. Buck's fame always preceded him, and the reader is amazed at first but soon familiar with the royal reception he is always given: in the tiny town of Nicodemus, Kansas (population 40); in the halls of the U.S. Congress in Washington, D.C; in radio studios all over New York City; in Minneapolis at the Twins monstrosity of a ballpark, the Metrodome; in Gary, Indiana, for the Northern League All-Star Game banquet; at an elementary school in Atlanta with two other former Negro Leaguers; in Chicago for the funeral of Ted "Double Duty" Radcliffe. In these and other locales, fans, current players, celebrities, and children all rushed up to greet O'Neil, to hug him, to get his autograph, to absorb some of the positive, loving spirit that emanated from his person like a light beam.

Hugging was mandatory. If someone hung back, Buck would open his arms wide and issue the command, "Give it up!" Buck especially liked hugging women, and he even persuaded the rare ones who had no idea who he was. Buck's affection for hugging was only one of many endearing characteristics that Posnanski notes over and over again. There was his sartorial exuberance (when Buck wore a bright blue jacket, he had blue shoes to go with it); his favorite sayings ("Good black don't crack."); his ability to immediately fall asleep on airplanes; his love for singing and of jazz ("Buck always said the two greatest things in this world are baseball and jazz."); his insatiable desire to help get others the credit he felt they were due; and his refusal to be seen as a victim. The last characteristic, the one he expressed whenever he said things like "Don't feel sorry for me. I was right on time," ... that's the one which ennobled him. (Buck's repeated admonition to his fellow travelers, "Don't be late," serves as an ironic counterpoint to the world's view that he'd been born too early.)

While he wasn't a musician, Buck O'Neil had met, befriended, and enjoyed in person the music of many of jazz's greatest practitioners (such as Charlie Parker). He shared memories with Posnanski of all the legendary jazz joints of Kansas City's past, and he seemed to waltz through life every day of their journey, as if that music were still playing in the background, until his age would catch up with him and he would have to retire from exhaustion. Nevertheless, his stamina was amazing and possible only coming as it did out of an abundance of caritas. Sensitive to these vibes, Buck's utter rejection of victimhood, and the simple wisdom of his spontaneous utterances, Posnanski frames O'Neil's words throughout the book into song lyrics or found poems perhaps.

Where does bitterness take you?
To a broken heart?
To an early grave?
When I die
I want to die from natural causes.
Not from hate
Eating me up from the inside.

Everywhere this Traveling Love Show went, Buck knew gobs of people and even more of them knew him, or claimed to (Out of consideration, Buck never admitted he didn't remember somebody or had never met the person before). Famous players abound, many of whom Buck coached in the Negro Leagues (Willie Mays); scouted (Ernie Banks) as the first black scout in the Major Leagues; or brought back to the game (Billy Williams) when prejudice had pushed him close to quitting ("It's going to change," Buck keep assuring Williams). But the star of the book is the pretty good Negro Leagues first baseman who never played one pitch in the white Major Leagues.

With everything that O'Neil had done for the game and with everything he'd meant to so many people there was a crusade of sorts to get him into the Cooperstown Hall of Fame before his gigantic heart gave out. There was even an expectation that he would finally get his due when it became known that a huge class of Negro Leaguers would be going in *en masse* in the summer of 2006. The climax of the book comes when it is learned that 17 Negro Leaguers are elected but not Buck O'Neil. The author, Kendrick, and fans around the country are incredulous, even angry, at what they perceive to be the final injustice; yet O'Neil receives the disappointment with the soft hands of the slick-fielding first sacker he'd been as a young man. After sharing the journey through Buck O'Neil's America, the reader is hardly surprised at such a reaction. So while *The Soul of Baseball* is not a history, one gets as good a sense from it of what the Negro Leagues were all about as from a shelf of historical treatises of the subject. And while it is not a biography, the book enables one to get to know and appreciate the subject as if he were a beloved family member. That's as much as we can expect any book to do.

Spalding's World Tour: The Epic Adventure That Took Baseball Around the Globe— And Made It America's Game

◆

Mark Lamster

◆

New York: Public Affairs, 2006. Cloth, 341 pages, ISBN: 978-1-58648-311-1. Map of the Tour, Prologue: A Galaxy of Stars. Epilogue: The Globe Trotters Club, Appendix I: The Spalding Tourists, Appendix II: Game Results of the Tour, Notes, Bibliography, Acknowledgments, Index, 29 black & white photos scattered throughout the book.

If *Spalding's World Tour: The Epic Adventure that Took Baseball Around the Globe—And Made It America's Game* by Mark Lamster and Public Affairs is not regarded as a classic of baseball literature, then the term has no meaning or usefulness at all. For the book, which sources material from Albert Goodwill Spalding's own account in his quasi-autobiography, *America's National Game*, as well as from the published accounts of several other participants and a plethora of contemporary newspaper reports, improves exponentially upon them all by synthesizing their various contributions and multiple viewpoints into one marvelous, richly-evoked story that rivals the edification and excitement which the highlights of the bold journey provided for the tourists themselves.

As Lamster makes clear, it took someone as ambitious and audacious as Spalding to have even conceived as grand an idea as a trip around the world to spread the gospel of baseball. Tellingly, Spalding's motto, which also serves as the book's frontispiece, was "Everything is possible to him who dares." By 1888, the year of the big sojourn, Spalding had graduated from pitching (at which he was exceptional) to ownership of the Chicago White Stockings as well as the largest and eponymously-named sporting goods company in the country. Intelligent, savvy, and capable, Spalding was his own biggest fan, and he sometimes took more credit than he deserved for the accomplishments of others (such as the establishment of the National League). He was also a master promoter and propagandist, baseball's equivalent of P.T. Barnum: a characterization first made by Spalding biographer Peter Levine, whom Lamster acknowledges.

Long-distance travel towards the close of the nineteenth century was still slow, difficult, and risky, and it took a lot of planning, cajoling, and optimism by the tour's leader to get the project off the ground. Spalding not only had to convince his own players to make the trip for modest remuneration (but on an all-expenses paid basis), but he had to also assemble an All-Star aggregate of players from other National League teams (the "All-America" squad) to join the tour and provide the competition for the games which were to be the point of the expedition. Surely, Spalding reasoned, people around the globe would adopt baseball as their favorite sport if they were only given the opportunity to witness the game's beauties and intricacies first-hand as displayed by top professionals. Sensibly, Spalding hired competent help to make travel arrangements, schedule games, reserve the most suitable playing fields available, and generally beat the drum ahead of the traveling band of baseballists; and these men (James Hart, Harry Simpson, and Will Lynch) did top notch work. As did three top journalists of the day (Simon Goodfriend, Newton MacMillan, and Harry Palmer) who accompanied the teams and sent generally glowing dispatches back to their respective papers stateside.

While full of glorious possibilities, the trip around the world would not be a profitable venture, as Spalding well knew. (Allowing the captain of his White Sox team, Cap Anson, and tour general manager Leigh Lynch to "invest" in the tour was hardly Spalding's finest moment.) The daring magnate was willing to spend (and lose) a sizeable amount of his own money in the hope, not that the tour would make money, but that he would be able to expand his sporting goods business into new markets. In addition to his genuine missionary motivation, Spalding also desired to atone for the financial and aesthetic failure of an earlier such excursion in 1874 to England and Ireland which he had led on behalf of organizer Harry Wright. Finally, he desired to settle the question of baseball's origins by demonstrating that it was the "American game *par excellence*," the embodiment of a well-known alliterative catalog of virtues he rattles off in *America's National Game*.

Everyone was not impressed with the idea, and Spalding's rival Al Spink (who favored the American Association over the National League) tried to discredit it in *The Sporting News*, dubbing it the "Chicago Fake," and predicting that "Not one half of the men mentioned in the All-America team will make the trip." National League stars Mike Tiernan and King Kelly did in fact break their commitments to Spalding and stay home, but Spalding was able to put together a formidable opponent for the White Stockings, and the tour departed on schedule on October 20, after the two teams first played the tour's initial game in Chicago (Kelly actually played in this game but never re-joined the tour in Denver as promised).

Spalding's gang of road warriors, which included Spalding's mother and a number of wives and well-to-do fans, first barnstormed west across the United States by rail and played a total of 15 games in St. Paul, Minneapolis, Cedar Rapids, Des Moines, Omaha, Hastings (NE), Denver, Colorado Springs, Salt Lake City, San Francisco, and Los Angeles. Everywhere they went, they were hailed as celebrities, given august receptions by local authorities, feted at sumptuous banquets, and lodged in the finest hotels available, all the while engaging in as much sightseeing as possible. Initially, the tour was billed as a junket to Australia alone, but from the beginning

Spalding had planned to extend the itinerary. It was only after the success of the first leg of the trip while the party was bound for Hawaii aboard the *S.S. Alameda* from San Francisco that Spalding cagily made known his intentions in the form of a leak. He let the tourists think that continuing around the world was their idea; and when he finally made an open declaration, the players erupted in applause. Quite shrewdly, Lamster imitates the charade, leaving the reader in some confusion, until he narrates the scenes described above; a device which serves to reinforce Spalding's chutzpah and supreme self-confidence.

In all, the baseball world tourists would sail upon five other ships, as they moved their traveling show from Australia to Ceylon and Aden, up the Suez Canal to Cairo and Port Said, then on to cities in Italy and France, England and Ireland, before crossing the Atlantic to New York City, where they began the final leg of the trip: a second barnstorming jaunt by rail to every city with a team in the National League plus Brooklyn and Baltimore before receiving a triumphant welcome back home in Chicago. The White Stockings and All-Americas played 57 games against each other, some of which were shortened because of weather or field conditions, while other scheduled contests were cancelled altogether. An additional string of competitions took place during which one of the sides played against a local contingent, and a few exhibitions were held when the two teams playing together as the Spalding Tourists deigned to take on the local experts in games of rounders or cricket. The players usually did their best not only to put on a good show but to win the games and the series; and often, as when they played a game in front of The Great Pyramid, Cheops, they had the sense of making history as strongly as did Spalding. On the other hand, when the players mailed it in, as the All-Americas did after a night of partying caused them to lose to a California League team of minor leaguers, they were rightly criticized. Referring to this lackluster performance, *The Sporting News* gleefully tweaked Spalding, saying that before he "attempt[s] to introduce base ball in a foreign land with the All-Americas [he] should introduce the game to them first." As the reader is not at all invested in which side won or lost the tour's games, it is to Lamster's great credit that he is able to keep the reader interested in his descriptions of them and the circumstances under which they were played. One example: Spalding wanted to stage a game at the Roman Coliseum but was denied. In regard to the Vatican piazza, Lamster quips: "It would have made a far more commodious playing field than the Coliseum, but this was a request too cheeky even for Spalding."

Spalding had the foresight to bring along some additional entertainment: comedian Frank Lincoln, balloon aerialist/stuntman Professor C. Bartholomew, and the White Stockings' diminutive black mascot Clarence Duval, whom Spalding dressed in ostentatious costumes and put at the head of the tourists' parades. The games usually drew big crowds although it was not always possible to charge admission due to some of the venues being unenclosed. The game of baseball itself got mixed reviews, although the tourists, as in America, were always welcomed as conquering heroes, with one exception: when an American diplomat posted in Italy rudely declined to roll out the welcome mat. Amazingly, there were no catastrophes or even serious injuries on the trip, other than the knee injury to Chicago shortstop Ned Williamson, from which he never fully recovered. The players also avoided acting like ugly

Americans, with a few exceptions, such as the time they attempted to hurl baseballs over the pyramid and did pelt the right eye of the Sphinx with fastballs.

More troublesome was the minor crisis that unfolded in Hawaii when American officials there would not permit the tourists to play their game because it was scheduled on a Sunday, much to the displeasure of King Kalakaua and his subjects. Somehow, Spalding defused the situation, prompting one of the players to muse, "What Al does not know about diplomacy is of no possible use." The biggest controversy to affect the tour was not even anything that happened on the tour but word from home that National League owners had voted to impose a salary classification scheme (in effect, a salary cap). Upon hearing about the scheme, some of the players and particularly Giants shortstop John Montgomery Ward, who was the Marvin Miller of the day, suspected that the tour was in part a ploy to keep them away while the owners pulled a fast one behind their backs. Predictably, Spalding was able to calm the waters and keep the tour together, although Ward did abandon it and return to New York after the second of three games scheduled in London in order to attend to his duties as the leader of the Baseball Brotherhood.

All along the trip, from beginning to end, Lamster serves as the ultimate tour guide, enabling us to vicariously partake of the same culturally broadening experience the tourists had; while pointing out instances when the tourists, representing the best of America, ironically exhibited attitudes and beliefs that seem un–American to today's sensibilities. In addition, many readers will painlessly have their geography quotient raised by many factors; particularly helpful is the map of the tour at the front of the book. The book concludes with an Epilogue in which Lamster tells us what happened in the years following the tour to the principals, especially Spalding himself. He also provides an assessment as to the degree to which the tour accomplished its main goal, judging by the status of baseball around the world today. A clue to the author's opinion is embedded in the book's subtitle which states that the tour "Made It (baseball) *America's* Game." How ever one wants to view the matter, there is no question that Albert Spalding's World Tour accomplished something remarkable and unsurpassed in the history of sports promotion. It should elicit our wholehearted modern admiration, as should the book which so artfully chronicles it.

Spitballing: The Baseball Days of Long Bob Ewing

◆

MIKE LACKEY

◆

Wilmington, OH: Orange Fraser Press, 2013. Paper, 343 pages, ISBN: 9781 939710055. Acknowledgments, Introduction, End Notes for every chapter. Appendix: Bob Ewing's Career Pitching Record, About the Author, Bibliography, Index, 15 black & white photos scattered throughout the book.

Simply put, *Spitballing: The Baseball Days of Long Bob Ewing* by Mike Lackey is the most beautiful baseball book of an expository nature ever published. In regard to the cited qualification, it has no rivals, yet even very few of the most sumptuously produced books of baseball art and photography, whose raison d'etat is the presentation of visual delights, manage to provide the reader the pleasure offered by *Spitballing*. An appreciation of books as beautiful objects (as opposed to utilitarian packages or formats) is evident in every design decision made by the publisher (Orange Fraser Press of Wilmington, Ohio); such as, Jeff Suntala's evocative water color art on the cover, the exquisite calligraphy used for chapter titles, and the silhouettes of a pitcher in the various stages of his windup and delivery used to mark chapters and even stand in for the first "i" in the title. The perfect melding of subject, text, and graphic elements displayed on every page makes this biography a triumph of the bookmaker's art.

Of course, Orange Fraser Press could not have produced this masterpiece of baseball literature had the author, an experienced newspaperman, not first provided them with a first-rate manuscript: a deserving untold story unearthed by the most rigorous research and related with verve, keen insight, and a masculine style, characterized by precision and economy. Bob Ewing, a forgotten Dead Ball-Era pitcher, came to the attention of Mike Lackey because of geographical proximity: Ewing having spent his entire life in and around Wapakoneta, Ohio, the county seat of Auglaize County and a mere 15 miles from Lima, the midsize city where the author resided for the 16-year period he worked on the book.

Curiosity may have drawn author to subject, but a deeper dive into Ewing's life and career convinced Lackey that the forgotten pitcher's story was worth telling

precisely because he was *not* a famous superstar but a pretty typical ballplayer, one of the thousands who are not continuously spot-lit in glory but one who has his moments and without whom the game cannot exist. Lackey also believed Ewing was deserving of a biography because he was the Reds' winningest pitcher of the Dead

Ball Era and Cincinnati's most prominent spitball artist ever. In properly telling Ewing's personal story, Lackey would per force bring to life for contemporary readers the times in which the pitcher lived; a fascinating layer of detail which the author continually weaves into the narration. For instance, to convey how long ago the Bob Ewing story began, Lackey reminds us that the National League began in 1876, just three years after Ewing's birth and that the country itself was only 100 years old. The Shawnee Indian tribe had been moved out of the state not that long before (in 1832); both Ewing's grandfather and father had fought in the Civil War; and Auglaize Country had come into being just a few years before that in 1848. Presented with these facts and Lackey's divulgence that Ewing grew up in the farming community of Goshen Township near the unincorporated hamlet of New Hampshire, the reader is not surprised to learn that Ewing's formal education ended after the eighth grade.

Ewing went 124–118 as a major league pitcher (mostly for the Cincinnati Reds), but Lackey knew there was a lot more to the story than that unimpressive record. In short, Ewing was an underrated pitcher, for several reasons. He played for bad teams almost his entire career and lost many a game for lack of run support; working in Cincinnati, he labored for what we call today a "small market" team, an habitually under-funded and poorly-supported franchise; and he was a quiet, respectful individual who not only shunned the various vices so common among his more "colorful" cohorts but could not even bring himself to display pique at questionable ball and strike calls by the umpires. Furthermore, Ewing was no youngster when he finally got his shot in the show. As Lackey demonstrates, despite the Wapakoneta area being a hot bed of baseball talent, its closeness to Cincinnati, and the Reds persistent desperation for quality pitching, Ewing somehow remained under the radar for the longest time. At age 24 he was still pitching amateur ball until he finally broke into the pros with Toledo in 1897. He won 20 or more games each of the next four seasons, compiling a composite record of 88–36, before a strong performance against the barnstorming Reds in a post-season exhibition finally motivated Cincinnati manager Bid McPhee to sign him to a contract for the upcoming campaign. Long Bob made his major league debut on April 19, 1902, five days before his 29th birthday.

Ewing did have talent, a good fastball and a sharp curve, as well as the physical attributes deemed necessary for a pitcher. He was dubbed "Long Bob" precisely because he was tall and lanky (for his day) and possessed lengthy arms and fingers. Almost everyone liked him, and he was respected by Cincinnati's sportswriters and insufferable Reds fans who often made life a misery for other players. But he never seemed to be regarded as a top flight moundsman by a succession of managers, despite the blighted no-hitter he hurled against the New York Giants (a controversial scoring decision resulted in the performance being officially recorded as a one-hitter). That changed when, on September 23, 1904, the 31-year-old Ewing, sporting a 26–31 career record, suddenly added a new pitch to his repertoire, the spitball. Long Bob baffled Boston batters all day and came away with a 2–1 victory. He struck out 12, walked only one, and scattered seven hits, all described as "flukes," "scratches," or "bloops."

Ewing did not gradually develop the spitter during championship competition but unleashed it when he was fully in control of it. Lackey wisely surmises that he had to have perfected his control of the unpredictable pitch through much diligent practice on the sidelines. In any case, the pitch saved his career, he became acknowledged as the National League's first "master of the spitball," and before long sportswriters were referring to him as "Spitter Bob" or "Spitball Robert." This development is the heart of Ewing's biography, as well as a major theme of the book, as the pitch was extremely controversial. The Dead Ball Era, another theme expounded brilliantly by the author, was already a period when runs were precious and usually had to be manufactured via small-ball tactics. Ewing's career ERA of 2.49, for example, appears superb today, and a century after he retired it ranked 28th on the all-time list, but it was only 22nd among his Dead Ball contemporaries. If usage of the difficult-to-hit spitball became widespread, many feared that offense would disappear altogether from the game. Other pitchers did adopt the spitter, and some prospered with it, but the myriad difficulties that accompany the pitch prevented it from dominating the game as dreaded: all of which Lackey covers in absorbing detail.

While the essence of the game, the constant battle between hitters and pitchers, was the same then as now, many things were different; and the time Lackey devotes to matters such as the following is never wasted: "syndicate" baseball, the practice of some magnates having ownership of multiple teams in the same league; the formation of the National Commission to broker peace between the warring National and infant American League; barnstorming junkets, including the ground-breaking six-week tour of Cuba made by the Reds after the 1908 season; and the experiment with night baseball made by Reds president Garry Herrmann.

As exhaustive as Lackey's research efforts were, the details of some matters remained buried by time. Yet, Lackey deals honestly with such difficulties, providing the reader with surmises amounting to the most reasonable guesstimates possible to make. We don't know exactly how George Lemuel Ewing came to be called "Bob," but Lackey says this nickname probably derived from the youngster's fondness for his grandfather, Robert. Apparently on the manager's trading block during a 1907 house cleaning/youth movement, Ewing was ultimately retained by the Reds either because Herrmann or influential business manager Frank Bancroft protected him or because other teams' interest in the pitcher caused a re-evaluation of his value to the team. And Ewing won the heart of his wife, Nelle Hunter, because he regarded her as a competent equal whereas his main competitor treated Nelle as a helpless child in need of protection.

When Ewing's career did finally fizzle out, he returned home to his farm, as he did after every season, to resume the simple life. He trained harness horses and bred hunting dogs, leased and operated a billiards parlor, and served two terms as sheriff of Auglaize County. His being elected to the office as a Republican in territory overwhelmingly occupied by Democrats testifies to the high regard in which he was held. Two sensational murder cases challenged him with more than he'd probably bargained for, but his reputation survived unscathed and he lived out his days on the farm the same way he'd built a successful career as a major league pitcher: quietly and contentedly.

Of the book's many virtues, Lackey's straightforward sharply-honed prose ranks very high. Especially delightful are those moments, often chapter-enders, when he punctuates an idea or theme with a very short period. At the end of Chapter

Six, which concludes with a discussion of Ewing's inability to ever wring much of a raise out of the parsimonious Reds, Lackey writes, "He wanted to play, so they had him." That's good writing, another example of which occurs at the end of the book proper (a final chapter extolls the long-lived Nelle who loved baseball as much as her husband). No better summing up is imaginable for Long Bob Ewing than what his kindred spirit, Mike Lackey, writes about his demise: "His death certificate, under 'usual occupation,' listed 'ball player.'"

Steinbrenner: The Last Lion of Baseball

◆

Bill Madden

◆

New York: Harper, 2010. Cloth, 457 pages, ISBN: 978-0-06-169031-0. Introduction. Notes and Acknowledgments, Bibliography, Index, 38 black & white photos between pages 206 and 207. Other baseball books by the author: Damned Yankees: A No-Holds-Barred Account of Life with Boss Steinbrenner with Moss Klein *(Warner Books, 1990),* Zim: A Baseball Life with Don Zimmer *(Total Sports, 2001),* The Zen of Zim: Baseball, Beanballs and Bosses with Don Zimmer *(Thomas Dunne Books, 2004)*, 1954: The Year Willie Mays and the First Generation of Black Superstars Changed Major League Baseball Forever *(Da Capo Press, 2014),* Lou: Fifty Years of Kicking Dirt, Playing Hard, and Winning Big in the Sweet Spot of Baseball with Lou Piniella *(Harper, 2017), and* Tom Seaver: A Terrific Life *(Simon & Schuster, 2020).*

Comments: Madden was the recipient of the Baseball Hall of Fame's 2010 J.G. Taylor Spink Award.

Michael Shapiro, *New York Times*: "What we see, almost from the beginning of Steinbrenner's tenure, is a man of overweening self-importance and callousness, with a breathtaking absence of empathy. Reading the book feels like the literary equivalent of passing a traffic accident; it is all but impossible to turn away. Steinbrenner could be charming and generous. But these good qualities do little to mitigate what is, finally, a devastating account."

Over the final three decades of the twentieth century there was no more important figure in baseball than George M. Steinbrenner, the heir to a Great Lakes shipping company headquartered in Cleveland, Ohio, who purchased the moribund New York Yankees in 1972, restored the team to its former glory, and rebuilt the brand to such a degree that today the Yankees, worth $7.1 billion, rank as the second most valuable of all sports franchises. There was also no one more controversial than Steinbrenner: a mercurial embodiment of the Dr. Jekyll/Mr. Hyde duality, a verbally abusive boss renowned for the impetuous firing and often re-hiring of employees (especially managers, such as Billy Martin), and a pathologically competitive egomaniac whose outlandish spending on contracts ushered in the era of high stakes free agency. Steinbrenner's long, chaotic, and sensationalistic career, which played out in newspaper headlines, was unlike anything else in baseball history; which makes the book that brilliantly captures the man and his complicated story,

Bill Madden's *Steinbrenner: The Last Lion of Baseball*, one of the game's most unforgettable biographies.

As Maddon demonstrates in the second chapter about the subject's early life, Steinbrenner was already a man of significant accomplishments and talents before he became owner of the most storied team in baseball–surprisingly, he was a superb organist and pianist. After graduating from prestigious Williams College, where he hurtled and played football, he served two years in the Air Force (time spent mostly running an athletic program at the Lockbourne base in Columbus, Ohio), earned a master's degree in physical education from Ohio State University, and then coached football at Northwestern and Purdue Universities. Most importantly, he proved his business acumen by taking over the struggling family shipping business and making it profitable again. He also was a founding member of Group 66, an association of philanthropic business leaders who did much to revitalize a declining Cleveland. By any reasonable measure, he was a success, yet apparently, he never felt like one. This was due to his father, Henry, "a strict disciplinarian" who made his son feel that nothing he ever did was good enough. According to a "close friend" cited by Maddon, "George was permanently scarred by his father's rigidity and lack of affection, and I have no doubt he'd have given up all his championship rings just to have gotten a hug and an 'I love you, son,' from the old man." Sad as this father-son relationship was, as Steinbrenner himself recognized, it instilled in him the over-the-top "perfectionist, will-to-win competitiveness" that would come to define his Attila-the-Hun management style.

Of course, Steinbrenner's track record was not without blemish. He originally tried to purchase the Cleveland Indians but at the last minute, after he'd assembled the necessary group of investors, was rebuffed by owner Vernon Stouffer. He did acquire the Cleveland Pipers of the National Industrial Basketball League, but the team went bankrupt. Before it did, his meddling and questionable business tactics drove both the team's GM and its beloved coach into resigning. In addition, his furious in-game referee baiting caused the *Cleveland Press* to declare him "congenitally unsuited to own a sports franchise." The assessment amounted to a prescient warning that went unheeded.

Maddon opens the book with an arresting account of the turning point in the subject's life: the meeting at which Steinbrenner sealed the deal to purchase the Yankees from CBS, which wanted out of the baseball business. Steinbrenner had to convince CBS chairman William S. Paley that he not only headed up a financially sound group of investors, but that he would also run the franchise in a responsible manner; being always respectful of how much the team meant to the city. Steinbrenner allayed Paley's concerns mostly by claiming that he intended to leave running the team up to the baseball professionals, while he continued to concentrate on the family shipping business in Cleveland. Readers with even a basic familiarity with Steinbrenner's subsequent history may be forgiven for laughing at that proposition.

As it happened, Steinbrenner quickly asserted himself as the unquestioned authority over the team, instigating the almost immediate resignations of two CBS executives meant to facilitate the franchise transfer, and by the end of the 1973 season, the exodus of hold-over high-ranking team officials and three limited partners who eagerly divested themselves of their Yankees stock. The latter's cutting ties with

Steinbrenner presaged the same move by investor John McMullen, who a few years later famously said, "I came to realize there is nothing in life quite so limited as being a limited partner of George Steinbrenner."

Ironically, just as Steinbrenner was figuring out his new business, he was suspended from the game for two years by baseball commissioner Bowie Kuhn for being convicted of making illegal contributions to the Nixon presidential re-election campaign. Another suspension (actually a lifetime ban) and numerous fines for all sorts of infractions and ill-advised comments lay in the future. Fortunately, Steinbrenner had ex-Reds and Indians GM Gabe Paul, whom he had installed as team president, to run the team in his absence, and it was, in fact, Paul who made the shrewd trades that provided the nucleus of the roster which won three straight AL pennants and the World Championships of 1977 and '78. Still, Steinbrenner remained involved and made his own contributions to the revival of the team; directing from afar the hiring of Billy Martin as manager and the historic free agent signing of A's pitcher Catfish Hunter; a deal that opened the financial flood gates and signaled to other owners that remaining competitive was going to be much more expensive in the future. Steinbrenner spent as if he were parting with Monopoly money, and some more of his early signings ... of Reggie Jackson and Goose Gossage ... and even a few of the later ones (Dave Winfield) paid off; but as time went on a lot of money was wasted on players who did not produce. The Yankees during Steinbrenner's long tenure operated as a revolving door. Players came and went with dizzying frequency, as did managers: when Dallas Green was fired in August of 1989, it was the Yankees 17th managerial change in 17 years. The problem was Steinbrenner's uncontrollable need to meddle and his unrealistic expectations, his belief that well-paid employees should *automatically* produce results commensurate with their compensation; the latter an especially inane idea in regard to ballplayers.

In addition to the initial revival of 1976–1981 (the Yankees won the AL pennant in '81 but lost the World Series to the Los Angeles Dodgers), Steinbrenner was at the helm for the team's second, more spectacular run, when between 1996 and 2009, they won eight pennants and five World Championships. Despite these successes, Steinbrenner seemed unable to avoid controversy, demeaning conflicts with employees and even friends, and crazy, embarrassing situations, such as: his fight in an elevator with two Dodgers fans and his newspaper apology to Yankees fans for the team's loss of the 1981 Series; his trying to justify the firing of manager Lou Piniella, a personal friend, by falsely accusing him of stealing furniture from the team; and his having to endure thousands of New York fans shouting "Steinbrenner sucks! Steinbrenner sucks! Steinbrenner sucks!" after the traded Reggie Jackson homered for the California Angels in his initial return to Yankee Stadium.

The low point for Steinbrenner came in the aftermath of a tawdry financial dispute he had with Dave Winfield and his involvement with Howard Spira, a gambler and disgruntled former employee of Winfield's charitable foundation who shopped around purportedly pejorative information about the All-Star outfielder. Although Spira was convicted of attempting to blackmail Steinbrenner, commissioner Fay Vincent sought to punish Steinbrenner for "conduct detrimental to baseball." Vincent originally intended to suspend Steinbrenner for two years, but because he feared the word "suspension" might affect his involvement with the U.S. Olympic Committee (an organization some believed he loved more than the Yankees), Steinbrenner allowed Vincent to place him on baseball's "permanent ineligible list." As in the case of Pete Rose, this amounted to a lifetime ban from baseball. Only Vincent's own outrageous behavior got Steinbrenner off the hook. While interviewing Steinbrenner about the Winfield/Spira affair, Vincent had run roughshod over him, clearly violating "baseball's rules of procedure"; and after the owners executive council, already tired of what they considered to be Vincent's abuse of power, went to bat for the Yankees owner, Vincent rescinded the ban.

As his age began to slow him down, Steinbrenner slowly relinquished control of the team to others (including his sons, Hank and Hal) to the point that when the Yankees won their 27th World Championship in 2009, he happily watched the Series from his home in Tampa, Florida; an achievement in its own right in that he realized he'd righted the ship and was finally content to allow others to steer it. He died less than a year later (July 13) at age 80.

As one would expect from a veteran sportswriter such as he, Maddon keeps the momentum of the book going by discussing the Yankees' fortunes, year by year, and by offering expert analysis of how they won and what went wrong when they didn't. To his credit, he remains neutral in his reporting. When the subject is depicted in a negative light, the negativity is provided by the words of some of the 150+ people he interviewed for the book. The reader is left to decide for himself exactly what kind of person George Steinbrenner was. And so, we may ask, Was Steinbrenner a great man? If having a significant impact on the times in which one lives is the main criterion, then yes, Steinbrenner was a great man. He was a visionary with a monumental sense of the Yankees' place in history and an unshakeable will to be a good custodian of that specialness. Was he good man? On balance, despite his many flaws, particularly his unexplainable penchant for lying, he was as good or better than most of us. One very positive aspect of his character that comes through repeatedly is his extreme generosity and his willingness to forgive and forget. Time after time, Maddon describes George heatedly firing an exasperated employee one day and expecting him to be back at work the next day as if nothing had happened. The book also abounds with examples of Steinbrenner doing his best to help people in need; the most redeeming examples of this virtue being his setting up a foundation to send children of fallen New York policeman and firemen to college and the way he sprang into action to deal with the tragic death of catcher Thurman Munson, putting all the assets of the Yankees into play to assist and comfort Munson's wife and family and to honor the fallen captain. Maddon writes: "In terms of being a leader, boss and commander in chief, even 30 years later, those who were there in that time of crisis would still agree that it had been George Steinbrenner's finest hour." Finally, if the most pertinent question is Was Steinbrenner a fascinating man? … about that there can be no dispute. Steinbrenner lived every day of his life as if the world might end tomorrow. By sheer will power and determination he put and kept himself for most of his adult life at the center of the nation's national pastime and enjoyed every minute of it. Bill Maddon understood all this, and anyone who reads *Steinbrenner: The Last Lion of Baseball* will find himself full of deep appreciation not only for the subject, but for its author as well.

Summer of Shadows:
A Murder, a Pennant Race, and the Twilight of the Best Location in the Nation

◆

Jonathan Knight

◆

Cincinnati: Clerisy Press, 2011. Paper, 464 pages, ISBN: 978-1-57860-467-8. Prelude: Summer 1969. End Notes, About the Author, 44 black & white photos scattered throughout the book.

   Comments: "I grew up in Cleveland, a city where we feed on love of misery, of near misses and tragedy. *Summer of Shadows* captures those moments in time that last forever in our collective imagination and reminds us that this often-maligned town was once one of America's greatest. Captivating, engaging, you won't put it down"—Craig Heimbuch

   There are many notable books which attempt to pair baseball with a subject other than the game on the diamond but none more fascinating than Jonathan Knight's *Summer of Shadows*, a brilliant account of the two headline-dominating stories that transfixed the populace of northern Ohio during the summer of 1954: the Cleveland Indians' record-setting march to the American League pennant and the ghastly murder of Dr. Sam Sheppard's pregnant wife, Marilyn, both of which occurred at the height of and signaled the end of Cleveland's status as "The best location in the nation." While the baseball season receives priority over the murder in the narration, the true crime element of the book differentiates it from all other books on baseball. Indeed, the sensational murder and subsequent highly publicized trial threaten at times to overshadow the exploits of the Indians, and they serve as a sobering reminder, just as they did in 1954, that there are more important things in life than baseball.

   In the book's prelude, Knight cites the Cuyahoga River's catching on fire and burning for several hours on June 22, 1969, as the symbol of Cleveland's fall from grace and the impetus for the sardonic nickname it became saddled with, "Mistake by the Lake." Readers familiar with the poor image that has dogged Cleveland since that time may be surprised to learn that the City was once held in much higher esteem. By the mid-nineteen fifties it was the seventh-largest city in the nation and, according to

Knight, hummed along energetically as "one of the industrial capitals of the world." It exulted in a new state-of-the-art lakefront airport, an efficient rapid transport system, its glow as the "best-lighted metropolitan area in the world," and its ability seemingly to continually birth innovation in numerous fields; examples of which the author continually alludes to in the course of his narrative. The pride Clevelanders had in their city was boosted and reflected by the success of its professional sports teams; not just that of the Indians but also of the football Browns and the Barons who dominated the American Hockey League. All these factors combined to make Cleveland an idyllic place to live, as well as a glaring contrast for the events of the summer of 1954 which shocked its citizens and put the City on a downward trajectory.

The thing that made the Indians' defeat in the 1954 World Series so devastating was that it was totally unexpected. The Indians not only finally outpaced their nemesis, the New York Yankees, after finishing second to them the previous three seasons; the Tribe also eventually, after a tough pennant race for most of the summer, smoked their despised rivals, besting them by eight games and setting an American League record for most wins in a season with 111. Few people thought that the other team with "New York" embroidered across their jerseys, the National League Giants, would beat the Indians in the World Series, much less pull off a four-game sweep.

During the regular season, the Indians indeed were a great team. The offense boasted the winner of the League batting title (second baseman Bobby Avila), the League leader in home runs and RBI (center fielder Larry Doby), and the previous year's AL MVP, Al Rosen; who, despite an injury, put on a show at Cleveland's Municipal Stadium in front of the home crowd during the 1954 All-Star Game, going 3–4 at bat with two home runs and five runs batted in. The pitching was even better. The big three of Early Wynn, Bob Lemon, and Mike Garcia won 65 games and prevented extended losing streaks; Bob Feller and Hal Newhouser at the end of their careers added 20 more wins; and Don Mossi and Ray Narleski formed the best relief combination in the League. As good as the team was, the Indians still had to prove it. GM Hank Greenberg, who built the team, and manager Al Lopez, who was tired of losing to mentor Casey Stengel, were especially under pressure to win; and Knight's accounts of the important games and series over the long season are masterfully reported and blended perfectly into the other series of events which captured the attention of Clevelanders. Instead of all together at the end, Knight covers the four games of the '54 World Series separately as "Autumn Interludes" placed before each of the four Parts of the book. Spacing the detailed accounts of the four contests out this way creates an appropriate sense of foreboding and heightens the disastrous effect of the Indians' mammoth October failure.

The key to the Series, Game One, was decided by, of all things, the Giants' odd, bathtub-shaped ballpark, the venerable Polo Grounds, which allowed Willie Mays to rob Vic Wertz of a 440-foot home run and then awarded Dusty Rhodes a "Chinese" homer on nothing more than a 258-foot can of corn. Emphasizing this amazing contrast, Knight writes: "The preposterous nature of Rhodes' homer further underlined the injustice of Wertz's robbery. 'Wertz hits the ball as far as anybody ever will,' Lopez sighed later, 'and it's just an out.' Indeed, just as Wertz's blast would have been a home run in any ballpark but one, Rhodes' game-winning home run would have been a routine fly ball in any baseball park in America. Except one." The loss stunned the Indians, but they lost the Series simply because they were out-hit and especially out-pitched throughout.

Tragically, the Indians' great summer was interrupted by the grisly murder of Marilyn Sheppard in the early hours of July 4. Until that time, her handsome husband had been living the American dream. He and Marilyn resided in a paid-off home in upscale Bay Village, and he shared a thriving medical practice with his father and two brothers at a nearby hospital owned by the family. Sam immediately became the prime suspect; primarily because the story he told investigators was so suspicious and hard to believe.

That story, which never changed, was that Sam fell asleep in a living room chair at the end of a dinner party, while his wife went upstairs to bed. He was awakened by a scream and ran upstairs to check on Marilyn. On the landing outside the bedroom door, he was knocked out by a blow to the head from behind. When he groggily regained consciousness, he looked into the room and saw his wife lying on the edge of the bed, her face pulverized beyond recognition, her pillow soaked in blood, with more blood splattered throughout the room. He felt for a pulse and found none. After checking on his 7-year-old son who slept peacefully in an adjoining bedroom, he heard a noise downstairs, ran to investigate, and wound up chasing after a shadowy figure escaping onto the Lake Erie beach behind the house. There in the dark he struggled with the unknown assailant, who gradually overpowered him and again rendered him unconscious with a choke hold. When he awoke, he was soaking wet, in considerable neck pain, and bereft of the tee shirt he'd been wearing. He staggered back into the house, found the place ransacked, and covered the partially unclothed body of his wife with a sheet. Then at 5:45 a.m. he called not the police but his friend and neighbor Spencer Houk, the mayor of Bay Village, crying, "For God's sake, Spen, come quick! I think they've killed Marilyn."

Making the horrible situation even more bizarre, the investigation into the murder was an incompetent fiasco. Policemen, reporters, family members, and neighbors ... not just Houk and his wife but others too, including famous Browns quarterback Otto Graham ... traipsed all over the Sheppard house contaminating the crime scene. Admitting that they were out of their league, the small Bay Village police department quickly turned the case over to the Cleveland homicide unit, but the case was essentially prosecuted in the court of public opinion by two powerful Cleveland figures: Cuyahoga County coroner Dr. Samuel Gerber and the highly influential editor of the *Cleveland Press*, Louis B. Seltzer. Both men concluded almost immediately that Sheppard was the murderer. Seltzer was particularly zealous, publishing front page editorials with suggestive headlines such as, "Somebody Is Getting Away with Murder," and publicly pressuring Gerber to hold an inquest and later for authorities to arrest Sheppard. The inquest presided over by Gerber, whose questions were blatantly accusatory, was a circus; and the subsequent nine-week trial, the longest in county history which concluded a few days before Christmas that year, reached a verdict that was almost pre-ordained given the extensive newspaper coverage the case had received not only in Cleveland but in papers around the country as well. The 30-year-old Sheppard was found guilty on a charge of second-degree murder and sentenced to life in prison in the Ohio State Penitentiary; despite the trial never producing a murder weapon, an eye witness, a confession, or even a plausible motive. Members of the press, law enforcement, and the legal profession in Cleveland by and large felt that Sheppard received a fair trial; but ten years later, after a young lawyer named F. Lee Bailey had taken over for the Sheppard's original family counsel, the Supreme Court heard an appeal and vehemently disagreed. The court said that the case in 1954 had been infected by "massive, pervasive, and prejudicial publicity" and that "bedlam had reigned at the courthouse," and taken on a "carnival atmosphere." Bailey handily won a re-trial and Sam was set free after having served ten years of his sentence. As in the O.J. Simpson case and unlike the television series based on the Sheppard case, *The Fugitive*, no one else was ever charged with Marilyn Sheppard's murder. Though free, Sheppard had been severely damaged by the experience. Two subsequent ill-advised and short-lived marriages, a brief career as a wrestler using the self-mocking nickname "Killer," a disastrous attempt to resurrect his medical practice, and heavy bouts of drinking were parts of his downward spiral which ended in an early death a mere six years after his release from prison. His murder case, whether the original verdict was correct or not, became "the embodiment of everything that can go wrong with the American justice system," and led to important changes in American jurisprudence.

In the final pages of the book Knight describes the steady demise of Cleveland since the City's heyday of 1954, and the recitation of woes undergone is depressing indeed. Whether the 1954 World Series and the Marilyn Sheppard murder were causative to some degree of this decline, as the book maintains, or merely emblematic of it, Knight makes the reader feel the powerful emotions that both events unleashed on the people who lived most intimately through them. Right after the '54 World Series, Louis Seltzer ran a defiantly optimistic editorial in the *Press*, insisting that Cleveland, though bowed at the moment, would never relinquish its title as "The City of Champions." Knight, a person who also clearly loves the City, echoes that optimism in the final words of the book: "Yes, as always, Cleveland perseveres, its citizens cherishing their city no matter what its perception and appreciating the golden days when they come. In the meantime, they're left with memories of what once was, and the hope that even in the depths of the darkest winter, someday summer will come again."

21: The Story of Roberto Clemente (A Graphic Novel)

◆

WILFRED SANTIAGO

◆

Seattle, WA: Fantagraphics Books, 2011. Cloth, 182+ pages, ISBN 978-1-560 97-892-3. Selected bibliography.

The point of the graphic novel is to tell with sequential pictures as well as with words, a story worth telling. Indeed, when the story to be told or the subject of the story is already very familiar, the pictures can be said to take precedence over the text; and if the art is not exceptional, then the graphic novel is without a true purpose. As baseball is such a highly visual activity … with its colorful uniforms and highly recognizable logos, the iconic stances, positions, and motions of the players, and the unmistakable look of its classic ballparks … the game makes a perfect match for the genre. While only a handful of artists and writers have picked up the gauntlet so far, several baseball graphic novels qualify as Diamond Classics, with the most scintillating, captivating, and dramatic of them being "*21*": *The Story of Roberto Clemente*, written and illustrated by Wilfred Santiago.

Because "*21*" purports to be a biography rather than a more focused account of one season or seminal event, Santiago was faced with the necessity of having to carefully choose those parts of the life that he considered to be most meaningful. The longest of the six "sections" of the book (to facilitate the flow of the narrative, the author eschews clearly demarcated "chapters") is the first one, devoted to Clemente's boyhood in Puerto Rico up to the time of his departure for the United States and his foray into professional baseball, as a farmhand of the Brooklyn Dodgers. Much of the detail in this section appears to have been drawn from David Maraniss' brilliant and definitive biography, *Clemente: The Passion and Grace of Baseball's Last Hero* (a title listed in "*21*'s" bibliography). Santiago has the members of Clemente's large family refer to him as "Momen," his nickname derived from his inquisitiveness as a boy which caused him to continually interrupt others by saying, "Momentito" (i.e., wait a moment), because he always wanted to know the reason behind something. He shows us the baseball-crazy Clemente using almost anything and everything (such as bottle caps) as makeshift baseballs. He depicts the boy troubled by insomnia and nightmares and haunted by the terrible death by fire of older sister Anairis (who perished before he became aware of her existence). We see Roberto's mother comforting him by reminding him of the words of her favorite hymn: "Life is nothing, life is fleeting, only God makes man happy." Santiago includes a two-page, 12-panel sequence illustrating the 12-year-old's heroism, his pulling a man out of a crashed and burning automobile, and later having a classmate tease him for being "the Lone Ranger on two wheels" (the young hero arrives on the scene by bicycle). And we get a glimpse of the 17-year-old's self-confidence when he throws out the car window on the way to the airport the new hat his father had given him as a farewell present. His brothers say he should have given away the hat which he does not like to someone else, but Momen replies, "Are you crazy? Then I become famous and someone tells everyone that it belonged to me. Papa will kill me." All of these details, these telling moments are meant to convey the things that formed Clemente's character ... his dedication to baseball, his concern for others, and his love of God, family, and his native land.

Of course, there is plenty of dialogue in "21" (encapsulated in dialogue bubbles of all shapes and sizes) but very little direct narration by the author. Instead, what is not conveyed by dialogue is transmitted by news broadcasts; snippets of radio game play-by-play; signage ("WE SERVE WHITE PEOPLE ONLY"); the reproduction of actual telegrams (one sent by Clemente's father to the Dodgers), letters (one of Roberto's home-sick missives to his mother); historical newspaper front pages; tickets and ticket stubs; advertising; an image of the 45 rpm record of the song that was the musical soundtrack of the Pirates' 1960 World Championship season; and excerpts from magazines and programs. All of this done in an effort to *show* us instead of merely telling us.

And then there is the artwork by Santiago. He himself on the book's first page calls the novel a "comic book," and so it should come as no surprise that his drawings, particularly of people, are somewhat cartoonish in style. But how exquisitely expressive they are! It is also worth noting that the artist takes more liberties with the minor cast of characters than he does with those holding down major roles. Santiago also usually loosens his style when drawing ballplayers (including Clemente); perhaps as a way to emphasize both the stresses of competition and the fans' view of the players as comic book super heroes. In any case, the novel is a ceaselessly stimulating and beautiful piece of art to behold.

The book's odd but hand-friendly size (6¼"× 8") and its arresting cover (Clemente in left-sided profile, black number 21 prominently displayed on the back of his sleeveless cream-colored Pirates uniform vest) immediately signal something special; and inside the basically black and white drawings are accentuated by numerous soothing shades of brown, cream, and gold ... with bright orange used for many of the dialogue bubbles. As he does with the dialogue bubbles, Santiago greatly varies the shape, size, and orientation of the panels, as well as the number of panels on any particular page. He uses every viewpoint imaginable (such as bird's-eye, worm's-eye, rear views, and closeups), as well as numerous other tricks of the cartoonist's trade, such as onomatopoeia (Pow! Thud! and "K-KRK" for the sound of Roberto twisting his neck), emanata (hearts "literally" bursting out of Pirates' fans as the Yankees trounce the Bucs 16–3 in Game Two of the 1960 Fall Classic), grawlix (jibberish substitutes for swearing), and splash paging (a page with a single panel). The cumulative effect of the use of all these striking elements is the temptation to not merely read but to *study* page after page of the marvelous world re-created by the artist.

After the opening section, the next one focuses on Clemente's early career: his frustration at not getting much playing time in Montreal or Brooklyn (the Dodgers were trying to hide Clemente from other clubs, his coming out party playing for the Santurce Crabs, his being drafted by the Pirates, and the car accident in Puerto Rico which resulted in his chronic spine and neck problems). The remaining sections cover his courtship of wife, Vera, and the critical moments and years of his career: 1956 before he had established himself as a star; the World Series Championship seasons of 1960 and 1971; Roberto Clemente Night in 1970; and the final game of his career on September 30, 1972, when he got the base hit that made him the 11th member of the 3,000 Hit Club. Santiago shows us Clemente's humility when he is honored but also his anger when he is disrespected, if not discriminated against (such as his finishing eighth in the 1960 NL MVP voting). What will surprise some readers is the brevity with which Santiago handles the subject's death, a mere five pages or so; with most of that dealing with Clemente's preparations for the doomed mission-of-mercy flight in aid of Nicaraguan earthquake victims. However, this is a case of "less being more," as if the details of the mistakes made which caused the plane to crash, the futile search for Clemente's body, and the universally sorrowful response to the tragedy are just too painful to dwell on.

The final pages are stark indeed but extremely meaningful: two blackish-green splash pages, the complete darkness on the left-hand page illuminated only by the image of a tiny white airplane in the night sky above the sea, indicated by a single "wavy" squiggle towards the bottom; and on the right-hand page slightly above the level of the plane, three bright stars towards which the plane seems to fly. These stars are the ones said to represent the Magi, the three Kings Balthazar, Gaspar, and Melchior, who traveled afar to find, worship, and present gifts to the baby Jesus, the new-born Savior of the World. This story is introduced in the first section of the novel when Momen's mother over six wonderful pages points out the three stars and explains their significance as a way of comforting the nightmare-disturbed boy; concluding wisely that "To be absent from this life, is to be in the presence of the Lord." The feast day of the Magi, the Epiphany, celebrated on January 6, recurs several times in the rest of the book so that it becomes the motif which unifies "21" and elevates it above the level of the sports pages.

Clemente had a premonition of an early death, something Santiago alludes to in a sequence which has Clemente finally falling asleep and dreaming on a Pirates' flight. Clemente is awakened by a teammate who says, "Look at the old Rip Van Winkle. You finally did it! And you don't look a day old."

"I'm no worried about that," replies Roberto.

"Right. You shouldn't worry," says the teammate. "Not everyone grows old." Careful readers will also notice Santiago foreshadowing Clemente's death by placing small, easily unnoticed airplanes in several seemingly arbitrarily places.

In the preface to his great biography, Maraniss describes a huge cenotaph erected in Clemente's honor which stands across the street from the baseball stadium in Carolina, Puerto Rico. Referring to the central panel which depicts Clemente holding a lamb, Maraniss says, "In sainthood, his people put a lamb in his arms, but he was no saint, and certainly not docile. He was agitated, beautiful, sentimental, unsettled, sweet, serious, selfless, haunted, sensitive, contradictory, and intensely proud of everything about his native land, including himself." Maybe, but while it is certainly true that the Catholic Church has not canonized Roberto Clemente, Wilfred Santiago makes clear in "21" his belief that Clemente enjoys the beatific vision. At a minimum, it is impossible for anyone to gainsay the truth that Clemente did indeed honor the credo by which he lived: "If you have a chance to help others and fail to do so, you are wasting your life on this earth."

Walter Johnson: Baseball's Big Train

◆

HENRY W. THOMAS

◆

Washington, D.C.: Phenom Press, 1995. Cloth, 458 pages, ISBN: 0-9645439-0-7. Acknowledgments, Introduction, Foreword by Shirley Povich. Appendix I: Was He the Greatest, Appendix II: The Best Games, Appendix III: The Numbers, Notes, Bibliography, Index, 22 black & white photos between pages 90 and 91, 26 black & white photos between pages 138 and 139, and 28 black & white photos between pages 298 and 299.

Comments: *Walter Johnson* won the 13th CASEY Award in 1995.

Thomas found so much great material in the family scrapbooks on his grandfather that he used some of it as interludes and some as snippets to introduce chapters. Here is an anecdote by Ed Grillo that introduces Chapter 5: "Another instance which shows the character of the great pitcher occurred in Boston one day when McAleer had the club. Walter was pitching brilliantly against the Red Sox in a very close game when a couple of errors and a base on balls filled the bases with no one out. It looked as if the game would be lost at this stage and the crowd went wild. But Johnson buckled down to business and struck out Hooper, Speaker, and Lewis, Boston's big guns, and then with his head down walked to the bench. I was sitting with McAleer at the time, and as Johnson walked from the mound, McAleer poked me in the ribs and shouted, 'Look! Look! He's ashamed he did it.'"

Baseball literature is a treasure trove of great biographies, and if there is one work among these literary gems that may be described as perfect ... in its pairing of worthy subject and talented, empathetic author, in its judicious management of a wealth of relevant information, and in its complete triumph in executing its mission ... it surely is *Walter Johnson: Baseball's Big Train* by Henry W. Thomas. The prowess of the subject had always been a given, his name rattled off methodically whenever pitching greats were being discussed, yet prior to this book Johnson's life and career had never been adequately laid out like a map which accurately delineates the features of a recently explored territory. As we know now, no one was more qualified to revivify Walter Johnson than Henry "Hank" Thomas, who just happens to be, besides a superb researcher and storyteller, the grandson of the great pitcher. Amazingly, much of the raw material that Thomas the biographer needed had been close at hand in the family home his entire life in the form of 30 thick scrapbooks of newspaper clippings, letters, documents, and other types of ephemera covering most of

Walter Johnson

Baseball's Big Train

Henry W. Thomas

Foreword by Shirley Povich

Johnson's 21-year major league career (all of it spent with the Washington Senators); meticulously assembled by the pitcher's wife Hazel and pretty much ignored for decades by his descendants. Until one day Thomas, as an adult, out of a combination of boredom and curiosity delved into the scrapbooks. He immediately realized the opportunity and obligation before him when he read glowing descriptions of his grandfather, such as this by sportswriter Frank Graham, found in the February 1947 issue of *Baseball Magazine*: "He was, beyond doubt, the greatest pitcher that ever scuffed a rubber with his spikes. But he was much more than that. Walter Johnson had all the virtues commonly but not always truthfully attributed to athletic heroes: honesty, decency, dignity, thoughtfulness and a genuine modesty. A simple man, he was, in his way, a great man." After completing years of research into the periods of Johnson's life not covered in the scrapbooks, Thomas had the complete story and was thus able to produce the biography that is the literary equivalent of one of Walter Johnson's many mound masterpieces.

And the number of the latter is staggering, as is the entire corpus of Johnson's statistical big league record. While the Big Train pitched only one no-hitter (an error prevented it from being a perfect game), he threw 110 shutouts, 38 of them 1–0 victories, both major league records that no one else has even come close to equaling. As Thomas posits in an appendix on "The Best Games," which briefly recounts 15 of Johnson's most impressive games "…a list of fifty of Walter Johnson's greatest games would leave out many brilliant performances." Included in the 15 (in addition to the no-hitter) are an Opening Day one-hitter against the Philadelphia A's on April 14, 1910 (Johnson's other one-baserunner game); the 18-inning 1–0 win over Chicago on May 15, 1918 (the longest shutout victory ever; matched later by Carl Hubbell); Johnson's whitewash of the Pittsburgh Pirates in the 1925 World Series on October 11, making him, at 37 years and 11 months, the oldest pitcher to throw a World Series shutout; a 15-inning 1–0 win on Opening Day 1926 against the powerful A's which Johnson himself considered his masterpiece, as no runner reached second base; the June 9, 1907, perfect game win for the Weiser, Idaho, minor league team that convinced Washington Senators manager Joe Cantillon that he had to have the 19-year-old on his team; and the 27-strikeout game (in fifteen innings) for Fullerton (California) Union High School on April 15, 1905. Thomas includes the latter two, non-major league games because they demonstrated Johnson's enormous talent in the form of a practically unhittable fastball right from the beginning. Fifty years after that school boy game, a member of the opposing Santa Ana High School team said, "I remember we all keep saying to the next batter, 'He ain't got a thing but a fast ball' and that was true. But what a fast ball! It came up to the plate like a pea shot out of a cannon."

Everybody who ever batted against Johnson said something similar, even jaded major leaguers who thought they'd seen it all. What made Johnson's inhuman speed all the harder to believe as well as difficult to catch up with was the ease with which he delivered the ball: a sweeping sidearm delivery that appeared to require no exertion whatsoever. As Detroit Hall of Fame outfielder Sam Crawford said, "That's what threw you off. He threw so nice and easy–and then swoosh, and it was by you. Easily the greatest pitcher I ever saw." Thomas found gobs of such testimonials, all of them worth sharing ... so many of them that he sets them off as chapter "Introductories" so as not to interrupt the narrative.

In addition to confounding batters, Johnson's effortless motion bestowed on him a bionic arm, enabling him to pitch often and frequently deep into extra-inning games. Throughout his career, Johnson was a starting pitcher; but, always ready to help the team, he came out of the bullpen 138 times. The quintessential workhorse, he threw 300+ innings and started 40+ games for nine consecutive years. On top of all this activity, he pitched in numerous benefit exhibition games during the off-season; and through it all he suffered only a pair of somewhat serious sore arms, both of which eventually came around with rest and non-surgical treatment.

Johnson eventually developed a curveball to complement his blazing fastball, but what made him more than just a spectacular thrower was his great control and his lack of obsession with strikeouts. No one knew better than Johnson how potentially lethal his fastball was, and in fact he was terrified of killing somebody with a pitched ball. He knocked down only one batter, Frank "Home Run" Baker, and refused to throw "purpose pitches" afterwards or even "work inside," much to the relief of American League batters (Thomas provides the figures to show that after that one knock down, Baker could hardly touch Johnson the rest of his career. The author does the same to show how Ty Cobb successfully exploited Johnson's fear of killing a batter. Ironically, despite his caution, Johnson racked up 203 hit batsmen, the ML record). It's clear that had Johnson been willing to intimidate hitters, most of them would have fared much worse against him than they did. Johnson was also content to let his fielders help him, and he often saved his arm by letting up when the Senators had given him a nice lead; a practice he referred to as "artful loafing." Thomas cites the game of July 3, 1913, against Boston as a good example of the strategy: a 1–0 Washington victory in 15 innings during which Johnson gave up 15 hits, still the record for hits allowed in a complete game shutout. Obviously, the "loafing" also cost Johnson in personal statistics; the best example of that being a season finale "joke game" during which Senators played out of position all over the diamond. Johnson started in center field but relieved late in the game by popular demand. Lobbing the ball in, he surrendered two hits and was charged with two earned runs when the hitters came around to score off another reliver. For years Johnson's ERA that year was listed as 1.09 until those two runs were added, raising his ERA to 1.14. Without those "joke game" runs, Johnson would hold the record for lowest ERA in a season instead of Bob Gibson who compiled a 1.12 ERA in 1968.

Of the numerous contributions this book makes to our understanding and appreciation of Johnson, the most important are Johnson's status in his own time and the high caliber of the man's character. Johnson was almost universally regarded as the greatest pitcher of all time, Christy Mathewson being the challenger championed by a few dissenters. The Big Train, in fact, was seen as the mound equivalent of the Bambino, and had Johnson spent his career in New York rather than Washington, he could very well have been as big a media sensation as Babe Ruth.

This, despite the glaringly obvious fact that Johnson's personality and character were diametrically opposed to those of Ruth. Johnson, whose idea of a big time away from the diamond was working his gentleman's farm or tromping through the woods with his prized hound dogs, was a devoted husband and father and a loyal friend to everyone he ever met. As talented as he was, humility and stoicism were his defining characteristics. He wouldn't leave Idaho for the big time until his parents gave him the okay. Even as a huge star, he never complained or did anything even marginally dishonest. He never alibied, never blamed teammates for errors or a lack of run support, and never pitied himself when all too often the breaks did not go his way. The admiration of Johnson was so deeply felt and widespread as to have been unique in baseball history. There is no more affecting illustration of this than the numerous times Thomas describes opposing fans openly rooting for Johnson against their own boys. Opposing players and managers were not immune from similar compulsions either. Boston's Harry Hooper, retired on a hot smash to first as the final out of Johnson's no-hitter, told the pitcher, "I'm glad to lose that hit for your no-hit game." Johnson offered the press a typically modest reaction: "Goodness gracious sakes alive, wasn't I lucky!"

It might seem as if Walter Johnson led a charmed life but not quite. Life subjected him to some tough times and dark nights as it does us all, namely: Johnson's embarrassing flirtation with the upstart Federal League; his being jacked around in his unsuccessful attempts to buy a minor league team; his toiling for second-rate ballclubs until the end of his career when the Senators finally assembled championship quality teams; his failures in the 1924 and 1925 World Series (despite his triumph in relief in Game Seven of the 1924 Fall Classic); and, most poignantly, in the space of nine years, the loss of his father, a daughter, a grandfather, his mother-in-law, a sister, and, most cruelly of all, his beloved soul mate, Hazel. Johnson's courage in facing these blows only endeared him all the more to his adoring public.

In addition to the Appendices on Johnson's Best Games and on his stats and many records (Johnson retired with a 417–279 record and a lifetime ERA of 2.17), Thomas concludes this epic biography with a third Appendix, "Was He the Greatest?" The latter, which examines the honors accorded Johnson as well as opinions about great pitchers expressed in various studies, is as needed as a pair of sunglasses in the blackest of thunderstorms. For the reader has already been convinced and needs no urging to agree with the sentiment expressed at the time of Johnson's death by his old friend Clark Griffith, who managed and later owned the Senators for most of the pitcher's career: "We'll never see his like again."

We Are the Ship: The Story of Negro League Baseball

◆

KADIR NELSON

◆

New York: Jump at the Sun/Hyperion Books for Children, 2008. Cloth, 88 pages, ISBN: 978-0-7868-0832-8. Foreword by Hank Aaron. Negro Leaguers Who Made It to the Major Leagues, Negro Leaguers in the National Baseball Hall of Fame, Author's Note, Acknowledgments, Bibliography, Filmography, Endnotes, Index.

 Comments: *We Are the Ship* is the only children's book to be nominated as a finalist for and also to win the CASEY Award for Best Baseball Book of the Year. With an almost unanimous low score of 4 points (1 + 1 + 2) it won handily over the competition, including *Ballet in the Dirt: The Golden Age of Baseball* by Neil Leifer (second place) and *Ed Barrow: The Bulldog Who Built the Yankees' First Dynasty* (third) by Daniel R. Levitt.

 The book also won the Coretta Scott King Author Award, the Robert F. Sibert Informational Book Medal, and the CSK Illustrator Honor Book award.

 Sometimes it takes an artist to really open our eyes (and minds), and that is exactly what Pratt Institute graduate Kadir Nelson did when he published *We Are the Ship*: his anecdotal history of Negro League Baseball which is highlighted by the reproduction of a series of his stunningly beautiful and evocative oil paintings about the subject. The visual impact of this book is virtually impossible to overestimate; as the sensitivity and loving respect on display in the paintings, not to mention their technical brilliance, have the effect of making the Negro Leagues seem like an entirely new discovery and an extremely exciting one at that.

 It's not like authors had neglected the Negro Leagues. In fact, the amazing institution born out of discrimination which served as a refuge for the hundreds of talented African American men who were banned from the white major leagues yet remained determined to play the game they loved at as high a level as possible had already been for years a favorite subject for accomplished researchers and writers, such as Richard Bak, John Holway, Larry Lester, Robert Peterson, and Don Rogosin who are all listed in the book's Bibliography. Yet, Nelson's paintings elevate the idea of the Negro League player to a whole new level that words alone cannot reach.

Take for instance the cover painting of catcher and slugger Josh Gibson, a majestic home run masher known as "the black Babe Ruth." It is a portrait of strength personified; evident not just in the bulging-veined hands and forearms strangling the bat laid over his shoulder or in the pumped-up biceps accentuated by the rolled-up sleeves of his jersey but in the hard cast of Gibson's penetrating gaze, aimed directly at the viewer. It is the uncompromising, determined visage of an undaunted spirit, forged by the crucible of discrimination, hardship, and triumph against all odds. It is the look of a batter to be feared, of a man not to be trifled with. In this portrait, there is nothing behind Gibson to distract us other than barely noticeable wisps of clouds in an otherwise clear sky, but later in the book, we get a look at the complete painting. This time we see that those lumberjack arms are even bigger than they appeared to be on the cover, and we notice in the right corner of the background a telling detail that serves as an ironic comment by the artist: an American flag flying above the outfield wall, supposedly symbolizing "liberty and justice for all."

The arresting, defining characteristics displayed in the Gibson painting are similarly to be found throughout the book in portraits of other important Negro Leaguers. The early days are represented by pioneers, such as pitcher "Smokey" Joe Williams, Negro National League founder Rube Foster (who uttered the famous words of the title), and shortstop John Henry "Pop" Lloyd; while the heyday is represented by superstars Oscar Charleston, Willie Foster, Pittsburgh Crawfords owner Gus Greenlee, Wilbur "Bullet" Rogan, William Julius "Judy" Johnson, Raleigh "Biz" Mackey, Norman "Turkey" Stearnes, Martin Dihigo, Hilton Smith, Buck Leonard, James "Cool Papa" Bell, and Ray "Squatty" Dandridge. Jackie Robinson, attired in his Dodgers uniform and standing on the edge of the outfield grass of Ebbets Field, comes near the end of the book, for it was his courageous integration of the major leagues which hastened the bitter-sweet demise of the Negro Leagues.

One may legitimately ask where the smiles are in these paintings, for with the exception of a candid scene inside the bus of the Newark Eagles which depicts the players joyfully singing to pass the time, they are absent; even from the wonderful group and team paintings of which there are several. The answer lies in the artist's keen awareness of the hard-won identity of his subjects and his determination to emphasize, beyond anyone's ability to miss it, his subjects' inherent dignity and heroic stature. As the text duly indicates, there was plenty of fun and joy to be had in the playing and watching of Negro League–style baseball, and in simply be*ing* a Negro Leaguer; but between the lines it was all business the majority of the time (clowning was sometimes a part of the Negro League game, especially when teams barnstormed against inferior, small-town competition). This truth is easily deduced from the dead seriousness apparent in the several action scenes depicted in the book: a grimacing Jackie Robinson of the Kansas City Monarchs sliding safely across home plate underneath the catcher's outstretched arms, the umpire standing over both players, his arms spread emphatically wide; "the mighty Josh Gibson," from the on-deck circle, intently watching Satchel Paige deliver a pitch to Buck Leonard from the mound of Washington, D.C.'s Griffith Stadium; and the lanky Satchel in his stretch atop the mound of Yankee Stadium staring towards home plate, a lonely but indomitable figure, all eyes in the New York Cubans' dugout lasered on him.

Other paintings in the book more directly illustrate specific aspects of the history narrated by the text. For example, one painting spread across adjacent pages shows Rube Foster and his Chicago American Giants (circa 1920) dressed to the nines and emerging from their own train car, testimony that the players did not always travel by car or bus. A four-page fold-out reproduces on one side a ticket to the "First Colored World Series" dated October 11, 1924, and on the other it depicts the two competing teams, the Monarchs and Hilldale Club (Philadelphia), lined up along both base lines of Kansas City's Muehlebach Field before the game. And then there are paintings which illustrate exhibition play against major league all-star teams, Negro Leaguers being the first to play night baseball, Latin America as a more hospitable (but also sometimes dangerous) place for Negro Leaguers to play ball, the annual must-see Negro League all-star game known as the East-West Classic, and the post-integration folding of the entire industry. It all adds up to a spectacular feast of consummate artistry produced for the dual purposes of honoring the men depicted and of drawing others into an appreciation for the world those men inhabited and conquered.

A word about the text. Originally, it was to be written by someone else, but Mr. Nelson decided to give it a shot himself. His first and, as it turned out, fortuitous decision was to write in the voice of a reminiscing "everyman" Negro League player. As soon as we "hear" his first words, we are hooked and we know that we are listening to a knowledgeable, friendly voice we can trust: "Seems like we've been playing baseball for a mighty long time. At least as long as we've been free. Baseball's the best game there ever was. It's a beautifully designed game that requires a quick wit, a strong body, and a cool head." This narrator takes us briskly through the entire history of the Negro Leagues, explaining everything we need to know and giving us plenty of examples to illustrate his points, and he does it all in nine innings, which some folks prefer to call "chapters."

Finally, *We Are the Ship*, with its near-square shape (approximately 11" × 11"), reinforced library binding, and the conversational tone of its text was conceived of and designed as a children's book; yet there is no doubt of its immense appeal to adults as well as children. In fact, if one were limited to owning a single volume on the Negro Leagues, this would be the one for everyone in the family to treasure and return to time and again.

The Wizard of Waxahachie: Paul Richards and the End of Baseball as We Knew It

Warren Corbett

Dallas: Southern Methodist University Press, 2009. Cloth, 430 pages, ISBN: 978-0-87074-556-0. Foreword by Brooks Robinson, Introduction by Tony La Russa. Notes at the end of chapters, Epilogue: The Beauty of the Competition, Bibliography, Index, 16 black & white photos between pages 208 and 209. Other baseball book by the author: One Game at a Time: The 1959 National League Pennant Race *(Scarecrow Press, 2013).*

Comments: The winner of the Aviation/Space Writers Association award for his writing on the U.S. space program, Corbett was for a brief time a minor league play-by-play broadcaster.

It is easy to understand why today the name Paul Richards is recognized only by true students of baseball history and older fans still possessed of spry memories. The man has not been elected to the National Baseball Hall of Fame, nor is he likely to be elected in the future; and he never guided one of the major league teams he ran as a manager or general manager (or both) to a pennant, much less a World Series Championship. Yet he was unquestionably one of the most important and influential figures in the game for three decades (if not a highly popular one); and that is the presumptive theme any fair-minded reader will concur with after reading Warren Corbett's measured and perceptive biography of Richards entitled *The Wizard of Waxahachie*.

In 1908, the year Paul Rapier Richards came into this world, the town of his birth thirty miles south of Dallas, Texas, billed itself as the Queen City of the Cotton Belt. While cotton was important to its economic success, Waxahachie was crazy about baseball, mainly because the Detroit Tigers trained there for several years. Richards caught baseball fever from the Tigers and never recovered. The account of his watching Ty Cobb drop a routine fly ball at Waxahachie's Jungle Park became a staple of Richards' oft-repeated tales; as it taught him an early and important lesson: "not to worry about mechanical errors, because even the great Cobb could muff the simplest chance." The story is one of several partly-true Richards' remembrances corrected by Corbett (Richards undoubtedly saw what he remembers but not during an exhibition game between the Tigers and NY Giants, who trained in nearby Marlin, Texas, because, as Corbett discovered, the teams never played at Jungle Park).

In Richards' day, Waxahachie not only loved baseball; the town also somehow produced baseball talent like an assembly line. The Waxahachie High School Indians won sixty-five straight games and nine consecutive state championships, and eight of Richards' Indians' teammates went into professional ball; five of them all the way to the big leagues. Richards, who played third base for the varsity as an eighth grader, was considered the best of the lot. He was signed by the Brooklyn Dodgers after his junior year and sat on the Dodgers' bench for a couple of weeks as a 17-year-old before he was assigned to Pittsfield (MA) of the Class A Eastern League, where he actually began his professional playing career.

Richards played minor league baseball for a total of 17 years with intermittent stints in the major leagues. He was that most common type of baseball failure: an excellent all-around bush leaguer who got stuck behind established players at his position in the major leagues (in his longest big league stay, a four-year stretch with Detroit when he was past his prime, he played an average of 83 games and hit a composite .203). Nevertheless, as Corbett makes clear with defining statements, Richards' playing career was all preparation for his true vocation of managing. Becoming a catcher (which he did while playing for the Macon Peaches) "would be his only distinction as a major league player and helped to establish him as a candidate to manage" (Richards had a great arm and handled pitchers brilliantly). Playing for Donie Bush in Minneapolis was "the first time a manager had taught Richards the nuances of the game." And getting demoted to the Atlanta Crackers from Detroit was "the third move that shaped his career and the rest of his life" because it was in Atlanta that he first assumed the managerial reins of a professional ball club.

With Atlanta and later in the high minors with Buffalo and Seattle the self-educated, highly intelligent Richards showed himself to be an effective leader, an innovator, and a strategist who was always an inning or two ahead of the guy in the other dugout. Patient and low key with his players, he was also a terrible baiter of umpires. In eleven seasons as a major league manager Richards received 80 ejections, placing him sixth on the all-time list ahead of managers who had much longer careers. When Richards finally got his chance to manage in the majors, with the Chicago White Sox in 1951, he had been in professional baseball for 25 years. It was in Chicago that the baseball world at large began to take note of the philosophy he'd spent so many years developing. Richards believed that most games are lost, not won and that good teams are those that capitalize most effectively on the other guys' mistakes. Getting the other guys out is the most important thing, and so Richards emphasized pitching, speed, and defense. He also had a defined philosophy of pitching which stressed control, change of speeds, and sufficient rest between starts (because of the latter belief Richards favored five-man rotations). And long before it became a common practice, he instituted pitch counts for his starting pitchers. With Chicago and after that with Baltimore, Richards consistently brought together failures, has-beens, and unproven prospects and molded them into effective, over-achieving pitching staffs that kept his teams in contention much longer than the experts ever thought possible. As for the offensive side of things, Richards recognized the importance of on-base percentage, again, well before the popularity of "Moneyball," and he liked to put pressure on the defense with speed which enabled his teams to consistently rank high in stolen bases, triples, and close games. He was also willing to give young players a chance; most notably the White Sox's Nellie Fox, when the youngster resembled an under-developed high school freshman more than a major league ballplayer; the Orioles' Brooks Robinson who was all-glove as a youngster; and the Orioles' Jim Gentile, who became the one legitimate power threat he had always sought and usually never managed to acquire. After the auditioning Gentile had a miserable 1960 spring training, Richards told him: "Son, you can't be as bad as you look.... I'm going to give you 150 at-bats. If you hit, you're my first baseman. If not, on the thirtieth day, you'll be back with the Dodgers."

Richards' teams in Chicago and Baltimore (the formerly hapless St. Louis Browns) almost always improved but never enough to win a pennant. The Orioles' second-place finish in 1960 was the best showing and earned Richards Manager of the Year laurels. Despite this "failure" to win a championship, Richards left his stamp wherever he went. The "Go-Go" White Sox, who won the AL pennant in 1959 after Richards' departure, were born under his tutelage, and the "Oriole Way" manual/playbook which laid the foundation for Baltimore's dynastic success in the 1970s was created by Richards. Not all of Richards' ideas panned out: having the pitcher and catcher exchange gloves as the pitcher backed up a long throw to the plate seemed like a good idea until the pitcher gave the righthanded catcher a lefthanded glove. But plenty of them amounted to real innovations. The Richards ploy of a baserunner allowing a ground ball to hit him to avoid a double play resulted in a rule change; his tactic of moving his pitcher to another position for a batter or two and then putting him back on the mound was way ahead of its time; and his invention of the "elephant ear" catcher's mitt to handle knuckleball pitchers such as Hoyt Wilhelm made him famous.

By the end of his reign in Baltimore, Richards' genius for the game of baseball "commanded wide respect," and that's why the expansion Houston Colt 45s were so keen on hiring him as the team's first GM to get the franchise off the ground. Richards believed by this time that GMs (who control player acquisitions) are more important than dugout managers; plus he was thrilled to be returning to his home state. Sixteen of Richards' players eventually became major league managers, and in Houston, as elsewhere, he placed his guys throughout the organization. Yet, his dictatorial tendencies and utmost confidence in his own views and ideas wore thin rather quickly, and a nasty feud with principal owner Judge Roy Hofheinz led to his departure. His succeeding tenure as the GM in Atlanta did not turn out any better; his taking the job being described by Corbett as "a ghastly mistake." He managed one more year, in 1976 for Bill Veeck's White Sox, when a bit of a generation gap emerged between him and the players; and afterwards as farm director, he trained Tony La Russa in the fickle art of managing a major league baseball team. His final courtship with the game came in 1981 when he labored as "a scout, instructor, and troubleshooter" for the Texas Rangers.

While the author admires his subject, and with good reason, he is not blind to his faults. Richards' habit of making his team practice on off days and sometimes even after games would never fly today, and his practice of having struggling pitchers get teeth pulled and undergo tonsillectomies was downright medieval. He wasn't a good judge of prospects (his preference for a kid named Arne Thorsland caused the Orioles to lose Dean Chance); he was misguided in his disdain of Marvin Miller and his belief that the players' union would ruin the game; and he was not above breaking rules (such as those governing bonus babies) if he thought the cheating would help his team. The latter trait even surfaced in his cheating and hustling at golf, a game he became obsessed with in his senior years.

Despite these flaws, Corbett's well-balanced, empathetic portrait makes it impossible not to appreciate and even like Paul Richards, a basically good person who fulfilled his destiny of becoming what insiders call simply "a baseball man." With brilliant precision the author unravels the subject's long career and reveals the meaning of every important step along the way. In the end, Paul Richards did with his life exactly what he was born to do. White Sox GM Frank Lane defined Richards the manager perfectly when he said that he got the best out of the material he had to work with. Pitcher Saul Rogosin, one of Richards' successful reclamation projects, said the same thing from a player's point of view: "He conned all of us into thinking we were better than we were."

Index

Aaron, Hank 281
Abrams, Harry N. 24
Abreu, Bobby 221
Academy Awards 9
Achorn, Edward 108–111
Adams, Doc 134
Adams, Franklin P. 148
Alderson, Sandy 183
Alexander, Charles 153
Alexander, Grover Cleveland 178, 205–208
All Americans (Spalding's world tour) 254–256
Allen, Blake 201–202
Allen, Dick 44, 83–87
Allen, Era 86
Allen, Ethan 193
Alpine Cowboys 5–9
American Association (major league) 254
American Association (minor league) 178
American Hockey League 268
American League 16, 65–69, 82, 90, 99–102, 170, 196–199, 222–226, 260, 263–265, 266–269, 277–279
America's National Game 253–256
Anaheim Angels 201–204
Anderson, Sparky 28–32, 194, 213
Andrews, Mike 101
Anson, Cap 90, 254
Aponte, Luis 43
Appalachian League 93
Appel, Brian 221
Appel, Marty 2, 218–221
Archer, Jimmy 26
Arkansas Gazette 86
Arkansas Travelers 85
Arnold, Dorothy 143
Asheville Tourists 77
Astacio, Hector 202
Atlanta Braves 46, 170
Atlanta Crackers 284
Atlantic Monthly 57
Atlantics (Brooklyn) 135–136
Aucker, Elden 114

Austin, Jimmy 25
Avila, Bobby 268
Aybar, Erick 202

The Babe Ruth Story 16
Bailey, F. Lee 270
Bak, Richard 2, 280
Baker, Frank "Home Run" 221, 278
Baker, Gene 167
Ball, Phil 152
Ball Four 44–47, 181–185, 213
Balthazar, King 273
Baltimore Orioles 76, 93–95, 102, 160, 284–285
Bancroft, Frank 110, 260
Banks, Eloyce 166
Banks, Ernie 165–167, 176–180, 241, 252
Banks, Jan 166
Banks, Jerry 166
Banks, Joey 166
Barbarians at the Gate 168
Barber, Red 162
Barnum, P.T. 125, 253
Barrow, Ed 174, 216
Barry, Dan 40–43
Bartholomew, Professor C. 255
Baseball: A Comprehensive Bibliography 29
Baseball Before We Knew It: A Search for the Roots of the Game 134
Baseball Brotherhood 256
Baseball Encyclopedia 70, 193, 238
Baseball in the Garden of Eden: The Secret History of the Early Game 134
Baseball Magazine 193, 277
Baseball Reference 93
Baseball: The Writers' Game 116
Baseball's First Inning: A History of the National Pastime Through the Civil War 134
Bavasi, Buzzie 156, 189
Beane, Billy 181–185, 194
Bears Stadium (Denver) 29

Becker, Leonard 38
Beer, Jeremy 205–209, 241
Belinsky, Bo 94
Bell, James "Cool Papa" 281
Bell, Stuart 14
Bench, Johnny 18, 31, 54, 170
Bender, Chief 30
Bennett, Eddie 160
Benteen, Frederick 159
Berg, Alan 16
Berg, Ethel 59
Berg, Morris "Moe" 15–16, 56–59
Berg, Sam 59
Bergen, Bill 25
Berger, Sy 23
Berra, Yogi 19, 198, 220, 244
Birmingham Barons 216
Blackface 17
Block, David 134
Blue, Vida 100–101
Bodie, Ping 221
Boggs, Wade 40
Bonds, Barry 18, 174
Bonds, Bobby 86
Boone, Bob 212
Borders, Ila 249
Boros, Steve 194
Bostock, Lyman 54
Boston Braves 146, 148, 214, 216, 241, 259
Boston Red Sox 8, 26, 54–55, 90, 103–07, 109–110, 123–126, 176, 194, 196–199, 214, 221, 222, 224, 241, 278, 279
Bouton, Jim 44–47, 201
Bouton, Laurie 47
Bouton, Michael 47
Bowen, Sam 42
Bowman (baseball card company) 22
Boyer, Clete 198
Boyer, Ken 162, 197
Bozymowski, Michael 114
Bradford, Chad 185
Bradley, Anna 205
Bradley, Hugh 105
Bragan, Bobby 155
Brecheen, Harry 93

Brennan, Marty 28
Brett, George 34, 63
Bridwell, Al 146
Brock, Lou 197
Brooklyn Brown Dodgers 207
Brooklyn Dodgers 11, 28, 120–122, 138–139, 160, 168, 186–190, 193, 239–241, 224–225, 271- 273, 281, 284
Brooklyn Superbas 26
Brosnan, Jim 162
Brought, James K. 97–98
Brown, Jeremy 184–185
Browne, Byron 154
Browning, Reed 88–91
Browning, Robert 63
Buchholz, Mike 41–42
Buffalo Bisons 239
Bull Durham 75–78
Bunning, Jim 198
Burden, Randy 203–204
Busch, August III 162
Busch, Gussie 196–199
Busch, Niven, Jr. 231
Busch, Susan Hornibrook 162
Bush, Donie 284
Byrne, Tom 53–54

Cagan, Joanna 11
California League 50, 185, 255
Callaspo, Alberto 202
Callison, Johnny 84–85
Camden Yards 11
Cammeyer, William 9
Campanella, Roy 207
Campbell, Jim 42
Cantillon, Joe 277
Cape Cod league 214
Capone, Al 179–180
Caray, Chip 163
Caray, Harry 2, 161–164, 197
Caray, Skip 163
Carew, Rod 18
Carolina League 72
Cartwright, Alexander 134
CASEY Award 1–2, 12, 33, 36, 82, 88, 103, 127, 194, 200, 205, 210, 211, 214, 227
Casey Stengel: Baseball's Greatest Character 2
Cash, Norm 8
Castro, Fidel 160
Chadwick, Henry 134, 184, 191–193
Chalmers, Hugh 65–69
Chambliss, Chris 220
Chance, Frank 144–147, 176
Chapman, Kate (née Daly) 224, 225
Chapman, Ray 222–226
Charleston, Janie 205
Charleston, Katherine 205
Charleston, Oscar 205–209, 281
Charlotte Hornets 72

Chaucer, Geoffrey 51
Chicago American Giants 282
Chicago Black Sox 151, 179
Chicago Colts 90
Chicago Cubs 36–39, 67, 97–98, 144–148, 154, 161–164, 165–168, 176–180, 189, 197, 217, 235–238
Chicago Sun-Times 165
Chicago White Sox (aka White Stockings) 10, 37, 54, 57, 84, 86, 106, 160, 162, 179, 226, 247, 253–256, 284–285
Cicotte, Eddie 26
Cieradkowski, Gary 157–160
Cincinnati Red Stockings 135–136
Cincinnati Reds 28–32, 34, 38, 101, 170, 198, 211–213, 258–261, 264
Citi Field (New York) 11
Clary, Ellis 160
Clavin, Tom 120–122
Claxton, Jimmy 159
Clemens, Roger 18, 110, 221
Clemente, Anairis 272
Clemente, Roberto 271–274
Clemente: The Passion and Grace of Baseball's Last Hero 271, 274
Cleveland, Grover 150
Cleveland Barons 268
Cleveland Browns 268, 269
Cleveland Indians 221, 222–226, 241, 263, 264, 266–270
Cleveland Naps 27, 65–69
Cleveland Pipers 263
Cleveland Press 263, 269–270
Cleveland Spiders 90
Cobb, Herschel Roswell, Jr. (grandson of Ty Cobb) 127–131
Cobb, Herschel, Sr. (son of Ty Cobb) 128–131
Cobb, Kit (brother of Herschel Cobb, Jr.) 131
Cobb, Madelyn (daughter of Herschel Cobb, Jr.) 127–128
Cobb, Susan (sister of Herschel Cobb, Jr.) 127–131
Cobb, Ty 25, 65–69, 88, 127–131, 147, 152, 155, 207, 213, 278, 283–284
Cobb, Ty (son of Ty Cobb) 10
Cobb, Ty (son of Herschel Cobb, Jr.) 129
Cole, Thomas 125
Coleman, Jerry 220
Collins, Jimmy 216
Collision at Home Plate: The Lives of Pete Rose and Bart Giamatti 210
Comerica Park (Detroit) 115
Comiskey Park 247

Concepcion, Dave 31
Conlon, Charles M. 24–27
Connie Mack Stadium (Philadelphia) 84
Considine, Bob 16
Continental Baseball League 8
Cook, Earnshaw 184, 193
Cooper, Alice 114
Cooper, Gary 81, 231–234
Cooper, Harold 43
Cooper, James Fenimore 125
Corbett, Warren 283–286
Corbitt, Claude 159
Corriden, Red 67–69
Costner, Kevin 76–78
The Court Martial of Jackie Robinson 137
Cramer, Dick 184
Cramer, Richard Ben 141
Crawford, Sam 277
Creamer, Robert 2
Creighton, James 135–136
Crosby, Bing 30
Crosley Field (Cincinnati) 30, 105, 212
Curry, Duncan 134
Custer, George Armstrong 159
Cuyahoga River 266–270
Cuyler, Kiki 178–179

Dalkowski, Pat 95
Dalkowski, Steve 76, 92–95
Dandridge, Ray "Squatty" 281
Dark, Alvin 101
David, John Lee 115
Davis, Bette 232
Davis, Jody 37
Davis, Tommy 101, 154–156
Davis, Willie 154–156
Dawidoff, Nicholas 7, 56–59
Dawson, Andre 37–38
Day, Doris 155
Dean, Charlie 146
Dean, Elmer 96
Dean, Jay Hanna "Dizzy" 96–98, 161
Dean, Pat 97
Dean, Paul 97
Deery, Jerome 10
DeJesus, Ivan 54
deMause, Neil 11
Dembski, Bill 92–95
Denver Bears 29
DePodesta, Paul 181–185
Desire 17
Detroit Tigers 34, 42, 65–69, 98, 102, 114–15, 266–270, 277, 283–284
Devine, Bing 197
Dewan, John 194
DeWitt, Bill 244
Diamond Classics: Essays on 100 of the Best Baseball Books Ever Published 1

Index

Diamond Classics II 1–3
Dickey, Bill 81, 232
Dickinson, Emily 63
Didion, Joan 247
Dihigo, Martin 281
Di Ionna, Mark 123–26
DiMaggio, Joe 17, 35, 141–143, 175, 211, 220–221, 244, 245
DiMaggio, Joe, Jr. 143
DiMaggio, Vince 142
Dismukes, William "Dizzy" 207
Doby, Larry 268
The Dodgers Move West 189
Doolittle, James "Jimmy" 57
Doran, Bill 38
Doubleday, Abner 134
Downing, Al 198
Drew, Bob 43
Drew, J.D. 249
Driessen, Dan 31
Drysdale, Don 18, 97, 156
Dugan, Joe 221
Dunn, Jack 26
Durango Alacranes 46
Durham, Leon 38
Durocher, Leo 165–166, 240–241, 269
Duval, Clarence 255
Dvorsky, Alex 202
Dyja, Thomas 227–230

Eagles (New York) 135
Eastern Colored League 207
Eastern League 240, 284
Ebbets Field 189, 240, 281
Eckersley, Dennis 46
Eckfords (Brooklyn) 135
Eig, Jonathan 172–175
Elysian Fields 136
Emperor Meiji 15
Empires (New York) 135
English, Woody 178
Epstein, Eddie 184
Epstein, Mike 101
Epstein, Theo 194
Erardi, John 28–32
Ergott, Roberts 176–180
ESPN.com 48
Euchner, Charles 11
Evans, Billy 68, 147
Evers, Johnny 26, 144–148, 176
Ewing, George Lemuel ("Long Bob") 257–261
Ewing, Nelle (née Hunter) 260–261
Ewing, Robert 260
Excelsiors (Brooklyn) 135

Fashion Race Course (Queens) 135
Faubus, Orval 85
Federal League 151, 279
Feezle, Stan 121

Fehler, Gene 60–64
Feller, Bob 18, 268
Fenway Park (Boston) 103–107
Ferguson, Robert 134
Fewster, Chick 224
Field of Dreams 72
Field of Screams: How the Great Stadium Swindle Turns Public Money into Private Profit 11
Fielder, Prince 203
56: Joe DiMaggio and the Last magic Number in Sports 211
Fingers, Rollie 18, 79–81, 99
Finley, Charlie 99–102, 162
Fisk, Carlton 18–19
Fitts, Robert K. 12–16
Fitzgerald, Ed 170
Fitzgibbon, Helen 148
Flood, Curt 44, 197
Florida Hotel League 207
Forbes Field (Pittsburgh) 216
Ford, Whitey 23, 34, 220
Forr, James 214–217
Fosse, Ray 212
Foster, Dick 35
Foster, George 31
Foster, Rube 207, 281–282
Foster, Willie 281
Fostoria (OH) Redbirds 235
Fox, Nellie 285
Foxx, Jimmie 14
Fresno Grizzlies 203
Friedlander, Brett 70–74
Frost, Robert 63
The Fugitive 270
Fullerton, Hugh 146
Furillo, Carl 241
Fusin, Grady 184

Gaedel, Eddie 82
Gaherin, John 169–179
Gallico, Paul 172, 232
Galloway, Will "Hippo" 159
Gammons, Peter 191
Garagiola, Joe 138–139
Garcia, Mike 268
Garson, Greer 232
Gaspar, King 273
Gefre, Sister Rosalind 248
Gehrig, Christina 174
Gehrig, Eleanor (née Twitchell) 15, 174, 231–234
Gehrig, Lou 14–16, 26, 81, 142, 158–159, 172–175, 220–221, 231–234, 244
Gehringer, Charlie 14
Gentile, Jim 285
George, Bill 41
Gerber, Dr. Samuel 269
Geronimo, Cesar 31
Gerst, Bob 100–101, 197
Giamatti, Bart 170
Gibson, Bob 18, 197–199, 278
Gibson, Josh 160, 207–208, 281

Gibson, Kirk 18
Gietschier, Steve 24
Gilbert, Thomas W. 132–136, 227
Gilhooley, Frank 221
Gilligan, Barney 110
Glynn, Jeff 203
Glynn, Sarah 203
Goldberger, Paul 9–11
Goldklang, Marv 247
Goldman, Delores "Dutchie" 163
Goldwyn, Samuel 231–234
Gomez, Lefty 14
Gonzalez, Mike 57
Goodfriend, Simon 254
Gossage, Goose 220, 264
Gothams (New York) 135
Gould, Elliot 46
Gould, Stephen Jay 194
Graham, Archie "Moonlight" 70–74
Graham, Frank 172, 219, 277
Graham, Otto 269
Grand Forks Chiefs 95
Grant, Ulysses S. 227
Gray, Pete 160
Great Falls Dodgers 203
Greater New Yorks (alternate name for Highlanders) 219
Green, Dallas 38, 264
Green, Dick 100
Greenberg, Hank 268
Greenlee, Gus 208, 281
Gregory, Robert 96–98
Gresham, Walter Q. 150
Griffey, Ken 31
Griffith, Clark 279
Griffith Stadium (Washington) 281
Grimm, Charlie 178–179
Groat, Dick 197
Grossklaus, Gary 39
Grove, Lefty 160
Guillo, Nemesio 159

Habana Base Ball Club 159
Halberstam, David 196–199
Hall, Anthony Michael 77
Hamilton, Milo 163
Harper, Tommy 213
Harridge, Will 82
Harrisburg Giants 208
Hart, James 254
Hartnett, Gabby 178–180, 217
Harwell, Ernie 114
Hatteberg, Scott 185
Hayhurst, Bonnie 50
Hayhurst, Dirk 48–51
Heathcote, Cliff 179
Helyar, John 168–171
Hemingway, Ernest 143
Hemstreet, Terry 38
Henderson, Rickey 18

Hendley, Bob 154
Henry, John 225
Henry, Orville 86
Here Comes the Nelsons 76
Herman, Babe 233
Herman, Billy 82
Herrmann, Garry 260
The Hidden Game of Baseball 191
Higginson, Bobby 114
Hilderbrant, George 152
Hilldale Athletic Club 282
Hillerich, John "Bud" 14
Hilltop Park (New York) 219
Hitler, Adolf 186
Hitler Moves East 17
Hodges, Bob 121
Hodges, Gil 120–122, 166
Hodges, Joan (née Lombardi) 122
Hoffman, Trevor 50
Hofheinz, Judge Roy 285
Holtzman, Ken 100
Holway, John 280
Holy Cow! 162
Homestead Grays 208
Hooper, Harry 279
Horio, Jimmy 15
Hornbaker, Tim 2
Hornsby, Rogers 176–179
Houk, Spencer 269
Houston Astros 38, 46, 251
Houston Buffaloes 160
Houston Colt .45s 285
How to Play Second Base 144
Howard, Elston 198
Howe, Steve 247, 249
Howsam, Bob 28–32, 170
Hubbell, Carl 27, 97–98, 216, 277
Huggins, Miller 26, 219, 225
Huhn, Rick 65–69
Hulbert, William 10
Hull, George 125–126
Humphrey, Hubert 139
Hunt, Estella 59
Hunter, Catfish 18, 99, 101, 264
Hunter, Charles 8
Huntington Grounds (Boston) 104
Hustle: The Myth, Life, and Lies of Pete Rose 210

Indianapolis ABC's 207
Indianapolis Clowns 207
Information Please! 57, 148
The Iowa Baseball Confederacy 116
International League 40–43, 240
Interstate League 160

Jackson, Reggie 99, 101, 229, 264

Jackson, "Shoeless" Joe 27
Jacobs, Lori 17
James, Bill 183–185, 193–194, 205
Jenkins, Ferguson 235
Jersey City Giants 240
Jesus Christ 273
Jeter, Derek 18, 220, 221
Johnson, Ban 68–69, 90, 104, 152, 219, 224
Johnson, Davey 194
Johnson, Ed 29
Johnson, Hazel 277, 279
Johnson, Lou 154–155
Johnson, Randy 18
Johnson, Walter 106, 216, 275–279
Johnson, William "Judy" Julius 281
Jones, Dr. Josepf B. 135
Jordan, Pat 201
Jordan, Tim "Big City" 26
Joyce, John 134
Judge Landis and 25 Years of Baseball 150
Jungle Park (Waxahachie) 283
Jurges, Billy 179

Kahn, Roger 137, 210
Kalakaua, King 256
Kaline, Al 18, 114–115, 245
Kansas City Athletics 33, 99–100, 221
Kansas City Monarchs 138, 166, 250, 281, 282
Kansas City Royals 212
Karlen, Neal 246–249
Keane, Johnny 197, 199
Keeler, Wee Willie 26
Kelly, Jerome 105
Kelly, Mike "King" 254
Kendrick, Bob 251–252
Kennedy, John Fitzgerald 139, 154–155
Kennedy, Kostya 210–213
Kennedy, Robert 139, 154
Kerrane, Kevin 235
Kieran, John 57
Kinch, Michael 41
King, Martin Luther 154
Kings of the Mound 193
Kinsella, W.P. 70–74, 116–19
Knight, Jonathan 266–270
Koenig, Mark 179
Kokernot, Herbert L., Jr. 5–9
Kokernot, Herbert L., Sr. 5
Kokernot Field 5–9
Koppert, Leonard 207
Koshein Stadium (Japan) 15
Kotchman, Tom 202–203
Koufax, Sandy 101, 154–156
Koza, Ann 42
Koza, Dave 42
Krichell, Paul 174

Kuhn, Bowie 46, 69, 100–101, 169, 264
Kurman, Paula 47

Lackey, Mike 257–261
Lajoie, Napoleon 65–69
Lake Elsinore Pirates 50
Lamster, Mark 253–256
Lancaster, Burt 72
Landis, Abraham 150
Landis, Kenesaw Mountain 149–152, 170, 179–180
Lane, F.C. 193
Lanigan, Ernie 193
Lanning, Michael Lee 137
Lardner, Ring 96
Laribee, Russ 41
Larkin, Barry 211
LaRoosh, Ebby Calvin 78
Larsen, Don 241, 245
La Russa, Tony 285
Laux, France 162
Leahy, Michael 153–156
Lee, Bill "Spaceman" 44
Lee, Robert E. 227
Leerhsen, Charles 2
Lemon, Bob 268
Leonard, Buck 281
Lester, Larry 280
Levine, Peter 253
Levinthal, David 17–19
Lewis, Duffy 105
Lewis, Michael 181–185, 194
Lieb, Fred 174, 233
Lincoln, Abraham 156, 227, 229
Lincoln, Frank 255
Lindsey, Charles 193
Lindsey, George 193
Linz, Phil 198
Lloyd, John Henry "Pop" 281
Logue, Charles 105
The Long Goodbye 46
Lopez, Al 268
The Lords of Baseball 168
Los Angeles Angels (PCL) 189
Los Angeles Coliseum 190
Los Angeles Dodgers 34, 38, 86–87, 101, 120, 122, 153–156, 168, 169, 186–190, 235, 264
Louisville Colonels 178
Lovelace, Richard 63
Lowry, Philip J. 9
Lucadello, Tony 235–238
Luebber, Scott 41
Luque, Dolf 240–241
Luther, Heath 202
Lynch, Leigh 254
Lynch, Will 254

Mack, Connie 14–16, 178
Mackey, Raleigh "Biz" 160, 281
MacMillan, Newton 254
Macon Peaches 284
MacPhail, Lee 102

Index

Madden, Alecia Vicentia 73
Madden, Bill 262–265
Maddux, Greg 38
Madison Black Wolf 249
Magadan, Dave 37
Maglie, Sal 239–242
Maglie, Sal, Jr. 241
Mahler, Jonathan 17–19
Mallory, "Bulldog" 97
Malone, Perce "Pat" 179
A Man Called Peter 76
Mankiewicz, Herman 232
Mantle, Mickey 21–23, 33–35, 62, 137, 169, 197–198, 220, 221, 237, 243–245
Mantle, Mutt 212, 244
Maraniss, David 271, 274
Maranville, Rabbit 146, 216
Marichal, Juan 82
Maris, Roger 18, 245
Marlins Park (Miami) 11
Marquard, Rube 106
Martin, Billy 33–35, 63, 86, 262, 264
Martinez, Pedro 18
Mate, Rudolph 233
Mathewson, Christy 106, 147, 160, 278
Matsui, Hideki 18
Mattingly, Don 18, 220
Mauch, Gene 84–86, 198
Mays, Carl 222–226
Mays, Willie 18, 160, 252, 268
Mazeroski, Bill 18–19
McAleer, Jimmy 104, 106
McCabe, Constance 24–27
McCabe, Neal 24–27
McCarthy, Joe 173, 178–179
McCarthy, Matt 200–204
McCarver, Tim 18, 164, 196–199
McCormick, Harry 146
McCovey, Willie 18
McCoy, Thomas P. 41
McCoy Stadium 40–43
McCracken, Voros 184
McCue, Andy 186–190
McDonald, George 147
McGraw, John 25, 73, 106, 148, 175
McGreevy, "Nuf Ced" 106
McGwire, Mark 18
McKechnie, Bill 216
McLain, Denny 60
McLaughlin, George V. 188
McLaughlin, James (Boston architect) 104–105
McLaughlin, Jim (Cincinnati Reds scouting director) 30
McMahon, Billy 134
McMullen, John 264
McPhail, Larry 188
McPhee, Bid 259
McRoy, Robert 104, 106

Meade, Gen. George Gordon 227
Medwick, Joe 160
Melchior, King 273
Melton, Bill 162
Merkle, Fred 25, 146–147
Mesa, Pablo 207
Messersmith, Andy 169
Metrodome (Minneapolis) 251
Mexican League 46, 240
Michael, Gene 38
Mikkelsen, Pete 198
Miller, Marvin 101, 169–170, 256
Mills, Eldon 193
Mills, Harlan 193
Milwaukee Brewers 170
Minneapolis Star-Tribune 248
Minnesota Twins 34, 248, 251
Mitchell, Mike 147
Mlicki, Dave 114
Molori, John 20
Monday, Rick 100
Mondor, Ben 42
Monroe, Marilyn 143
Montreal Expos 31
Montreal Royals 138
Moore, Wadie, Jr. 86
Morgan, Joe 31, 213
Morgan, Joe (Pawtucket manager) 42
Morris, Carl 184, 194
Moscow Foreign Workers' Club 159
Moses, Robert 188–189
Mossi, Don 268
Muehlebach Field (Kansas City) 282
Municipal Stadium (Cleveland) 268
Munson, Thurman 18, 220, 221, 265
Murcer, Bobby 220
Murphy, Eddie 146
Murphy, Mike 37
Murray, Bill 246–249
Musial, Stan 23
My Favorite Summer 243
My Prison Without Bars 213
Myer, Buddy 82

Narleski, Ray 268
Nathanson, Mitchell 44–47
National Baseball Hall of Fame/Famers 35, 79–82, 87, 88–89, 120, 122, 123–126, 144, 148, 152, 156, 166, 193, 210–213, 214–217, 226, 235, 237, 251–252, 277, 283
National Industrial Basketball League 263
National League 73, 90, 108–111, 146–147, 153–156, 176–180, 196–199, 216–217, 245, 253–256, 259–261
Ned Skeldon Stadium (Toledo) 238
Neff, Marty 248
Negro American League 207
Negro League Museum 251–252
Negro Leagues 205–209, 250–252, 280–282
Negro National League 207, 281
Nelson, Kadir 280–282
Nelson, Rob 46
Nettles, Graig 220
New York Americans (alternate name for Highlanders) 219
New York Cubans 282
New York Daily News 174
New York Giants 18–19, 25–26, 70–74, 97–98, 103–106, 146–147, 175, 219, 239–241, 256, 259, 268–269, 284
New York Knickerbockers 134–136
New York Metropolitans (American Association major league) 111
New York Mets 37, 57, 101, 122, 156, 166, 183, 198, 248
New York Mutuals 136
New York State League 72
New York Times 9, 21, 168, 216, 219
New York Yankees (aka Highlanders) 21–23, 25–26, 28, 31, 33–35, 44–46, 54, 62, 81, 122, 141–143, 158–160, 176, 179, 196–199, 201, 218–221, 222, 224–226, 239–241, 243–245, 248, 262–265, 268, 273
Newark Eagles 281
Newhouser, Hal 114
Neyer, Rob 184
Nixon, Richard 139, 264
Norfolk Tars 158
Northern League 246–249, 251
Nottle, "Singing" Ed 249
Nye, Rich 37

Oakland Athletics 34, 81, 99–102, 162, 181–185, 194, 264
Oakland Oaks 33, 159–160
O'Connor, "Rowdy Jack" 67–69
O'Day, Hank 146
O'Doul, Lefty 14, 233
Ohio Baseball Hall of Fame 238
Oliver, Ted 193
O'Malley, Edwin 188
O'Malley, Walter 156, 169, 186–190, 248
Oms, Alejandro 207
O'Neil, Buck 207, 250–252
Oracle Park (San Francisco) 11
Orange Fraser Press 257

Osborn Engineering Company 10
Oswald, Bob 154
Otero, Reggie 235
Ott, Mel 26

Pacific Coast League (PCL) 142, 189
Page, Ted 208
Paige, Satchel 62, 160, 161, 281
Paley, William S. 263
Palmer, Harry 254
Palmer, Jim 193
Palmer, Pete 184, 191, 194
Parker, Charlie 252
Parker, Wes 155
Parrish, Victor 68
Parrott, Harold 139, 168
Paul, Gabe 264
Pawtucket Red Sox 40–43
Peary, Danny 120–122
Peckinpaugh, Roger 221
Pecos League 8
Peeler, Tim 60
Pennington, Bill 33–35
Pepe, Phil 243
Percentage Baseball 193
Perez, Tony 30–31
Perry, Gaylord 7, 82
Petco Park (San Diego) 11
Pete Rose 31, 211–213
Pete Rose: My Story 210
Peterson, Robert 280
Pettite, Andy 220
Pfeffer, Jeff 224
Philadelphia A's 15, 28, 67, 73, 136, 146, 179–180, 277
Philadelphia Phillies 31, 83–87, 197–198, 212, 235–238, 249
Philadelphia 76ers 83
Piersall, Jimmy 162
Pietrusza, David 149–152
Pileggi, John 241
Pileggi, Kay 241
Pileggi, Mae 241
Pioneer League 200–204
Pipp, Wally 26, 221
Pitler, Jake 121
Pittsburgh Crawfords 207–208, 281
Pittsburgh Pirates 95, 147, 214–217, 272–274, 277, 279
Player Win Averages 193
Playing the Field: Why Sports Teams Move and Cities Fight to Keep Them 11
Polo Grounds (New York) 219, 268
Populous (formerly HOK Sport) 10
Portland Mavericks 46
Portsmouth Truckers 215–216
Posada, Jorge 220
Posnanski, Joe 250–252

Poulson, Norris 189
Povich, Shirley 57
Powell, Jake 160
Powers, Jimmy 174
Pratt, Del 21
Preedin, Arnold 159
Preedin, Walter 159
Pritikin, Henry 38
Pritikin, Jerry 38
Proctor, David 214–217
Providence Grays 108–111
Provo Angels 200–204
Public Affairs (publisher) 253
Pueblo Parrots 240
Pulitzer Prize 9
Purcell, Ed 194
Putnams (Brooklyn) 135

Quinn, John 14

Radbourn, Charles "Old Hoss" 108–11
Radcliffe, Ted "Double Duty" 251
Ramos, Pedro 198
Rampersad, Arnold 137–140
Rapoport, Ron 165–167
Ray Winder Stadium (Little Rock, AR) 85
Reagins, Tony 203
Reed, John H. 150
Reed, Winifred 150
Reese, Harold "Pee Wee" 122, 138
Reiser, Pete 155
Reising, Robert 70–74
Reston, James, Jr. 210
Reusse, Patrick 248
Rhodes, Dusty 268
Rhodes, Greg 28–32
Richards, Paul Rapier 93, 283–286
Richman, Hal 193
Rickey, Branch 30, 85, 95, 97–98, 110, 121, 137–139, 152, 185, 188, 190, 197
Rickey, Branch, Jr. 121
Rickey & Robinson 137
Ripken, Cal, Jr. 40
Rivera, Mariano 220, 236
Riverfront Stadium (Cincinnati) 30
Rizzuto, Phil 159
Robbins, Tim 76–78
Roberts, Randy 243–245
Roberts, Robin 81–82
Robinson, Brooks 285
Robinson, Edwin Arlington 63
Robinson, Jackie 18–19, 85, 87, 122, 137–140, 159, 207, 230, 245, 250, 281
Robinson, Mallie 137
Robinson, Phil Alden 72
Robinson, Rachel 139

Robinson, Ray 172
Robison, Frank 91
Rochester Red Wings 40–43
Rockefeller, John D. 151
Rockefeller, Nelson 139
Rodriquez, Alex 220
Rogan, Wilbur "Bullet" 281
Rogers, Will 96, 98
Rogosin, Don 280
Rolling Stone 247
Roman Coliseum 255
Ronan, Kernan 203
Roosevelt, Theodore 150
Roosevelt Stadium (Jersey City) 189
Rose, Harry 212
Rose, Pete 210–213, 265
Roseboro, John 154
Rosen, Al 268
Roth, Allan 184, 193
Runyon, Damon 98
Ruppert, Jacob 220
Ruth, Babe 12–16, 26–27, 88, 137, 151, 152, 172, 174, 175, 176, 178, 207, 220–221, 232, 244–245, 278–279
Ruth, Julia 14
Ryczek, William J. 134

Sabathia, C.C. 220
Sadecki, Ray 197
Sagel, Art 38
St. Louis Browns 10, 67–69, 82, 152, 160, 162, 285
St. Louis Cardinals 11, 54, 86, 96–98, 138, 162, 164, 178, 196–199, 201
St. Louis Perfectos 91
St. Louis Post-Dispatch 67
St. Paul Saints 246–249
Sal Maglie 241–242
Sal Maglie 241–242
San Antonio Missions 50
San Diego Chicken 117
San Diego Padres 38, 48, 50
San Francisco Giants 155
San Francisco Seals 142
San Jose Bees 247
Sandomir, Richard 231–234
Santa Clara Leopardos 207
Santiago, Wilfred 271–274
Santurce Crabs 273
Sarandon, Susan 76–78
Sawamura, Eiji 14
Scales, George 208
Schanker, Steve 38
Schecter, Leonard 46
Schley, Van 237
Schmidt, Mike 86, 213, 235, 237
Schott, Marge 30
Schraf, Mark 1, 79–82
Schultz, Barney 197
Schwarz, Alan 191–195
Schwechheimer, Lou 42

Scott, Marty 248
Scranton Miners 72
Scully, Vin 162
Seattle Pilots 46, 241
Seaver, Tom 18
Seitz, Peter 169–170
Selig, Bud 181
Seltzer, Louis B. 269–270
Service, Scott 238
Sewell, Joe 226
Shannon, Mike 197
Sharon, Dick 54
Shelton, Ron 75–78
Sheppard, Marilyn 266–270
Sheppard, Dr. Samuel "Sam" Holmes 266–270
Shires, Art 179
Shoeless Joe 70, 116, 117, 228
Shoeless Joe Jackson 27, 97
Shor, Toots 143
Shore, Ray 30–31
Shoriki, Matsutaro 14
Short, Chris 198
Simmons, Curt 197
Simpson, Harry 254
Simpson, O.J. 270
Simpson, Wayne 30
Sinatra, Frank 143
The Sinister First Baseman 194
Sioux City Explorers 249
Sioux Falls Canaries 249
Siwoff, Seymour 194
Skipper, James J. 184
Slaughter, Enos 23, 82, 138–139
Slouching Towards Bethlehem 247
Smith, Dave 194
Smith, Hilton 281
Smith, John L. 188
Smith, Johnny 243–245
Smith, Lee 37
Smith, Myron J. 29
Smith, Tal 194
Snelling, Dennis 144–148
Society for American Baseball Research (SABR) 2, 12, 154, 191–195
Sokolove, Michael Y. 210
Sosa, Sammy 18
South End Grounds (Boston) 10
Southern Association 216
Sowell, Mike 222–226
Spalding, A.G. 10, 134, 253–256
Speaker, Tris 104, 152, 207, 221, 225
Spink, Al 254
Spink, J.G. Taylor 150
Spira, Howard 264–265
Spitball: The Literary Baseball Magazine 1–3
The Sporting News 24, 30, 254, 255
Sports Illustrated 75, 86

Stahl, Jake 104, 105
Stalin, Joseph 159, 186
Stallings, George 148
Stanhope, Carrie 111
Stankiewicz, "Ma" 114
Stankiewicz, "Pa" 114
Stanton, Joe 114–115
Stanton, Tom 112–115
Stanton, Zach 115
Starfin, Victor 15
Stargell, Willie 18
Stearns, Norman "Turkey" 281
Steinbrenner, George 34, 100, 219–220, 262–265
Steinbrenner, Hal 265
Steinbrenner, Hank 265
Steinbrenner, Henry 263
Stengel, Casey 33–35, 221, 245, 268
Stengel: His Life and Times 2
Stephenson, Riggs 178
Stevens, Dave 248
Stone, Howard 114
Stottlemyre, Mel 62
Stouffer, Vernon 263
Stout, D.J. 5–9
Stout, Doyle 7
Stout, Glenn 103–7
Strawberry, Darryl 183, 246, 248
Stump, Al 131
Stuper, John 201–202
Sullivan, Neil 189
Sun Trust Park (Atlanta) 11
Suntala, Jeff 257
Suzuki, Ichiro 18
Suzuki, Sotaro 14
Sweeney, Charles W. 110, 205–208
Swerling, Jo 232

Taft, Marty 115
Tamburro, Mike 42
Tanner, Chuck 84, 162
Target Field (Minneapolis) 11
Taylor, Charles 104
Taylor, C.I. 207
Taylor, John I. 104
Tener, John 147
Tennyson, Alfred Lord 63
Terwilliger, Wayne "Twig" 248
Testa, Judith 239–242
Texas League 50, 97
Texas Rangers 248, 285
Thomas, Alex 92–95
Thomas, Dylan 64
Thomas, Frank (National Leaguer) 84–85
Thomas, Henry "Hank" 275–279
Thompson, Hunter S. 247
Thomson, Bobby 18, 241
Thorn, John 134, 136, 191, 194
The Thrill of the Grass 116

Tiernan, Mike 254
Tiger Stadium (Detroit) 112–115
Tinker, Joe 82, 144–147, 176
Toney, Fred 38
Toppen, Monica 249
Topping, Dan 220
Topps (baseball card company) 20–23
Torborg, Jeff 155
Total Baseball 194
Touching Second: The Science of Baseball 144
Tracewski, Dick 155
Traynor, Eve 217
Traynor, Harold Joseph "Pie" 214–217
Trenton Giants 160
Tripp, Steven Elliott 2
Trout, Steve 37
Troy Haymakers 136
Turbow, Jason 99–102
Turner, Ted 46, 170
Ty Cobb: A Terrible Beauty 2
Ty Cobb: Baseball and American Manhood 2
Ty Cobb: His Tumultuous Life and Times 2

Ueberroth, Peter 170
Umbarger, Jim 41
Union Association 110
Union Grounds (Brooklyn) 9, 135
USA Today 46, 194

Van Cott, T.G. 134
Vaughn, Hippo 38
Veeck, Bill, Jr. 246–249, 285
Veeck, Bill, Sr. 178–179
Veeck, Mike 247–249
Veeck as in Wreck 247
Verdi, Bob 162, 164
Vikander, Brian 92–95
Vincent, Fay 170, 213, 264–265
Virginia League 216
Vizquel, Omar 18
Vogt, Fritz 125
Von der Ahe, Chris 10

Wadsworth, Louis 134
Wagner, Charlie 104
Wagner, Dick 30
Wagner, Honus 21, 26, 148, 216
Waikus, Eddie 179
Walker, Eric 183, 194
Wall Street Journal 168
Walsh, Christy 231–232
War on the Basepaths: The Definitive Biography of Ty Cobb 2
Ward, John Montgomery 256
Wardlow, Don 248
Washington, Harold 37
Washington, Herb 100

Washington Nationals 136
Washington Senators 56, 106, 122, 160, 216, 220, 277–279
Weaver, Buck 151
Weaver, Earl 94, 194
Webb, Del 220
Weinman, Paul 60
Weiss, George 30, 169, 197
Wenner, Jann 247
Wertz, Vic 268–269
Western League 97
Wheaton, William 134
Wheeler, Lonnie 36–39
Where the Buffalo Roam 247
Whitaker, Tim 83–87
White, Bill 85, 197
White, Jo-Jo 114
White, Ray 158–159
Whiting, Robert 12
Whitman, Walt 63, 77
Wild West 17
Wilhelm, Hoyt 285
Wilker, Ian 53–55
Wilker, Jenny 53–54
Wilker, Josh 52–55
Wilker, Louis 52
Wilkers, Ronnie "Woo Woo" 38
Williams, Billy 252
Williams, Dallas 41
Williams, Dick 101
Williams, Joe "Smokey" 281
Williams, Ted 23, 95, 137, 245
Williamson, Ned 255–256
Wills, Maury 154–156
Wilson, Hack 26, 178–179, 194
Wilson, Jud 160
Winchester '73 76
Winegardner, Mark 235–238
Winfield, Dave 220, 264–265
Witkowsky, Art 114
Woltman, Dr. Henry W. 173
Wood, Joe 106
Wood, Wilbur 53
Woodward, Rick 216
Wordsworth, William 63
Wright, Craig 184
Wright, Dave 248
Wright, Harry 134, 254
Wright, Teresa 232–234
Wrigley, Philip K. 180
Wrigley, William, Jr. 167, 176–180, 262–265
Wrigley Field (Chicago) 36–39, 163, 167, 176–180, 217
Wrigley Field (Los Angeles) 189
Wynn, Early 268

Yankee Stadium 17, 47, 63, 141–142, 173, 219–221, 233, 244, 264, 281–282
Yastrzemski, Carl 55, 105
York, Sgt. Alvin Cullum 232
Young, Cy 82, 88–91
Young, Dick 122
Young, Robba 91

Zappala, Ellen 20–23
Zappala, Tom 20–23
Zito, Barry 184
Zminda, Don 161–164